Joseph Smith's Translation

Joseph Smith's Translation

The Words and Worlds of Early Mormonism

SAMUEL MORRIS BROWN

OXFORD
UNIVERSITY PRESS

Oxford University Press is a department of the University of Oxford. It furthers the University's objective of excellence in research, scholarship, and education by publishing worldwide. Oxford is a registered trade mark of Oxford University Press in the UK and certain other countries.

Published in the United States of America by Oxford University Press
198 Madison Avenue, New York, NY 10016, United States of America.

© Oxford University Press 2020

All rights reserved. No part of this publication may be reproduced, stored in a retrieval system, or transmitted, in any form or by any means, without the prior permission in writing of Oxford University Press, or as expressly permitted by law, by license, or under terms agreed with the appropriate reproduction rights organization. Inquiries concerning reproduction outside the scope of the above should be sent to the Rights Department, Oxford University Press, at the address above.

You must not circulate this work in any other form
and you must impose this same condition on any acquirer.

CIP data is on file at the Library of Congress
ISBN 978-0-19-005423-6

I dedicate this book to my wife, Kate Holbrook, who makes my efforts at translation worthwhile.

Contents

Acknowledgments	ix
Chronology	xi
Key Abbreviations Used in Footnotes	xiii
Introduction: Language, Time, and the Human Cosmos	1
Nineteenth-Century Contexts	4
Smith's Goals and Aspirations	7
Implications	11

SECTION 1 CONTEXTS

1. The Quest for Pure Language	19
Language and Its Origins	21
The Sacred Pictogram	29
Joseph Smith on Language	31
Conclusion	48
2. The Nature of Time	51
Time in History	54
Flattening Time	57
The Primordium and Historylessness	59
The Saints and the Collapse of Time	61
Life in Yon Time	69
The First and Eternal Theology	74
Time and Space	76
Conclusion	78
3. Human and Divine Selves	81
Nineteenth-Century Selves	83
Smith's Modernist Sensibilities	89
The Modern Prison of Individualism	96
Escape Routes from Individual Isolation	97
Conclusion	120

SECTION 2 TEXTS

4. The Task of the Book of Mormon: To Save the Bible, First You Must Kill It	127
The Bible in Crisis	130

The Gold Bible	132
The Problems of Language	135
Transmitting the Bible	137
Canon and Completeness	141
The Acts of Translation	144
Self-Interpreting Scripture	146
Saving Evidential Christianity	150
Evidence in a Modern Age: The Problem of Miracles	155
Getting from Bible to Church	158
Conclusion	160
5. Rereading the Bible: Joseph Smith's New Translation	163
Taxonomy of Smith's Bible Translations	164
Smith's Bible Timeline, 1829–1833	166
Context and Competition	170
Expanding Smith's Bible Translation	173
Interpretation	183
Marvelous Literalism and the Metaphysics of Reading	185
Conclusion	190
6. The Egyptian Bible and the Cosmic Order	193
Egypt in America	195
Immediate Contexts and Continuities	197
Overview of the Texts	199
Themes of the Egyptian Bible	211
Secularity and the Egyptian Bible	229
Conclusion	231
7. The Transcendent Immanent Temple	233
A Brief History of Temples	235
The Harmony of the Cosmos	246
Divine Anthropology in the Temple Endowment	248
The Right Name of Things	252
That Which Must Not Be Spoken	256
Living the Temple	260
The Immanent-Transcendent God	263
A God Split in Two (or More)	265
Conclusion	269
Epilogue	271
Bibliography	275
Index	295

Acknowledgments

Undergraduate theoretical syntax courses from Samuel Epstein and Noam Chomsky taught me to wonder systematically about the structures of language. While I did not pursue linguistics formally after college, I have ever been grateful for their influence on the care and rigor of my thinking. Those two scholars are among the most consummately intellectual people I have ever met.

This book grew out of conversations with colleagues and friends, most prominently Jared Hickman. During the writing of *In Heaven as It Is on Earth: Joseph Smith and the Early Mormon Conquest of Death* and its kindred projects, I was impressed by the extension of the principle of metaphysical correspondence in early Latter-day Saint thought and the sense in which translation as a source of scriptural texts mirrored translation as a process by which humans became assimilable to the divine presence. This juxtaposition called out for an explanation that could deal with the deep connections of these two modes of translation. Jared and I discussed these questions at length from our respective intellectual traditions and even for a time contemplated a coauthored book on the topic. While Jared and I interpret many of these questions differently, he has taught me much over the many years of our close and stimulating friendship.

I am also grateful to the many friends and colleagues who have improved this work, often through careful and wise reading of drafts. I specifically and alphabetically thank Michael Austin, Jacob Baker, Phil Barlow, Diann Brown, Spencer Brown, Richard Bushman, Zachary Gubler, Grant Hardy, Michael Haycock, Kate Holbrook, Robin Jensen, Jason Kerr, and John Durham Peters. Jana Riess, John Turner, and James Egan led the pack in their thorough comments on the entire manuscript. I also thank the able young scholars who have helped me as research assistants, including Nicholas Shrum, Brady Winslow, and Brett Dowdle. I thank The Faith Matters Foundation for funding much of the work of my research assistants. I thank Cynthia Read and her expert staff at Oxford University Press for their consistent support and excellent insights.

I thank the editors of *Church History* for allowing me to incorporate revised material originally published in their journal. Chapter 6 uses and revises my "Joseph (Smith) in Egypt: Babel, Hieroglyphs, and the Pure Language of Eden," *Church History* 78:1 (March 2009): 26–65, which I explored in a different key in chapter 5 of my *In Heaven as It Is on Earth*. Some portions of chapter 1 update and expand material from aspects of those same works.

Chronology

December 1805 Joseph Smith Jr. born in Sharon, Vermont
Summer 1820 Smith's First Vision of Deity
Fall 1824 Smith's initial vision of angel Moroni
1826 Smith on trial for vagrancy in New York
1827 Smith meets and marries Emma Hale
Fall 1827 Smith obtains Book of Mormon plates
Winter 1827–1828 First transcripts of Book of Mormon "characters"
1827–1828 Smith dictates Book of Lehi
1828 Book of Lehi manuscript lost; Smith's son Alvin stilborn; Emma appears near death
April 1829 Smith dictates Mosiah to Moroni
Spring 1829 Smith dictates Doctrine and Covenants 4–10
May 1829 Smith dictates 1 Nephi to Words of Mormon
March 1830 Book of Mormon published
April 1830 Church of Christ officially founded
May 1830 Indian Removal Act signed
September 1830 Smith dictates Doctrine and Covenants 29
ca. June 1830 Smith dictates Visions of Moses, formally launching the New Translation of the Bible
December 1830 Smith dictates Prophecy of Enoch
December 1830 Sidney Rigdon joins New Translation effort
1831 Smith moves to Kirtland, Ohio
February–March 1832 Smith dictates Sample of Pure Language
February 1832 Smith dictates Doctrine and Covenants 76 ("the Vision")
February–March 1832 Smith dictates Doctrine and Covenants 77
December 1832–January 1833 Smith dictates Doctrine and Covenants 88 ("Olive Leaf"), which anticipates human equality with Christ
January 1833 School of Prophets founded
July 1833 Sidney Rigdon declares New Translation complete
1833 Attempted publication of Book of Commandments
1834 Camp of Israel paramilitary march to save Zion
February–September 1835 Publication of Doctrine and Covenants
May 1835 William Phelps creates Edenic language document

May–August 1835 William Phelps uses biblical codenames for Church leaders named in Doctrine and Covenants

July 1835 Smith buys Egyptian mummies and funerary papyri

ca. July–ca. December 1835 Abraham 1:1–2:18 dictated; grammar documents drafted

January–March 1836 Kirtland Hebrew School

Spring 1836 Kirtland temple preparations and dedication

1838 Missouri Mormon War and Smith's incarceration in Liberty Jail

April 1839 Smith escapes jail and moves to Commerce/Nauvoo, Illinois

1839–1841 Smith uses material related to Abraham 3 in multiple contexts

March 1841 Smith uses material related to Abraham 5 and Sample of Pure Language in Lyceum speech

March 1842 Abraham 3–5 completed and published

March 1842 Smith inducted into Freemasonry

May 1842 Smith introduces Nauvoo temple rites

November 1843 Proposal to publish Egyptian grammar

April 1844 Smith retranslates Genesis 1:1 to prove plurality of Gods and human deification

June 1844 Smith uses John to prove plurality of Gods

June 1844 Joseph and Hyrum Smith murdered by vigilante mob

Key Abbreviations Used in Footnotes

CHL	Church History Library, Church of Jesus Christ of Latter-day Saints, Salt Lake City, UT.
D&C	Doctrine and Covenants of the Church of Jesus Christ of Latter-day Saints (Salt Lake City, UT: Intellectual Reserve, 1981).
EMD	*Early Mormon Documents*, ed. Dan Vogel, 5 vols. (Salt Lake City: Signature Books, 1996–2004).
EJ	*Elders' Journal of the Church of Latter Day Saints*, Kirtland, Ohio, October–November 1837, Far West, Missouri, July–August 1838.
EMS	*The Evening and the Morning Star*, Independence, Missouri, June 1832–July 1833, Kirtland, Ohio, December 1833–September 1834.
EoM	Daniel Ludlow, ed., *Encyclopedia of Mormonism* (New York: Macmillan, 1992).
EPB	H. Michael Marquardt, comp. and ed., *Early Patriarchal Blessings of the Church of Jesus Christ of Latter-day Saints* (Salt Lake City: Smith-Pettit Foundation, 2007).
HBLL	Harold B. Lee Library, Brigham Young University, Provo, UT.
JSP	The Joseph Smith Papers project (https://josephsmithpapers.org) has transformed the accessibility of the archives of the Church of Jesus Christ of Latter-day Saints. The series include Journals (*J*), Histories (*H*), Documents (*D*), Manuscript Revelation Books (*MRB*), and Administrative Records (*AR*). Each of the volumes is referred to as *JSP*, followed by a letter designating the series (e.g., *J*) and a number (e.g., *2*) indicating the volume within the series. Thus, *JSPD3* refers to the third volume in the Documents series.
M&A	*Latter Day Saints' Messenger and Advocate*, Kirtland, Ohio, October 1834–September 1837.
MS	*Latter-day Saints' Millennial Star*, Manchester, England, May 1840–March 1842; Liverpool, April 1842–March 3, 1932; London, March 10, 1932–December 1970.
NewT	Scott Faulring, Kent Jackson, and Robert Mathews, *Joseph Smith's New Translation of the Bible: Original Manuscripts* (Provo, UT: Religious Studies Center, Brigham Young University, 2004).
T&S	*Times and Seasons*, Commerce/Nauvoo, Illinois, November 1839–February 1846.
WJS	Andrew Ehat and Lyndon Cook, comp. and ed., *The Words of Joseph Smith: The Contemporary Accounts of the Nauvoo Discourses of the Prophet Joseph* (Provo, UT: Grandin Book Co, 1991).
WWJ	Wilford Woodruff, *Wilford Woodruff's Journal, Typescript*, ed. Scott Kenney, 9 vols. (Midvale, UT: Signature Books, 1983–1985); original at CHL.

Introduction

Language, Time, and the Human Cosmos

In 1938, Marjorie Courtenay-Latimer, the curator of a tiny museum on the southeastern coast of South Africa, discovered a stunning, five-foot-long blue fish among the haul of a local trawler. She secured the find, transporting it in a taxicab back to the museum, and introduced it to a local gentleman scientist, J. L. B. Smith. The amateur ichthyologist proposed a new genus, *Latimeria*, of an ancient order of fishes with lobed tails called the coelacanth. Soon dubbed a "living fossil," this creature came to be seen as a close relative to the fish that made its way onto land, the shared ancestor of most terrestrial life, including us, the readers and writers of books.

In the minds of many observers, these prehistoric-looking fish represented a discovery as stunning as a colony of dinosaurs. The coelacanths seemed to hold out the possibility that pockets of biological order could resist the relentless pressures of natural selection. Now a zoological celebrity hounded by a determined paparazzi that threatens its final extinction, the coelacanth has inhabited the popular imagination precisely as a living fossil.

But this claim is, instructively, quite wrong. The modern coelacanth is as distant biologically from its ancestors of 70 to 80 million years ago as bats are from whales. These odd-looking fish aren't living fossils at all. The whole concept of a living fossil is incoherent. No species stays the same over millions of years, and the specimens whose hematite-coated skeletons are found buried in rock are long dead. The coelacanths are distant cousins from an ancient aunt whose descendants were lost and presumed dead. And, yet, the image of a living fossil persists, carried on the backs of the humble and elusive *Latimeria*.[1]

Whatever the details of evolutionary history, "living fossil" is a way to talk about an entity that doesn't belong in its current time. Some prior epoch has greater claim on it than the present. Such a being carries an imprint of an ancient history that has otherwise been obliterated. Even if, by token of living, it is *not* in fact its ancient antecedent, such an entity recalls the past in a way that makes its place in the modern world seem uncertain. Simultaneously, it may call

---

[1] Thomson, *Living Fossil*, reviews this history. I thank Steven Peck for teaching me coelacanth evolution.

us to reassess what we think we know about the modern world. Living fossils are caught between times; they resist the tidy classification into the primitive before and the modern after.

I've spent two decades studying the formal structures and documentary legacy of the churches and communities deriving from the religious career of Joseph Smith and his family and close friends—most famously the Church of Jesus Christ of Latter-day Saints (often called "Mormon").[2] This study has persuaded me that this American religious tradition is a cultural coelacanth. No more a living fossil than the giant blue fish with the lobed tail, the religion of the Latter-day Saints nevertheless seems to be torn out of time. It often appears more ancient than modern. Many Church members believe in angels and demons, seer stones and mystical scrolls, a God who not only exists physically but also is essentially anthropomorphic, and a Great Chain of Being (albeit, crucially, expressed in genealogical rather than ontological terms). It's as if the Latter-day Saints didn't get the memo about modernity.

But, of course, the Church of Jesus Christ of Latter-day Saints isn't even medieval. In many respects it is consummately modern, with an intense focus on human agency and potential, an ardent anti-Calvinism, and by most reports a thoroughgoing materialism that collapses body and spirit into matter. Such modern elements were present even when the Saints operated a polygamous theocracy in nineteenth-century Utah. In the twentieth century, the Church came to seem more modern than ever, as it abandoned polygamy and formal theocracy, grew and bureaucratized, and applied business techniques to its operations and self-presentation. The twentieth-century Church dressed its public face—young male missionaries—as conservative businessmen, traveling two-by-two in suits and ties as they spread their message of reform and human perfectibility.[3] Especially as the century progressed, the Church became technologically savvy and methodically corporate at its large headquarters in Salt Lake City, Utah. Its members even came to define their existence as a church as dependent on the Protestant Reformation and the secularization (as church-state separation) that it unleashed.[4] After World War II, many Church leaders and members aligned themselves politically and often culturally with America's Religious Right.

---

[2] In 2018, Church president Russell M. Nelson deprecated the term "Mormon" and the abbreviation "LDS Church" for usual discourse among members of The Church of Jesus Christ of Latter-day Saints. He also urged journalists to avoid those terms. Out of respect for Latter-day Saint readers, I've limited as possible my use of the terms, admitting that in certain cases, "Mormon" is perhaps the best and clearest scholarly designation, even though it was an abbreviation of the derisive term "Mormonite." Where possible, I use "Saint," "Latter-day Saint," and "Church member" interchangeably and occasionally use "Restoration" as an adjective meaning Mormon. My goal is to strike a reasonable balance between academic clarity and respect for the subjects of study.

[3] Bowman, "Eternal Progression."

[4] See, e.g., *EoM*, 1171–72, and *Ensign* (June 1999): 34–40.

Through their complex encounter with Protestant fundamentalisms, some Latter-day Saints embraced modern biblical literalism and New Earth creationism. Latter-day Saint marriage became a perfect instance of the Victorian ideal that it once radically rejected. Even in its apparent exceptions from modernity, no church could be more modern.

The story of what became the Church of Jesus Christ of Latter-day Saints begins with the Smith family, poor farmers occasionally on the verge of middle-class stability, parented by a devout Presbyterian mother and an unchurched Universalist father. A middle son, Joseph Jr., possessed spiritual gifts and a questing mind. By his teens, he was describing encounters with heavenly visitors that culminated in the late 1820s in a scriptural account of ancient American Christianity translated from an otherwise unknown hieroglyphic script inscribed on gold plates. This Book of Mormon in turn launched a Restorationist Church of Christ in 1830, led by the prophet-translator Joseph Smith Jr. That new church decried Protestantism as a corrupt distortion of the original Gospel of Christ, drawing converts especially from among seekers and other critics of the Protestant mainstream. In addition to establishing church and doctrine, Joseph Smith transformed or established a handful of settlements for his followers so that they could live in physical, "gathered," community in preparation for Christ's Second Coming. Each such town collapsed as a result of violent resistance, whether as vigilante attacks or state-sanctioned suppression. After Smith's death in 1844 at the hands of a mob, the main body of the Church abandoned the United States for what was then Mexico, establishing a religious empire in territory that became the state of Utah.

In support of his Restoration and the community it engendered, Smith produced a corpus of sacred texts, the vast majority of them dictated to assistants. Generally, Smith described his process for generating scripture as translation effected by the "gift and power" of God.[5] He began in 1829–1830 with the 588-page Book of Mormon—an American Bible that revealed the deep, Christian history of America's Natives. He immediately transitioned to two interrelated scriptural projects—a set of modern revelations ultimately called the Doctrine and Covenants, and a New Translation of the Bible later termed the Joseph Smith Translation. From 1835 to 1842 he worked to interpret a collection of two-thousand-year-old Egyptian funeral papyri. The 1842 publication of the resulting Book of Abraham came in support of an expanded temple liturgy, a multitextured ritual drama in which his followers acted out the sacred texts Smith had been revealing. The temple rites and their foundation in Smith's scripture and an otherworldly power the early Saints called priesthood highlight

---

[5] This phrase is in the preface of the 1830 Book of Mormon and, e.g., *JSPD2*, 354.

the merger of humans with sacred texts in Smith's Restoration project. This was a central attribute of his religious career and my preoccupation in the present book: translation was about more than words and sentences. Translation was also concerned with the transformation of human beings and the worlds they were capable of inhabiting. These twin senses of translation run together in early Latter-day Saint thought.

Smith and his associates came of age in America's nineteenth century, at a crossroads in the development of what has become modern society. Core questions relevant to modernity were being extensively debated among traditional Calvinists, populist revivalists, freethought skeptics, marginalized and enslaved peoples, learned Unitarians, and scores more schools and groups. What was the appropriate relationship between individuals and society? What was the Bible, and how reliable was it as a guide to life or afterlife? What did it mean to be a human being, and how should human and divine will interact? For a few radical critics, the question became whether there was still a place for God as such in the world. Joseph Smith, among others, thought he had compelling answers to those questions.

Nineteenth-Century Contexts

Implicit in the image of a living fossil is the division of time into the fossilized past and the living present. In the case of Latter-day Saint history, that dividing line is the nineteenth century. Smith and his disciples were deciding to what extent they belonged in the world they inherited from their parents and grandparents. The century began a generation after the American Revolution, in the midst of cultural, political, and religious conflicts that centered on questions about how a new world order would differ from the old. The axes of perceived cultural conflict and change were multiple: economic, philosophical, sociological, theological, scientific, and spiritual.[6]

The French aristocrat and amateur social scientist Alexis de Tocqueville (born four months before Joseph Smith in radically different circumstances) toured America in the early 1830s to understand the American penal system, a trip that also resulted in a two-volume work on *Democracy in America*.[7] His perspective, two generations after the American and French revolutions, provides a view from across epochs. Tocqueville's accounts of life in early "democratic" America are informal and biased by his class and ethnicity, but they suggest how America

---

[6] Howe, *Transformation of America*. On eighteenth-century contexts, see Brekus, *Osborn's World*, 7–11, and Hindmarsh, *Early Evangelicalism*, esp. 5, 9, 44–45, 273.

[7] Brogan, *Tocqueville*.

looked to someone connected to older modes of being and thinking. The early American Republic felt like a strange and exciting sociocultural experiment. Three axes in particular seem relevant to understanding Smith and his theology of translation: language, time, and identity.

For the first time in human history the printed word became essentially ubiquitous, as publishers disseminated religious tracts, newspapers, and titillating fictions in the millions.[8] Although universal literacy was more aspiration than reality, the written word was linking writers and readers across vast scales of space and time. Associated disruptions to class distinctions and societal centers of gravity meant (to Tocqueville, among others) that language was shattering into incompatible pieces as partisan newspapers became the mechanism of social influence.[9] At a deeper level, while many Americans still believed in what critics call magic, educated elites were actively losing interest in metaphysically potent language.

Ideas about time were also in flux. Independent America saw itself as a new order for the ages. Partisans of Enlightenment thought proselytized a world of technology and experimental science that, in their view, overturned the superstitions of the past.[10] A Protestant theological consensus favored cessationism, the belief that miracles had only happened during the time of the Bible and no longer occurred in the modern world.[11] This cessationism was an intentional abruption from the past—in Tocqueville's elitist and hyperbolic terms, learned Americans had "an almost insurmountable distaste for whatever is supernatural."[12] Cessationism meant that the wild times of antiquity were safely remote, even from people of faith. In a parallel erasure, Euro-Americans sought to eliminate the Native ways of life that preceded European society on the continent with special intensity in the horrors of Indian Removal in the 1830s.[13] With the constriction of Native territorial claims, the uncolonized element of a precontact world also became less accessible. Following eighteenth-century precedent, the Euro-American democratic experiment sought to forget the past in favor of a progressive future.

Stories about identity are perhaps the most complex and multivalent of the cultural transitions of the period. Many politicians, intellectuals, and reformers saw themselves as implementing, broadly speaking, the political philosophy of John Locke (1632–1704), which drew the center of authority away from the

---

[8] Brown, *Evangelical Writing*; Moore, "Culture Industry"; Schantz, "Religious Tracts."
[9] Tocqueville, *Democracy in America*, 2:106–14.
[10] Schmidt, *American Enlightenment*.
[11] On cessationism, see Turner, *Mormon Jesus*, 64, 94; Buck, *Theological Dictionary*, 376–79; and chapter 2 *infra*.
[12] De Tocqueville, *Democracy in America*, 2:4.
[13] See, e.g., Purdue and Green, *Trail of Tears*; Howe, *Transformation of America*, 414–23.

harmony of the traditional Chain of Being and its hereditary rulers to the self-determination of individual citizens.[14] Tocqueville popularized the term "individualism" to describe the culture that such a politics caused to flourish in the young American Republic.

Religion—a plastic word then as now—was changing too, in a variety of ways.[15] Calvinism was under attack from multiple camps. Disestablishment of churches, begun in the last decades of the eighteenth century, was entirely on the law books by 1833, simultaneously creating limits to traditional churches and encouraging the flourishing of revivalist denominations like the Baptists and Methodists.[16] Tocqueville observed the anti-institutional spirit of American religion: "a democratic people will not easily give credence to divine missions; . . . they will laugh at modern prophets; and . . . they will seek to discover the chief arbiter of their belief within, and not beyond, the limits of their kind."[17] He was wrong about large swaths of the population—who embraced, like the early Saints, the ongoing presence of divine power[18]—but he understood a substantial proportion nevertheless.

Many Americans at the time saw themselves as turning the world upside down politically, theologically, and culturally. That perception may matter as much for the present story as the more complex realities of contingency and disruption. The ultimate outcome wasn't apparent at the time—assumptions and connections that now seem automatic were then controversial at best. Even as we might begin to recognize the world we now inhabit in these glimpses of nineteenth-century cultural controversies, we also must acknowledge the fact that late modern culture is an artificial pastiche of historical postures, none of which was inevitable.[19] There were many paths through and out of the nineteenth century.

Into this disputed world came Joseph Smith Jr. in the late 1820s. While he took on the controversies of his day in brash and idiosyncratic ways, he did so in the hopes of achieving particular ends. Those ends depended to some extent on his ideological opponents—especially the learned clergy, evangelical revivalists, and freethought skeptics. Smith and his followers charted an alternative path through antebellum American culture.

---

[14] De Tocqueville, *Democracy in America*, 2:99. Frances Trollope similarly complained about this shift in identity: *Domestic Manners*, 253, as did, in a different key, Andrews Norton: Norton, *A Statement of Reasons*, xxiii.
[15] Grasso, *Skepticism*, 6, 10, 361, 387–88.
[16] On disestablishment, see, e.g., Marty, "Living with Establishment," and Green, *Second Disestablishment*.
[17] De Tocqueville, *Democracy in America*, 2:9.
[18] Grainger, *Church in the Wild*; Butler, *Sea of Faith*.
[19] Taylor, *Secular Age*, and Grainger, *Church in the Wild*, 7, 154.

Smith's Goals and Aspirations

For Joseph Smith, the fundamental problems of the human condition were alienation and separation. The nature of human beings and their worlds in the modern age left him uneasy. He feared the possibility that humans could be isolated from each other in life and in death. And he worried that humans were estranged from God and their divine nature. While he was never comfortable with the doctrine of original sin, he nevertheless suffered the pangs of loss associated with the primordial Fall from the divine presence. Focused on cosmic origins as the key to life's ultimate puzzle, Smith was haunted by the loss of Eden. That separation intensified in the Curse of Babel and the fallen language that afflicted the world in Babel's aftermath, not even sparing Scripture.

Smith saw serious flaws in the modern world, even as he appreciated the freedom it provided for him, a rural heretic, from the dominance of urban and provincial elites. The nature of human beings and their worlds in the modern age appeared incomplete, even dangerous to him. He sought solutions in ontologies that blurred common dualisms.[20] The project that draws my attention in *Joseph Smith's Translation* is something he and his disciples called translation, a metaphysical mode of rereading and recreating the Bible—especially its first eleven chapters, which scholars call the Primeval History. This translation was concerned with transforming readers and bringing them into relationship with the ancients. Smith sought to make sense of the world by making durable connections with human and greater-than-human beings in defiance of the constraints of space and time.[21] This concept of translation came to fruition in the Nauvoo temple liturgy, in which his followers enacted scripture with their bodies and became thereby capable of life in the direct presence of God. When an early Latter-day Saint hymn announces that Smith "translated sacredly" the Book of Mormon, the adverb is pregnant with implication.[22] Smith's translation is much more complex, and interesting, than observers have traditionally given it credit for.[23]

Smith and his disciples used this translation to attempt an escape from the modern prisons of language, time, and space. He fought against the brokenness of language, the stifling horizon of time, and the walls erected between individuals.

---

[20] On related Evangelical projects of blurry dualism, see Hindmarsh, *Early Evangelicalism*, 124, 138–140.
[21] Orsi, *Heaven and Earth*, suggests this relationship as central to religious experience generally.
[22] Smith, *Sacred Hymns*, 33.
[23] Kathleen Flake's masterful "Translating Time" is an exception to the general rule.

Smith's Approach

A core concept necessary to understanding Smith's Restoration and its cultural contexts is what some scholars term metaphysical correspondence, from its particular expression in Renaissance thought.[24] Synonyms for these beliefs include cosmic harmony, analogy, sympathy, microcosm:macrocosm, and "as above, so below."[25] In Smith's 1844 rereading of 1 Corinthians 15, "that which is Earthyly is in likeness of that which is Heavenly."[26] Correspondence organized natural philosophy and religion for centuries if not millennia, with special prominence in Christian Platonism. The underlying notion is that symmetries and harmonies can be mechanisms for powerful connections. Similarity is deeply nutritive, even constitutional—essential powers and natural histories of objects are disclosed and potentially *made* through that similarity. The historian-philosopher Remi Brague and the religious theorist J. Z. Smith have correctly seen correspondence as historically ubiquitous and deeply cosmological.[27] Recent historians have espied this pattern of thought even in the Atlantic Protestantism that ostensibly banished it.[28] The elimination of such connection was one of the central metaphysical assumptions grafted onto Newtonian mechanics in the eighteenth and nineteenth centuries.[29]

The correspondent world crackles with power and connection for its participants. Expressed in sympathetic magic, correspondence maintains that like affects like. A spell whose prosody is airy, perhaps coupled with a feather, may permit flight; deer testicles may confer human fertility. In nature mysticism, correspondence sees the divine presence throughout space and the celestial bodies that populate it. More generally, correspondence carries the sense that there is an overarching cosmic order and humans belong to it. The structure of the universe (macrocosm) thus dictates and animates the parallel structure of humanity (microcosm). Such correspondence underlies much of Smith's worldview and makes possible the interdependence of texts and humans in his thought.

Translation, Smith's metaphysical escape route from the prisons of language, time, and individualism, included two related activities. In the first aspect, Smith repeatedly rendered ancient texts—known and previously unknown, material and visionary—into American English, a process by which he overcame the constraints of language and time that otherwise separated ancient people from

---

[24] Taylor, *Secular Age*, 35, unduly limits correspondence to learned circles.
[25] See Albanese, *Mind and Spirit*, 13–16, 26–27, 59–62; Goodrick-Clarke, *Esoteric Traditions*, esp. 8–9, 23, 72, 155–72; Brown, *Body and Society*, xliv, 199; Hazen, *Village Enlightenment*, 98; Hindmarsh, *Early Evangelicalism*, 109–11; Grainger, *Church in the Wild*, 8, 98.
[26] *WJS*, 380.
[27] Brague, *Wisdom of the World*, esp. 93–96, and Smith, *Map Is Not Territory*, 132.
[28] Grainger, *Church in the Wild*, 4, 6, 8, 74, 98, 144, 172, 179–80; Hall, *Worlds of Wonder*, 66.
[29] Gregory, *Unintended Reformation*, 223; Hindmarsh, *Early Evangelicalism*, 5, 178, 273.

their modern heirs. The second aspect of translation concerned the human essence. Smith argued for the ontological transformation of human beings, both theologically—as he preached the equality of humans and gods—and practically, as an apocalyptic transformation by which certain individuals could be suddenly prepared to tolerate the direct presence of God. The translation of humans into divine beings brought the ancient principle of metaphysical correspondence to whole-bodied life. (One hears in these doctrines echoes of esoteric transmutation—by which special knowledge transforms a person—as well as the Evangelical interdigitation of the books of nature and revelation.[30])

For Smith the two modes of translation aimed at healing the rent at the center of existence, the isolation that became central to the experience of late modernity.[31] Smith employed translation to resist spatial and temporal alienation. He made the ancients his contemporaries, directly accessible to his disciples. Different times and realms bled into each other. His Book of Mormon described American Jews worshiping Christ long before his birth, and his latter-day followers were called to live the ancient ways themselves.

Smith was arguing a practical metaphysics of translation. I use the term "metaphysics" to describe that which complements the physical, to evoke some sense of a realm or power beyond the everyday. For the Saints and many of their peers, metaphysics was a more-than-metaphorical source of power and order associated with the fabric of the cosmos and the divine presence.[32] In translation Smith had in mind both physical and metaphysical transformations.

By invoking metaphysics, I don't mean to suggest that Smith's translations aren't *real*. Not at all. But they aren't merely *physical*. I argue, in other words, that a recent suggestion by a prominent Latter-day Saint scholar that translation is a "misnomer" when it comes to Smith's scripture is radically too flat.[33] Smith's translations are bound up with a world beyond the everyday. Smith was, to borrow the historian of religion Robert Orsi's terminology, concerned with manifestations of real divine presence in a world some hoped had turned its back on such abundance.[34] This divine presence came through texts, and it also came through the humans that Smith increasingly saw as divine. This merger of texts and humans in the context of a metaphysically thick cosmos draws toward the possibility that humans might obtain direct contact with God. Such contact would require transformation—in Smith's phrase near the end of his life, if his disciples "wish to go whare God is" then they "must be like God."[35] That path to the divine presence and the changes it requires are the work of translation.

[30] Goodrick-Clarke, *Esoteric Traditions*, 9; Grainger, *Church in the Wild*, esp. chap. 2.
[31] Barlow, "Fractured Reality."
[32] In this regard, I differ from Hickman, "Reconfiguration."
[33] Givens, *Greatest Price*, 32.
[34] Orsi, *History and Presence*.
[35] *WWJ*, 2:169.

As part of my effort to understand the metaphysics of translation, I engage several questions. What is Smith's most famous scripture, the Book of Mormon, doing as a text? What is the relationship between that Book of Mormon and Smith's subsequent engagement of biblical texts? What was Smith doing when he handled Egyptian funerary papyri and then dictated ancient stories in the name of Abraham? What problems was Smith trying to solve with his divine anthropology, which equated gods and humans through a cosmic-genetic force he called priesthood? How did Restoration scripture relate to Smith's temple liturgy? Answering these questions requires understanding broader contexts in America and in Latter-day Saint thought.

In part because Smith's efforts at translation were so intimately connected to words and their contexts, I read his scriptures closely. The content mattered to Smith and his followers, and so did the form and context. Prior scholars have used terms from Bible studies, especially "pseudepigrapha" and "midrash," to describe Smith's scriptures. Pseudepigrapha are pseudonymous writings that borrow the authority of a more famous prophet, while a midrash is a meticulous and creative reading of a sacred text.[36] Following the Swedish theologian Krister Stendahl's characterization of the Book of Mormon, I see Joseph Smith's textual translations as occupying another category. They are, to my eye, *targums*.[37]

A targum (from a Semitic root meaning to translate or interpret) was a parabiblical oral text that mediated the meaning of an ancient Hebrew text for a community that no longer understood biblical Hebrew. The status of targums was controversial, as the faithful wondered whether such texts could ever match the Hebrew scriptures, and whether they should be written or remain forever as oral tradition. Ultimately, targums entered the written record and persisted, in some communities attaining an almost scriptural status. Most important for my purposes, a targum was a translation that tapped into creative energy in the interface between written and oral scripture, extending among many generations of linguistic and cultural communities.[38]

Understanding the metaphysical rather than merely linguistic facets of translation provides a better understanding of Smith's anthropology and the nature of scripture in America. It also illuminates the shapes of religion in the early

---

[36] Price, "Prophecy and Palimpsest," advocates pseudepigraphy. On midrash, see, e.g., Hardy, *Reader's Guide*, 69–70, with expansion in Hardy and Hardy, "Perceptions of Isaiah." On the distinctive possibility of *haggadah*, see, e.g., Blenkinsopp, *Creation*, 163, or (as "aggadic exegesis") Frederick, *Rhetoric of Allusivity*, 57.

[37] Stendahl makes the argument in "Third Nephi." Stephen Stein, following Stendahl, suggested that both Latter-day Saints and Shakers were "targumizing." *Shaker Experience*, 182, cf. Stein, "America's Bibles," 172.

[38] Although to my knowledge Smith never used the term, targums were known in the early nineteenth century, as in Buck, *Theological Dictionary*, 567–68, or John Witherspoon's "To the Reader," which introduced many American Bibles after 1791 including at least one Smith owned: Perry, "Many Bibles," 763.

Republic. Exploring a group outside the usual binary of Protestants versus freethinkers or religious versus secular exposes a new and useful vantage on many of the cultural stakes for antebellum Americans. Establishing the core contexts and concerns will be essential to making sense of the corpus of Smith's scriptural texts and their implications. To really understand what translation was for, we have to know what problems the early Saints were trying to solve. We ought to understand the attributes of the modern world they found oppressive, what traps they were trying to avoid.

Implications

What might Smith's metaphysics of translation mean for understanding the Latter-day Saint experience and nineteenth-century America? Most basically, my account reframes prior accounts of translation in Latter-day Saint history.[39] The dominance of merely textual models of translation—in writings by both practitioners and critics—is a legacy of assumptions that are alien to the documents and people involved. Within a distinct strain of biblicism that mixed esotericism and Common Sense rationalism, these translations are comfortable with and dependent on the interweaving of physical and metaphysical realms. Early Latter-day Saint thought proves to be much more complex, creative, and interesting than has often been allowed. Antique modes of thought clearly persist in the idea worlds of Smith and his disciples. The Latter-day Saints straddled modern and premodern worlds with substantial ambivalence. They used forms and techniques borrowed from modernity—human perfectionism, religious voluntarism, commonsense reasoning, among others—to argue for antique ends. The early Saints were not allowing the universe to be measured by the canons of modern culture, but Smith was glad to use whatever tools were lying around the shop. And, often, he used those familiar tools in ways his compatriots found odd, if not absurd.

Joseph Smith's Translation also reinterprets a handful of familiar concepts within Latter-day Saint history. Priesthood, anthropology, materialism, the theology of scripture, the role of the Book of Mormon, the nature of the New Translation of the Bible, the purpose and mechanics of the Egyptian Bible, and the nature of religious community within the Latter-day Saint tradition all look different when viewed from the lens of the metaphysics of translation.

Exploration of the metaphysics of early Latter-day Saint translation also sheds light on broader questions about religion in America, particularly questions

---

[39] The main exception to the rule is Hickman, "Reconfiguration." Hickman and I agree about the importance of metaphysics to translation. We disagree about the metaphysics.

about the "religious" and the "secular."[40] Scholars now maintain that the two words are plastic and contextual,[41] but their polarity mattered to historical figures and to their modern observers, even if they often seem hopelessly overlapping. As I argue in section 1, the spaces Smith and his disciples carved out within American idea worlds demonstrate the vast space beyond and between traditional stories about the oppositions of religion and secularity. The Latter-day Saint tradition—the most successful of the Christian heresies of America's nineteenth century—has been relatively unexplored for insights into the disparate paths available through the thickets of modernity.

By way of example, believers can use fastidious rationalism to interact with supernatural visitors; the correspondent cosmos can support an aggressive emphasis on human this-worldly flourishing. Agitators for religious tolerance can desire local theocracy. Time can be flattened into eternity rather than away from it. The required polarities of modernity don't have to exist and often will not in concrete lives. I am thus not exploring "the secular" in any traditional sense. Instead I'm asking how lives were lived and ideas thought in defiance of specific dichotomies, even as I acknowledge that actual experiences of actual cultural change have shaped what we mean by secularity.

The Saints' distinctive place within Protestant America illuminates in novel ways what was at stake conceptually and ideologically even as it troubles and teases aspects of modernity itself. Perhaps most importantly it shows that our current society wasn't inevitable—many different paths were available in the nineteenth century but ultimately foreclosed. We are now living what happened to survive the nineteenth century at large scale. But other cultures survived too, including that of the Latter-day Saints. People trying to understand the twenty-first-century Saints may benefit from understanding their early alliances with and hostilities toward core tenets of modernity.

Some readers may worry that I take Smith too seriously or have created a robust theological system from his incoherent ideas. He was, after all, a migrant agricultural worker in the mystical wilds of western New York, and his followers were often cut from the same cloth. According to critics and disciples alike, he was a man of limited formal education. Beyond the scriptural texts he dictated, his thought is fragmented across audits and recollections of oral sermons, ghost-written essays, coauthored editorials, and a handful of letters. Although many thousands of pages have been written about his teachings in retrospect, the truly contemporary documentary record is sparse. So why does Smith look so interesting and his thought so full-bodied in my account? Primarily, I think he was

---

[40] See, e.g., Grasso, "Religious and Secular," 369–70.
[41] Smith, *Map Is Not Territory*, 179–97; Orsi, *Cambridge Companion*, 3–8; Modern, *Secularism*; Coleman, "Secularization"; Moore, "Culture Industry."

a fascinating thinker comfortable manipulating complex conceptual structures in practical and relevant ways. And, even in his eclecticism, he operated within a now less accessible but historically coherent view of the cosmos. I'm aware that at some level all scholars and interpreters practice eisegesis, inserting themselves and their sensibilities into the texts they study. I've worked to limit such intrusions to the extent possible. My goal is to be both sympathetic and rigorous—what I report here appears to be what the documents tend to mean when they are read within their cultural contexts. I'm trying to recover what Smith's Restoration looked like to the people involved at the time it happened. At the same time, I worry that concerns about overly coherent scholarly treatments bespeak a smoldering elitism that sees folk intellectuals as inferior to traditional scholars. I believe that my treatment is consistent with recent historiography that emphasizes the odd and marginal folk, discovering the rich complexities and integrity of their lives outside the mainstream. Smith and his followers had that "lived religion" in spades.

Similarly, my account of the words and worlds of the early Saints is intended to be of complementary use to academics and other observers or practitioners, regardless of their often substantial methodological and epistemological differences. I make no requirement of readers as to the truth claims of Smith and the religious traditions deriving from him. A sympathetic curiosity and a willingness to understand foreign conceptual contexts opens a view across cultural differences.

Living fossils can be difficult to comprehend because they span incommensurable epochs. Their ancient aspects can be disorienting for modern observers. If you think you've caught a rainbow trout, a coelacanth is a terrible shock, gruesome even. If you're looking for a coelacanth, though, they are lovely and wild. I have sought to provide a field guide to this distinctive fish.

I suspect that many of us are curious about people of the past primarily because we wrestle, in our own very different ways, with the hard, big questions ourselves. We came from the people of the past, however remote and hazy the ancestry. The answers we seek and accept have changed, to be sure, but we will continue, necessarily, to wonder. *Joseph Smith's Translation* adds texture and clarity to that quest.

SECTION 1
CONTEXTS

Before moving into Smith's scriptural texts, we ought to engage the conceptual and cultural contexts in which they came to be. Those contexts are dominated by a loose and conflicting agglomeration of ideas that are often evoked by some combination of "secular" and "modern" in opposition to their antonyms "religious" and "ancient." An old consensus, especially in sociology, held that Western society was progressing from a superstitious past to a future free of religion. The German sociologist Max Weber (1864–1920), under the guise of "disenchantment" and the "iron cage" of consumer capitalism led the charge. This core conceit was an early twentieth-century story about the postmedieval period that sought to understand industrial capitalist societies. Proponents called the process "secularization."

Traditional secularization stories focused primarily on societal structures, including the legal barriers between church authority and state power, and secondarily on the number of people who report that they are no longer Christian. Where legal barriers are high and many have left Christianity, a society is secularized. Many early advocates of secularization saw the final purgation of "religion" from society as the inevitable outcome of the secularization juggernaut. That boosterism has proved inaccurate. The world is more complex than all that.

The word "secular" itself (from an Etruscan word for a human generation) means "of an age" or "of a century."[1] It means this-worldly concerns that are appropriate to a mortal context. Traditionally, secular was a member of a complementary pair; in Catholicism, for example, the secular clergy were those who ran parishes, while the religious were the nuns and monks who lived apart from the world. After the Reformation (albeit with antique precedents[2]), "secular" increasingly referred to the authority of state apparatus in opposition to church hierarchies. At the individual level, secular was the press of the everyday—work and wages and practical objects—complementing that which enriched

---

[1] Feeney, *Caesar's Calendar*, 145–46. I thank Jim Faulconer for this source.
[2] Wilken, *Religious Freedom*.

the everyday: love and worship and wonder. Until late in the nineteenth century, "secular" had no special polemical or partisan connotation.[3] It was, like "temporal," a neutral account of aspects of human existence that mattered but weren't the whole story. Over the twentieth century, secular came to mean a particular flavor of elite Western modernity, coloring the preceding centuries and predicting the subsequent ones. But what exactly the term meant even then wasn't clear.

In a sprawling book that capped decades of intellectual work, the Canadian Catholic philosopher Charles Taylor argued that the traditional secularization story is deeply misleading.[4] Instead of chronicling politics and legislation or tabulating church attendance, Taylor asked about the types of important questions people in the West could ask and what intellectual and emotional resources they might bring to bear on those questions. He also asked what shaped their modes of being and their experience of themselves. He drew special attention to the nature of religious plurality, individual identity, epistemology, and the shape of the cosmos. In a subtle move that is often misunderstood, he shifted attention away from sloganeering and toward modern Western structures of thought and their essential contingency. "Secular" means so many things, shared between religious and nonreligious folk, that it's difficult to analyze. But the ideas still matter, however difficult to pin with a single word. Taylor proposed that we consider those ideas and abandon any stable modernist notion of the secular.

Taylor's philosophical work enriches historical analyses by others to understand the aftermath of Protestant Reformation[5] and its medieval roots[6] and to better characterize the nature of faith and its critics in early America. The historian Christopher Grasso especially has evoked the unsteady dynamics, including battles and truces, between "faith" and "skepticism" in the American Republic before the Civil War.[7] Others have sought to more firmly establish the role of skepticism in shaping American culture.[8] With Taylor (albeit sometimes while ostensibly arguing with him[9]), some scholars have observed that secularity and religion don't easily disentangle and aren't even coherent categories.[10] The secular is born of the religious both genealogically and taxonomically, borrowing many of its conceptual and ethical sensibilities from Western Christianity. Modern religious folk (both liberals and fundamentalists) are often quite secular, and modern secularists think religiously.

---

[3] See, e.g., Webster, *American Dictionary*, s.v. Sacred, Secular.
[4] Taylor, *Secular Age*.
[5] Gregory, *Unintended Reformation*.
[6] Gillespie, *Theological Origins*.
[7] Grasso, "Religious and Secular," and Grasso, *Skepticism*.
[8] Thus Schmidt, *Village Atheists*, and Porterfield, *Conceived in Doubt*.
[9] Thus, e.g., Butler, "Disquieting History."
[10] Moore, "Religion, Secularization," 237; Grasso, *Skepticism*.

All along, the secular was one aspect of life; only with time and in some hands did it make claims as an independent ideology. Religious people lived in the secular world and were generally glad to do so. They grew crops, went to school, voted in elections, bought clothing, and played games. They did so as people who also worshiped, sang hymns, and talked to suprahuman agencies. The later ideology at play—one thread among many in the Atlantic Protestant tapestry—was the fiction that the secular could and indeed must stand on its own, rather than existing within a religious and human ecosystem. In the secularization stories, the very notion of the secular took on radically different meanings.

Taylor's account is fundamentally philosophical and theological (and admittedly focused on Western Christendom rather than broader global contexts), but he raises questions that merit exploration in American religious history. We need not see Taylor as a historian of American religion to find his conceptualizations useful in triangulating some of the stakes and tensions confronting those who lived in the nineteenth-century Atlantic world.[11]

In using some of Taylor's ideas as lenses for viewing nineteenth-century America, I explore multiple axes of tension and differentiation rather than attempting to place individuals or groups into distinct adversarial camps. People may certainly have seen themselves as belonging to warring groups, but those divisions were fluid and map poorly onto modern terminology. Reality is always murkier than ideal, and I will explore that murkiness.

In fact, the Latter-day Saints often stood askew of modern dualisms like secular versus religious. They tended for example to occupy a radical third category between the faith and skepticism that Grasso chronicles.[12] They were advocating, all at once, too much faith and too much skepticism. Skeptics used the Saints as evidence of the risks of faith, and traditional Protestants denounced Smith's followers as the lunatic products of "infidelity."[13] Latter-day Saints didn't fit within the usual polarity, and this disoriented the groups arrayed on either side; it probably still does. The Saints were deeply and strangely both secular and religious. Their views on and experiences with three major axes of cultural difference contextualize the scriptural translation that is the focus of this book. I devote one chapter to each of those axes.

Chapter 1 begins this section with perspectives on the power and meaning of language. As best we can tell, humans have attributed special power to language since the first time they spoke. Many nineteenth-century Americans still believed that language could be charged with great power, even as critics argued

---

[11] Mullen, *Chance of Salvation*, 19, correctly describes Taylor's account as genealogical rather than historical.
[12] Grasso, *American Faith*.
[13] Grasso, *American Faith*, 218, 418–19. See also Bacheler, *Mormonism Exposed*, 24; Hunt, *Mormonism*, iv–v; and Fluhman, *Anti-Mormonism*, 73–74, 82.

that language was flat and conventional. Smith sought to master hieroglyphs in their antique sense and recover the sacred, primordial language God spoke in the Garden of Eden. The Saints hoped that this primordially pure language could take them beyond the fallen world to a persistent identity with God. Smith treated language as both metaphysically essential and entirely conventional.

In chapter 2, I explore time. The explosive debates about the nature of time associated with the new physics of the twentieth century were still in the future, but a modern flattening of time and an associated indifference to deep or sacred history was already being cultivated when Smith began dictating his translations and revelations. Early Latter-day Saint views of time reflected and disputed prevalent ideas about the nature of time and history. Latter-day Saint primordialism veered toward the entire disruption of time. In the final period of earth's history, kicked off by Smith's time-defying Book of Mormon, all dispensations would come together in sacred simultaneity. While Latter-day Saint primordialism is well known, much remarked, and consistent with other Restorationist movements in the Atlantic world, it hasn't been appreciated how much this primordialism was part of an overall attitude toward time that was tightly bound to human relationships across generations. He flattened time, but with a radically different purpose than purely "secular" approaches.

In chapter 3, I consider the nature of human identity in early Latter-day Saint thought. According to Taylor, the old self was born into its identity, which it derived as God's creature, situated within the Chain of Being. The modern self, on the other hand, is buffered against the encroachments of God, society, magic, and demons.[14] This buffered, independent self is also, profoundly, alone. Smith and his followers were not well buffered, not by a long shot. They were susceptible to suprahuman agencies, whether as afflicting providences, spiritual possessions, or personal visits from demons pretending to be angels. They were also porous to their coreligionists, as manifested by multiple, notorious attempts at communal living. These communitarian experiments unfolded in the shadow and pattern of the ancient Enoch's city of Zion, a story told in Smith's New Translation of the Bible, in which an entire city was taken corporately to heaven before the desolation of Noah's flood. The story of Enoch's city was thus a *scriptural* translation about *human* translation. Worshipers melded into each other and into the presence of God. The Saints were utterly porous and wholly divine.

---

[14] Taylor's arguments are spread across a substantial corpus, including especially *Sources of the Self*, *Secular Age*, and *Language Animal*.

1
The Quest for Pure Language

In January 1855, Eliza R. Snow (Figure 1.1), the best-known priestess of nineteenth-century Utah and plural wife of the first two Church presidents, delivered an address to a social group gathered in her brother Lorenzo's hall.

The Saints had been in the Great Basin for less than a decade and were still reeling from the vigilante execution of Joseph Smith and his brother Hyrum in 1844. They had initially settled in the less fertile lands beside a giant salty lake rather than the better location beside the freshwater Utah Lake controlled by the local Timpanogos Nuche band.[1] Even as they expanded their geographical basis, the Saints struggled to survive physically in a complex disequilibrium with Natives and white Gentiles.

But the Utah Saints also saw themselves as building heaven on earth. And that heaven would involve social gatherings, gaiety, and—especially for Snow, a prolific writer—hymns and poetry. She was no stranger to sublime language, having long since become the Latter-day Saints' most famous poet and having recorded many of the most important events of the faith's history with her own pen. In her address at the social hall, she intoned,

> Father Adam, our God, let all Israel extol,
> And, Jesus, our Brother, who died for us all:
> All the praise is imperfect, we *now* can bestow—
> Our expression is weak, and our language *too low*:
> But when Zion that dwells on a planet in light,
> With the Zion perfected on earth, shall unite;
> Sweet, rich, high-sounding anthems, all heav'n will inspire,
> As the pure language flows from the lips of the choir.[2]

In her expectations for the coming age of perfection, Snow was a part of a long tradition among Latter-day Saints and their predecessors. The anticipation of a pure language to be sung in a millennial hymn was the hope of a cure for an ancient curse that condemned human language to fallen inscrutability. When

---

[1] Farmer, *Zion's Mount*, chapters 1–2.
[2] Derr and Davidson, eds., *Complete Poetry*, #244. I thank Jill Mulvay Derr for this source.

Figure 1.1 Eliza Roxcy Snow (Smith Young), one of the most prominent nineteenth-century Latter-day Saints, a poet, theologian, and Church leader. Image courtesy of the Church History Library, The Church of Jesus Christ of Latter-day Saints.

the sanctified city Zion (chapter 3) returned with Christ, language would be perfect again.

Snow was true to Joseph Smith's legacy. He spent his religious career in pursuit of the possibility of a pure language that could liberate believers from the prison of human language. His approaches to the problem were spirited, wide-ranging, and in continuity with ancient traditions.

Language has been a puzzle since antiquity—we cannot imagine human consciousness or community without language, but it regularly fails, betrays, and isolates us.³ Language, to borrow from Walt Whitman, is large; it contains multitudes. Beyond the mere fact of infinite potential (e.g., any sentence can be extended ad infinitum), language exists both as a theoretical system of constraints and the instances of that system every moment it is spoken. It is the present moment and deep history. It is sound waves and marks on durable media.

Smith believed that his task was to discover the language beyond human language, a pure language he thought was once present on earth but had been lost through human sin. The primordial language promised freedom and power. As he puzzled over existence, ontology, and community, he saw the lost pure language as the solution.⁴

Through access to the pure language shimmering beneath the surface of conventional language, Smith and his disciples sought access to the divine realm. The hieroglyph is a central component of their strategy to retrieve pure language, but the web of meaning in which the glyphs are situated and from which they draw their power matters as much as the glyphs themselves. Pure language relied on metaphysical correspondence and an understanding of hieroglyphs as essential names. The story of this language was always a story of beginnings as well as endings.

Language and Its Origins

Although by Smith's time the traditional quest for the original language had fallen under an academic anathema (albeit with some learned holdouts⁵), many commoners continued to wonder what the primordially pure language had looked like. In that Edenic tongue,⁶ there was no separation between the desire to be unified and the words to communicate that unity, no distinction between oral and written.⁷ That primordial language promised fidelity to nature,⁸ simplicity of interpretation,⁹ the unity of thought and word,¹⁰ and the possibility of

---

³ Plato's *Cratylus* and *Phaedrus* consider these questions. See also, e.g., Burnett, *Origin and Progress*, and Irwin, *American Hieroglyphics*, 49.
⁴ Brown, "(Smith) in Egypt," 47–50, and Brown, *In Heaven*, 136–37.
⁵ Miller, *Brief Retrospect*, 2:122, and Burnett's *Origin and Progress of Language* and *Antient Metaphysics*, 4:322–23. Hobbes and others argued influentially against the primordial language: Lewis, *Artificial Languages*, 136.
⁶ Although many sources use "Adamic" to refer to the first language, I propose Edenic as more accurate, since the language was spoken by all in Eden, not just the first man. Eliza R. Snow called it "Eve's tongue": Beecher, "Eliza Enigma," 38.
⁷ Knowlson, *Universal Language*, 10, 13; Clarke, *Holy Bible*, 1:43.
⁸ Knowlson, *Universal Language*, 12, 14; Lewis, *Artificial Languages*, 12, 70, 113, 121; Ebeling, *Hermes Trismegistus*, 20, 79; Taylor, *Secular Age*, 760–61.
⁹ Lewis, *Artificial Languages*, 126; *EMS* 2:18 (March 1834): 141–42.
¹⁰ In many respects, pure thought unencumbered by human language is what Christian mysticism aimed for. See Bernard McGinn's *Presence of God* series.

an end to ethnic or denominational strife.[11] It also, for some, promised access to the power by which God created the earth, by which "chaos heard, and worlds came into order."[12]

The stories about this powerful language at the beginnings of the world come first in the earliest chapters of the Hebrew Bible that were central to Smith's understanding of the potential of divine language.

Language in the Primeval History

Readers have long debated how precisely God created the world in the Hebrew Bible. The Genesis text is clear, if laconic: God spoke, and the world came into being.[13] The specific theology of the divine Word changed significantly over the centuries, but whatever the ultimate interpretation, "God said 'Let there be light': and there was light."

Once God had created heaven and earth and the humans and animals to populate earth, God began speaking to the humans (1:28–30). Humans seem never to have existed without language. The capacity to understand language may well have been part of what was intended in the report that humans were created in God's "image" (1:27).

The garrulous human couple soon called together every specimen of animal creation and bestowed on each a name. In the succinct language of the King James Bible (Genesis 2:19–20), God "brought" all the newly created animals "unto Adam to see what he would call them." While God had apparently named everything else, humans had to name the animals themselves. According to this early Hebrew account, "whatsoever Adam called every living creature, that *was* the name thereof." These terse sentences contain and partially obscure a rich network of meaning and presupposition stretching over millennia. If God created humanity and named the first humans, why could he not also name the animals he had created? Did God reveal Adam's name (the literal sense of the Hebrew is probably "the human") to Adam? If so, did Adam follow a similar methodology in naming the animals? Did Adam develop written signs or just spoken names? Most importantly for the themes of this chapter, is language natural or conventional? Does any word, any name, have a scope or power beyond its mere capacity to designate an object in the world?

---

[11] Knowlson, *Universal Language*, 15: Peters, *Speaking into the Air*, 18–20; *The Christian Baptist* 4 (March 1827): 312–14.

[12] *JSPR2*, 318.

[13] This is distinct from other ancient Near Eastern creation stories, like the Babylonian *Enuma elish*. Instead of winning a battle with swords, spears, and lightning, God subdued chaos for the Hebrews with the power of his voice. I thank Jana Riess for this juxtaposition.

Jewish mystics, Christian philosophers, mainline clerics, Western esoteric thinkers, and many lay believers all maintained that Adam commanded a sacred language, and the naming episode expressed metaphysical power.[14] Specifically, Adam chose names that reflected the true nature of a given animal. In other terms, Adam's language is *natural* rather than *conventional*. Would a rose by any other name really smell as sweet? In God's language, no.

According to traditional narratives, the primordial purity of Eden ended with the Fall, but for many Bible readers, language did not follow suit for several of the notoriously long generations of Bible characters. For many, the fall of language came instead at Babel (Babylon), after God had destroyed and then recreated the world through the Flood.[15]

Genesis 11:1–9 tells the story of an attempt to build a "city and a tower" on the plain of Shinar (possibly the area adjacent to the Chebar Canal in modern Iraq) in Babylon that would establish a "name" strong enough to protect the civilization.[16] God apparently realized that a unified language made possible the imperial dominance of Babylon. The possession of a unified language may have blurred the distinction between God and humans, by giving the civilization a name on par with the name of God. So God settled on the "confusion of the ancient language," or the "confound[ing of] the language of men."[17] Thenceforth, language would separate rather than unite humans, preventing their aspirations to make a name for themselves as against God.

Some saw the Curse of Babel as the reason national languages exist, while others viewed the curse as something inherent to the nature of language itself. Not just a multitude of languages, in other words, but language in and of itself had fallen at Babel.[18] Smith found both aspects important.

Language Origins in Christianity

For centuries, the sparse texts of the Hebrew Bible's Primeval History dominated thinking in the West about the nature of human origins and the meanings of language. Christianity had multiple traditions and reasonable consensus on the topic. The great Christian thinker Augustine (354–430) believed that human

---

[14] Among Smith's near-contemporaries, see Priest, *American Antiquities*, 19; Clarke, *Holy Bible*, 1:43; Bellamy, *All Religions*, 28–29.
[15] *Babel* in Genesis 11 is an etiological pun ("jumble" or "confuse") meant to refer to Babylon (which etymologically means "the gate of the gods").
[16] Blenkinsopp, *Creation*, 1, 165–67.
[17] Priest, *American Antiquities*, 22; *EMS* 2:13 (June 1833): 102.
[18] Bauman, *Speaking and Silence*, 1–2, 21; *The Christian Baptist* 2:11 (June 6, 1825): 159; Cornelius, *Languages*, 7–9. Bushnell, *God in Christ*, 13–14, takes the opposite view. See also Gray, *Babel*.

words had been stripped of their meaning and power.[19] While he hoped to situate the power of language in the transcendent word of Christ, he still distinguished fallen human language from the language spoken in Eden. Many of the main streams of Christian thought hewed closely to Augustine's distinction, including the Reformed tradition of John Calvin (1509-1564) and his most famous American interpreter, Jonathan Edwards (1703-1758). For them, nothing human could compare to God; language was as lost as the rest of humanity. Believers could only hope for a regenerating experience beyond human language. Even as Christians tempered their hopes for the here and now, they could anticipate an eventual restoration of divine language when Christ returned, as fulfillment of Zephaniah's (3:9) prophecy that God will "turn to the people a pure language."[20]

For early American believers, the primordial language of Eden—often as the millennial language of Zephaniah—continued to carry substantial weight. Edenic language represented a time of clarity, when the human mind was liberated by language rather than fettered by it. Humans had enjoyed free intercourse with God in Eden: they manifestly had no such access in early America.[21] The memoirs of the African American women Jarena Lee (1783-1864) and Zilpha Elaw (ca. 1790-1873) exemplify the Christian yearning for wholeness in pure language. Lee, for example, recalled her sanctification experience as "past description. There is no language that can describe it, except that which was heard by St. Paul, when he was caught up in the third heaven, and heard words which it was not lawful to utter."[22] Using the precedent of 2 Corinthians 12, she both reported her spiritual experience and admitted that without the heavenly language she could not communicate it. Elaw, for her part, witnessed the recovery of her sister from near death followed by glossolalic singing that signaled true recovery and the call to preach. As she worked her way through her preaching mission (and similar to many Quakers[23]), Elaw became increasingly convinced that the prize was the language beyond human languages. That pure language, she wrote, "seems to be essential for the associations of glorified spirits."[24]

Most believers made do with alternative access to essential truths. The combination of the Bible and the Holy Spirit, as they were mediated by the moral sense shared by all human beings, predominated in antebellum America.[25] Some hoped

---

[19] See especially Book XI of *Confessions*. The philosopher and communication theorist John Durham Peters thinks of Augustine as "the key figure in semiotic theory between Plato and Saussure." *Speaking into the Air*, 67-69.
[20] On Calvin, Huijgen, "Divine Accommodation." I thank Ben Spackman for this reference. On Edwards, Marsden, *Edwards*, 111, and McDermott, *Edwards*, 82.
[21] Thus, e.g., EMS 2:18 (March 1834): 141 and *The Christian Baptist* 4 (March 1827): 312-14.
[22] Ernest, "Governing Spirit," 271-72, and Andrews, *Sisters of the Spirit*, 34.
[23] Bauman, *Speaking and Silence*, 7.
[24] Ernest, "Governing Spirit," 270, 272.
[25] Ahlstrom, "Scottish Philosophy"; Noll, "Common Sense."

that ancient languages, especially Hebrew, still retained connections to the first language.[26] For some—perhaps as part of a spiritual exercise—glossolalia might provide brief and ecstatic access.[27] Others anticipated that righteous efforts to bring about Zephaniah's pure language could help bring the Millennium to pass.[28] For those more prone to limit language's horizons, artificial universal language schemes attempted to mitigate if only at a grammatical level the effects of linguistic diversity.[29] For those open to esotericism, other threads of Hebrew and Christian tradition promised alternative access to that language.[30]

Language in Western Esotericism

Western esoteric traditions are among the most robust modes of preserving ancient ideas about language. Persisting through the nineteenth century, Western esotericism drew on ancient Mediterranean precedents, including alphabetic mysticism, as well as the texts and oral traditions of ritual specialists, the cunning folk traditions of the English-speaking Atlantic and, most proximate to Joseph Smith, treasure quest, Freemasonry, and Swedenborgianism.[31]

For a variety of reasons, many related cultural practices were once termed "magic." The terminology has fallen into scholarly disrepute, largely because it communicates more about relative social status than about the substance of belief or practice.[32] Magic, in other words, is a name people call those they look down on. Not everyone agrees with the scholars. For many readers, even when "magic" is stripped of polemic, it retains the ability to communicate something important to do with supernatural power outside the churches. Such practices employ powerful language that operates beyond understanding and may bind suprahuman agencies. Following scholarly conventions, I won't rely on the term "magic," but I acknowledge the power of words, sometimes as spells or incantations, to shape the cosmos and the nonhuman agencies that inhabit it.

---

[26] Goldman, *Sacred Tongue*, 23–25, 80–82; cf. Buck, *Theological Dictionary*, 298.
[27] Schmidt, *American Enlightenment*, 201–202; Juster, *Doomsayers*, 167–68; *M&A* 1:4 (January 1835): 60; Howe, *Mormonism Unvailed*, 133.
[28] Edward Irving, the founder of the Irvingites in Britain to whom the Saints were justly compared, translated a seventeenth-century millenarian text, published in London in 1827, in which this millenarian interpretation of Zephaniah is advanced. See Lacunza, *Coming of Messiah*, 2:317–19. Cf. *EMS* 1:6 (November 1832): 45; *EMS* 2:18 (March 1834):141–42. Even mainstream thinkers like Samuel Hopkins endorsed this view: Juster, *Doomsayers*, 159.
[29] Knowlson, *Universal Language*, 9–14, 16–17, 29–31, and Lewis, *Artificial Languages*.
[30] Grainger, *Church in the Wild*, 6, 68, 74, 96, 98, 209.
[31] Hanegraaff, *Esotericism*, and Brooke, *Refiner's Fire*.
[32] Styers, *Making Magic*.

(An ancient, less polemical term for words and rituals powerful enough to shape the behavior of suprahuman agency is theurgy, or "divine work."[33])

More recent scholarly work has emphasized continuities with ancient learned traditions, especially as "Platonic Orientalism" (following the historian of esotericism Wouter Hanegraaff).[34] These fragments were most accessible to Smith within the wisdom of cunning folk and treasure hunt, Freemasonry, and Swedenborgianism. This is not to say that esoteric traditions belonged only to fringe thinkers—notables like Yale president Ezra Stiles (1727–1795) practiced versions of Kabbalah, and other scholars continued the traditions of Renaissance esotericism.[35] Pietists and evangelicals also drew on Kabbalah and alchemy.[36] Nevertheless, these three domains are the most relevant tributaries to early LDS thought.

Before his formal religious career, Smith was known as a treasure seer. He worked to locate wells, salt mines, Native artifacts, and buried treasure.[37] The seer's role was to identify propitious locations for a dig and guide attempts at extraction. Treasure seekers sometimes managed demons (often as ghosts or treasure guardians) who protected the treasure. Ritual silence could make or break a treasure dig, while incantations might protect both the dig and its participants.[38] The treasure quest was, among other things, a popular strain of ancient theurgy.

Freemasonry, the most easily accessible and relatively coherent repository of Western esoteric tradition in antebellum America was accessible to Smith throughout his life, albeit with greater intensity in the 1840s.[39] Multiple nineteenth-century treatises proclaimed the close affinity of Freemasonry and the ancient Mediterranean mystery religions—theurgic rites connected to a patron deity and often concerned with ritual access to immortality.[40] The Masonic

---

[33] See Shaw, *Theurgy and the Soul*. The early American Deist writer John Fellows distinguished benign theurgy from necromancy: *Exposition*, 191–93.

[34] Hanegraaff, *Esotericism*, 12. Kabbalah, while an intriguing possibility, became potentially relevant late in Smith's life and can't be disentangled from his interactions with Freemasonry. Owens, "Occult Connection" (the lengthiest attempt to see Smith as a Kabbalist) isn't grounded in expected rules of evidence or interpretation. The arguments in Fleming, "Christian Platonism," are similarly strained.

[35] On Stiles, see Brown, "Chain of Belonging," 6. On the persistence of the Renaissance magus, see Leventhal, *Shadow of the Enlightenment*. Interest in these themes persisted into the twentieth century: Taylor, *Secular Age*, 760.

[36] Grainger, *Church in the Wild*, 6, 98.

[37] Dillinger, *Treasure Hunting*, summarizes an outdated historiography of folk magic within the frame of treasure hunting. More sophisticated treatments of magic include Styers, *Making Magic*, and Hanegraaff, *Esotericism*. Smith only ever minimized his involvement in the treasure quest: *EJ* 1:3 (July 1838): 43.

[38] On the specifics of treasure hunts, see, e.g., Dillinger, *Magical Treasure Hunting*; Taylor, "Supernatural Economy," 4; Taylor, "Smith's Treasure Seeking."

[39] Homer, "Freemasonry" is a useful summary.

[40] Brooke, *Refiner's Fire*, is correct in seeing Masonry as the most relevant link between Smith's Restoration and western esoteric traditions. On connections to mystery religions, Fellows, *Exposition*; Ramsay, *Travels of Cyrus*; Bernard, *Light on Masonry*, 333; Cole, *Freemason's Library*, 16.

writer William Hutchinson proposed that the word "Mason" derived from *mysta*, the Greek name for a participant in the mysteries.[41] The antiquarian hobbyist and Deist activist John Fellows maintained that Masonic secrecy itself derived from hieroglyphs and the mysteries.[42]

Masonic rituals were often concerned with the possession of powerful words. A key goal of lodge work, especially within the Royal Arch, was to discover and then protect the sacred name of God.[43] According to Fellows, "He who pronounces it, say they, shakes heaven and earth, and inspires the very angels with astonishment and terror. There is a sovereign authority in this name; it governs the world by its power."[44]

Though some Masons were concerned with the reconstruction of an entire language, most saw special words as tokens to facilitate their entry into a celestial fraternity.[45] Others held that Masonic codes and ciphers represented a special reprieve from the curse of Babel. In Hutchinson's phrase, Masons "retained the *universal language*, uncorrupted with the confusion of the plains of Shinar, and preserved it to posterity."[46]

The hope of language and clear sight in Masonry was that the observer could see all the way to the reality of things. Quoting the early Christian writer Clement of Alexandria (150–215), Fellows argued, "*Things are seen as they are*; and nature, and the things of nature, are given to be comprehended."[47] Alongside the identification of the names of deity came the use of a new name for individual Masons. In this regard, too, Masonry had something in common with contemporary understandings of the mystery religions.[48]

This is not to say that most Masons were invested in the pursuit of powerful language. According to Fellows,

---

The mystery religions existed in parallel with and occasional subversion of state religion: Burkert, *Mystery Cults*.

[41] Hutchinson, *Spirit of Masonry*, 12–13; Bernard, *Light on Masonry*, 467; cf. Fellows, *Exposition*, 225, 234.
[42] Fellows, *Exposition*, 233, cf. Ebeling, *Hermes Trismegistus*, 122–24. On Fellows, Grasso, *American Faith*, 118, 123.
[43] Fellows, *Exposition*, 153, claimed that the word is *Emmanuel* and the quest for that word is central to Freemasonry. Cf. the critical Bernard, *Light on Masonry*, 429, 454, 516, and Morgan, *Illustrations of Masonry*, 84. Sources aren't always clear about the nature of the "Master's Word."
[44] Fellows, *Exposition*, 242; cf. Bernard, *Light on Masonry*, 549.
[45] Hutchinson, *Spirit of Masonry*, 12–13, with discussion in Fellows, *Exposition*, 225.
[46] Hutchinson, *Spirit of Masonry*, 5; Cole, *Freemason's Library*, 11, 290; compare Hackett, *Freemasonry*, 51. Complexly, some traditions saw the builders of Babel as proto-Masons: Bernard, *Light on Masonry*, 326.
[47] Fellows, *Exposition*, 114.
[48] Fellows, *Exposition*, 236.

> The universal language of Masons, so much vaunted of, extends no further than to a few words, signs, and grips, by which they can communicate to each other that they are Masons, and have been initiated into certain degre[e]s. They may also learn a cypher that is given in the royal arch, but which not one in a thousand takes the pains to acquire.[49]

This disclaimer is worth remembering in treatments of Masonry and Smith's Restoration. Whether to take mystical language traditions (indeed any of the mystical traditions[50]) seriously may have been a minority affair among practicing Masons.

Smith had a more casual acquaintance with Emanuel Swedenborg (1688–1772), who played an outsized role in both esoteric and mainstream cultural contexts.[51] A scientific dabbler, engineer, and bureaucrat in Sweden, Swedenborg turned in middle age to visionary pursuits. In visions he generally made his way across galaxies that were configured—in antique, correspondent style—as a body. He called this humanized cosmos *Maximus Homo* (often rendered the "Universal Human"). Swedenborg propounded an interpretive approach grounded in the hieroglyph to support metaphysical readings of the Bible.[52] In the historian Leigh Schmidt's artful phrase, "Everything harbored hidden correspondences" for Swedenborg; "all the world was a hieroglyph."[53] While in many respects, he was a typical practitioner of Western esotericism, the Swedish mystic became especially widely known as a cultural progenitor of séance spiritualism and the Protestant domestic heaven, both cultural phenomena that merged the earthly and heavenly realms in antebellum America.[54] His contributions to and visions of the nature of pure language have been historically underappreciated: that language was an infrastructure for his metaphysics, eschatology, and hermeneutics.[55]

These three sources are important to the context of early Latter-day Saint ideas about language. While Smith only ever acknowledged using Freemasonry as a conduit to esoteric pasts, the other two, even if indirectly, provide relevant contexts. All three esteemed a vital, powerful language. All three were skeptical that modern human language was adequate to existence. And for all three,

---

[49] Fellows, *Exposition*, 269–70.
[50] Morgan, *Illustrations of Masonry*, 48, 89.
[51] Admitting that documentation is sparse, on intersections between Swedenborg and Latter-day Saints, see Hunter, *Hunter*, 316; Pratt, *Mormonism Unveiled*, 7–8; July 27, 183,9 letter from Isaac Galland, Joseph Smith Letterbook 2, 70–71, CHL.
[52] Meyers, *Swedenborgian Experience*, 28–29.
[53] Schmidt, *American Enlightenment*, 201; Gura, *Transcendentalism*, 60; Goodrick-Clarke, *Esoteric Traditions*, 162–63.
[54] McDannell and Lang, *Heaven*, esp. 183, 217–21.
[55] Wilkinson, *Absolute Language*; Juster, *Doomsayers*, 159.

hieroglyphs played a central role in the quest for pure and powerful language. These sacred pictograms were among the most identifiable, familiar, and persistent markers of the first language.

The Sacred Pictogram

Beliefs about powerful hieroglyphs weren't just in the esoteric currents of society, although such concepts were popular on the margins. While it is reasonable to claim that the hieroglyphic tradition "was everywhere intimately connected with Neo-Platonism, and Christian mysticism,"[56] it's also true that hieroglyphs mattered to many beyond the mystics and formal Platonists.[57] This was especially true in connection with pure language.[58] Though observers included other languages (most often Hebrew, Chinese, and Mayan[59]) in their list of mystical scripts, Egyptian glyphs exemplified the deep meaning of pictograms. These small images, which established a one-to-one correspondence between a physical object and its representation, demonstrated language at its most primal and powerful.[60]

Even if they weren't interested in mystical pictography, people understood glyphs as esoteric symbols in a special kind of language different from modern language. The English Methodist Bible commentator Adam Clarke (1760/2–1832), whose Bible commentary was apparently Smith's favorite, maintained that the Egyptian "magicians" of the Bible were "interpreters of abstruse and difficult subjects; and especially of the Egyptian hieroglyphics, an art which is now entirely lost."[61] Noah Webster (1758–1843) agreed in his 1828 dictionary.[62] Such was common knowledge. Others had uncommon knowledge of hieroglyphs.

When the African American prophet Nat Turner (1800–1831) was trying to understand his call to launch a holy war of Black restoration around 1830, he turned to heavenly hieroglyphs. After realizing that Christ and humanity occupied the stars (the constellations favored by ancients, he argued, were a misprision), he witnessed Christ's blood returning to earth in the form of dew on

---

[56] Iversen, *Myth of Egypt*, 75. See also Brooke, *Refiner's Fire*, 28, 196.
[57] Albanese, *Republic of Mind and Spirit*, 6, 13–16, 26–27, 141, 147, 164; Quinn, *Magic World View*, 151–52.
[58] Ramsay, *Travels of Cyrus*, xv. See also Harkness, *Conversations with Angels*; Oliver, *Antiquities*, 59–61; McDermott, *Edwards*, 95, 127.
[59] On Mayan, Wauchope, *Lost Tribes*, 10–12, 21, 25; on Chinese, *Nauvoo Neighbor* 1:32 (December 6, 1843); McDermott, *Edwards*, 211; and Knowlson, *Universal Language*, 16, 24.
[60] One influential theorist saw them as pointing to the Platonic Forms themselves: Iversen, *Myth of Egypt*, 95.
[61] Clarke, *Holy Bible*, 1: 231. On Smith's relationship to Clarke, see Huggins, "Contemporary Source," and Wayment and Lemmon, "Recently Recovered Source."
[62] Webster, *American Dictionary*, s.v. "hieroglyphic."

the corn. Along with the bloody dew, Turner saw "hieroglyphic characters and numbers, with the forms of men in different attitudes, portrayed in blood, and representing the figures I had seen before in the heavens." These hieroglyphs and a solar eclipse persuaded Turner, in a potent expression of cosmic correspondence, that it was time to launch his own bloody insurrection in 1831.[63] Within a few years of the time Turner was learning his mission from hieroglyphs, Joseph Smith was learning his from similar pictograms, engraved on his gold plates.

In the 1840s and 1850s the early and prominent spiritualist, the Poughkeepsie Seer Andrew Jackson Davis (1826–1910) was finding similar glyphs in nature, albeit with less sanguinary implications. Found on the ground or in the folds of a handkerchief or on a visionary scroll, these were messages direct from the spirit world, which Davis "interpreted" for his audiences as early aspects of the spiritualist revolution. As a mark of the common interest in finding scientific terminology for mystical mergers of the two realms, Davis saw spirits as writing the glyphs electrochemically, much as the daguerreotype functioned to preserve images.[64]

Another critic of the Protestant mainstreams, Ralph Waldo Emerson (1803–1882), was a learned Unitarian dissenter from Boston most closely identified with the post-Christian Romantic movement called Transcendentalism.[65] Fighting against both traditional clergy and critics who sought science in place of spirituality, Emerson and his colleagues argued for a life open to transcendence that came through a turn inward. In this quest, he viewed pictography as the deep history of language.[66] "Every word which is used to express a moral or intellectual fact, if traced to its root, is found to be borrowed from some material appearance," he argued in his seminal 1836 essay *Nature*.[67] He seems to have believed that physical objects, captured in correspondent words, were the "original elements" from which language fell into its modern corruption.[68] The primordial language in Nature had for Emerson a deep and ancient power. Something similar was true of the liberal Presbyterian minister Horace Bushnell (1802–1876). In his sprawling 1849 "Dissertation on Language," Bushnell argued that language derived from the body, sensation, and space—from the encounter with nature as

---

[63] Gray, *Nat Turner*, 9–10. Demonstrating the close ties between hieroglyphs and metaphysical correspondence, when Turner tells his vision to a white man, he is converted and instantly afflicted by a condition in which his skin weeps the same blood, afflicted with the hieroglyphic dew portending Christ's return. Our account of Turner's experience comes filtered through Gray, but this separation from the source doesn't limit the relevance of this hieroglyphic image to the culture of the time.

[64] Davis, *Spiritual Intercourse*, 55–60, 65, 67.

[65] Gura, *Transcendentalism*.

[66] Irwin, *American Hieroglyphics*, 3–13, 28.

[67] Emerson, *Nature*, 23, with discussion in Irwin, *American Hieroglyphics*, 12. See also Holifield, *Theology in America*, 458–59; Conkin, *Uneasy Center*, 236; Marsden, *Edwards*, 111.

[68] Emerson, *Nature*, 27.

it truly was.⁶⁹ Both knew that the original language that partook of sacred pictography was lost. Only fossils remained in modern human languages. Bushnell and Emerson were writing eulogies to lost words and worlds.

The early Saints agreed with traditional ideas about hieroglyphs. The Book of Mormon was written in glyphs they called Reformed Egyptian. Smith's right-hand man for linguistic matters, William Wines (W.W.) Phelps (1792–1872), wrote that the "Egyptians . . . concealed their arts in mystical characters or hieroglyphics."⁷⁰ Early apostle Wilford Woodruff (1807–1898), touring the British Museum on an evangelizing mission in 1840, emblematically admired the papyrus collection "more . . . than any thing" else, realizing that they contained "many glorious things Sacred & historical concerning the early ages of the world Abram & the Prophets &c."⁷¹ Hieroglyphs mattered to Smith's Restoration from beginning to end.

Joseph Smith on Language

Prior to cultural changes associated with modernity, a formidable, pictographic language existed behind a curtain separating it from language's current broken and conventional form. Believers knew that most human language was mundane; they just believed that there was more to the story. Ideas about language thus in some respect paralleled the broader distinctions between immanent and transcendent (and the attendant queasiness about transcendence; see chapter 7). The Saints and others were keen to find access to a language that touched on the transcendent realm and forged connections across time and space. Hieroglyphs were an especially conspicuous and powerful mechanism for preserving that power. The philosophical and ethical positions that became increasingly prominent over the eighteenth and nineteenth centuries tended to resist that power, deeming metaphysical correspondence a superstition. The familiar, flat, arbitrary language everywhere visible in the contemporary world, they announced, was all there was to language.⁷² Although this view would later hold sway in educated Western society and certainly had partisans at the time, such an exclusively

---

⁶⁹ Holifield, *Theology in America*, 458–59; Bushnell, *God in Christ*, 22–25. See also Durfee, "Horace Bushnell," 57–70.
⁷⁰ *EMS* 2 (July 1834) 22: 173. See also *M&A*, 2:3 (December 1835): 235, amplified in *The Wasp* 1:4 (7 May 1842): 3 and *T&S* 3:13 (2 May 1842): 774.
⁷¹ *WWJ*, 1:535, cf. *T&S* 3:22 (September 15, 1842): 925.
⁷² This is the classic position of the modern consensus attributed to Hobbes, Locke, and Condillac in Taylor, *Language Animal*. Gura, *Transcendentalism*, 24–25, 37, attributes this tradition to Locke's 1689 *Essay Concerning Human Understanding*. We should acknowledge that even Locke imagined that an angelic language was free of these constraints: Peters, *Speaking into the Air*, 87.

secular position didn't satisfy many in the pews, let alone radical critics like Joseph Smith.

For Smith the problem was personal, as well as theoretical. Although naturally intelligent, Smith was poor and uneducated. A popular orator as long as his audience wasn't too urbane, he always struggled to write. He resented the highbrow professors that had seemed to make of the Bible and Christianity a Babel of denominational strife. His friends often misunderstood or betrayed him despite his charisma, and he felt alone in the crowd, unable to make his mind known. In one of his last sermons, he summarized this theme in his life. After stating, "I have no enmity against any man. I love you all," he sighed, "you never knew my heart; no man knows my history; I cannot tell it."[73] Smith yearned throughout his life for a time when language could connect rather than divide and hoped that others could see with him the ways that heavenly language crackled with power. While he—advertently or not—made his way into philosophical controversies of sophistication and antiquity, he came at the questions with the practical enthusiasm of a frontier autodidact.[74] He brought together a number of threads in a quest for the perfect clarity and power that God could bestow on believers. Although his methods varied over time, the problems with language were apparent to Smith from the very earliest phase of his career. His ways out of that bind included glossolalia, visionary hieroglyphic scripture, direct access to Eden's language, and a temple ritual that ultimately recapitulated the naming of animals in Eden (chapter 7). Fundamentally, Smith was concerned to overcome the aftermath of the curse of Babel.

Fallen Human Language

The curse of Babel bothered Smith. It was the reason language had become a prison from which he struggled to be free. That curse was the reason humans were alienated from each other and at least part of the reason they were estranged from God. In June 1832, he worried to his first wife Emma about "[his] inability in convaying [his] ideas in writing."[75] The next month, he wrote to Phelps, "[I] cannot write my feelings, neither can toungue, or language paint them to you. I only can observe that I could wish, that my heart, & feelings thereof might for once be laid open before [you], as plain as your own natural face is to you by looking in a mirror."[76] In an 1839 letter to Emma, he indicated that

---

[73] T&S 5:15 (August 15, 1844): 617.
[74] Brown, "Ghostwriter."
[75] JSPD2, 256.
[76] JSPD2, 261.

"with immotions known only to God, do I write this letter, the contemplations, of the mind under these circumstances, defies the pen, or tounge, or Angels, to describe, or patint, to the human being, who never experiance what we experience."[77] He could never get fallen language to work.[78]

Smith's frustrated yearning never went away. Even after finishing all his major translation projects, Smith still mused in his journal in 1843, "I cannot find words to express myself I am not learnd. but I have as good feelings as any man. O that I had the the [sic] language of the archangel to express my feelings once to my frends. but I never expect to."[79] The linguistic failure wasn't from a lack of trying; nor did his increasing exposure to ancient languages solve the problem with words. What he needed was the language of archangels, the language of God.[80]

The Tower of Babel and its aftermath registered in complex ways in Smith's writings.[81] It wasn't just that fallen language was inadequate; it could be dangerous. A key problem within the Book of Mormon is a band of criminals named for its ancient leader Gadianton, a disciple of the devil. These Gadianton robbers used language as a code to hide criminal conspiracies, thus apparently reinstating a primordial transgression recounted in the Visions of Moses (Moses 5:51; see chapter 5). The Gadianton band embodies the dangerous uses of language: deception, secret schemes, and exploitation. According to Helaman 6:28, the cursed Babylonian builders on the Plain of Shinar were inspired by Satan just as the Gadianton robbers had been. They were kindred spirits—those who got language cursed, and those who used language in accursed ways—and both would be punished. This passage implicitly adds a new valence to the old story; perhaps the proto-Babylonians had already corrupted language for nefarious purposes, and God just brought that corruption to its natural conclusion. Similarly, Gadianton-like "secret combinations" were the downfall of the Jaredite civilization, a society that preceded the Lehites and derived from the only tribe to have even temporarily escaped the curse of Babel (Ether 8:15–26). Language imbued with evil power was an existential threat.

The Jaredite narrative itself provides another key view on Babel. This central narrative-within-a-narrative tells of the archetypal people of Jared (perhaps named after Enoch's father) who fled the curse of Babel. The Jaredites were protected only by their tribal leader's brother (named Moriancumer[82]), whose soul was so well aligned with God's that he was able to see God's body and know

---

[77] *JSPD6*, 403; see also *JSPD7*, 57.
[78] He shared this experience with others, including the famously pious Methodist Sarah Jones: Grasso, *American Faith*, 76.
[79] *JSPJ2*, 361.
[80] Compare Alma 29:1.
[81] See also Brown, *In Heaven*, 129–31.
[82] *T&S* 2:11 (1 April 1841): 362, and Ether 2:13.

God's language (see chapter 3). Theirs was a story of escape from language's curse. The key to their freedom was a prophet with seer stones, profound faith, and a command of metaphysically powerful language. The Jaredite story resonated in the lives of Smith and his disciples. The early apostle Thomas Marsh wrote in 1831 of his anticipation that "the Lord God will turn to the people a pure language; this is the first language, and it is still preserved on the plates of Jared, and will be the last language that will be."[83]

After the Book of Mormon, Smith's scriptures continued to engage Babel. In his New Translation of the Bible (chapter 5), as he transitioned from the Noachian flood narrative of Genesis 6–10, Smith recited the Babel story with brief but significant modifications. Where the biblical narrative left punishment for pride as an implicit theme, he added two clauses to emphasize that the confusion of languages was a direct consequence of transgression. The sin was disobedience, as the people "hearkened not unto the Lord," and the loss of "the same language" for all humanity occurred "because the Lord was displeased with their works."[84] Smith clarified the Bible text: the change in language at Babel was indeed a curse.

Smith's closest collaborators agreed. Phelps wrote in an 1832 essay later attributed to Smith, "We can hardly find a language, written or spoken, on earth, at this time, that will convey the true meaning of the heart to the understanding of another." In an essay the next year, Phelps cautioned "as to the meaning of words, we are sensible, many contradictions in terms exist, and will till wickedness is destroyed, and the Pure Language returned."[85] Adam Clarke made much the same argument, while a Latter-day Saint editorialist later complained that "language has become confounded, corrupted, changed, mixed and adulterated, so that words are very unintelligible signs of ideas."[86] Even if language was conventional, as the philosophers, freethinkers, and linguists increasingly claimed, it was a mangled convention. Mortal language was nothing to be proud of. While Smith would have abhorred the elitism of Tocqueville—who saw linguistic failings as "a deplorable consequence of democracy"—he would have agreed that language was imprecise and prone to betray its speakers.[87]

In 1832 Smith wrote to Phelps, "Oh Lord God deliver us in thy due time from the little narrow prison almost as it were totel darkness of paper pen and ink and a crooked broken scattered and imperfect language."[88] In the past I've

---

[83] *Hopkinsian Magazine* 4:18 (December 31, 1831): 285. I thank John Turner for this source.
[84] *NewT*, 120–21 (Genesis 11). The Book of Mormon (Helaman 6:28) announced that Satan had directly orchestrated the plans to build the tower at Babel.
[85] *EMS* 1:4 (September 1832): 25, cf. *T&S* 5:19 (October 15, 1844): 672. See also *EMS* 2:14 (July 1833): 111; and *EMS* 1:11 (April 1833): 88.
[86] Clarke, *Holy Bible*, 1:88; *T&S* 4:7 (February 15, 1843): 105.
[87] Tocqueville, *Democracy in America*, 2:64–70, esp. 67.
[88] *JSPD2*, 320.

understood this tiny prayer as Smith struggling, like the biblical Moses, with his lack of facility with English, especially its written form. That's almost certainly true. He often complained of feeling self-conscious about how poorly his writing measured up to the educated elite of his age.[89] But Smith wasn't just hoping to be a better writer. He was also praying to inhabit a world in which language had recovered its primal power. In other words, he was asking not just for his own capabilities to increase but also for the capacity of language itself to expand. The preceding paragraph in the letter to Phelps provides the relevant context. "Oh Lord when will the time come when Brother William thy Servent and myself behold the day that we may stand together and gase upon Eternal wisdom engraven upon the hevens while the magesty of our God holdeth up the dark curtain until we may read the round of Eternity to the fullness and satisfaction of our immortal souls[.]"[90] Language needed to recover its facility at interconnecting human beings, not just with each other but also with the cosmos at large. To "read the round of Eternity" in the fullness of the soul was Smith's overarching linguistic project. He seems to have understood that sacred truths were written in a realm beyond earth, and developing the capacity to read those truths promised an escape from the prisons of language, time, and mortal identity.[91]

The curse of Babel also manifested, according to critics, in the dizzying plurality of disestablished American Protestantism. Many critics saw language as the cause of doctrinal plurality and sectarian strife; this had been true for centuries.[92] The early American Republic contained an intensity of instability and disruption that many felt was unprecedented.[93] Smith and his followers, ardent critics of "the wickedness of sectarianism," agreed.[94] The early apostle Parley Pratt referred to American Protestantism as "the plains of Babel."[95] The missionary Erastus Snow noted that after Babel, "different nations sprang up in Idolatry, speaking different dialects, and . . . in their idolatrous condition counterfeited the true priesthood, and the religion of heaven."[96] Snow was revisiting an argument from the Book of Mormon: as human language drifts away from the scriptural standard, infidelity grows in tandem.[97] The fact that Christian theology

---

[89] Thus, e.g., *JSPD3*, 356, 359, with other sources reviewed in Brown, "Ghostwriter."
[90] *JSPD2*, 320 reads, against the textual evidence, "sound of Eternity." The letter is reprinted in *T&S* 5:19 (October 15, 1844): 674 with "round of eternity," which better matches the manuscript evidence. This reference to eternity has resonance with Alma 7:20.
[91] "Reading the round of eternity" was similar to the panoramic visions in Smith's scriptures: Brown, "Voice of God."
[92] On Reformation concerns, see, e.g., Wilken, *Religious Freedom*, 108. More proximately, see Buck, *Theological Dictionary*, 88.
[93] Howe, *Transformation of America*.
[94] *JSPD3*, 9.
[95] *MS* 2:1 (May 1, 1840): 9, cf. Clarke, *Holy Bible*, 1:87.
[96] *T&S* 2:19 (August 2, 1841): 490.
[97] 1 Nephi 3:19–20, 4:13.

depended on the Bible—limited, as critics observed, by the language in which it was written[98]—made the American religious landscape unstable.

Smith was skeptical that the Bible could survive being encoded in fallen language. Nevertheless, the ancient languages of scripture still held fragments of antiquity that promised, in a hieroglyphic key, access to the primordium.

Sacred Human Languages

Smith took at least two approaches in his quest for primordial language: attention to Bible languages and access to the mystically powerful language of Eden. The day before his thirtieth birthday, as he was initiating formal study of Hebrew, Smith wrote in his official diary, "O may God give me learning even Language and indo[w] me with qualifycations to magnify his name."[99] A few months later, now fully immersed in Hebrew lessons, he wrote, "My soul delights in reading the word of the Lord in the original, and I am determined to persue the study of languages untill I shall become master of them . . . so long as I do live I am determined to make this my object."[100] He found the process spiritually invigorating—describing his 1836 engagement with the Hebrew text, his journal records, "it seems as if the Lord opens our mind, in a marvelous manner to understand his word in the original language."[101]

Smith studied voraciously. I've argued in the past that he was trying to derive authority and respect from his study of ancient languages,[102] but I now find that argument incomplete. He was also trying to gain access to the sacred purity of primordial language, using whatever resources were available to him. In this respect, he was similar to, if more mystical than, his contemporary restorationist Alexander Campbell (1788–1866), a Reformed Baptist primitivist who cofounded what became the Disciples/Churches of Christ movement. Mainstream clergy had been at this project for centuries, albeit generally without the restorationist impulse.[103] Scriptural languages mattered.

Smith believed that the biblical languages were the closest available approximations to the holy language.[104] In this respect he differed radically from his learned, liberal compatriot, Emerson. In his epochal *Self-Reliance*, Emerson argued for a self separated from all antecedents, including those of the cultures

---

[98] Holifield, *Theology in America*, 167.
[99] *JSPJ1*, 135.
[100] *JSPJ1*, 186.
[101] *JSPJ1*, 164.
[102] Brown, "Ghostwriter."
[103] See, e.g., Goldman, *Sacred Tongue*, and Buck, *Theological Dictionary*, 372.
[104] Brown, "(Smith) in Egypt," 54–56.

whose stories are told in the Bible. "If, therefore, a man claims to know and speak of God, and carries you backward to the phraseology of some old mouldered nation in another country, in another world, believe him not."[105] Emerson was interested in primordial ideas and communication, but he would have none of the intercession of biblical languages. In his way, Emerson was not unlike Quakers, who thought that "learning old languages to read other men's words in old books in order to understand God's Word in the original was the extreme of folly."[106]

In a different key, the autodidact preacher Jarena Lee struck a more purely spiritual pose: "it may be with such as [I] am, who has never had more than three months schooling; and wishing to know much of the way and law of God, have therefore watched the more closely the operations of the Spirit, and have in consequence been led thereby."[107] Lee saw her mind as relatively unpolluted by traditional education. This was a strength for her: she was able to see and understand clearly as a result. That wasn't true for Smith. He wanted formal education in scriptural languages.

Even though most of his early work relied on supernatural access to pure language, Smith believed that study could help him understand the sacred languages standing between the present and the primordium. He included formal Hebrew instruction in his frontier fraternity-cum-seminary, the School of the Prophets, hiring an apostate Sephardic Hebraist, Joshua Seixas, to lead classes. He lectured to his family on "the science of grammar."[108] He dabbled in Greek.[109] When the Saints made a list of the valuables lost in the Missouri Mormon War as part of their quest for restitution in 1839, they highlighted "a Library of books part of which were in the Hebrew and Syriac languages."[110] In his last two years of life, Smith hired a German tutor. In that context, Smith came to see even his limited facility with German as part of his scriptural knowledge.[111] Human language was fallen, but some were less fallen than others.

Even as he respected biblical languages, he had his eyes on a target beyond them. He wasn't satisfied with the languages that sufficed for Campbell and other learned Protestants. Smith wanted to cure the schism in the heart of the world, a rupture that grew in part from the distortions of human language.[112] He wanted the ultimate prize: the language of Eden.[113] As he studied Hebrew, he did so with an eye to what lay beyond. He reflected the belief that Phelps endorsed in 1832,

---

[105] Emerson, *Essays*, 58.
[106] Bauman, *Speaking and Silence*, 37–38, quoting George Fox.
[107] Ernest, "Governing Spirit," 263.
[108] On grammar, see *JSPJ1*, 84, 96. On Seixas, see Goldman, "Jewish Apostasy."
[109] *JSPJ1*, 135.
[110] *JSPD6*, 337.
[111] *WJS*, 342, 351, 355, 359, 366, 371.
[112] Barlow, "Fractured Reality."
[113] Brooke, *Refiner's Fire*, 195–97, 212.

that "the sacred poets came nearer the standard of truth . . . because the Hebrew, in which they wrote, was nearer the pure language, with which Adam gave names, than any other since used by man." "Who can read it," he asks, "without being almost led within the veil."[114]

At several points, especially as part of the Egyptian project of 1835–1842 (chapter 6), Smith and his confidants revealed words that they understood to be the language of Eden merged into and modulated by the ancient languages of scripture. Hieroglyphs allowed them to span the gap between biblical and primordial languages. Such was the power of pictographic representations—they could unite languages as seemingly diverse as Egyptian, Hebrew, New Testament Greek, and Edenic through the immutable association of objects and names. Beyond the uses of special names and Edenic phrases in the temple (chapter 7), the vestiges of Edenic power are visible in traditions about mystically powerful speech acts in Latter-day Saint scripture.

The Power of Language

Smith's Book of Mormon deals frequently with the question of supernaturally powerful language, starting with its Reformed Egyptian glyphs and including several prophets who possess divine speech. The Jaredite narrative of Moriancumer casts a long shadow. When the final Book of Mormon editor Moroni complains to God about his personal weakness in writing, he says of his Jaredite antecedent, "thou madest him that the things which he wrote were mighty even as thou art, unto the overpowering of man to read them."[115] Moroni is describing a capacity greater than rhetorical skill. For Moriancumer, whom Moroni so admired, freedom from Babel's curse (Ether 1:34–37) imparted to his words a supernatural force. While the scriptural text doesn't make the connection clear, Moriancumer's capacity with language apparently came from his transformative experience early in the narrative (chapter 3). In that encounter, the finger of God illuminates special stones to guide the Jaredite exodus. Those stones, we discover, become the Gazelem seer stones that make possible translation within the Book of Mormon.[116] They are handed down with the plates, and possession of them constitutes seerhood.

The genesis of those stones is thus a scriptural account of hieroglyphs. The stones were physical remnants of a prophet's direct encounter with God's writing

---

[114] *EMS* 1:6 (November 1832): 45. Goldman, *Sacred Tongue*, provides additional cultural context for American reverence for Hebrew. See also Knowlson, *Universal Language*, 12.
[115] Ether 12:20, 23–24, 30.
[116] On the *Gazelem* stones, Brown, "Voice of God," esp. 149–52; Ashurst-McGee, "Prophethood," 275–76, 310; D&C 17:1.

finger. This is what ancient glyphs do: they merge physics and metaphysics at their confluence with the primordial language. From Moriancumer's faith to God's finger to Smith's seer stones to the English scriptures he created, we trace a braiding of glyphic instruments and otherworldly meanings.

Centuries after Moriancumer, a prophet named Nephi (named after the original Nephi, so, following Grant Hardy, I'll call him Nephi$_2$) acquires a similar power of language. Just as Moriancumer, Nephi$_2$ trusts in God and is a faithful servant. Nephi$_2$ is agonizing over his failures to convert fallen Nephites, when the voice of God tells him, "behold, I will bless thee forever; and I will make thee mighty in word and in deed, in faith and in works; yea, even that all things shall be done unto thee according to thy word, for thou shalt not ask that which is contrary to my will" (Helaman 10:5). In a further extension of this power, Nephi$_2$ learns that he will have the ability to exercise Providence itself, commanding famine, pestilence, and other divine punishments (10: 6–10).

The Old Testament seems to have allowed such power only to Joshua, when he commands the sun to stop (Joshua 10:14). The New Testament provided more examples and antecedents. John 1 suggests that the divine Word created the earth and came to dwell there. In a private consultation in Matthew 17:20 (cf. Mark 11:23 and Matt 21:21), Christ tells his closest disciples that if they have "faith as a grain of mustard seed" they will be able to tell a mountain "Remove hence to yonder place," and it will obey their command. "Nothing," Christ tells his faithful followers, "shall be impossible unto you." That promise may have served as a template for the powerful speech revealed in Smith's scriptures.

During his New Translation of the Bible, Smith again engaged the primordial language. In 1830, he revealed that Enoch had a gift like Moriancumer's (Moses 6:34, 7:13). Enoch spoke with God and, in a sense, with God's voice. That latter attribute meant that "the earth trembled, and the mountains fled, even according to his command." This passage makes it clear that these are intended as typological explorations of the promise Jesus made regarding the implications of "faith as mustard seed" in Matthew. Given Enoch's position in the Hebrew Bible's Primeval History, it seems likely that Smith would have understood Enoch to be speaking the Edenic language.

Sometimes Latter-day Saints were to be recipients of this power. Thus J. B. Smith received a blessing in which he learned "if you shall command the wicked to be smitten they shall be smitten."[117] Similarly, Smith promised his brother, Hyrum, when he became Church Patriarch, that "who ever he blesses shall be blessed, and who ever he curseth shall be cursed."[118]

---

[117] *JSPD4*, 259.
[118] *JSPD7*, 524 [D&C 124: 93].

There were potential downsides to this powerful language. An 1838 church court considered the case of a rural elder preying on a vulnerable woman, who thought she might be a widow. The elder threatened her with a curse if she wouldn't marry him—he knew certainly that her husband was dead and she was thus marriageable. He told her that he had the power of Nephi$_2$'s language, which explained both his knowledge and his ability to curse her. In the event, the missing husband returned, and she prevailed in church court—the creepy elder was disciplined.[119]

Being able to speak the word to the world was one facet of the primordial language. Another was the power of that language when written. Smith's 1830 Visions of Moses is carefully concerned with assuring that the primordial language be preserved in scripture. Father Adam and Mother Eve kept a "book of remembrance" that was "recorded in the language of Adam, for it was given unto as many as called upon God" (Moses 6:5). Though Smith never gained access to the specific text, his New Translation of Genesis made clear that the Book of Remembrance was the first human scripture.[120] The connection between God's creative word and scripture, made rhetorically in an 1839 letter to Edward Partridge, further suggests this connection: "he that said let there be light, and there was light hath spoken this word."[121] This phrase tied Latter-day Saint scripture directly to God's first generative words.

"Book of remembrance" is a biblical term from Malachi 3:16.[122] Malachi 3 is concerned with the sudden return of God to his temple in the messianic future. The book of remembrance there appears to be a heavenly record of the pious acts of believers on earth. The tradition about a heavenly book listing those who have been loyal to God is attested (albeit imprecisely) in Exodus 32:31–33, in which Moses and God discuss how much of Israel will be erased. That seems to be the plain sense of Smith's December 1833 reference, in a letter to Edward Partridge and others, to such a book, and it matches typical Protestant interpretations.[123] There's more to it than that, though. In Smith's scripture, there's a generational component that merges genealogy with sacred language.

The early Latter-day Saint concept of intergenerational connection within sacred books is a sustained exegesis of Ezra 2:61–63. Smith made this connection explicit in his November 1832 letter to Phelps.[124] The key verse is 2:62, in which

---

[119] The elder, a widower himself, informed the object of his lecherous intentions that "Br Joseph told him to be cautious who he cursed in the name of the Lord, for who he cursed was cursed, and who he blessed was blessed." *JSPD6*, 124.

[120] Brown, *In Heaven*, 124–28.

[121] *JSPD6*, 363.

[122] Notably, Malachi 3 is one of the few Bible texts spoken aloud by Jesus during his visit to America in the Book of Mormon: 3 Nephi 24.

[123] *JSPD3*, 381, cf. Hindmarsh, *Early Evangelicalism*, 182.

[124] *JSPD2*, 320.

people "sought their register among those that were reckoned by genealogy, but they were not found: therefore were they as polluted, put from the priesthood." One's priesthood and salvation was thus tied to whether one had a family entry in the books of remembrance. Smith expounded this connection further in the letter to Phelps. In his view, believers "should have there names enrolled with the people of God, neither[r] is the geneology to be kept or to be had where it may be found on any of the reccords or hystory of the church there names shall not be found neithe[r] the names of ther fathers or the names of the children writen in the book of the Law of God."[125] Entire kindreds would stand or fall together. They would fall if their "book of remmemberance" was incomplete or incorrect.[126] This makes clearer why Smith felt such urgency to be sure people's names were written into these special books and the ongoing reliance of his teachings on specific readings of the biblical text.

According to Smith's scripture, Eve and Adam used the book to teach their offspring "to read and write, having a language which was pure and undefiled." Centuries later according to Smith's scriptural chronology, the mysterious figure Enoch reported that the sacred text originated with "the first [human being] of all ... even Adam. For a book of remembrance we have written among us, according to the pattern given by the finger of God." That reference to the divine finger is a partial echo of Moriancumer's experience with seeing the embodied Christ, finger first, as part of his protection from the curse of Babel.[127] This also (e.g., Moses 6:5–6) was a way to explain how the primordial language could persist down to the time of the confounding of language in Genesis 11, solving a textual problem within the Bible. The sacred book provided both a memorial and a way to preserve language so that later generations could read it. Adam's Book of Remembrance was not an esoteric manual of hermetic secrets but a sacred vessel to preserve the ancient dead, their voices, and the language they spoke.[128] As happened consistently, language and human identity intermixed. While Smith didn't recover that specific text, he did make an early attempt to recover the Edenic language.

---

[125] *JSPD2*, 319.
[126] *JSPD2*, 320.
[127] Moses 6:5–6, 45–46. Manuscript 1 for 6:5–6 has Moses "write with the finger of inspiration," just as God would in 6:45–46, and in an echo of Ether 3. Manuscript 2 corrects it to the published "spirit of inspiration." *NewT*, 97, 100, 608.
[128] Brooke, *Refiner's Fire*, 195–97, misunderstands the Book of Remembrance in early Latter-day Saint thought.

Samples of Pure Language

Perhaps most striking in the quest for primordial language is Smith's "A Sample of Pure Language," dictated in Spring 1832 as part of his targum of the Book of Revelation and the Gospel of John.[129] In this revelation, Smith provides a tiny glimpse of the language of Eden. In this unfinished dictation (as suggested by a string of related words without syntactical structure at the end), Smith reveals that one of God's names is "Awmen," corrected to "Awman" in the original manuscript and spelled "Ahman" in later publications.[130] This *Awman* is "the being which made all things in all its parts."

This sacred name is one that God shares with Jesus ("Son Awman"), humans ("Sons Awman") and angels ("Awman Angls-men"). These beings are all members of the same species, denominated *Awman*. This odd, brief catechism and Edenic language primer ends abruptly, but in just a few brush strokes it has summarized a central theme within early Latter-day Saint scripture and biblical exegesis: the conspecificity of God and humans, with Christ as the fulcrum for that identity.

The relevant context for the Sample of Pure Language is the New Testament translation project, especially the Gospel of John and Revelation. By their report (D&C 76:15), a visionary experience of February 16, 1832, was meant to clarify John 5:29 for Smith and Rigdon, alongside two dozen other scriptural passages.[131]

"The Vision," as the revelation became known, reported that a hierarchy within the afterlife would assure that basically universalist principles would prevail. Traditional hell was temporary, and the permanent hell, called perdition, was vastly empty. Participants in heaven would be divided into large kindreds bound to specific members of the Godhead based on their degree of righteousness in life. God, Jesus, angels, and human beings were an interconnected host of heaven (esp. 76:20–24). They are (76:58–59) "gods, even the sons of God." In a strong allusion back to the 1830 Prophecy of Enoch (Moses 7), they will enter

---

[129] *JSPR* 1, 264–65. On dating, tradition suggests March 1832, but The Vision (D&C 76) is dated February 16, and as I indicate below The Vision and The Sample share a similar set of concerns. D&C 77 is similar to The Sample in its structure and obvious dependence on the work of the New Translation so presumably came contemporaneously. While they are entered in the Manuscript Revelation Book 1 (MRB1) after a revelation dated March 15 (D&C 81), MRB1 was not kept in real time, and these two revelations are in the part of MRB1 in which entries are commonly placed out of chronological order (*JSPR1*, 5). On the basis of current evidence, neither a February nor a March date takes priority. On the portions of the New Translation occupying Smith at the time, see the tentative dating of *NewT*, 58.

[130] See notes on the history of this manuscript in *JSPR1*, 265.

[131] Isaiah 14 and 66, John 1, John 17, 1 Corinthians 15, Ephesians 1:13, and Hebrews 12 are some of the Bible passages on which Smith and Rigdon drew in their account of The Vision. On the influence of The Vision in the early church, see Bushman, *Rough Stone*, 196–202.

THE QUEST FOR PURE LANGUAGE 43

the heavenly City of Enoch (76:66–67). In a complementary vein and a similar format, D&C 77 deals with various oddities in Revelation, including the angel of 7:2–3 (D&C 77:9), who is tasked with "seal[ing] the servants of our God in their foreheads," a seal that implicitly connects to the "name written in their foreheads" of Revelation 14:1 and the promise of Revelation 3:12 to "write upon" believers "the name of my God."[132] These contemporary texts allow a sketch of a likely etymology for *Ahman*.

On the basis of text and context, the most persuasive interpretation of the Sample of Pure Language is that, using the vehicle of Edenic language, the text reinterprets John 5 in the context of The Vision and Smith's exegesis of references to the name of God in John's Revelation.[133] This pattern of exegesis and intertextuality is typical of Smith's scriptural practice.[134]

For more traditional readers, John 5 begins with Christ's healing miracle at a sacred spring near the Sea of Galilee on a Sabbath. He thereby identifies himself as a miracle worker and a competitor to traditional healers. He also scandalizes the Second Temple *cultus* by plying his trade as a healer on the divinely mandated day of rest. In explaining why he feels authorized to break the rules, Jesus makes clear, in multiple lines of reasoning, that he bears God's name and authority. Jesus and his father are united; "all men should honour the Son, even as they honour the Father" (5:23). His critics accuse him of claiming that "God was his Father, making himself equal with God" (5:18). This reasoning continues to an arresting use of the term *man*: "as the Father hath life in himself; so hath he given to the Son to have life in himself; And hath given him authority to execute judgment also, because he is the Son of man" (5:26–27). Christ then continues to indicate his unity with God, his power over life and death, and his embodiment of God (5:28–43). Christ has come "in [his] Father's name" (5:43). In Protestant hands, this was straightforward Trinitarianism.[135]

That title, "son of man" (*ben 'adam* in the Hebrew, *huios tou anthropou* in the Greek, understood by most biblical scholars now as a prophetic title indicating a human servant of God), seems to have stuck in Smith's craw. It emphasized the humanity rather than divinity of Christ. How could Christ be claiming that he came in his "Father's name" and then use a title that appeared to say the opposite? In other words, How could the "Son of *Man*" be *God*?[136] The Sample of Pure Language solves the problem by proposing that "Son of Man" is an incorrect translation of a cross-linguistic homophony. In other words, Christ is saying that

---

[132] *JSPD2*, 214.
[133] *JSPD2*, 214 misses the crucial connection to John 5.
[134] Frederick, *Allusivity*.
[135] Clarke, *New Testament*, 270–71.
[136] The claim is especially striking in light of 5:34 and 5:41 and is intensified by 5:43, in which Christ specifically states that he is coming in his father's *name*.

he can "execute judgment" in the Father's name because he is the "Son (Awman),"
not the "Son (of Man)." Suddenly the apparent incongruity fades, and we realize that in John 5 Christ was revealing the genetic identity by which he and the Father were one. Instead of Trinitarianism, Smith has located his signature polytheism (chapter 7).

Further evidence for this interpretation comes in the 1830 Prophecy of Enoch, which revealed that "in the language of Adam, Man of Holiness is [God's] name, and the *name* of his Only Begotten is the Son of Man" (Moses 6:57; emphasis added). The text positions "Son of Man" as a name rather than a title or description, consistent with the Sample of Pure Language. Smith seems in 1830 to have seen "Son of Man" as a name, and to have realized in 1832 that the name was misspelled in King James English. Roughly, there seems to have been a phonetic transition in Smith's mind from "son of man" to "son av man" to "son aw man" to "son awman."

Similarly, in the Visions of Moses (Moses 1:12–13), Smith positions Son of Man in contrast to Son of God, consistent with his interpretation of John 5.[137] Nor was this the only time Smith used an unexpected proper name to solve a theological puzzle. In 1829, he had revealed (D&C 19) that the "endless" in "endless torment" (2 Nephi 9:26, 28:23, translating Revelation 20:10) was not an adjective but a proper name for God. It was not the case that hell lasted forever, Smith said. That was mistaking a name of God for an English adjective. Instead, endless punishment was God's punishment.[138]

The *Ahman* etymology contains an apparently genetic claim. God and Jesus (and through the logic of the Vision and the odd phrase in Revelation 3:12, all the saved, including the ministering angels whose status from D&C 76:88 is echoed directly in the Sample of Pure Language) share a single, sacred name, *Ahman*.[139] This was a long-standing exegetical commitment to which Smith returned in his final sermons. Even through his June 1844 Sermon in the Grove, Smith used John 5 to explore the ontological unity of God and Christ.[140]

With the Sample of Pure Language, Smith also addressed an important theological problem vexing Atlantic Christianity. Unitarians had been complaining for decades that orthodox Christians had misinterpreted the New Testament by claiming that Jesus was God. The claim for Jesus's divinity had forced mainline Christians into the doctrine of Trinitarianism, which Unitarians saw as a

---

[137] It's also possible that this sequence has Moses misidentified as Christ (when Satan refers to him as "Son of Man"), and this motivates the counter that he is Son of God instead. Later exegesis of Revelation 14 and 22:4 maintained this approach: Brown, *In Heaven*, 269–70.

[138] I thank Jared Hickman for this observation. Smith wasn't alone in understanding "eternal" punishment as having an end: Daniell, *Bible in English*, 647, and Holifield, *Theology in America*, 221.

[139] I speculate that the ultimately canonical spelling, "Ahman," brought the prefix into accord with King James transliterations of the divine particle "yah."

[140] *WJS*, 378–82.

misinterpretation of language and gross corruption of religion. Some critics characterized Trinitarianism as naked polytheism.[141] Smith's Sample of Pure Language thus directly approached Unitarian criticisms—in John 5, Smith maintained that Jesus had unequivocally claimed his own divinity, using a name in the primordial tongue. As was common for Smith, his solution broke the arguments of both opponents in traditional debates. In the same stroke that answered Unitarianism, the *Ahman* revelation exploded Trinitarianism by rejecting the requirement for strict monotheism. Why talk of a triune God at all when humans and angels were of the same species as God?

Smith made this basic argument against Trinitarianism and Unitarianism on multiple occasions. In an anti-Calvinist amplification of John 6:44 within the New Translation, an effort he likely undertook contemporaneously with the Sample of Pure Language, he again suggested that God and Jesus were one. The King James text is spare—"No man can come to me, except the Father which hath sent me draw him: and I will raise him up at the last day." Smith had the verse read instead, "No man can come to me, except he doeth the will of my Father who hath sent me. And this is the will of him who hath sent me, that ye receive the Son; for the Father beareth record of him; and he who receiveth the testimony, and doeth the will of him who sent me, I will raise up in the resurrection of the just." For humans to be resurrected (implicitly into a God-like status), they had to receive Jesus—there is no initial dependence on the Father.[142] Smith's amplification thus tied John 6:44 back to John 5, The Vision, and the ontology of the Sample of Pure Language. Similarly, in his New Translation of Romans 9:5, Smith adjusted language to indicate that Christ "is God over all"[143] rather than simply God's son. In John 17:12 (a verse partially reinterpreted in D&C 76:31–39), Christ indicates that he has "kept" people in God's "name," another subtle allusion to *Ahman*. In that sacred name in the first language, Smith merged text and ontology.

Although the Sample of Pure Language itself faded from memory—largely subsumed by the Egyptian project that followed in 1835 (chapter 6)—that special word, which identified the ancient sacred name of the divine species, persisted among the Saints. Its central message remained important to the Church in multiple settings.[144] Most famously, Smith deployed *Ahman* in the name

---

[141] This is the core argument, for example, of Joseph Priestley's famous treatise, *Corruptions of Christianity*.

[142] *NewT*, 456–57. Smith is quibbling in this revision with the suggestion of election in the King James text indicating that God would draw people to himself. But the revision is not simply an Arminian rejection of predestined election but also the requirement that God be approached through Jesus.

[143] *NewT*, 490–91.

[144] See, e.g., D&C 78:20 (where the name was added by William Phelps as a code name in the 1835 *Doctrine and Covenants*), D&C 95:17, and *JD* 2:342. Brent Metcalfe ("Adamic Q&A") has identified two additional manuscript copies of this revelation: Orson Pratt, Notebook, 1835–36, MS

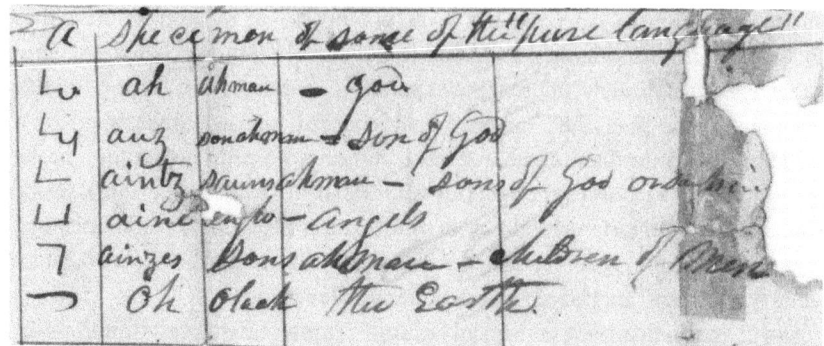

Figure 1.2 Aspects of the pure language in an 1835 letter of W. W. Phelps to his wife Sally Waterman Phelps. Image courtesy of Harold B. Lee Library at Brigham Young University.

Adam-ondi-Ahman, a valley in Missouri where Adam stood as grand patriarch to his descendants shortly before he died. Bringing the Vision's promise of a millennial reunion at Mount Zion full circle, *Adam-ondi-Ahman* was also the site at which Jesus would one day present the human race to God after his Second Coming.[145] Smith returned to the name, albeit in modified form as "the first man or first God," in the last months of his life.[146] Over time, *Ahman* grew from an esoteric homophony to an ontological claim to an intimate geography linking past, present, and future. Such was the promise of pure language and its promise of human communion.

Smith continued to work on the problem of pure language throughout his career. In May 1835, William Phelps sent his wife Sally a letter, in which he (and perhaps Smith) were trying to puzzle through the nature of the primordial language. In it, Phelps reused several of the words from the Sample of Pure Language (Figure 1.2).[147]

In the 1840s Smith revisited this issue with his temple liturgy, in which people learned phrases in the Edenic tongue and received training in the most powerful and direct way to escape the constraints of human language in addressing

---

4812, CHL, penultimate leaf (verso) and Frederick G. Williams, Questions and Answers, circa 1832, Thomas Bullock Collection, MS 27307, bx. 2, fd. 12, CHL.

[145] On Adam-ondi-Ahman, see Brown, *In Heaven*, 111–12. Smith may have proposed in 1838 that the term meant "The valley of God, in which Adam blessed his children" in the original language: *JSPD6*, 163.
[146] See *JSPAR*, 48, 81, 113. The phrasing at *JSPAR*, 81 is a likely source for some of Phelps's verbiage in his 1845 "Paracletes." Brown, "Paracletes."
[147] W. W. Phelps to Sally Phelps, May 26, 1835, MS 810, Box 2, Folder 1, *HBLL*.

God (chapter 7).[148] Until the end, Smith worked with the possibilities of pure language in his preaching. His sermons in the last year of his life became even more emphatic about the power of ancient words, covering an array of Hebrew, hieroglyphic, and Edenic words and their meanings.[149] He was not alone in his commitment to pure language.

Early Latter-day Saints hoped that the pure language would come again as they worked to create the conditions promised to arrive with Christ at his Second Coming.[150] Looking forward to the return of Christ, Parley Pratt's early hymn anticipates, "loud hosannas we'll proclaim / And sound aloud our Savior's name. // Our hearts and tongues all join'd in one, / A loud hosanna to proclaim, / While all the heav'ns shall shout again, / And all creation say, Amen."[151] This is a millenarian hymn, to be sure, and the Saints were enthusiastic millenarians. But Pratt is also hoping that two schisms would be healed. The cleft in the middle of humans, whereby their hearts and their tongues are disunited, must be repaired. And the rising barrier between humans and the cosmos must be torn down. As each person's tongue joins her heart, so will she sing with the earth in renewed union. This was the promise of pure language restored in fulfillment of Zephaniah's prophecy. Phelps thought this was a "glorious prospect of holiness" that was "worth living for, or worth dying for."[152] The dream did not soon die—Smith's followers introduced the short-lived Deseret Alphabet in the 1850s as an homage to language reform and the power of pure language.[153]

For early Latter-day Saint women, the most consistent access to pure language came through the spiritual gift of glossolalia. In their hymn-singing, praying, and preaching in the language of angels (coupled generally with a sermon, called an "interpretation," which sought to reduce the ecstatic hymnody to familiar human language), women experienced power, divine direction, and alternative states of consciousness.[154] Lovina Fairchild Wilson described her 1830s experience with the mystery of glossolalia: "I tried and was filled with words I understand not—language in many tongues I know not. I cannot understand much of it myself."[155] Sarah Cleveland reflected in an April 1842 sermon that "she many

---

[148] On the special mode of communication, see Quinn, "Prayer Circles"; on Edenic language, see Brooke, *Refiner's Fire*, 248.
[149] See, e.g., *WJS*, 187, 203, 213, 215, 230, 244, 247, 341, 351, 358–59, 366, 379–80 for uses of Hebrew and Greek. Many Egyptian usages are discussed in Brown, "Ghostwriter."
[150] *EMS* 1:9 (February 1833): 69.
[151] Smith, *Sacred Hymns*, 26–27, cf. Ibid, 37.
[152] *M&A* 1:9 (June 1835): 131.
[153] Watt, *Mormon Passage*, 144–46.
[154] On glossolalia, see Williams, *Pentecostal Glossolalia*; Garrett, *Spirit Possession*; Mills, *Speaking in Tongues*; Schmidt, *American Enlightenment*, 201–202. On Latter-day Saint glossolalia, see, e.g., *MS* 25:28 (July 11, 1863): 439; *Contributor* 3:5 (February 1882); *M&A* 1:4 (January 1835): 60; Copeland, "Tongues"; Howe, *Mormonism Unvailed*, 133.
[155] Johnson, *Female Religiosity*, 34.

times felt in her heart, what she could not express in our own language, and as the Prophet had given us liberty to improve the gifts of the gospel in our meetings, and feelings the power resting upon, desired to speak in the gift of tongues; which she did in a powerful manner."[156] Glossolalia was important in the Church for decades, from Kirtland through Utah.[157] Consistently believers saw themselves as approaching the Edenic language in their tongue speaking.[158] More than other outlets for public spirituality, glossolalia met with approval from church leaders, including Joseph Smith and others,[159] albeit with typical concerns that incautious glossolalia could destabilize the Church.[160]

As so often, women had in this case to build their religious experience and traditions from ephemera.[161] Rather than the engraven glyphs of the Book of Mormon or the millennia-old ink-on-papyrus of the Book of Abraham, women encountered the pure language in the evanescent sounds made when they sang in angelic choruses. This glossolalia isn't so terribly different from the experience Joseph Smith had with translation: a mystical encounter beyond words, followed by an attempt to reduce that ecstatic revelation into human language.[162] Once again, the problem was in seeing through everyday language to states of knowledge and communication beyond the merely physical. This hunt for language beyond language was a central component of the Latter-day Saints' straining toward the primordium and through it to the world's ending.

Conclusion

Language is puzzling, like an unsteady combination of water and air. We swim in it and breathe it, but sometimes we choke and might even drown. As it flashes in and out of our awareness, we catch glimpses of the limits of our minds and their perceptions. And those limits just make us hungrier for true awareness and actual communion. That struggle with language is very old, and it's an overriding concern for Joseph Smith and his followers. Smith blamed Babel for that state of affairs, and he and his followers waged pitched battle against it.

---

[156] Derr et al., *First Fifty Years*, 51.
[157] Ellingson, "Beliefs and Practices," 43–48; Corrill, *Brief History*, 9.
[158] Brown, *In Heaven*, 136–37; Lewis, *Artificial Languages*, 128.
[159] Newell, "Women's Share." At the conference of January 22–23, 1833, Smith "spake in an unknown Tongue" along with "all the Elders" and "several of the members of the Church both male & female." The glossolalia included hymns, sermons, and prayers: *JSPD2*, 381. See also *JSPH1*, 103.
[160] Thus, e.g., *WJS*, 3–4, 12, 119; *JSPD6*, 548; *JSPD3*, 167.
[161] The Shaker founder Ann Lee was also drawn to language mysticism, for which she was criticized by the Deist Ethan Allen: Holifield, *Theology in America*, 327.
[162] Brown, "Language of Heaven."

Correspondence, hieroglyphs, and the pure language that embodies them drove Smith's aspirations for linguistic translation and undergirded the connection he saw between linguistic and human transformation. He fit within long-standing intellectual traditions in both mainstream and esoteric thought. He seemed to agree with modern philosophers of language that contemporary human language was flat, conventional, and devoid of metaphysical power. He just didn't believe that was all there is.

Smith proved hungry to move from bare human language back to the primordial language from which it was estranged at Babel. Struggling persistently against that curse, he worked to develop the ability to "read the round of Eternity." The building blocks of this work were often the limited words of the King James Bible whose unsolved problems led Smith directly to that primal realm. Most notably, his 1832 Sample of Pure Language simultaneously solved a puzzle within the text, identified humans as God's literal children, and placed readers within the language beyond language. This possibility that words on a page contained identifiable echoes of the pure language motivated Smith in his desire to apply folk-scholarly techniques to his linguistic work. He was an autodidact scholar and a mystic and had no compunction about merging the two categories, however anachronistic that merger appeared in antebellum America. He saw his job as a seer to map out the relationships between the two realms, using words, intellect, and inspiration as his tools.

Smith used the sacred language, especially in his notion of books of remembrance, as a connection between humans and language that held the capacity to penetrate the haze of time. His need to defy the ravages of time is a key motivation in his quest for pure language. It's natural, therefore, to follow sacred language into sacred time. The metaphysically potent understanding of time shared by Smith and his followers also placed them at odds with polite modern society.

2
The Nature of Time

In 1845, Parley Pratt, one of Smith's earliest collaborators and a key systematizer of his thought, published an account of an apocalyptic vision. Called "One Hundred Years Hence. 1945," it was printed in both the American and English Church papers and was subsequently published as a freestanding pamphlet.[1] "God, through his servants, the prophets, has given all men a clue to the future," begins Pratt, who moves promptly to describing a panoramic vision of the world's past. With that introduction, the "angel of our presence" (a dual reference to a personal guardian angel and the angel of God's presence[2]) then conveys Pratt from his bed to a vantage point beyond the constraints of usual human time, a movement in space that sets off a movement in time.[3] Pratt and his angel guide arrive at a city built around a "most splendid building," the "TEMPLE OF THE LORD IN ZION" whose name was written "in letters of a pure language, and sparkling like diamonds." As a stunned Pratt marvels at the sublime scene, his escort informs him that he is witnessing the fulfillment of Isaiah.[4] With a start, Pratt realizes that he is inhabiting apocalyptic time a century in the future, and the veil hiding his "view from the glory of the upper deep, has been taken away," such that "all things appeared to" him as they did to God.

From this vantage point—freed of the constraints of space and time often depicted as a veil over human perception—Pratt discloses many oddities, largely couched as a fulfillment of John's Revelation. The worthies of the world, now Gods bearing the name of God on their crowns, have assembled to celebrate the annual martyrs' feast (April 7, the day after the anniversary Church members associated with the founding of their church) devoted to Joseph and Hyrum Smith.[5] The deified humans celebrating the feast represent "the worthy of the

---

[1] See *Nauvoo Neighbor* 3:19 (September 10, 1845): 2, and *MS* 6:9 (October 15, 1845): 140–42. Pratt's authorship is affirmed in later editions of the pamphlet. It's possible but not likely that the author was W. W. Phelps based on Phelps's role as assistant editor of the *Nauvoo Neighbor* at the time; no contemporary sources decide the question. I have followed the traditional attribution.

[2] The angel of God's presence was interpreted by some as the "God angel" or Jesus presenting himself as Jehovah. Thus, e.g., Allen, *Spiritual Exposition*, 650. Kugel, *God of Old* describes its history in ancient Hebrew writings.

[3] The Nephi visit is in 1 Nephi 11.

[4] Isaiah 60:17.

[5] This wording echoed the exegesis in *T&S* 6:3 (February 15, 1845): 808–809.

Joseph Smith's Translation. Samuel Morris Brown, Oxford University Press (2020). © Oxford University Press.
DOI: 10.1093/oso/9780190054236.001.0001

earth, with Adam at their head; the martyrs of the different dispensations, with Abel at their head; and honourable men from other worlds."[6]

Pratt then moves to the peripheral cities, the stakes of Zion, where he discovers perfect unity, facilitated by the receipt of news published in a newspaper that coordinates information across spatial distance.[7] In a fascinating anticipation of the science fiction film, *Planet of the Apes*, the newspaper reveals that premillennial New York City is essentially rediscovered during excavation of the foundation for the temple of the 124th City of Joseph (the first City of Joseph was Nauvoo). For convenient reference of celebrants whose recent memory may not have been intact, a time capsule provides clear evidence of the depravity of the world before Christ's return—including a jab at the 1844–1845 disgrace of a liberal Episcopalian minister for sexual indiscretion—as well as detailed newspaper accounts of the apocalyptic conflagration.[8]

Jesus, we discover, is the grand King of the Millennial Empire, but the Church is run by Joseph Smith and John of Patmos, who supervise the semiannual church conferences. The meeting venues alternate between the Old and New Jerusalems, which are now connected by a highway dotted with villages every ten miles and decorated by trees planted from seeds that the Angel Gabriel retrieved from the Garden of Eden. The new church newspaper is called *Zo-ma-rah* or *Pure News*, an apparent reuse of *Zomar* (a word in the Edenic language that according to Smith meant Zion), Enoch's sacred city filled with the pure in heart.[9] Items as banal as weather forecasts are drawn from the biblical books of Joel and Amos, a breathtaking merger of the timelessness of scripture and the ephemerality of weather.[10]

The vision concludes as Pratt's guardian angel provides him the opportunity to gaze through the "urim and thummim of God," recalling Smith's exegesis of Revelation 2:17 in which, after Christ's return, each person will have a seeric stone and the earth itself will be such a stone.[11] Through this looking glass, Pratt

---

[6] These individuals had implicitly achieved this exalted station via their anointing as "kings and priests" in temple rites. On the anointing as kings and priests, see Turner, *Mormon Jesus*, 224–28.

[7] The role of print in dissemination was important in that period. See Brown, *Word in the World*; Gutjahr, *American Bible*; and Howe, *Transformation of America*, 231–32.

[8] Reverend Benjamin Onderdonk, a reformer who, in the midst of internal controversy over the Oxford Movement to guide Episcopalianism in a more Catholic direction (among other reforms), was accused of what we would now term sexual harassment and removed from office. Pratt lists "onderdonking" as one of the sins of Protestant orthodoxy. On Onderdonk, see Butler, *Against the Whirlwind*, 115–18. Latter-day Saint elders actually met with Onderdonk in New York before his fall: *JSPD2*, 287, 305.

[9] On *Zomar*, see Brown, *In Heaven*, 136. On "pure in heart," see D&C 97:21.

[10] Joel 2:23 and Amos 9:13. Pratt phrases it as derived from the Law of the Lord. One would be forgiven for seeing overlap with the almanacs used to forecast weather in early America.

[11] *JSPJ2*, 404 and *MS* 26:8 (February 20, 1864): 118–19.

witnesses human history in panorama, a mechanism by which many of Smith's prophetic figures created scripture.[12]

Pratt's idiosyncratic vision thrums with ideas relevant to Latter-day Saint understandings of time and translation. The living and the dead feast together, incorporating guests from all tribes and epochs, including other planets. Past, present, and future intermingle promiscuously. The Edenic language has returned for the Millennium. Eden's seeds are growing into roadside shrubs. The Church of Latter-day Saints has merged with the Church of Former-day Saints to create the infrastructure of a heavenly community. Time and space are jumbled up, in a structure organized by ecclesial forms and priesthood community.

This snapshot of a special moment in time inspecting other moments in time frames important issues at play in Latter-day Saint thought. These topics in turn abut directly on broader transitions later associated with modern secularity. The type of time that Pratt described—God-permeated and easily punctured, manipulated, and gathered up—was not long for the world by the time he was writing. What he did not know about 1945 was that time, for many, would by then be flat, linear, sequential, and invariant. Time would by and large lose its former capacity to shift from plodding linearity into utter simultaneity. Such changes in the metaphysical infrastructure of time were already underway by the early nineteenth century, although they didn't approximate their present form until the middle of the twentieth.

One standard narrative of modern temporality holds that time became profane and homogeneous: All time had to be like all other time. There was no room for liturgical time, no separate rules for yon time (the mythically ancient past), no belief that humans had ready access to God's temporal frame in the past or present.[13] Such secular time was crucial to the orderly function of the state and its industrial mechanisms, especially factory labor, but it could asphyxiate traditional religious aspirations. While these transitions are never complete and some groups have never abandoned nonsecular time, cultural expectations about and human experience of time do seem to have changed.

Joseph Smith, typically for him, approached the question of secular time from an unrelated plane. In striking distinction to the radical Protestant group, the Moravians,[14] he didn't much employ liturgical calendars except perhaps in occasional echoes of Presbyterian holy seasons or the Methodists' similar practice in the "general conferences" of his church.[15] Whatever sacralization or transformation of time he practiced, it was not effected through a return to the Catholic

---

[12] On panoramic visions, see Brown, "Voice of God."
[13] Taylor, *Secular Age*, 265.
[14] Mullen, *Chance of Salvation*, 80.
[15] Schmidt, *Holy Fairs*.

liturgical calendar.[16] He also sounded Protestant in his approach to celebrating the Lord's Supper as a memorial rather than a portal to the first Eucharist. Smith did not consistently endorse the atemporal God of classical Christianity and learned paganism, instead (intermittently and equivocally) arguing that God's time was dictated by the orbit of the star nearest him. In those respects, Smith seems to fit a secular model of time.

On the other hand, Smith didn't believe in the separation of yon time from the present—in fact he was living the ancient past so dramatically that he and his followers embraced biblical polygamy, anticipated the return of animal sacrifice, and ritually enacted life in the Garden of Eden. He presented scriptures that functioned as time machines. Smith was, in a nutshell, breaking up the homogenized timeline of modernity to allow the passage of sacred time into the present.[17] In those respects, he seems defiant of purely secular conceptions of time.

While understandings of time have never been univocal, and more dramatic changes in the philosophy of time came in the twentieth century, the story that occupies us here is of cultural shifts that may have felt relevant in the early nineteenth century, as time became more standard, linear, homogeneous, and regimented.[18] These changes weren't so much concerned with the content of time, but rather its container. Modernity, roughly speaking, called for a uniformity of linear sequence and strict isolation of temporal units. Every second lasted as long as every other second, and each second only had one position in the sequence of all other seconds. Once assigned a location in that system, a given moment stayed put. A time beyond time, or the possibility that certain moments bestowed access to many other moments, became conceptually impossible. No content could spill between disparate temporal containers. This modern story and the Saints' indifference to it are the subject of this chapter.

Time in History

For millennia, time has been understood as coming in at least two flavors: the time that mortals experience, and the time (or, often, the absence of time) that God inhabits. Some believers have attempted to place God in a much vaster expanse of time that is still basically temporal. But the philosophers and theologians have thought of God as entirely outside time, even if at times of particular abundance God's time and human time intersect. Temporality is seen in

---

[16] Barlow, "Mormon Time," 12.
[17] I believe that this phenomenon is what Shipps, *New Religious Tradition*, was centrally attempting to explore.
[18] See, e.g., Peters, *Marvelous Clouds*, chapter 5.

premodern thought as a constraint that can be easily overcome through God's atemporal scope. God (or the gods) represents the possibility of release from the prison of time.

Even for those who see God as beyond human time, tension and ambiguity persist: does Divinity rest atop time, like a timeline in a parallel dimension (what we might call transtemporal), or does Divinity exist entirely outside time (atemporal)? Similarly, does human contact with Divinity mean that a person has escaped time or merely been touched at a particular moment along a suprahuman timeline? If God can see future events from his perch outside time, could we visit them too? Why does time feel so inexorable, and what is the relationship between our individual perception of time and some entity or essence that might be called Time?[19]

For many human cultures, temporal heterogeneity has supported a division of the world into the everyday one we inhabit and an ancient world that operated differently. While Mircea Eliade, the Romanian mystic and academic who helped to found the twentieth-century History of Religions school, is no longer authoritative (with much of the most effective criticism coming from his successor at the University of Chicago, J. Z. Smith), Eliade's understanding of human ideas about time seems relevant here.[20] According to Eliade's epochal *The Sacred and the Profane*, *homo religiosus* (his term of art for premodern humans, painting ancestral humanity with a broad brush) distinguishes "yon time" from contemporary time. Life in that ancient time was bursting with the presence of God/gods. Yon time cast a long shadow on the flatter time that followed. In Eliade's framework, rituals, myths, scriptures, and liturgical calendars provided believers access to ancient time. This yon time can be difficult to imagine for moderns, let alone inhabit.

While it's fair to complain that Eliade made use of too-easy analogies between Western biblical traditions and "primitive" cultures, he has correctly apprehended dynamics relevant to the function of modern Western society and its scriptures. In the yon time of the Hebrew Bible, people lived for centuries, animals could speak, giants walked the earth, and God could pop over, unexpectedly and often in disguise, for dinner. In the time we moderns inhabit now, none of this seems possible. We are bound within secular time.

Charles Taylor, following and updating Eliade, proposes a story of secular time crowding out metaphysically charged ancient time.[21] In the grossest of simplifications, premodern time was nearer to God's beyond than modern,

---

[19] This distinction parallels, albeit partially, Saussure's distinction between *langue* and *parole*.
[20] Smith's criticism of Eliade is available in e.g., *Map Is Not Territory*, 88–103, and *To Take Place*, 1–23.
[21] See, e.g., Taylor, *A Secular Age*, 54–61, 96, 195–96, 207–209, 712–20.

secular time can be. That proximity made possible nonlinear connections, folds and twists in time, the kind of temporal mashups on display in Pratt's dream vision with which this chapter began.

Characteristically, Taylor focuses on the liturgical calendar as a primary infrastructure for the heterogeneity of time. For medieval Christians and their predecessors, the calendar was a temporal map that marked out eddies and recurrences—moments able to interconnect across vast expanses of flat time. During the Easter feast, worshipers were brought into abrupt proximity to the day on which Christ rose from his Jerusalem grave. As believers processed through Holy Week, they were moving through time as well as space and memory.

The liturgical calendar was also a way to unite a society comprising the otherworldly monks and the this-worldly parishioners, served by the secular clergy. During Lent or similar special moments, the laity, normally mired in the quotidian business of survival, could participate in the asceticism of the monastic religious, such as when fasting from meat on Fridays. Lay believers thereby had the opportunity to participate in antiquity and the divine presence.

While Taylor underexplores this theme, there's a sense in which the separation of antique from modern time has something to do with the understanding of agency in human culture, as the Czech ecological philosopher Erazim Kohák has argued.[22] When the world we inhabit is a gift obviously beyond our agency, we perceive it differently than a world we have made ourselves. This applies to the world's time as well as its objects and locations.

One way of understanding secular temporality is thus as artificially constraining time and the world it structures: human clocks, rhythms, and agency. Secular time is no longer really about cycles of light and dark, of natural fertility and fallowness. Instead, machines measure time to assure the synchronization of other machines that can support the flow of human production to human consumers. In other words, yon time had an authority that contemporary time does not because its gifts from yon time are beyond human agency. (I chart the arc of human agency further in chapter 3.)

Whatever the causes and tributaries, the time associated with antiquity was more-than-linear, powerful, and enchanted. Admitting that culture is never monolithic and that we are exploring, to a certain extent, how early nineteenth-century individuals might have understood the tensions in their society and its past, this model of flattening time seems analytically useful.

---

[22] See Kohák, *Embers and Stars*.

Flattening Time

The temporal culture of modern secularity has taken a familiar shape. Its development wasn't inevitable, but its origin is traceable. Two of the main avenues of temporal disenchantment were the Protestant erasure of special times from the calendar and the creation of mechanically measured, homogeneous time to coordinate industry and science.

The roots of difference may begin with Augustine, with a faint path to Luther and the other Reformers whose religious work was foundational to aspects of later Western culture. Early Christians depaganized the calendar, Christianizing the important holidays and abandoning the rest. Protestant Reformers in turn saw the Catholic liturgical calendar as a pagan remnant that had to be simplified if not wholly expunged. Luther's heirs—especially those who followed Calvin's lead—were able to eliminate almost all holy days but Sunday from general acceptance in Western Europe and America.[23] The Reformers were concerned with reining in the excesses of medieval Catholicism. They worried about ritual, the authority of the church, and the unruliness of Christian laypeople. They did not accept the societal transaction by which monks and nuns honored an ascetical moral code while commoners lived their less regulated lives.[24] The liturgical calendar was part of the problem they wanted to fix: it gave authority to the church, sanctioned the excesses of Fat Tuesday beside Ash Wednesday, and supported often indecorous liturgical feasts. The Puritans followed Luther's precedent, refusing any special holiness because everything was deemed holy. These Reformed (Calvinist) Christians found Catholic sacral heterogeneity both idolatrous and easily manipulated to justify immoral behavior. This was a strongly religious move with unintended consequences.[25] Some Protestants, like Puritans and Quakers, even tried to purge paganism from the names of the days and months.[26]

The homogeneity of time is more complex. Some date the totalizing experience of imperial time to the Seleucid Empire in the ancient Near East. For the first time according to the classical historian Paul Kosmin, years were no longer attached to isolated experiences or the succession of kings. There was one dating scheme that would, apparently, persist forever.[27] Such approaches came and went, tethered to Julius Caesar in the Julian calendar, to Christ (albeit with the

---

[23] Harline, *Sunday*, chapter 3.
[24] Taylor, *Secular Age*, chapter 3.
[25] Walsh, "Holy Time." Schmidt's *Consumer Rites* trains a gently sardonic eye on the commercialization of the new holidays, even as he acknowledges the important religious and theoretical issues independent of the function of markets for goods and services.
[26] This legacy continued into the nineteenth century in the religious practice of Jarena Lee, who avoided day names, following the "plain language of the quakers." Andrews, *Sisters in the Spirit*, 47.
[27] Kosmin, *Time and Its Adversaries*.

Julian system intact) in the early medieval period, and our current Gregorian calendar coming into common use in the West in the sixteenth century. The march of linear time in modernity is a recurrence of older ideas and concepts. Still, something felt new about the experience of time in the modern West.[28]

There are important exceptions to these generalizations. No model is perfect. There is no single force of disenchantment, and "misenchantment"—the channeling of the reverence due an enchanted world into the fetishes of modern capitalism—may be a more relevant framing.[29] Importantly, I'm interested in how early nineteenth-century Americans might have understood the range of possibilities when it comes to time, both the time they could imagine for themselves and time as they imagined their ancestors had conceived it in the past.

Many of the changes in temporal conceptions relevant to the nineteenth century occurred in the two or three centuries leading up to it. Philosophical, religious, social, and technical exigencies shaped ideas about time. The philosopher and communication theorist John Durham Peters meditates on the potentialities of "elemental" media, his compelling view on the broader problems of embodied consciousness and the ways that humans think "with" the world. Time structures such elemental thinking, as it always has. Using the repurposed language of Harold Innis's theories of language and empire, Peters argues that the nineteenth century "saw a revolution in both space binding and time binding."[30]

In the beginning of the nineteenth century, time was often still told by the shadow cast by the local sundial. Individual towns could differ in their time, and time was still tied to the rhythms of the planets and their stars. As late as the middle of the nineteenth century, the sundial still supplemented (and occasionally corrected) the timepieces that regulated railroads and telegraphs. According to the sundial, noon was the moment when shadows cast by the sun were at their shortest, and other times were derived from that noon. Because the earth's surface is (roughly) uniformly curved, that moment of time varied continuously; a mechanical clock was thus locally inaccurate within a few hours' journey. Time depended exquisitely on space, as it always has. By the end of the nineteenth century, time zones had been established, in part because trains could cover large distances quickly, and in part for the required simultaneity of communication at a distance using the telegraph.[31] Each locality thus sacrificed its own specificity for the convenience of mass transport and industrialization.[32] While Max

---

[28] Taylor, *Secular Age*, 54–59, 96–97, 194–96 and Gillespie, *Theological Origins*, 2–5, 18.
[29] McCarraher, *Enchantments of Mammon*.
[30] Peters, *Speaking into the Air*, 138.
[31] On the telegraph, see Carey, *Communication*, 201–30 and Howe, *Transformation of America*. On the railroad, see Thompson, "Industrial Capitalism," and Beniger, *Control Revolution*. On time more generally, see Mumford, *Technics and Civilization*, esp. chapter 1.
[32] Peters, *Marvelous Clouds*, esp. chapter 5.

Weber's account has likely been overemphasized, he was right that some synchronization and control was necessary to support the rise of capitalist society.[33] These industrial exigencies related to factories and transportation pushed toward a particular kind of evaluating and interacting with time. But they stood in tension with other ideas about time, especially the relevance of ancient times.

The Primordium and Historylessness

What, exactly, early nineteenth-century Americans thought about the past is controversial. Some influential accounts—both contemporary and much later—have seen Americans as wholly separate from ancestral traditions, following the Enlightenment-era Quarrel of Ancients and Moderns.[34] Others have acknowledged connections to the past from mild traditionalism to intense primordialism. Both movements rejected recent traditions and saw America as headed for future greatness largely under the influence of progress and reform in the present, but the primordialists thought there was a useful past that they could deploy in defiance of recent tradition.

Primordialist strains of thought provide an important window onto ideas about time. Some antebellum Protestants were inclined to stay true to the Puritan impulse to live, in the historian Theodore Dwight Bozeman's phrase, "ancient lives." Some, like the Protestants before them, agitated to remove from Christianity all the changes—in ritual, doctrine, scripture, and church service—that had been added after the death of Christ.[35] Despite the waning of formal Calvinism in the nineteenth century, groups of primitivists continued the old quest. The itinerant preacher Barton Stone was sufficiently primitivist that he wanted the Lord's Supper to be a single loaf of unleavened bread because that's precisely what Christ would have served.[36] This primordialism dovetailed with American fantasies about independence from Europe and a desire to keep the world pure from the incursions of industrialization.[37] Some Romantics endorsed such a bypass of proximate human history, even as they acknowledged that this vision was incomplete in their contemporary America. The opening lines of Emerson's 1836 essay *Nature* proclaim, "OUR age is retrospective. It builds the sepulchres of the fathers. It writes biographies, histories, and criticism. The foregoing generations beheld God and nature face to face; we, through their eyes. Why should not we also enjoy an original relation to the universe?"[38]

---

[33] Weber, *Protestant Ethic*.
[34] Hindmarsh, *Early Evangelicalism*, 44–45.
[35] Bozeman, *Ancient Lives*.
[36] Barton Stone, "The Lord's Supper," *Christian Messenger* 8 (1834): 176–77.
[37] Hughes and Allen, *Illusions of Innocence* and Hughes, *Primitive Church*.
[38] Emerson, *Nature*, 1.

Emerson expanded that view in his 1842 *Self-Reliance*, decrying the "centuries" as "conspirators against the sanity and authority of the soul." History to him was "an impertinence and an injury."[39]

In part following the line that Emerson and others charted, the historian Sidney Mead famously pronounced American Protestants "historyless."[40] Mead was emphasizing Americans' rejection of precedents after the primordium and the sense that they were anticipating the millennium. In the aftermath of independence from colonial rule, Americans saw themselves as self-consciously separated from prior traditions—politically, socially, and religiously. Though American historylessness has always been partly fictitious, it represented a potent narrative that has persuaded many subsequent historians. In the words of Nathan Hatch, these Protestants demonstrated "widespread disdain for the supposed lessons of history and tradition."[41] They were protecting themselves against the claims of prior generations.

This transition has been described as movement out of cyclical time and into progressive time.[42] Early Americans, or so the story goes, took earlier tendencies away from cyclic time to an extreme. They saw themselves headed for a grand future of progress. This emphasis on the present as always straining toward the future risked disruption with the past. Tocqueville, for example, saw Americans as abandoning the authority of the past. He worried that Americans (and European immigrants to America) were prone "to abandon the living and the dead in quest of fortune."[43] According to Tocqueville, "the woof of time is every instant broken and the track of generations effaced. Those who went before are soon forgotten; of those who will come after, no one has any idea: the interest of man is confined to those in close propinquity to himself."[44]

This wasn't really true, of course. It was an intermediate history that Americans ignored. Many American Protestants understood themselves to be the heirs of the remnant church, the invisible community of the faithful preserved by God across the history of Christianity. This quiet remnant had ridden out the waves of Roman Catholicism by divine providence. They were the heirs of the church created in the book of Acts by the descent of the Holy Spirit. That history constituted their basis of authority.

Recall that history can mean at least two partly competing things: reverence for specific time points—individuals, events, traditions—in the past; and an acknowledgment of the process by which the past has become the present.

---

[39] Emerson, *Essays*, 58.
[40] Mead, *Lively Experiment*, 108–11; Marsden, "One's Own Interpreter," 80.
[41] Hatch, *Democratization*, 7.
[42] O'Dea, "Experience of Time"; Brague, *Wisdom of the World*, 167.
[43] Tocqueville, *Democracy in America* (1839), 296.
[44] Tocqueville, *Democracy in America*, 2:99, cf. 105–106.

Protestants loved key aspects of the past (as essentially all people do), but they also resisted the intervening crush of history. They were uncomfortable with the vessels by which history persisted. Commonly in dispute with Catholics, Protestants rejected, in other words, the authority of a magisterium in an intermediate past, preferring unmediated access to the relevant aspects of the ancient past. They viewed the Catholic interlude as a nuisance, a distraction. American Protestants wanted to be free to imagine that they had unrestricted access to the truly ancient past. They wanted to be the masters of history.

This approach to history was also racialized, as whites' primordialism in America required selective blindness. Whites often saw America as Edenic because they thought it was empty of "civilization." But the order Euro-Americans preferred was only one of several variants of human habitation. Just as they denied the history of Catholicism, they were also negating America's Native history. Euro-Americans could find their own local primordium only by denying history to the Natives who had populated the lands for millennia. Beyond the denial of history there was also the reality that temporal cultures varied. White Protestants weren't the only people with ideas about time potentially relevant to the Latter-day Saint experience. Although generalization is treacherous, many Native groups saw time as markedly heterogeneous.[45] Similarly, many African Americans saw conversion and biblical typology as avenues for escape from the deadly strictures of merely earthly time.[46]

We oughtn't overstate Protestant primordialism. Many looked to the purer past as a way to correct the lapsed present, but few sought to inhabit the ancient past with perfect fidelity. That style of primordialism, the one that Smith and his followers embraced, rejected most modernist time, even as it ceded the flatness of the present time from which they hoped to escape.[47]

The Saints and the Collapse of Time

The religious historian Jan Shipps has argued that Latter-day Saints were historyless, and Joseph Smith returned so wholly to the primordium as to be something other than Christian.[48] Shipps contends that Smith was more concerned with *illud tempus*, or yon time, than he was with Christian history. He was

---

[45] See Richter, *Facing East*, chapters 3–4, and Nabokov, *Forest of Time*.
[46] Mullen, *Chance of Salvation*, 108.
[47] Hughes and Allen, *Illusions of Innocence*; Eliade, "Paradise"; and Sanford, *Quest for Paradise*, 82–85.
[48] Shipps, *New Religious Tradition*; cf. Flanders, "Transform History," 110.

taking Protestant primordialism to an extreme.[49] But Smith wasn't just returning to *illud tempus* or even replacing it. He was arguing that *tempus* could not be separated into *illud* and *hoc* in the first place.[50] The historian Robert Flanders is closer to correct when he observes, "Mormons, unlike other millenarians of their generation, were more anxious to fulfill time than merely to see it end"[51]—as long as the "fulfillment" of time is its final inability to separate human beings from others.

As we've seen, Smith expressed himself prophetically at a historical moment when conceptions of time were flattening in the interests of science, technology, and market capitalism. Bible critics simultaneously stole from the Bible its distinction in time while emphasizing its distinction in culture. Within secular time, the Bible era was locked too far back for straightforward access. Smith was heir to a Protestantism that despised the Catholic liturgical calendar. And he had sympathy with primordialist strains of Christian thinking within a nation that was generally uninterested in the intervening centuries of European or Native history.

Smith's engagement with time is complex and various, but he was first and foremost concerned with abolishing temporal boundaries. Time threatened to render individuals extinct and to separate them from multiple pasts both near and far. He sought to inhabit a comprehensive interweaving of time and challenged the notion that various epochs should stay segregated. Where Emerson saw himself as needing to be saved from the tyranny of the ancestors, Smith welcomed them into community. Smith's primordialism was concerned with connection with the intervening generations rather than liberation from them. He spoke often about dispensations and was emphatic that he was the seer of "the dispensation of the fulness of times" (his interpretation of Ephesians 1:10). In Christian dispensationalism, different ages of humanity are governed by distinct "economies" (a calque of the Greek term meaning the rule of a household) or administrations of God's covenant.[52] This approach explained how an unchanging God could have established such patently different regimes as Old Testament Judaism, New Testament Christianity, and American Protestantism.[53]

Smith rejected standard dispensationalism. He understood dispensations as restorations of a fundamentally unchanging system that disappeared and reappeared through the millennia. That sense of the old made new again was

---

[49] O'Dea, "Experience of Time," judges early Restoration thought by the lights of twentieth-century theologies. Bozeman correctly emphasizes the ways that Puritans used Bible time as an *illud tempus*: *Live Ancient Lives*, 14–15.

[50] I agree with the spirit of Barlow, "Sense of Time," and Barlow, "Fractured Reality."

[51] Flanders, "Transform History," 113.

[52] See, e.g., Buck, *Theological Dictionary*, 150–51.

[53] While current practice refers to the Hebrew and Christian Bibles, I sometimes use Old and New Testaments to match nineteenth-century usage.

precisely evoked by Smith's choice of the term "new and everlasting covenant" to describe the way his church would bring into being an ancient-modern dispensation. Each dispensation was guided by a prophet-seer, the sacerdotal parent of an epoch, who could integrate his charges into the great human family and deal with temporally specific problems like floods, Egyptian bondage, or modern economic change.[54] After an apostasy (which happened distressingly often) a fundamentally identical system would be restored by another such seer. Smith's call, then, had been to restoration. Parley Pratt's influential *Voice of Warning* taught that under Smith's prophetic leadership "the religion of ancient days" was "returning to the earth in this enlightened age."[55] An old-new dispensation had arrived.

"Dispensation" as such is nowhere in the Book of Mormon, although the rules regulating dispensations are ubiquitous. Even when they are broken, traditional understandings of dispensation are acknowledged (e.g., in the stipulation in Mosiah 13:29–35 that the ancient American Jews who worship Jesus must do so from within the confines of a Mosaic Law that was radically misunderstood by the ancient Hebrews). In the shadow of the Law of Moses, the ancient American Jews are baptized and assemble in Christian churches. Most consistently and obviously, the Book of Mormon inveighs at length and in multiple locations against the Protestant doctrine of cessationism, which indicated that God's miraculous interventions in the world had ceased by the end of the New Testament. The much-remarked anticessationism of the Book of Mormon (chapter 4) is in fact an avowal of transtemporal dispensationalism. Cessationism was a relationship to time and an attempt to hold yon time at bay. Protestants did so in part to limit their exposure to Catholic "superstitions" and the authority of the Catholic magisterium. For critics like Smith, cessationism was too much of a rupture with yon time.

Smith's mergers of disparate dispensations manifested in various ways in early Restoration history. In August 1830, he announced a revelation (D&C 27) allowing the Latter-day Saints to deviate from Protestant precedent in celebrating the Eucharist. He made explicit that the Eucharist is a preparation for the grand banquet on Mount Zion (a theme Pratt expanded in his 1845 dream vision and present in multiple Latter-day Saint sources[56]). The revelation then recited the guest list for that sacred meal: Moroni, Elias, John, Elijah, Isaac, Abraham, Adam, and the New Testament apostles, who had vouchsafed to Joseph Smith

---

[54] *JSPD4*, 15; *EMS* 1:2 (July 1832): 13; *EMS* 1:4 (September 1832): 29.

[55] Pratt, *Voice of Warning*, 122. From the outside, Andrew Jackson Davis saw Smith as "convert[ing] all past revelations into the Mormon system of faith." *Harmonia*, 5:182.

[56] Thus an anticipation of the last days when the Saints will be "gathered together upon mount Zion, to enjoy each others society forever": *JSPH1*, 169. Similarly, Smith hoped to stand with his father on Mount Zion: *JSPJ2*, 116. See also Smith, *Sacred Hymns*, 88.

"a dispensation of the gospel for the last times; and for the fulness of times, in the which I will gather together in one all things, both which are in heaven, and which are on earth" (27:13). The simultaneity of those sacred figures and the movement of the familiar celebration of the Lord's Supper into the eschatological future both indicate the shape of Smith's dispensationalism.

In his report of an 1836 vision, he returned to the 1830 Eucharist revelation—the angels had "committed" the "Keys of this dispensation" into his hands.[57] In his 1840 discourse on priesthood, Smith preached that the practices known "at any former period shall be had again" in his current dispensation, the one that summarized and united all of history.[58] He thought "all things pertaining to that dispensation should be conducted precisely in accordance with the preceeding dispensations" and called for every dispensation to be "gathered together in one."[59]

Time was an unstable structure awaiting a prophet's clear vision to oversee its entire collapse. Smith wanted his people directly connected across all the dispensations. He preached in the 1840s that "those who are baptised for their dead ... must receave their ... anointings for their dead ... till they are connected to the ones in the dispensation before us."[60] In this context, it made sense that the biblical Adam underwent baptism (Moses 6:64) because Joseph Smith and his father did. The priesthood family to which they both belonged had not changed. If the veil were rent, Joseph would welcome Adam directly into the Church, with no awkward moment of incomprehension. Smith, as seer, would not only speak Adam's language if he came, but know his ways, his times.

Smith's collapse of time appears nonsensical from the perspective of Protestant dispensationalism. Attempting to characterize this approach, the historian Richard Hughes describes an "amalgamation of sacred time ... so complete that it appears as sheer confusion."[61] Smith's contemporaries agreed. The Presbyterian Jonathan Baldwin Turner wittily criticized Smith in an 1842 anti-Mormon book for engaging in "utter mockery and defiance of all chronology, all history, sacred or profane, all order of time, place, or style."[62] Turner was making, with more bombast, a point Campbell had made about the Book of Mormon a decade earlier.[63] What such critics have seen as weakness, though, Smith understood as strength. He was self-consciously uniting all time in one.

---

[57] *JSPJ1*, 222 (April 3, 1836).
[58] *JSPD7*, 440.
[59] *JSPD7*, 436.
[60] England, "George Laub's Journal," 174. Cf. *WWJ*, 2:388, and *WJS*, 365–69. Brigham Young was true to that impulse, preaching that he would "extend the Chain of the Pristhood back through the Apostolic dispensation to Father Adam just as soon as I can get a temple built." *WWJ*, 3:131 (16 February 1847).
[61] Hughes, "Soaring," 35.
[62] Turner, *Mormonism*, 203.
[63] "Delusions," *Millennial Harbinger* 2:2 (February 7, 1831): 85–96.

Smith's project, however manifestly primitivist, was to create a simultaneous human family, liberated from the prison of time.[64] In the phrase of the disciple Warren Cowdery, the Saints looked forward, with John's Revelation, to the period "when time itself shall be swallowed up . . . when Adam and his youngest son will be contemporaries."[65] Smith's amalgamation of sacred time aimed to conquer chaos, not to create it. He was resisting one type of temporal homogeneity—the linear flattening of modern time—with a radically distinct homogeneity—the entire accessibility of all time. He didn't attempt to recover liturgical calendars. But he wanted no part of a time that was locked into mere linear sequence. Any given year's calendar could be flat, but nothing must keep the years apart. He wanted to be able to fully inhabit the past and allow the past to inhabit the present.[66] As an early editorialist had it, the modern prophet "gathers up the history of all generations, by which he can compare the present with the past, and the past with the future, and bring the two ends of men's earthly existence together."[67] Smith's Restoration would heal the rifts of time. In doing so, it reopened questions about the nature of divine time.

The Time of God

In addition to his peculiar and ardent primordialism, Smith also pondered time itself and the relationship between human time and divine time. Did the early Saints believe that God was atemporal, as most traditional Christians would have it?[68] Or did they believe that God was transtemporal? Admitting that atemporal and transtemporal can shade into each other—indeed commonly did in Western culture[69]—the documentary record is mixed.

In a sermon to his son Corianton, the Book of Mormon prophet Alma describes his attempts to know the timing of death and resurrection. Equivocating, Alma nevertheless reports that God knows "all the times which are appointed unto man." In his attempt to answer the question of how long dead souls wait for resurrection in the Book of Mormon, Alma takes a stand in favor of atemporality: "all is as one day with God, and time only is measured unto men" (Alma 40:8). Toward the end of the book, Moroni, addressing antebellum unbelievers, argues against cessationism by saying that "God is the same yesterday, today, and

---

[64] I agree with Sayre ("Books Buried," 26–29) that contact with the dead was a key mechanism by which Smith allowed ancient time to persist.
[65] M&A 3:2 (November 1836): 411.
[66] Barlow, "Mormon Time," 27.
[67] M&A 2:8 (May 1836): 308.
[68] Buck, Theological Dictionary, 169, provides a typical Christian account of divine atemporality.
[69] Noll, The Word, 50.

forever" and that "in him there is no variableness neither shadow of changing." God is an "unchangeable Being" who "changeth not" (Mormon 9:9-10, 15-19). Whatever its other rhetorical implications, the Book of Mormon language suggests divine atemporality.

A subsequent canonized document offers another nod toward divine atemporality. The 1829-1830 *Articles and Covenants* (D&C 20) engage the question directly: "we know that there is a God in heaven, who is infinite and eternal, from everlasting to everlasting the same unchangeable God" (D&C 20:17). This specific text was not present in Cowdery's draft, suggesting that it may have come from Smith. An 1830 revelation (D&C 29) reconceives Genesis 1-3 in terms of parallel creations, temporal and spiritual. The divine voice explains that humans can't understand divine atemporality—"Speaking unto you that you may naturally understand; but unto myself my works have no end, neither beginning; but it is given unto you that ye may understand" (29:33). In his autobiographical sketch from 1832, Smith characterized God in fairly traditional terms as "a being . . . who filled Eternity who was and is and will be from all Eternity to Eternity."[70]

In his 1832 Olive Leaf revelation—an extension of the Vision—Smith revealed that when Christ returned temporality would dissolve into atemporality: "there shall be time, no longer."[71] Shortly thereafter, he revealed (D&C 109:77) that God has "an infinity of fulness, from everlasting to everlasting." In 1834 Sideny Rigdon took a firm stand in favor of atemporality in "the unseen world and eternity."[72] The 1835 Church hymnal included the claim, common among Methodists,[73] that "time began" when God initiated creation.[74] Another hymn described death as the "remov[al]" from "time."[75] In an 1840 comment about the importance of being committed to God, Smith promised to believers blessings "both in time and in Eternity."[76] In an 1842 discussion of the ritual of baptism for the dead, Smith indicated that "the past, the present and the future, were, and are with him one eternal now."[77] In his final public sermon in 1844, Smith pointed again to the vastness of time: "no man can limit the bounds, or the eternal existence of eternal time."[78] Smith's pronouncements appear to be endorsing something like divine atemporality; eternity and time differ substantially.

---

[70] *JSPD2*, 281.
[71] *JSPD2*, 345.
[72] *EMS* 2:19 (April 1834): 146.
[73] Clarke, *Holy Bible*, 1:27.
[74] Smith, *Sacred Hymns*, 90.
[75] Smith, *Sacred Hymns*, 63.
[76] *JSPD7*, 469.
[77] *T&S* 3 (April 15, 1842): 760.
[78] *WJS*, 379.

On the other hand, divine time could be a puzzle, and the Saints liked to solve theological conundrums. Often they wrestled metaphors into strongly literal terms. The second epistle of Peter (3:8) left a tantalizing clue on the nature of divine time: "one day is with the Lord as a thousand years." Phelps used that heuristic in a New Year essay for 1845 to calculate the earth's age as approximately 2.5 billion years: 7,000 divine years (7,000 was the earth's lifespan according to the then-dominant Bishop Ussher chronology used in Adam Clarke's magisterial commentary) at 1,000 human years per divine day.[79] Whatever the precise details, Phelps's calculation relied on divine transtemporality. In this view, God's days have duration: they are just very long when viewed from a human perspective.

Phelps's idiosyncratic calculation was part and parcel of a broader notion that time was an attribute of the orbits of particular celestial bodies, which he and Smith developed at length in 1835 and 1836. Crucially, they placed God under the temporal influence of a star named Kolob, whose orbital dominance was supreme (see chapter 6). Such was the theoretical/astronomical underpinning of Phelps's calculation, and it suggests that possibility that God was in fact bound by time.

In a set of later-canonized aphorisms from 1843, Joseph Smith indicated that angels were once governed by earthly time but in their angelic status were governed instead by divine time because they lived in a "great Urim and Thummim," suggesting that their angelic living situation combined celestial bodies with seer stone interpreters. On that divine stone, they saw that "all things for their glory are manifest, past, present, and future, and are continually before the Lord" (D&C 130:4–8). Here again, Smith is teaching divine transtemporality. The angels experienced their own time but could look through a seer stone to view all the other times (recall the importance of seer stones in Pratt's vision). These parallel modes of time—one human and one divine—persisted in a March 1841 sermon, in which Smith proposed a solution to the puzzle of Adam's longevity after the fall—God had promised after all that Adam would die the same day he fell. "At the time the Lord said this to Adam there was No mode of Counting time By man, as man Now Counts time."[80] Human time only began with the fall from the temporal modes of paradise.

Eliza R. Snow published a blank verse poem in 1841 called *Time and Change*. In her mind, creation was the moment when time separated from eternity, a rupture that would be healed at Christ's final return, the time of the "grand

---

[79] *T&S* 5:24 (January 1, 1845): 758. James Ussher, an Irish professor and archbishop, outlined a Protestant version of a preceding Catholic chronology, in his 1650 *Annales Veteris Testamenti*. See McCarthy, "Ussher."
[80] *JSPD8*, 66.

ecclaireissement 'Twixt Time and vast Eternity."[81] Snow sees a primordial unity ruptured by the Fall—"Ever since the great Co-partnership of Light and Darkness was Dissolv'd: and youthful Day and Night, no more Commingling" time pursues its relentless course, battering away at all human beings, both the righteous and the wicked.[82] Following Smith's unity of peoples, records, and time, Snow sees Christ's Second Coming as the moment when all the records, "leaf by leaf" will "Compris[e] all that Time has seen."[83] She thus seems to see divine time as both atemporal and transtemporal—atemporal at the beginning and end of time and transtemporal in between. Though Smith himself was not quite so explicit, her interpretation seems representative of much Latter-day Saint theology.

The Saints left a conflicting conceptual legacy. For the Latter-day Saints, God may have been wholly beyond time, atemporal. Or God may have been transtemporal, still contained within time but operating at a distinct level. Smith and his followers probably tended toward the latter interpretation but weren't comfortable setting themselves free from the former. The predilection toward the transtemporal model of God's time probably indicates the extent to which Smith's anthropomorphic gods and theomorphic humans (see chapter 3) were tied to a conception of time that spanned the categories of premodern atemporality and modern temporality. The emphasis on transtemporality also dovetailed well with Smith's earnest hope that he and his followers could be present within different epochs of time. They believed they could bring the past back to life in the present. As so often, the categories strain under the force required to apply them cleanly to Smith and his disciples.

Independent of God's atemporality, the Book of Mormon models an interwoven approach to temporality that has bemused readers since its publication. Ancient American Christians are seen reading the New Testament centuries before Christ. They often speak directly to nineteenth-century Native ("Israelite" or "Lamanite") and White ("Gentile") audiences. Nephi, for example, pauses in his interpretation of Isaiah around 550 BCE to indicate that his Hebrew community knows the law, but through their time-piercing prophecies, "the law hath become dead unto us, and we are made alive in Christ because of our faith" (2 Nephi 25:25). The Book acknowledges what an odd position its participants occupy. Caught between two epochs, America's ancient Saints take what is best from each and live in temporal fluidity. Jared Hickman has commented that the Book of Mormon is "a wormhole right from the get-go."[84] He is onto something important with that playful phrase. The text points toward an ultimate merger of all

---

[81] Snow, *Time and Change*, 5.
[82] Snow, *Time and Change*, 3–4.
[83] Snow, *Time and Change*, 4.
[84] Fenton and Hickman, "Learning to Read," 7.

times in one.⁸⁵ Smith aimed, with many another Christian, for a time when time, as separation, will be no more.⁸⁶

The Book of Mormon thus contributes to Smith's long-standing mixture of transtemporal and atemporal imagery. Smith's immediately subsequent work on the New Translation of the Bible continued the work begun in the Book of Mormon. There the Old and New Testaments again intermingle as if they were contemporary to each other. The notorious intertextuality of his work was also fundamentally concerned with intertemporality. What appeared to matter most to Smith—whatever proved true about the deep nature of time—was the capacity to inhabit the lives of those who came before and those who would come after, to "liken" as the Book of Mormon has it, ancient stories "unto" present readers.⁸⁷ This likening would take the Saints in surprising directions.

Life in Yon Time

Joseph Smith's primordialism is staggering; for him, the past had to be fully available in the present. With this as a goal, he implemented or proposed at least two striking practices that indicated the extent to which he expected that he and his followers would live in yon time. Both sound outrageous to a modern ear: biblical polygamy and animal sacrifice. (I discuss a third revival, the Nauvoo temple liturgy, in chapter 7.)

Smith's polygamy arose for multiple reasons. It resisted the shrinking Victorian nucleus, solved a logical puzzle from the Bible (the Sadducean thought experiment on remarriage after bereavement), served as a test of commitment that strengthened members' resolve, integrated the ecclesiastical family, concentrated power in the hands of the Latter-day Saint hierarchy, and much else.⁸⁸ Many practicing Latter-day Saints have argued that, most importantly, God commanded it. But this polygamy also invited Smith and his followers to observe, bodily, certain customs of the Hebrew Bible. Abraham, Jacob, and David were notorious polygamists, and so would the Latter-day Saints be. (This was not the first time that Christian primordialism resulted in polygamy, as many critics observed, citing especially the sixteenth-century Munster Anabaptists.⁸⁹)

---

⁸⁵ Fenton's otherwise insightful consideration of alternative histories in the Book of Mormon ("Open Canons") fails to engage the merger of times, which is the substrate in which cyclical history resides in Smith's scriptures.

⁸⁶ Augustine, *Confessions*, 7–8, 45, 62, 241–57

⁸⁷ 1 Nephi 19:23–24.

⁸⁸ Flake, "Priestly Logic"; Daynes, *More Wives*; Ulrich, *Plural Marriage*.

⁸⁹ Thus Alexander Campbell, "Delusions," *Millennial Harbinger* 2:2 (February 7, 1831): 85–86, and Bennett, *History of the Saints*, 302–307, with discussion and sources in Brown, *In Heaven*, 238–39.

The relationship between polygamy and time is important to understanding Joseph Smith's theology. The main public argument justifying polygamy during Smith's lifetime was the temporal displacement of remarriage after bereavement.[90] Polygamy resisted the separation that time imposed on serial monogamy occasioned by premature death. But polygamy didn't just violate the separation of time in its anticipation that a widower would be married to all his wives in the afterlife; it also relived patriarchal antiquity in all its painful drama. In the official, confidential revelation sanctioning the practice (D&C 132), the Old Testament precedent played a central role. This intimate, odd dialogue between Joseph Smith and God begins with God indicating that Smith had been trying to "understand wherein I, the Lord, justified" the patriarchs' marital practices. That the Saints felt they needed to adhere to ancient Hebrew marriage practices demonstrated that they were living ancient lives to an outrageous degree.[91]

Early Church members weren't just attempting to pattern their lives on biblical templates. They were reworking time. The 1842 polygamy revelation takes an explicit stance against modern constraints on time. The rules of Smith's marriage system "were instituted from before the foundation of the world" (132:5) and they would last beyond time:

> All covenants, contracts, bonds, obligations, oaths, vows, performances, connections, associations, or expectations, that are not made and entered into and sealed by the Holy Spirit of promise, of him who is anointed, *both as well for time and for all eternity* . . . are of no efficacy, virtue, or force in and after the resurrection from the dead; for all contracts that are not made unto this end have an end when men are dead (132:7; emphasis added).

The same point recurs shortly (132:13): "thrones, or principalities, or powers, or things of name, whatsoever they may be, that are not by me or by my word, saith the Lord, shall be thrown down, and shall not remain after men are dead, neither in nor after the resurrection." This is the language of sealing and binding, of merging earth into heaven. This language is deeply antisecular: no marriage for time only is considered worthy. Eliza R. Snow made the same point in a poem in 1843: "death will sever every tie / That is not based above the sky."[92]

According to the polygamy revelation, that which is temporal dies when humans die. This is no surprise—the lack of postmortal human existence has been a tenet of secular-sounding traditions since at least the Epicureans and related Greek atomists. Essentially all modern secularists would agree that nothing

---

[90] Brown, "Levirate Widow," 10–12; *EJ* 1:3 (July 1838): 43.
[91] Hardy, *Solemn Covenant*, argues for polygamy as antiquity. See also D&C 132:1, 34–39.
[92] *T&S* 4:14 (June 1, 1843): 224.

materially human persists after death, and to believe otherwise is a delusion. Smith, ever worried about the implications of human mortality, made clear that he was, in polygamy, creating a system that would defy death by binding the transcendent realm by rituals performed on earth. As was typical for Smith, his protests against secular limitation employed modern concepts. In the bustling liminality of his thought, the rituals that could bind the transcendent to the earthly include the modern construct of "contracts." Recasting rituals at least partly as contracts, Smith pursued otherworldly aims.[93]

The marriage revelation takes the divide between temporal and spiritual so seriously that the penalty for purely temporal contracts of marriage is demotion from the status of married gods to eternally single angels (132:15–17). For Smith such secular-minded folk would continue to exist in the afterlife just like everyone else. But they would have a lesser status because they had failed to make their contracts aspire to anything beyond secular time. They had lived too much in the world's present, ignoring its future.

Polygamy expanded from Smith's initial nucleus and became an overarching social, ecclesiastical, and genealogical system that extended over three-quarters of a century in the main church and to the present day in offshoot sects. Polygamy has always defined people out of polite American society—the eradication of Latter-day Saint polygamy was one of the basic tenets of the Republican Party's first platform and generated seemingly endless recriminations and persecution—but what has been underappreciated is that it also yanked practitioners out of the *saeculum*. In the practice of polygamy, Latter-day Saints lived simultaneously in the past, present, and future.

Another radically primordial practice never made its way into Church life: liturgical animal sacrifice. In his 1830 Visions of Moses, Joseph Smith filled out the after-story of the Fall. He was addressing the question of what happened right after Eve and Adam were expelled from the Garden of Eden. Some of what transpired was straightforward: the first humans engaged in agriculture and raised families. They "multiplied" and "replenished" the earth, as the King James text puts it. This was perfectly innocuous and well-documented in the traditional texts of Genesis 3–4, as were powerful angelic figures assigned to prevent human return to the garden. But the Hebrew Bible immediately jumps to a confusing discussion about Cain and Abel and the relative merits of plant versus animal sacrifice.

In the Visions of Moses, though, we encounter an expanded treatment that emphasizes two things. First, Adam and Eve begin praying, and God responds aurally but not visually—he is hidden from sight. (We learn elsewhere that this

---

[93] In the interests of space, I ignore the precedent of suzerainty treaties and covenants with Yahweh in the ancient Near East.

is a mark of fallen humanity, which cannot tolerate the physical presence of God—see chapter 3.) Second, we learn the content of God's revelation to Eve and Adam: he instructs them to practice animal sacrifice, the same sacred rituals well known from the Hebrew Bible. So far we haven't heard much that would distinguish the Visions of Moses from the traditional Hebrew Bible.

Then an angel comes to Eve and Adam, leading them in a brief Socratic dialogue to ascertain the reason for animal sacrifice. It is, the angel indicates, "a similitude of the sacrifice of the Only Begotten of the Father, which is full of grace and truth. Wherefore, thou shalt do all that thou doest in the name of the Son, and thou shalt repent and call upon God in the name of the Son forevermore" (Moses 5:7–8). In this phrase, Smith's revelation sets the tone for both the Latter-day Saint understanding of time and the persistence of animal sacrifice after the coming of Christ. According to Joseph Smith and contrary to what traditional Christians have claimed (including those who read the New Testament in its standard form), animal sacrifice was wholly compatible with explicit knowledge of Jesus. That compatibility was present in the oldest available scriptures, which Smith had unearthed through his process of translation.

Smith left that liturgical strand unexplored for about a decade, revisiting it in his October 1840 sermon on priesthood, human translation, and the role of angelic patriarchs in scripture and restoration. In laying out the interdependence of all humanity and people's occupation of a world shared with suprahuman beings, he returned to the genealogies of the Hebrew Bible. Smith then turned abruptly to the Visions of Moses and the instructions to the first parents to engage in animal sacrifice. He observed that "all the ordinances and duties that ever have been required by the priesthood under the direction and commandments of the Almighty in the last dispensation at the end thereof in any of the dispensations, shall all be had in the last dispensation." This was Smith's signature antidispensationalist primordialism brought to its apogee. The Latter-day dispensation included even "the offring of Sacrifice which also shall be continued at the last time." Specifically, Malachi 3:3 required that the "sons of Levi" should "offer unto the Lord an offering," and Malachi had to be fulfilled.[94] This offering, Smith knew, was animal sacrifice, that powerful emblem of the sacrifice of Jesus that began right after the Fall. If baptism extended before Jesus, then sacrifice would have to persist after Jesus.[95] If Smith's merger of all times was going to be real, then it would have to include even the strangest and most ancient aspects of the Bible.

---

[94] *WJS*, 42–43, October 5, 1840. See also Wandle Mace, "Autobiography 1809–1890" (MSS 921, HBLL), 29, 37, and Oliver Huntington, "Sayings of the Prophet Joseph Smith," *Young Women's Journal* (March 1893): 275. See *JSPD7*, 440.

[95] See discussion in *JSPD7*, 441.

In this sermon and its associated interpretation, Smith wasn't just re-engaging his Visions of Moses. He may also have been sparring with the entry "Priest" in his favorite theological dictionary, a reference he used from the early 1830s through the end of his life.[96] In this popular Protestant reference work, Charles Buck claimed, "if the word priest ... denote[s] a person commissioned ... to offer up a real sacrifice ... [w]e may justly deny that there is a priest upon earth."[97] Buck's stray comment was smugly anti-Catholic, but Smith may have heard it differently. Smith's priesthood was assiduously concerned with returning ancient Hebrew priests to the modern world. If Buck required Levite practice to admit the existence of a priest, so be it.

Smith's Book of Mormon had suggested this much in its announcement that the "high priesthood" was "from the foundation of the world; or in other words, being without beginning of days or end of years, being prepared from eternity to all eternity." If an ancient priest ever had to sacrifice an animal to God, then a modern priest would have the same bloody duty.

A few months after his October 1840 sermon (D&C 124:39), Smith indicated that one reason for building the Nauvoo temple was to provide an authorized space for "your memorials for your sacrifices by the sons of Levi." The problem of dispensational restoration was still on his mind. He made similar reference to the restoration of "daily sacrifice" by priests in the Millennium in 1843.[98] Although Smith didn't talk in much detail in surviving documents about animal sacrifice, and I've been unable to uncover any credible accounts of the actual practice among Latter-day Saints, he clearly intended to recover the ancient Hebrew—indeed, Edenic, according to Smith's revelations—religion in its entirety. This would include all the trappings of ancient priesthood. These trappings would one day include real ritual sacrifice of animals at the temple.

Smith and his peers would have been more familiar with the slaughter of animals than we are in the twenty-first century. He had perhaps been around animal sacrifice in his treasure-seeking experience, and he was in any case intimately acquainted with the agricultural immediacy of life and death.[99] Smith preceded the Protestant campaigns to recast the slaughter of animals as a suspicious practice and long before food production was wholly separated by industrial

---

[96] On the popularity of Buck's dictionary, including Smith's use of it, see Bowman and Brown, "Theological Dictionary." Smith used Buck's in the 1834–1835 *Lectures on Faith* and again in 1842, drawing on it as a way to find precedents for his own heresies in ancient doctrines catalogued within Buck's *Dictionary*.

[97] Buck, *Theological Dictionary*, 487.

[98] *JSPJ2*, 405.

[99] Defamatory affidavits in the early 1830s argued that Smith practiced animal sacrifice during treasure quests. See, e.g., *EMD*, 2:61, 197; Anderson, *Reputation*, 49–53; Howe, *Mormonism Unvailed*, 239, 249. Animal sacrifice was occasionally practiced in early American treasure questing: Dillinger, *Treasure Hunting*, 180. On animal sacrifice in antiquity, see Smith, *Relating Religion*, 145–59.

techniques from the homes where it was consumed. What drove him in his prophetic career to consider the even-then-scandalous practice was his conviction that all times were to be made one. Granting that Charles Buck was right that priesthood meant the ability to sacrifice an animal to God, Smith's priests would need to perform the same sacrifices the ancient Hebrews had.

Note this time-erasing symmetry: Smith's Book of Mormon had ancient Hebrews worshiping Jesus in deprecation of the then-current Law of Moses, and his nineteenth-century Latter-day Christians could look forward to practicing key aspects of the Law of Moses and patriarchal Hebrew life. This is the temporal jumble that Smith brought into being. It was a homogeneity of time born of exhaustive intermixing. Smith was, in religious studies scholar Kathleen Flake's phrase, "translating time" as he made biblical narratives mythically real for his followers. In Flake's amplification, "Smith made more than a claim to history. He gave his believing readers a sense of what was experientially real, not merely philosophically true."[100] At least in the case of animal sacrifice Smith was doing both at the same time, his deep primordialism remaining true to the hunger to inhabit a sacred past while simultaneously answering the logical call of Charles Buck's provocation. Importantly, Smith wasn't just making history experientially real; he was arguing that time could not constrain his followers.

The First and Eternal Theology

Smith's primordialism drew on a set of ancient wisdom traditions. While the term has historically been applied to different ends, *prisca theologia* ("ancient" or "first" theology) reasonably applies to aspects of the early Latter-day Saint worldview. Under Smith's direction, the Saints sought out fragments of original Truth scattered throughout human history. In their *prisca theologia*, early Saints expressed ideas about both the nature of time and their relationship to the past. Their practice of *prisca theologia* was an approach to plurality that encompassed the past and attempted to place its disparate threads into harmony.

The basic idea of *prisca theologia* was that teachings of non-Christian philosophers that were deemed compatible with Christianity—most famously but not exclusively the writings of Plato—reflected a prior revelation of the Gospel.[101] In other words, Christianity wasn't Platonic, Plato was a crypto-Christian. Although the tradition is best known in early Christian and neoclassical Renaissance thought (often as the *philosophia perennis*), versions of

---

[100] Flake, "Translating Time," 525–26.
[101] See Hanegraaff, *Esotericism*, 7–26.

it persisted well into colonial America.¹⁰² These concerns weren't restricted to learned theologians: Buck's *Theological Dictionary* reiterated these topics for lay Protestants in its treatment of Isaac Casaubon (1559–1614), himself a major figure within the *prisca* traditions.¹⁰³

To practitioners of *prisca* traditions it seemed "as if all domains of knowledge were linked together by a web of secret, hidden, invisible connections," a phrase that draws out the continuity of *prisca theologia* with the more ancient traditions of metaphysical correspondence.¹⁰⁴ Among the esoteric practitioners of the perennial philosophy, the Freemasons were closest to the Latter-day Saints. Masonic rituals and texts brimmed with accounts of recovered secrets of antiquity.¹⁰⁵ Mainstream Protestants might decry it as drawing "disjointed fragments of atheism, Judaism, and Papacy" together into "a shapeless mass,"¹⁰⁶ but the Saints knew better than that.

Smith and his followers were devoted practitioners of the first theology. The Visions of Moses and Prophecy of Enoch lay out the story of the first parents in a way that makes clear that they received the original revelation. In the 1834–1835 Lectures on Faith—theological essays intended for "instruction in the principles of our Faith and religion"¹⁰⁷ coauthored by Smith and Sidney Rigdon—Lecture 2 devotes substantial energy to outlining the precise mechanisms by which the dramatically long lifespans of the earliest biblical figures allowed for the transmission of ancient wisdom. This is a deeply personal model of the *prisca theologia*: parents, grandparents, great-grandparents and the rest all lived together in those early years, assuring that all generations would know the original truth.¹⁰⁸ Such was the live connection that the Books of Remembrance (chapter 1) encoded in pure language. In a distinctive take that prefigures later teachings on the "Second Comforter," Lecture 2 then indicates that when necessary a personal visit from Jesus will assure that the righteous believer receives the first theology directly.¹⁰⁹

---

[102] Schmitt, "Perennial Philosophy"; Popper, *Historical Culture*, 91–93; Delph, "Venetian Visitor." See also Schmidt-Biggemann, *Philosophia Perennis*, xiii, and Hanegraaff, *Esotericism*, 118. On colonial America, see McDermott, *Edwards*, and Holifield, *Theology in America*, 106.
[103] Buck, *Theological Dictionary*, 401, 459–60.
[104] Hanegraaff, *Esotericism*, 63.
[105] Masonic uses of *prisca theologia* includes Cole, *Freemason's Library*, 290; Karl Reinhold, *The Hebrew Mysteries, or the Oldest Religious Freemasonry*; Town, *Speculative Masonry*, 131–33, 172; Fellows, *Exposition, passim*. The classic, idiosyncratic William Warburton, *Divine Legation*, makes a similar kind of argument. Some critics, e.g., Stearns, *Free-Masonry*, 36, 62, rejected such claims, attempting to distance Christianity from Western esotericism.
[106] Kidder, *Mormonism*, 228–29.
[107] *JSPD4*, 458.
[108] *JSPR2*, 325–34.
[109] *JSPR2*, 335.

The first-generation Latter-day Saint Joseph Fielding described the *prisca theologia* in an open letter in the Church newspaper, referring to "the gleams of light seen among the Pagans of various nations" which is "derived by them from some people who had the priesthood."[110] Notable is the tie, once again, to priesthood, the force that unites humanity across the epochs of time. When Latter-day Saints talked about priesthood they had in mind the merger of genealogy, angelic presence, and their Chain of Belonging (see chapters 3 and 6). For them priesthood was the authoritative line by which the secret knowledge and rituals of the primordially pure Gospel could be communicated over the generations. The genealogical nature of this priesthood provided a deeply human schema for the structure of the universe. The connections they made with the past were deeply human, even as they were also concerned with secrets and ritual power.

The Saints weren't content with the ancient wisdom of Mesopotamia and the Mediterranean. They also wanted to know the secret antiquity of America's *prisca theologia*. The Book of Mormon contained between its covers a treasure trove of ancient American wisdom, both good (early Christianity) and bad (the Gadianton robbers), even as it called out the things that could never be spoken or written. One way of reading the Book of Mormon is precisely as the detailed account of the trails of sacred wisdom through the world of ancient America.

The early Saints would braid together the many different wisdoms in their dispensation to end all dispensations. Many scholars have drawn attention to the careful attention to the chain of provenance in the Book of Mormon.[111] Seen in this light, this chain of textual transmission is like the patriarchal overlap posited in the second Lecture on Faith. The possessors of the gold plates had to be contemporaries in the historical record precisely so that they could communicate to each other the sacred teachings. Smith and his followers were careful to establish the names of every link in the *prisca theologia* chain. When Moroni hands over that compilation of lost wisdom of ancient America to Smith, he is connecting the modern prophet to that most ancient tradition.

Time and Space

In the dream that began this chapter, the apostle Parley Pratt moved in and out of space and time within a millennial vision. He began in his own bed and then bounced between the Old and New Jerusalems, dining with visitors from other planets. His visionary time was breaking up the boundaries of space. Although

---

[110] *T&S* 3:5 (January 1, 1842): 649; cf. Egan, "Flood of Light."
[111] Givens, *Hand of Mormon*, 51–55; Wells, "Provenance," 111–13.

he didn't engage Aristotle intentionally, one can imagine Pratt appreciating the idea that when mortal time no longer exists, it will be clear that what we have called "time" was an attempt to describe the separation of physical objects.[112] We moderns are accustomed now to think of physics as mandating that time is the "fourth" dimension right beside three spatial dimensions. But the experience of time either as space or movement through space is very old. The interconnection of time and space meant something very different in earlier generations.

Sacred astronomy—a core component of a robust nature-mystical tradition among early nineteenth-century Evangelicals among many others[113]—directed many of the early Latter-day Saint meditations on space and time. For Smith a crucial connection between time and space reflected his merger of folk astronomy and an exegesis of Genesis 1:14–16. He emphasized the close correlation between planets and time in his 1832 Olive Leaf revelation. The key passage describes the "law ... by which they ['the heavens and the earth ... and all the planets'] move in their times and their seasons." The next verse repeats in more insistent detail: "And they give light to each other in their times and in their seasons, in their minutes, in their hours, in their days, in their weeks, in their months, in their years—all these are one year with God, but not with man" (D&C 88:42–44). Smith was communicating that celestial bodies constitute time in their interdependence. To be within time means to be governed by a specific kind of celestial body in a particular way. The notion that planets (or things like planets) dominated the structure of time was far from new with Smith. The concept was as old as the Hebrew Bible and almost certainly much older. The idea continued in writing and thinking about the Hebrew Bible, especially in association with the patriarch Abraham.[114] Whatever the mediacy of that connection, Smith and his disciples shared these sensibilities with ancient predecessors.

The theme of space and time reached its zenith with Smith's temple liturgy. He created there a space modeled on Solomon's temple, that stood apart from all the world. He defied the Puritans' attempts to make all the world equally sacred and abolish special locations that would otherwise smack of shrines.[115] The temple was a place that was holier than any other on earth. Here was a ritual portal to the expanses of time and space. Smith's followers there traversed time to inhabit the minds and experiences of their first parents in the Garden of Eden. The primeval garden was both a place and a specific time, and in them the early Saints stepped

---

[112] Aristotle's core arguments on time are in *Physics*, Book 4, Parts 10–13.
[113] Grainger, *Church in the Wild*, 49, 76–77.
[114] Brague, *Wisdom of the World*, 51, citing Jubilees 12:16–18, where the stars point beyond themselves to God. See also chapter 6, *infra*.
[115] Walsh, "Holy Time," with nineteenth-century evangelical squeamishness described in Grainger, *Church in the Wild*, 57.

out of modern time and space.[116] In the temple they touched eternity. Their access to eternity came in the recreated primordium.

While I explore the temple liturgy in greater detail in chapter 7, it's worth sketching out the early contours of a treatment as it relates to Latter-day Saint primordialism. Little interested in the Masons' central narrative of the murdered temple builder, Hiram Abiff, the Nauvoo liturgy concerned itself overwhelmingly with the earliest phases of the primeval history. There the early Saints imagined themselves walking with Eve and Adam through the decisions and experiences that led to the present world. As they ritually walked through the simulation of the birth of the world, worshipers moved through the primordium to the eschaton. At the conclusion of this grand sequence, they found themselves crowned with divinity in the company of their first parents. Through the movements and adornments of their body, and through the words they used (some of which was self-consciously based on the Edenic language), early Saints participated directly in the primeval history of the world. Through that ritual performance they found themselves arriving at the eschatological end of time, drawn into a final salvation.[117]

Conclusion

The path early Latter-day Saints trod through the history of the world will seem idiosyncratic to many of us now. It struck many of their contemporaries as outrageous even then. In retrospect it was a protest against cultural norms that tended to allow modernity's temporal prison to squeeze the chest just a little tighter. As with all protests, Smith's temporal defiance depended on the phenomena it resisted—not just because to oppose means to oppose *something*, but because some aspects of secular temporality made sense to early Latter-day Saints and were incorporated by them into their strategies. Any hope the Saints had of understanding the primordium was colored by their experiences with post-Protestant time. They couldn't straightforwardly endorse the traditional atemporality of God but wanted a time they could control—specifically with the intent to make human contact possible across the epochs.

Even as they drew on Puritan roots and oriented themselves within the post-Calvinist landscape, there's something impressive about the position the Saints took in the scope of history. They lived among epochs and drew their power from their ability to flit back and forth between the world's beginning and its end. The

---

[116] Flanders, "Transform History," 116.
[117] Brown, *In Heaven*, chapter 8.

eschaton was always also the primordium, and they stood poised in the overlap, at which wild fragments of the past like polygamy and animal sacrifice could intrude. There, at the beginning and end of the world, the Saints found themselves transformed, body and soul. But what were they, exactly? What was the source and nature of their identity?

3
Human and Divine Selves

At the time of the confounding of human language in Genesis 11 (ca. 2000 BCE, according to traditional chronology), an ancient prophet unknown outside the Book of Mormon had to save his people, the Jaredites, from the pandemonium that ensued when God cursed the civilization that built the Tower of Babel. The solution would require both human ingenuity and miraculous power. I introduced this man, Moriancumer, briefly in chapter 1. I consider his multifaceted story in depth here.

The Book of Mormon's editor-narrator, Moroni, begins the Jaredite story at the end of the Hebrew Bible's Primeval History, with a typical Old Testament genealogy for a man named Ether. This Ether is the prophet responsible for the Jaredite chronicle. This genealogy tracks the history of this lost people back to the eponymous founder, Jared.

The leader's brother, Moriancumer, is "large and mighty" and "highly favored of the Lord." Given his status with God, Jared asks his brother to "cry unto the Lord" for the protection of their tribe from the incipient curse. God grants the request and commands a Jaredite exodus from Babel. The Jaredite flight from the Old World is patterned on Noah's escape from the flood (Ether 1:41) and the Israelite exodus from Egypt (1:42). As a result, the Jaredites will fulfill in part, and in advance, the Abrahamic covenant that in the Hebrew Bible comes after the Babel story. Specifically, God will "raise up" the Jaredite "seed" so that it will be the greatest nation on earth (1:43).

The Jaredites arrive in a valley named for Nimrod, as if to emphasize that the Tower of Babel is the foil for their tribal narrative.[1] There the Jaredites begin, as Noah, to prepare for a long boat ride. This righteous remnant of a prelapsarian people are accompanied in this journey by a God like the Yahweh of the Israelite sojourn in Sinai (Ether 2:1–5). This God hides in a cloud, speaking with Moriancumer but not making himself visible (cf. Exodus 13:21).

The Jaredites then settle a port city they name for their prophet (Ether 2:13) and wait there four years. At that point, the shrouded God returns to speak with Moriancumer, castigating him for backsliding (Ether 2:14). The prophet and his people repent, and God teaches them to build their versions of Noah's ark.

---

[1] Nimrod was understood to be the leader of the civilization at Babel: Clarke, *Holy Bible*, 1:84.

The shipbuilding is not without difficulty, though. Moriancumer discovers two problems—air circulation and illumination. God, still invisible, solves the respiratory issues with special plugs, like corks in a bottle of wine, that can be adjusted based on the craft's orientation. But Moriancumer must solve the lighting problem.

The prophet moves to a furnace on Mount Shelem, where he forges the translucent stones that prefigure the stones of John's Apocalypse (Revelation 2:17). The prophet asks that God touch the lantern stones with his finger so that they will "shine forth in darkness." God complies with the request matter-of-factly by touching the forged spheres with his finger. Moriancumer is shocked to realize that God's finger is no prayerful metaphor but is in fact a reality "like unto flesh and blood." God is an embodied being, not just a mist of other-worldly power. This is the glyphic transition for language and human bodies that we encountered in chapter 1.

In the Bible, God's finger is the stylus by which he writes scripture (e.g., Exodus 31:18; Deuteronomy 9:10)[2] and in early modern evangelicalism it was the points of contact between the heavenly and earthly realms.[3] But in this Book of Mormon story, the finger is, through metonymy, God's physical body. God then reveals that entire body to the perceptive prophet. This glimpse of the divine finger beckons Moriancumer to a transformation that will make the human seer able to bear the direct presence of God and bestows salvation on him. God tells the prophet, "ye are redeemed from the fall; therefore ye are brought back into my presence" (Ether 3:6–16). Moriancumer has been transformed.

Moroni speaks enviously of the Jaredite prophet, centuries later—"thou madest him that the things which he wrote were mighty *even as thou art*" (Ether 12:24; emphasis added). Moriancumer's linguistic power thus recapitulates the divine word of Genesis and John. The lantern stones were vessels for God's enfleshment and Moriancumer's ability to tolerate the divine presence.

This scriptural story of a prophet seeing God's body during an escape from Babel provides clues about the intimacy of human identity and language in Latter-day Saint metaphysics. The twin senses of translation as human and linguistic transformation are both present in this story, which is the tip of a theological iceberg. Smith and his disciples had a great deal to say about what human beings had been in the past, were at present, and would become in the future. The story was more than anything about communal deification situated within a mixture of ancient and modern anthropologies.

---

[2] Other uses of God's finger emphasize the power of God's physical manifestation in the world—Exodus 8:19, Psalm 8:3, Luke 11:20.

[3] Hindmarsh, *Early Evangelicalism*, 117.

Latter-day Saint anthropologies were vivid and strange, but they also developed within a cultural context in which ideas about individuals and communities and their respective vulnerabilities were under shifting pressures. Especially prominent were ideas about individual liberty, religious voluntarism, personal access to inspiration, and limitations to state authority. The Saints embraced many such modern arguments. But they also seem to have sensed tragic trade-offs at play. The early Latter-day Saints refused, loudly, to absorb the trade-offs made by many other Protestants (and, frequently enough, their freethought cousins) in pursuit of Lockean ideals of political liberty. The Saints saw the dark side of individualism just as they saw the promise of modern government based on consent.

Even as he absorbed the rhetoric of modern selves, Smith saw the promised individualism as a prison from which he hoped to liberate his followers. How and why Smith found individualism a prison is a crucial story in early Latter-day Saint thought. It also tells us something about the points of tension and dispute in antebellum American religion and society.

Nineteenth-Century Selves

A standard twentieth-century story holds that modern selves are isolated, protected from each other and from suprahuman agencies. This story maintains that these modern selves followed brightly lit paths from premodern bondage through the Enlightenment liberation to the present-day liberal consensus. This standard story is inaccurate in many respects, as scholars have recently emphasized,[4] even as it acknowledges key strains of modernist rhetoric. The paths to late modern selfhood were often hazy, with indistinct trail markers and multiple possible destinations. Still, some themes predominate.

Charles Taylor has drawn attention to the context and vulnerability of individuals as a core attribute of cultural change. The key questions were, according to Taylor, Are individuals points like stars in the sky, or are they like nodes in a lattice? Are individuals vulnerable to influences outside them, or are they shielded from such influence?

On Taylor's account, the premodern self was "porous" and contextual, while the modern self was increasingly "buffered" or "punctual" (i.e., like a point).[5] Others have suggested "bounded" or "immunized" as synonyms for this sense of personal insulation.[6] Taylor's terminology isn't especially historical—many

---

[4] Taylor, Sources of the Self; Seigel, Self; Coleman, "Secularization."
[5] Taylor, *Sources of the Self*, 49, 174, and Taylor, *Secular Age*, 27, 37–42, 134–42, 156, 262–64, 300–307.
[6] Modern, *Secularism*, 19.

antebellum Americans would have been surprised to hear that they were buffered, even as they became increasingly comfortable with slogans and ideas that supported such buffering.[7] Something as complex as human identity defies easy generalization. But, if only genealogically, questions of interdependence and porousness help to organize the mass of data regarding conceptions of persons in the nineteenth century. These questions focused particularly on agency and constraint, the issue of embedment in systems that preceded and overshadowed one. The porous self of Taylor's account is susceptible to the influence of supernatural forces and to human communities.

Suprahuman agencies and powers could bring happiness or, too often, tragedy. Terrible things happened, relentlessly. People fell off horses and broke their necks; they got cancer; their ships sank; they lost limbs and little children. For many believers, these were "afflicting providences," expressions of a sometimes inscrutable divine will;[8] for others they were senseless misery. Beyond tragic destinies, porous selves were at risk for bodily invasion. Demons and sprites could possess. An evil eye could penetrate the soul; a neighbor's curse could induce bodily illness. (We may recognize remnants of such beliefs in the circulation of popular histories of invocations of God's blessing in response to a sneeze on the grounds that a devil might enter the vulnerable face.[9]) Even as there were flashes of redemption, contentment, and even victory, an enchanted world was often dark, painful, and unpredictable. Little wonder that many moderns welcomed defenses against such terrors.

Beyond providential suffering and demonic intrusions, premodern selves were porous to societal influences. Put too simply, to know themselves, premodern Westerners were more likely to look outward than inward. Classically the Great Chain of Being provided an infrastructure of deep and lasting significance for Westerners. The Chain, deriving mostly from Aristotle, was a scientific concept: all biological entities fit within an ontological hierarchy. For Christians, God as the Ground of Being was made visible and intelligible through this Great Chain, and so were people, both collectively and individually.[10] For many Christians, the Chain encompassed a plural hierarchy of conscious beings to match the plurality of beings on earth. Angels (sometimes termed "intelligences"[11]) were greater than humans, who were in turn greater

---

[7] Grainger, *Church in the Wild*, 7, 44, 62, 66.
[8] Saum, *Popular Mood*.
[9] No one knows the origins of a custom that even Pliny commented as an old tradition beyond explanation. A treatment in 1895 rehearsed the standard explanations with only a hint of the possibility of cursing associated with the sneeze when it occurred on Sunday, according to a popular English rhyme. "Origin of Sneezing Customs," *Current Literature: A Magazine of Contemporary Record* 17:6 (June 1895): 511.
[10] Lovejoy, *Chain of Being*. See also chapter 6 herein.
[11] Lovejoy, *Chain of Being*, 191.

than horses, who outranked fish, themselves superior to flowers. This hierarchy had repercussions in human society, some of them malignant: The Chain was the explicit justification for divine kingship, social castes, and slavery. Each person's place in life was defined at birth, as part of the balanced harmony of the world. Even for those who didn't explicitly embrace the Chain, the harmonious correspondences of heaven and earth imposed constraints on human lives.

Under the Chain of Being, the reason for individual agency, to a first approximation, was to figure out how to make the best of one's particular lot in life. It was not generally to invent oneself. The porous self wasn't just prone to demonic possession, in other words, but to being constrained, coerced, and exploited. Roughly speaking, modern Western political theorists from Hugo Grotius (1583–1645) and John Locke on down were concerned in part with replacing the Chain of Being with structures based on individuals.[12] While it drew on multiple, often incompatible political thinkers and traditions, the republican ideologies of the American Revolution, especially in retrospect, brought Lockean political philosophy into the real world.[13]

In the first generations after Independence, new political structures, religious voluntarism, mechanistic views of nature, novel communication and transportation technologies, the evangelical revivalism dubbed the Second Great Awakening, and evolving market structures contributed to a mélange of loosely related concepts and phenomena relevant to selfhood.

Calvinist theologies—themselves complexly merging community covenants and the ineluctably individual stakes of salvation[14]—found numerous critics as American Protestantism shifted toward the Baptist and Methodist churches. Competing theological traditions went under various names, but Arminianism, often shading into Pelagianism, was the center of gravity for anti-Calvinism. The central concern was the role of human agency in salvation.[15]

Arminianism, most closely associated with the Methodists in antebellum America, maintained that humans didn't earn salvation per se, but they could refuse Christ's grace. (Such refusal was impossible within Calvinism, as salvation was a matter of divine election rather than human action.) For some, Arminian tenets were too moderate, as for the Latter-day Saint convert who derided Protestantism's "mongrel Calvinism, and crippled arminianism."[16] Pelagians— named for a fourth-century British monk whom Augustine lampooned— defiantly pressed beyond Arminianism for recognition that human beings could

---

[12] McClure, *Lockean Politics*; Seigel, *Self*, 109–10.
[13] Bailyn, *Ideological Origins*, chapter 2; Taylor, *Secular Age*, 160, 197, 208, 448.
[14] Noll, *America's God*, 38–39. Such church covenants persisted in a new key among, e.g., Baptists: Peck and Lawton, *Historical Sketch*, 11–13, 41.
[15] Hindmarsh, *Early Evangelicalism*, 275; Johnson, *Shopkeeper's Millennium*, 96.
[16] *M&A* 1:1 (October 1834): 10.

direct their own salvation. The human will mattered to the shape of eternity.[17] In the words of Latter-day Saint convert Almira Mack Scobey Covey in an 1835 letter to her sister, "it depends upon my faithfulness if I obtain a crown of Celestial Glory."[18] Covey was, in folk terms, endorsing American Pelagianism. In extreme cases, Pelagianism could become a view of human perfectibility that bordered on deification.[19]

Theologically, many free-thought advocates similarly rejected Calvinism, in concert with rising attachment to what we now call humanism. Early in life, Smith felt the draw of the Methodists' popular Arminianism; whatever his mother's commitment to Presbyterianism, he seems never to have liked the mainstream churches. He soon came to see the Arminians as too attracted to the God of the creeds and too open to the risk of backsliding out of salvation. They were neither sacerdotal nor sacramental enough for him.

Pelagian perfectionism was far from unanimous in America even outside Calvinist circles. Many traditionalists, including the fluid and infuriating public intellectual Orestes Brownson (1803–1876), hated the concept. Brownson demonized the modern idea of human "progress" as "the foolish notion that man is born, an inchoate, an incipient God, and that his destiny is to grow into or become the infinite God."[20] He rightly saw this heresy as violating traditional Christian theology, but he had an uphill battle when it came to persuading religious humanists like Smith.

The role of human will was one key question, but so was the context for human will. Ancient selves, however robust, weren't intended to be the whole story. They were tightly embedded into communities. People knew that to a substantial degree their selves were created by something other than themselves. Yet external constraints came to be seen as increasingly odious. Two contemporary observers we have encountered before highlight the stakes for participants: Alexis de Tocqueville and Ralph Waldo Emerson.

In his *Democracy in America*, Tocqueville described a pivot toward an ideology of "equality" that tended to express itself in "individualism" and a this-worldly focus, which he viewed as markers of the modern self being fashioned in America.[21] Tocqueville was an aristocrat writing for a French audience. His bias is evident; he expresses ways that participants in older modes of being might

---

[17] Some see, e.g., Finney's New Light Presbyterianism as Pelagian: Preston Graham Jr., "The Pelagian Controversy and Nineteenth-Century American Religion," n.d., https://s3.amazonaws.com/churchplantmedia-cms/christ_presbyterian_whitney/pelagian-controversy-3.pdf, Accessed July 12, 2018. Others saw Pelagianism in early America: O'Dea, "Experience of Time," 184.
[18] Johnson, *Female Religiosity*, 29.
[19] On Latter-day Saint perfectionism, Brooke, *Refiner's Fire*, 56–57, 67–71.
[20] Grasso, *American Faith*, 353.
[21] Tocqueville, *Democracy in America* 2:98–99.

imagine their differences from the American experiment.[22] Tocqueville distinguished this "individualism" from "egoism," a visceral selfishness into which individualism could descend if it weren't carefully controlled. He espied good and bad in American individualism.

The individualism Tocqueville observed was not philosophically new. Fights over these questions, while ultimately antique, could easily be traced to seventeenth- and eighteenth-century cultural claims in England and Europe. Thomas Paine (1737–1809), perhaps the most famous and popular of early Anglo-American critics of Christianity, pitted individualism against religion in his pithy phrase of 1794: "My own mind is my own church."[23] Reformers, both many Protestants and their critics, hoped to limit religious constraints on individuals.[24] Whether the religious culture that resulted could counterbalance egoism was an open question.

Whether, having rejected traditional hierarchical social models, Americans would re-aggregate in associations like nonestablishment churches, reform movements, or fraternal organizations (as Tocqueville thought they should) or drift toward further isolation and egoism (as Tocqueville worried they might) wasn't clear. Tocqueville worried that "not only does democracy make every man forget his ancestors, but it hides his descendants and separates his contemporaries from him; it throws him back forever upon himself alone and threatens in the end to confine him entirely within the solitude of his own heart."[25] Tocqueville focused attention on the loss of the Chain of Being—"democracy breaks that chain and severs every link of it."[26] Despite Tocqueville's disapproval, the image of an individual bravely breaking free of the constraints imposed by clerics and hierarchs was an animating vision of American individualism after the Revolution. In Grasso's memorable phrase, "the political deification of the democratic individual transformed the lives of even simple farm folk as much as canals and the coming of the railroad."[27] In the horrified rendition of the British observer, Frances Trollope, drunken American workmen bragged "we makes our own laws, and governs our own selves."[28]

Criticism of Smith and his followers from within the Protestant mainstream gives some sense of the devotion to independence present more broadly. One anti-Mormon diatribe quoted a newspaper editorialist as maintaining that Smith

---

[22] Witness the more acerbic tone of the British aristocrat Frances Trollope (1780–1863) in *Domestic Manners*.
[23] Paine, *Age of Reason*, 2, with discussion in Gregory, *Unintended Reformation*, 171. Paine mattered at least through the 1840s: Grasso, *American Faith*, 14.
[24] Wilken, *Religious Freedom*.
[25] Tocqueville, *Democracy in America*, 2:99.
[26] Tocqueville, *Democracy in America*, 2:99.
[27] Grasso, *American Faith*, 351.
[28] Trollope, *Domestic Manners*, 313.

had made "his voice to believers like the voice of God; trained to sacrifice their individuality; to utter one cry; to think and act in crowds; with minds that seem to have been struck from the sphere of reason."[29]

Admitting that Emerson expressed elite sensibilities, his writings on self-reliance have been seen in retrospect as epochal, if conflicted.[30] Emerson fulfilled and amplified Tocqueville's observations about individualism.[31] In reality, he was neither first nor last to make the arguments that selves must be free of historical or community constraint. The fact that the modern-sounding epigraph to *Self-Reliance*—instructing readers not to seek themselves outside themselves—was lifted from the Roman satirist Juvenal is telling.[32] Rather than looking outward at tradition, we should look inward to find truth, Emerson preached. Anyone who interfered with his personal truth quest—including "father and mother and wife and brother"—he explains, was invited to leave his social circle immediately.[33] Self-reliant individuals must belong only to the truth and not to other people. In his typically outlandish style, Emerson intoned, "Be it known unto you that henceforward I obey no law less than the eternal law. I will have no covenants but proximities."[34] He was, in the modern sense, a free man, seeking his "aboriginal Self, on which a universal reliance may be grounded."[35]

Tocqueville saw people like Emerson as representative practitioners of individualism and saw anticlerical rhetoric and political maneuvering as representing the way people lived. But this rhetoric wasn't reality for a large number of people. Tocqueville was blind to the Evangelical focus on the "extinction of the self"[36] and related anti-individualism,[37] perhaps in part because of prevalent rhetoric about salvation that was "in principle unmediated" except by the Bible.[38] Even where they aspired to negate their own fallen will in the worship of the perfect Christ, Evangelical Protestants still reported their lives as necessarily independent of most constraints short of God.[39] The tensions between rhetoric and reality perpetuated uncertainty about the nature and status of individuals.

What Tocqueville seems to have regretted, Emerson embraced with gusto. Within *Self-Reliance* Emerson recounts an exemplary encounter with a traditional believer. He asks the man, "What have I to do with the sacredness of traditions, if I live wholly from within?" The churchman replies by wondering

---

[29] Lee, *Knavery Exposed*, 5.
[30] On the conflict, Grasso, *American Faith*, 361.
[31] Thus, e.g. Bellah et al., *Habits of the Heart*, 55–56, 63.
[32] Emerson, *Essays*, 37.
[33] Emerson, *Essays*, 45, 48, 63–64, cf. Matthew 19:27–29.
[34] Emerson, *Essays*, 64.
[35] Emerson, *Essays*, 55–56.
[36] Grainger, *Church in the Wild*, 7, 44, 62, 81; cf. Grasso, *American Faith*, 67, 84, 87.
[37] Coleman, "Secularization," 379, 385–86, 394.
[38] Noll, *America's God*, 173.
[39] Hindmarsh, *Early Evangelicalism*, 55–57; Grainger, *Church in the Wild*, 7, 116.

whether Emerson's spiritual impulses come "from below." Emerson answers that he believes himself correct, but ultimately, "if I am the Devil's child, I will live then from the Devil."[40] With this tongue-in-cheek rejoinder, Emerson proclaims an individualism strong enough to favor hell over inauthenticity.

Emerson's claim to prefer hell to a constrictive heaven dovetails insightfully with a parallel witticism from Joseph Smith. In a July 1843 sermon, Smith preached, "let me be resurrected with the Saints, whether to heaven or hell or any other good place. . . . What do we care if the society is good?"[41] Both he and Emerson had a heady vision of human potential. Neither could tolerate the Calvinist story of original sin or human depravity.[42] Neither was willing to cede control of the afterlife to their Protestant cousins. But where Emerson focused on the idea of individuals improving themselves according to their inner meanings, Smith believed, as we will soon see, that selves were actualized in community.[43]

The image of Smith skipping heaven to stay true to his friends is the characteristic mix of human agency, scandalous anti-Calvinism, and intense communitarianism that he elaborated over his career. Such a tangled map onto modern sensibilities is characteristic of his thought.

Smith's Modernist Sensibilities

In many respects, Smith was as ardent a modernist as any other American of his era. He highlighted human agency as a cardinal virtue. He espoused a high anthropology that was explicitly anti-Calvinist. On the other hand, the Saints were anti-individualistic. This paradox—human perfectionism framed within anti-individualism—underlies a distinctive Latter-day Saint anthropology that ultimately reenvisioned the God of the Bible.

A High Anthropology

Something like extreme Pelagianism became part of Smith's vision over time, and it coexisted for him with a new status for God.[44] He proposed an anthropology so high it was divine and a theology so domestic it identified a wife—the

---

[40] Emerson, *Essays*, 44.
[41] *WJS*, 234.
[42] Smith reported his "total unbelief" in "Original Sin" in an 1840 sermon in Washington, DC: *JSPD7*, 178.
[43] Notably, the Mormon seceder John Corrill sided with Emerson: "I had rather enjoy liberty in hell than suffer bondage in heaven": LeSueur, *Mormon War*, 260.
[44] The claim of Davis, "New England Origins," 158, that Latter-day Saints were Puritan rather than Arminian fails to appreciate the Pelagian nature of Smith's theology.

Queen of Heaven or Heavenly Mother—for God the Father.[45] Smith has become famous for this merger of the divine and the human, what I call his divine anthropology. But he didn't exactly start out that way.

Judging by Smith's adult reminiscences about his teen years, he experienced human weakness personally. Reflecting on his life between his First Vision and his work on the Book of Mormon, Smith remembered the "corruption of human nature which I am sorry to say led me into divers temptations to the gratification of many appetites offensive in the sight of God."[46] However much he came to advocate human perfection, he knew well what it meant to fail morally.

The Book of Mormon, even if it sowed some Arminian-sounding seeds, was no perfectionist manifesto. While the historian Thomas Alexander probably overstates its Protestantism in a classic essay, he correctly observes the doctrinal distance between the Book of Mormon and Smith's subsequent divine anthropology.[47] Two sermons best illustrate the Book of Mormon anthropology: Lehi's deathbed instruction to his son Jacob (2 Nephi 2), and King Benjamin's final sermon to his Nephite people (Mosiah 3).

According to Lehi, the Fall has forced a total change in the conditions of human life. After the "fall of man" the law will tend to "cut [humans] off" and cause them to "perish" spiritually. Humans are corrupted, and Christ is the power for salvation. Benjamin for his part takes the position that the "natural man is an enemy to God, and has been from the fall of Adam, and will be, forever and ever, unless he yields to the enticings of the Holy Spirit, and putteth off the natural man and becometh a saint through the atonement of Christ" (Mosiah 3:19). The claim that in a state of nature humans are opposed to God would be familiar to the Arminian Methodists as well as orthodox Calvinists, even if the language of "putting off" and "yielding" tilts Arminian. These two sermons confirm a basic theology of human depravity.

Book of Mormon narratives confirm its theology. Much like the Israelites they've abandoned, the Lehites can't stop falling from grace and into God's curse (this cycle of blessing and cursing is a leitmotif of the Book of Mormon). Although some rare prophets, like Moriancumer, are godly, there is little talk of human divinity. Humans choose badly, and they do so consistently.

Although the Book of Mormon had little to say about divine anthropology, Smith introduced the teachings over the course of the next two years. In the 1830 Visions of Moses and Prophecy of Enoch, we see much more human perfectionism and early indications of human divinization. God confesses emblematically that humans are his work and his glory (Moses 1:39) rather than,

---

[45] Brown, *In Heaven*, 274–78.
[46] *JSPH1*, 220.
[47] Alexander, "Mormon Doctrine."

as traditional Christians would have it, creatures that derive from his glory.[48] Enoch's communitarian city Zion (see later in this chapter) becomes capable of tolerating God's presence as part of its translation to heaven (Moses 7:21, 69). The 1832 Sample of Pure Language we encountered in chapter 1 provides a lexicon for the divine anthropology in its identification of the species *Ahman*.[49] The 1832 Olive Leaf promised humans equality with God, generating substantial interest and controversy.[50] The seventh Lecture on Faith proposed that salvation was a process by which believers became more clearly God-like.[51] Smith's divine anthropology, well underway in the 1830s, grew more robust over time, including through a theology of bodies.[52]

Human souls were comprised, Smith said, of spirits and bodies, and Christians hadn't understood either of them. As he put it in the Olive Leaf, "the spirit and the body are the soul of man. And the resurrection from the dead is the redemption of the soul" (D&C 88:15–16). Spirit—transcendent, spiritual, supernatural—merges with body—immanent, temporal, natural. That ongoing, living merger is the soul, which will be redeemed in resurrection. The soul was not, as others might have it, the human spirit. Spirits could not meaningfully exist without bodies. This puzzling through of the nature of life and resurrection persisted throughout Smith's life even as it took variant forms over time. Specifically, the body became the aim of mortality and the locus of power. He saw spirit as very much like and complementary to body. Spirit was material at some level, even as it required the body for actual flourishing. This blurry dualism is sometimes mistaken for philosophical materialism, but Smith was more concerned with harmony among realms than with anything resembling materialism per se.[53]

In his 1841 "Observation of the Sectarian God," Smith noted that, "at the first organization in heaven," God chose Christ to lead the "plan of salvation," by which "we came to this earth that we might have a body." To bring the point home firmly, Smith reiterated, "The great principle of happiness consists in having a body."[54] In late March 1841, he reported of the pre-earth life that "God saw that

---

[48] I thank Phil Barlow (personal communication) for this observation. See also Flake, "Translating Time," 519.

[49] The Sample of Pure Language either breaks with or more likely supplements Moses (6:57, 7:35), which maintains that God's names include Man of Holiness, Man of Counsel, and Endless and Eternal.

[50] Brown, "Olive Leaf," 161–63.

[51] *JSPR2*, 375.

[52] Brown, *In Heaven*, 261–71.

[53] Nolan, "Materialism," does not make the typical mistake. See also Brown, "Materialists." Other Christian thinkers have proposed blurry dualisms. Thus, e.g., the Thomist view of hylomorphism or Evangelical vitalism (see Grainger, *Church in the Wild*). I thank Zack Gubler for thinking with me about hylomorphism. Christian materialism (Buck, *Theological Dictionary*, 345–46) may be a somewhat closer fit for Smith. For a contemporary Protestant critique of Smith's materialism, see Kidder, *Mormonism*, 234, 236–39.

[54] *JSPD7*, 496–97.

those intelligences had Not power to Defend themselves against those that had a tabernacle therefore the Lord Calls them together in Counsel & agrees to form them tabernacles so that he might Gender the spirit & the tabernacle together."[55] He seems to have seen the story of the Gadarene swine in Mark 5 (demons ask Christ to route them from a possessed man to a herd of pigs during an exorcism, as if they depended on a body, no matter how humble) as biblical evidence for the necessity of bodies to spirits.[56] In April 1844, Smith recounted human creation in terms of this same pairing, teaching that "God made a tabernacle & put a spirit in it and it became a Human soul."[57] This notion of the soul as unity of spirit and body became a commonplace among his followers. But if spirits needed bodies, then why not God?

Smith made a series of arguments in favor of divine embodiment, thereby sacralizing the physical world. Smith's account of the body is remarkable and often misunderstood. He clearly indicated—starting with Moriancumer's divine encounter and persisting throughout his career—that the God of the Bible was embodied. This fact by itself would suggest the importance of embodiment for happiness and salvation, even if the full development of the doctrine came in the 1840s.

In his January 1841 "Observations on the Sectarian God," Smith taught, "That which is without body or parts is nothing. There is no other God in heaven but that God who has flesh and bones."[58] About a month later, Smith took on Trinitarianism, arguing that orthodox Calvinists claimed to believe in "three Heads & but one body." In place of Trinitarianism, Smith taught that "the three were separate bodys, God the first & Jesus the Mediator the 2^d & the Holy Ghost."[59] In March 1841, he again taught that "the Son Had a Tabernacle & so had the father."[60] Not one shared body, but three distinct bodies.

Smith and his followers disliked the God of the creeds and philosophers. That Platonic-sounding God of pure Being was too remote for their taste. Smith emblematically mocked the Methodists and their "God of no body or parts."[61] If the Saints had asked their Protestant peers, they'd have replied that the creedal God without bodily form became proximate in the person of Jesus. The Saints didn't see that as a credible response because the New Testament gave at best an unsteady witness of Trinitarianism. They were more comfortable with the (intermittently) anthropomorphic God of the Hebrew Bible. Smith's teachings on

---

[55] *JSPD8*, 86.
[56] *JSPD8*, 87.
[57] *JSPD8*, 86.
[58] *JSPD7*, 494.
[59] *JSPD8*, 47–48.
[60] *JSPD8*, 65.
[61] *JSPJ3*, 12.

divine embodiment got more specific and emphatic over the next few years, culminating in the most radical statements in 1844 in which God the Father was not just embodied but was himself a deified human.[62]

One hears echoes of correspondence in Smith's insistence that humans and God had to be the same kind of being and live a similar embodiment. God had a body and a divine will, and so would his children. Situated within the merger of physical and spiritual, the Saints could move toward the expression of the purpose of their mortal lives, the righteous exercise of moral agency.

Free Agency

The capacity to choose, enshrined as a core virtue of modern political and social life, was also central to Latter-day Saint theology and anthropology.[63] The bodies that with spirits constituted souls had to make choices. Smith and his disciples couldn't get enough of human agency, starting with the Book of Mormon.[64] The two key passages concerned with anthropology (Lehi's deathbed sermon and Benjamin's final sermon) are again relevant. Lehi (2 Nephi 2:4–5, 11–16) argues that life requires the exercise of agency. He tells his son that the plan for human salvation mandates "an opposition in all things" partly expressed in a division of the universe into "things to act and things to be acted upon." Humans are meant from their origins to decide—"the Lord God gave unto man that he should act for himself." To exercise agency is to act rather than be acted on.

Centuries later, King Benjamin echoes Lehi's theology, calling his listeners to act "according to your own will" (Mosiah 2:21). Making explicit what was largely implicit in Lehi's message, Benjamin preaches that believers "are made free" in Christ. This freedom is the capacity to decide their own fate. Similarly, just before the arrival of Christ to the New World, Samuel the Lamanite prophet tells the wicked Nephites (Helaman 14:30) that they are "free," which means "permitted to act for yourselves."[65] Samuel's message is clear: humans are independent moral agents.

Shortly after he published the Book of Mormon, Smith dictated a revelation that revisited creation and the time before the world was (D&C 29). There he engages the introduction of free will into the Garden of Eden. "Behold, I gave

---

[62] *WJS*, 340–62, 378–83. See also Givens, *Wrestling the Angel*, 93–95.
[63] Grotius and Locke are often considered originators of this modern emphasis. Weber, *Protestant Ethic*, 26; Taylor, *Sources of the Self*, 159–76; Taylor, *Secular Age*, 127, 159–61.
[64] Flake, "Translating Time," 515–19, provides a religious studies perspective. Givens describes "moral agency" as the "capacity for independent virtuous activity" in *Wrestling the Angel*, 194–98. See also *EoM*, 26–27.
[65] Other sections of relevance to the posture of agency in the Book of Mormon include 2 Nephi 10:23; Alma 12:31, 13:3, 30:8, 41:7.

unto him [Adam] that he should be an agent unto himself." The devil immediately tests Adam's agency. That devil, we learn, instigated war in heaven and corrupted a third of the hosts of heaven. After his defeat in that heavenly war, Satan was allowed to roam the earth because "it must needs be that the devil should tempt the children of men, or they could not be agents unto themselves" (29:34–39), echoing Lehi's "opposition in all things." Around the same time, Smith in his Visions of Moses (Moses 4) depicts a conflict between Jesus and Satan in which the devil seeks to "destroy the agency" of humanity (4:3). Satan proposes to foreclose the exercise of will, while Christ defends human agency.

At the end of 1830, Smith revealed in his Prophecy of Enoch that God told Eve and Adam that people are "agents unto themselves" (Moses 6:56). In a restatement in the next chapter, God confirms that "in the Garden of Eden, gave I unto man his agency" (7:32). Smith's 1832 exegesis of the Prologue to John (D&C 93) announces the "agency of man" by which an individual's fate can be determined in the afterlife. In D&C 101 (December 1833), God refers to human "futurity, according to the moral agency which I have given unto him." An 1834 revelation reiterated that God has "given unto the children of men to be agents unto themselves."[66] In 1842 the Book of Abraham reconfirmed those familiar positions by casting human life as a test during which God will "prove" humans "to see if they will do all things God shall command them" (Abraham 3:25). This text also makes clear that God chose Jesus because he would protect human agency (3:27–28). Abraham thus completes the story started in Moses 4, tying it more clearly to the War in Heaven of Revelation 12:7–10. The world thus exists in large part to give humans bodies and a stage on which to exercise agency.

Smith wasn't alone in these controversies. Jonathan Edwards had influentially addressed Arminian critics (and modernist individualists) in his popular *Freedom of the Will*, an abridgement of which Smith owned.[67] Edwards maintained that God was the cause of humans, who could nevertheless choose to follow their appetites and characters (even if those choices didn't determine election).[68] While Smith positioned himself as anti-Calvinist, if he'd have understood Edwards's main point, he might have found himself in broad agreement—will and agency are coexpressions of humans and God. He would have denied Edwards's specific conceptions of the gulf between humans and God—Smith saw God and humans as interdependent in a way Edwards would have rejected as pagan. But the sense of agency as cocreation is likely something the two thinkers share. God created the context in which humans could express their will, as Smith had claimed from the very beginning.

---

[66] *JSPD4*, 23 [D&C 104:17].
[67] Jones, "Nauvoo Library," 164.
[68] Marsden, *Edwards*, 436–46.

With increasing clarity over time, Smith positioned agency as a specific response to Calvinist election. In a May 1841 sermon, he was explicit. Playfully, he redefined election as the establishment of rules of engagement before the mortal experiment rather than the eternal decree about who passed the test. "God did elect or predestinate, that all those who would be saved, should be saved in Christ Jesus, and through obedience to the gospel; but he passes over no man's sins, but visits them with correction, and if his children will not repent of their sins, he will discard them."[69] In other words, Calvinist election was an inaccurate model of what the Saints called the Plan of Salvation. How any individual fared in the Plan depended on how he or she wielded agency; what had been elected was the opportunity to try. By April 1844, Smith was even clearer. In an address to a closed group of devoted disciples, he taught that "God cannot save or damn a man only on the principle that every man acts, chooses, and worships for himself."[70] Where the Methodism in which he first experienced religion had been careful to remain within the Arminian orbit, in Smith's later pronouncements, he endorsed a full-throated Pelagianism. Humans worked within God's system and were sustained by God's love and power, but they had to choose salvation themselves.

Within the Church, agency bent to the needs of the community. Early Latter-day Saints followed their personal revelation and anti-Protestant inclinations into the Church, with its hierarchy of prophets, presidents, and priesthoods. The basic impulse of choosing to belong was not unique to them. This was one of Evangelical historian Nathan Hatch's most enduring observations in his treatment of "democratization" within American Protestantism—many people sought the right to decide to whom they could pledge their agency.[71] This fact alone suggests that agency needn't always be individualistic, even when it reposes in individuals. For the Saints, this juxtaposition seemed fitting rather than paradoxical. The God of pre-earth life who created the plan for agency crucially organized humans into dispensations of extended kindreds (Abraham 3:22, 4:26–27).[72] That organization both cultivated and constrained agency.

Latter-day Saint theologies of embodiment and agency sound quite modern, but in practice they were intensely cross-pressured.

---

[69] *T&S* 2:15 (1 June 1841): 429.
[70] *JSPAR*, 97–101.
[71] Hatch, *Democratization*, 16, 80, 122. Mullen, *Chance of Salvation*, chapter 4, expands Hatch's treatment.
[72] *JSPD7*, 495. An 1843 sermon (*JSPJ3*, 32) clarifies that God ordained that salvation of the dead would come through "gath[er]ing together," an implicit interpretation of the implications of the "organization" in Abraham.

The Modern Prison of Individualism

Modern in many respects when it came to human agency and perfectibility, Smith nevertheless seems to have had serious reservations about individualism. He resisted isolation, reconceived the Chain of Being in genealogical terms, and left his followers porous to, rather than buffered from, one another.

Weber famously overstated the individualistic nature of Calvinism in his seminal account of the rise of capitalism.[73] But he wasn't obviously wrong about the fact that Calvinism left many believers on edge, especially about their own salvation. The crisis was integral to the conviction of depravity that drew potential believers to Christ. To be sure, Calvinist and Evangelical societies, including in early America, were deeply communal as we just noted in discussing Tocqueville's blind spots. But individuals still had to struggle through salvation in their own hearts. Conviction and regeneration rested in individual souls. Weber thought the uncertainty about salvation drove Protestants to work harder in hopes that success would demonstrate their "elected" status. Whether Weber was right or not, his was a modern story. For Smith it wasn't just an individual's postmortal state that mattered, though. Much as the Puritans before him, he agonized over the status of kith and kin. It wasn't enough to be saved alone.[74]

At a personal level, Smith knew and hated loneliness. His mother remembered that he explained his decision to marry Emma Hale on the basis of his terrible lonesomeness after the death of his brother Alvin in 1824.[75] Writing to Emma from the road in 1834, he explained his decision to write her by hand because it was a "consolation" to feel connected to her during his "lonely moments which is not easily described."[76] After a day of unexpected visitors shortly after New Year 1836, he exclaimed, "I delight in the society of my friends & brethren."[77] When he was imprisoned in Missouri in 1839, he wrote to Emma, complaining that he felt like "Joseph in Egypt," wondering whether his "friends yet live" and "if they live . . . do they remember me have they regard for me if so let me know it."[78] In an 1842 letter to the Whitney family (including his new plural wife Sarah Ann) from hiding, Smith worried that he could "not live long" in his "lonely retreat." He pleaded that they would come to "comfort" him in his "time of affliction."[79]

Others noted this hunger for companionship. Heber Kimball wrote to Parley Pratt in June 1842 that, "Brother Joseph feels as well as I Ever seen him. one

---

[73] Weber, *Protestant Ethic*, with criticism in Gregory, *Unintended Reformation*, 269.
[74] Brown, *In Heaven*, 203–205, 208–11.
[75] Lucy Mack Smith, *History* (1845), 97, CHL.
[76] *JSPD4*, 50.
[77] *JSPJ1*, 147.
[78] *JSPD6*, 375.
[79] Joseph Smith, "Letter to the Whitneys, 18 August 1842," CHL.

reason is he has got a Small company that he feels safe in thare hands. and that is not all he can open his bosom to and feel him Self safe."[80] Kimball had in mind the temple-Masonic fraternity established that Spring. In 1843, Smith proclaimed that friendship was "the grand fundamental prin[c]iple of Mormonism," echoing Masonic teachings.[81] Smith's attachment to attachment does not determine his theology, but it provides important personal context for the work to create and support communities. His resistance to individualism was not just intellectual or spiritual. It was visceral.

With interrelated theologies and rituals in his religious career, Smith seems to have been asking why anyone would have required complete liberation from dependence on God, cosmos, and other humans. This clarion call of Enlightenment modernists seems to have mystified Smith. He saw an individual's escape to heaven as radically inferior to a community's salvation, a theology crystallized in the scandalous comment we encountered earlier that he preferred hell with friends to heaven alone. Individualism was as much a prison as hell.

Escape Routes from Individual Isolation

Smith sought to escape individualism through an anthropology that saw people as simultaneously porous and powerful. Broadly, (1) as part of his ongoing commitment to metaphysical correspondence, he worked out the parameters of the spatial and ontological factors that threatened to separate humans from God; and (2) he theorized and attempted to develop "theodemocratic" utopias to merge individuals into robust and eternal communities. In pursuit of these ends, he followed paths that were both this- and other-worldly. These approaches relied on concepts of movement through space and time as well as ontological transformation.

Other-Worldly Paths

As many of his predecessors and fewer of his peers, Smith saw modes of escaping the prison of individualism that relied on supernatural capacities or nonordinary access to the spiritual realm. The paths Smith and his colleagues embraced were part of a dance at the interface between earth and heaven that was a major feature of their worldview.

---

[80] Heber Kimball to Parley Pratt, June 17, 1842, CHL.
[81] *JSPJ3*, 66, cf. Cole, *Freemason's Library*, 121–23.

Traveling the Heavens

As a consequence of the Fall, human beings lost direct physical access to God. While talk about God's absence from the world (sometimes as the "hidden God" or *Deus absconditus*) increased over the modern period, that was one way of expressing an ancient concern about divine separation.[82] This separation was never complete. Many Protestants still saw the cosmos as full of God's presence, even if their access to God was generally indirect. Some Enlightenment reformers and freethinkers hoped to make the separation complete, to strip the material world of divinity. They were thus adding an Epicurean metaphysics to Newtonian physics.[83] In the phrase of historian Brett Grainger, partisans of this "mechanistic cosmology saw moon, sun, and stars as dead, distant cogs in the celestial machinery," while "antebellum evangelicals addressed them as tutors and coreligionists, as exemplars in holy living."[84] Smith and his disciples participated in that latter mode of being. They saw themselves as inhabiting the living cosmos alongside God.

Whatever the debates about mechanistic cosmology, for the Saints and many others, surely God was somewhere, and if he didn't walk the earth after the Fall, perhaps humans could learn to walk the heavens. As early as the 1830s, Latter-day Saints were tying human translation to a form of sacred movement that promised such access. Although (contrary to Emanuel Swedenborg, who spent decades in such travels) few if any Saints claimed to achieve this gift, blessings and priesthood ordinations advanced the capacity as a millennial promise.

Many of the earliest blessings were connected to supernatural evangelism. For example, Zebedee Coltrin, ordaining Wilford Woodruff a Seventy in 1837, promised that Woodruff would "waft [him]self (as did Philip) from River to river from Sea to sea & from Continant to Continant for the Purpose of Preaching the gospel of Jesus Christ."[85] Such blessings drew on the Christian Bible narratives of Philip, a missionary who escaped violence when God spirited him away (Acts 8:39–40).[86]

The scope of such sacred evangelism was not limited to this world. Many Saints received the blessing to be translated from planet to planet, to the moon and stars. Most pregnantly, faithful believers were to be translated to the special star Kolob, that orbited nearest to God.[87] The sequence of bodily translation was

---

[82] Gillespie, *Theological Origins*, 226; Coleman, "Secularization," 369, 373–76.
[83] Grasso, "Religious and Secular," 370; Wilson, *Epicureanism*.
[84] Grainger, *Church in the Wild*, 76.
[85] *WWJ*, 1:118.
[86] Thus, e.g., *EPB*, 4, 16, 17, 64, 67, 69, 70, 72, 89, 94, 96, 108, 119, 173.
[87] See, e.g., *EPB*, 64, 67, 96, 105, 124, 146, 149, 171. See also Oliver B. Huntington, "Resurrection of My Mother," *Young Woman's Journal* 5:7 (April 1894): 346. On Kolob, see *WWJ*, 1:118.

not obviously developmental—all forms are present from the early 1830s (except references to Kolob, which begin to appear after 1835). But there was a logical progression to the grand prize of human translation, the movement across the earth, among the stars, and ultimately to the heavenly abode of God, in a form capable of tolerating the encounter. The translation to heaven recapitulated the translation journeys of Enoch (with his city) and Elijah (on his fiery chariot). Benjamin Winchester heard, "if you desire it you shall be taken as Enoch [or] Elijah."[88] Zina Diantha Huntington heard that 'thou mayest tarry or translate thyself as seemeth thee good."[89] A dozen or more patriarchal blessings made similar promises.[90]

Often the translating power of Enoch and Elijah referred to the transformation of humans and the earth they would inhabit at the time of Christ's Second Coming. Darwin Richardson learned, "if you desire it you shall be changed in the twinkling of an eye, and enter upon the Millenial reign."[91] At least a dozen others heard the same thing.[92] The basic idea was of a power to defy death by living the stories of ancient predecessors. The eschatological connection intensified as many Saints expected to meet those ancestors during that millennial translation, rising through the air to meet Enoch and his city as the righteous are gathered to heaven.[93]

While most early blessings came from members of the Smith family, others followed precedent. In 1849, Presendia Huntington Kimball blessed Joseph Hovey (in reciprocation for a blessing from him to calm her nerves) that "you shall be blessed and become a mighty man in Israel and sit in the Council of the Just and noble spirits of Israel and be like the disciples, who did waft themselves from city to city and from clime to clime and remained to tarry, yea this shall be your mission."[94] While she emphasized the apostolic sense of translation, Kimball connected supernatural movement to an immortality attributed to the Apostle John in New Testament (John 21:22–23) and three American apostles in the Book of Mormon (3 Nephi 28:12; 4 Nephi 1:14, 37). Once again, sacred movement was associated with final transformation.

The Saints were not alone in their basic understanding of translation. Noah Webster defined it as "the removal of a person to heaven without subjecting him to death" in his 1828 *American Dictionary*. Other religious outsiders like the Public Universal Friend (born Jemima Wilkinson; 1752–1819) and Mother

---

[88] JSPD4, 276.
[89] Patriarchal Blessing 1319, CHL, copy in author's possession.
[90] EPB, 38, 40, 65, 78, 83, 85, 89, 90, 95, 96, 111, 123, 139, 177.
[91] JSPD4, 277.
[92] EPB, 40, 44, 49, 56, 65, 67, 76, 101, 120, 123, 128, 135, 146.
[93] EPB, 123; Smith, *Sacred Hymns*, 26, 38, 53, 86.
[94] Hovey Journal, 74–75 (March 4, 1849), CHL.

Ann Lee (1736–1784) aimed for similar translation.[95] Andrew Jackson Davis saw translation as referring to movement of spirits among planets and death as the transformation of people into spirits.[96]

The quest for human translation was most often eschatological, concerned with the world's wrapping up scenes. According to the 1832 Olive Leaf revelation, believers were being "prepared for the celestial glory; for after it [the human soul] hath filled the measure of its creation, it shall be crowned with glory, even with the presence of God" (D&C 88:19).[97] The same promise applied to the earth as well: "the earth abideth the law, of a celestial kingdom, for it filleth, the measure of its creation . . . it shall be quickened again, and shall abide the power, by which it was quickened" (88:25–26).[98] This *quickening* of the Olive Leaf was a synonym for translation.

The capacity to be physically proximate without being destroyed was important to manage the risk of madness or extinction posed by the divine presence. As had the ancients (and some of their charismatic peers[99]), the Latter-day Saints worried whether they could tolerate the glorious and annihilating presence of the divine.[100] Repeatedly Smith's revelations explore the transfiguration required for humans to abide the divine presence the way Moriancumer had on Mount Shelem. In the Visions of Moses and Prophecy of Enoch, Moses has to be "transfigured" within "the glory of God" so he can tolerate the divine presence (Moses 1:2, 9, 31). He admits that if he'd have seen God with his natural eyes "I should have withered and died in his presence." Eve and Adam after the Fall learn that they are "shut out from the presence of God" (5:4, 6:49) because "no unclean thing can dwell . . . in his presence" (6:57). The Book of Mormon similarly talks in terms of being "cut off" from the divine presence (1 Nephi 2:21; 2 Nephi 1:20, 4:4, 5:20, 9:6) and indicates that after the fall "there is no flesh that can dwell in the presence of God" (2 Nephi 2:8).

In 1831, Smith preached in the divine voice to a church conference, "you shall see me & know that I am not with the carnal neither natural but with the spiritual for no man hath seen God at any time in the flesh but by the Spirit of God neither can any natural man abide the presence of God neither after the carnal mind ye are not able to abide the presence of God now" (D&C 67:10–13).[101] In the 1832

---

[95] Turner, *Mormonism*, 92–93; Juster, *Doomsayers*, 65. See Juster, *Doomsayers*, 73, 99, 114; Buck, *Theological Dictionary*, 69 for other examples.

[96] Davis, *Spiritual Intercourse*, 73–74, 84.

[97] *JSPD2*, 338.

[98] *JSPD2*, 338.

[99] One woman described in a Reformed Methodist history feared in 1817 that even conversion might kill her until she was "made pure": Pitts, *Gospel Witness*, 65.

[100] Exodus 19:21, 20:19, 28:35, 33:20; Deuteronomy 5:24–25, 8:16; Leviticus 15:31; Numbers 8:19, 17:12–13; Judges 13:22.

[101] *JSPD2*, 110.

Vision, Smith and Rigdon reported that "to whom he grants this privilege of seeing and knowing for themselves; That through the power and manifestation of the Spirit, while in the flesh, they may be able to bear his presence in the world of glory" (D&C 76:117–18). In 1832, Smith revealed that without priesthood and its ordinances, "the power of Godliness is not manifest unto man in the flesh, for without this no man can see the face of God even the father and live" (D&C 84:21–22).[102] This aspiration was also present in Latter-day Saint hymnody from very early on.[103]

It wasn't just the divine presence per se, but also the pure intelligence associated with God that was inaccessible. When Phelps published a pastiche of material from the early revelations in 1833, he indicated that Enoch and his people received the blessing to "be able to bear the presence of God in the world of glory." They were, he said, "translated."[104] Taking a similar tack in an 1842 exegesis of Malachi 3:3, Smith explained that "the peryfying of the sons of Levi was by giving unto them inteligince—that we are not capable of meditating on & reciving all the inteligence which belongs to an immortal state."[105] Direct revelation and spiritual knowledge was a key aspect of the transformation of those priestly figures, and for the Nauvoo Saints this came to mean recipients of temple priesthood. Such was the promise of translation: unmediated access to divine presence and intelligence.

Smith used the Urim and Thummin, biblicized sacred stones, as a locus of connection between humans, texts, worlds, space, and time.[106] He first used the terms to refer to the interpreter stones he used for the Book of Mormon translation (connected directly to Moriancumer's sacred stones, as we saw in chapter 1), but they came to mean much more. Smith understood Revelation's "sea of glass" (4:6) as a reference to the resurrected earth. He was explicit about it in an 1832 question-and-answer session in Hiram, Ohio: the sea of glass was "the earth, in its sanctified, immortal, and eternal state" (D&C 77:1). Other than references to the interpreter stones through which he received translations and revelations, Smith didn't say much more about Urim and Thummim for several years.

In the 1839–1842 Book of Abraham, chapter 3, Smith reported that Abraham had his own "Urim and Thummim, which the Lord my God had given unto me, in Ur of the Chaldees." Using those stones, Abraham was able to see the "very great" stars and especially Kolob, which "was nearest unto the throne of God." Abraham then received a revelatory explanation of Kolob and the nature of its time "by the Urim and Thummim" (3:1–4). As we'll see in chapter 6, Abraham's

[102] JSPD2, 295.
[103] Smith, Sacred Hymns, 91, 101–102.
[104] EMS 1:11 (April 1833): 81.
[105] JSPJ2, 195.
[106] Brown, In Heaven, 82.

astronomical revelations are intimately concerned with the connections among people, earthly objects, and celestial bodies.

Smith expanded the treatment of Abraham 3 in an April 1843 instructional session (a version of which was canonized as D&C 130). There he extended the use of Urim and Thummim as devices for metaphysical astronomy. He confirmed that different kinds of beings (gods, angels, humans) observe time based on the planet on which they reside but could see other times through Urim and Thummim, as we saw in chapter 2. This solution presented a logical puzzle because of ministering angels, who obviously interact with earth-dwellers but may not be bound by earth time. Smith explained that "the Angels do not reside on a planet like our earth but they dwell with God and the planet where he dwells is like crystal, and like a sea of glass before the throne. This is the great Urim & Thummim whereon all things are manifest." He explained the role of correspondence in establishing this connection, "The Urim & Thummim is a small representation of this globe. The earth when it is purified will be made like unto crystal and will be a Urim & Thummim whereby all things pertaining to an inferior kingdom, or all kingdoms of a lower order will be manifest to those who dwell on it."[107] Another account of the same sermon recalled that the resurrected earth would "be a Urim & Thummim for all things below it in the scale of creation,"[108] making the association with the Chain of Being explicit. In parallel, Smith apparently explained (according to Brigham Young's official history) that each person would receive their own Urim and Thummim at the resurrection.[109] They would, in other words, become like Abraham and God, capable of seeing, knowing, and understanding themselves and the celestial bodies through these planetary seer stones. That was part of their final transformation. In a parallel line that was tied to the temple liturgy, Smith preached in June 1844 that Adam learned the "key word to which the heavens is opend" through the Urim and Thummim.[110]

The documents preserving Smith's theology of the Urim and Thummim is thus fragmentary but evocative. What seems clear is that these objects are (1) seerstones, (2) resurrected planets or stars, (3) conduits for revelation and divine language, and (4) the resurrection birthright of the righteous. These stones are thus a locus of connection within the cosmic Chain of Being and speak once more to the intimacy of humans and texts in Smith's theologies.

A specific problem arose in the interface between translation and resurrection, both of which facilitate direct access to God. Resurrection was both ontological

---

[107] *JSPJ2*, 404.
[108] *JSPJ2*, 324.
[109] *MS* 26:8 (February 20, 1864): 118–19.
[110] *JSPJ3*, 334.

(bodies became immortal) and spatial (resurrected beings moved to heaven). The Restoration theology of bodily translation left an unanswered question. If translation made divine proximity possible, was translation just a resurrection of the living rather than the dead? Or was it something else entirely? Smith didn't address that question directly until the 1840s.

In a public sermon on priesthood in early October 1840, Smith used a reference in Hebrews 11:35 to a "better resurrection" as the textual basis for a distinction between "translation" and "resurrection." He preached that "the doctrine of translation is a power which belongs to this priesthood," before suggesting that translated beings had not completed their mortal journeys. Translation was thus a lesser resurrection than the resurrection of the dead, he maintained. Translated beings served as "Ministring angels Unto many planets,"[111] echoing the connection between cosmic travel and translation. He returned to the same theme a year later, laying out a taxonomy of humans, angels, and spirits based on the degree and type of embodiment.[112] Translation was a mighty prequel; it was not the final act. Parley Pratt taught something similar, mixed with his belief that spirit replaced blood in the veins of resurrected beings.[113] Smith made a similar claim in an 1843 funeral sermon—"Flesh and blood cannot go there but flesh and bones quickened by the Spirit of God can."[114]

While this 1840 sermon placed some limits on bodily translation, it implied that translation was indeed a variant of resurrection. There were two forms of resurrection, one preliminary and the other, "better resurrection" final. In any case, the concept of human transformation remained a part of the ongoing community of humans and divine beings. In fact, in their status as ministering spirits, translated beings had the role of helping live prophets write scripture, again melding the twin senses of translation as the movement of ideas among peoples and of humans among states of being. In October 1839, Smith explicitly taught that scripture was written when the dead visited the living, in a complex exegetical merger of Jude 1:14–15 and Hebrews 11:4. As a "ministring Angel," he explained, Enoch "appered unto Jude as Abel did unto Paul."[115] This theology of translation made explicit the innate and permanent interconnection between humans and texts, and it recalled the image of Urim and Thummim as a locus for that unity.

---

[111] *JSPD7*, 438–39. Smith first broached the idea in August 1839: *JSPD6*, 552. Rigdon had discussed these concepts in general terms in *M&A* 1:11 (August 1835): 165 and *EMS* 2:19 (April 1834): 147.
[112] *JSPD8*, 288, 301, cf. *JSPD8*, 83
[113] Pratt, *Millennium*, 132–35, 139.
[114] *JSPJ3*, 110, October 9, 1843.
[115] *JSPD7*, 438. See discussion in Brown, "Read the Round." Protestants saw references to ministering spirits as generic references to angels: Buck, *Theological Dictionary*, 21–23.

Many Saints hoped for dramatic events like Moriancumer piercing the veil or Stephen being spirited away from harm but rarely if ever experienced such translation. But there was also a long game, a metaphysical and genetic force that transformed humans from their birth. The two modes of transformation seem to have merged in Smith's thought under the title of "priesthood."

Priesthood and the Seed of Abraham

"Priesthood" is a complex word that is especially fluid in the early Restoration. Among other types of priesthood, Smith proposed a genealogical version that expanded on Hebrew precedents of tribal priesthood within Israel. Something about this priesthood linked it to the passage and interconnection of human generations. In the past I've called it his "sacerdotal genealogy," while the liturgical historian Jonathan Stapley proposes "cosmological priesthood" and the historian Joseph Stuart prefers "temple priesthood."[116] Some Latter-day Saint commenters have called it the "patriarchal priesthood," following precedent in the early Church.[117] Whatever the term employed, the idea was that a metaphysical power available to the Saints could change humans ontologically as they came to participate in the family of heaven. Believers were transformed to the extent that they participated in this cosmic priesthood, an enhanced, sacerdotal parallel to Evangelical sanctification by the Holy Spirit.[118] This cosmic priesthood existed in parallel with an all-male ecclesiastical priesthood. The fact that the single word did double duty has led to confusion and underappreciation of the cosmic priesthood.

Abrupt transitions in Moses 6 (1830) confirm the tie between cosmic genealogy and priesthood. The text introduces a new line from Eve and Adam through Seth to replace the dead Abel and describes scripture and prophecy in the context of the Edenic Books of Remembrance and the "pure and undefiled" language they contained. "Now this same Priesthood, which was in the beginning, shall be in the end of the world also." It is at once primordial and eschatological. Adam makes this statement by "prophecy." In support of this priesthood, "a genealogy was kept of the children of God," the "book of the generations of Adam" (6:6-8).[119]

---

[116] Brown, *In Heaven*, 204, 220–25; Stapley, *Power of Godliness*, 22, 26–27; Stuart, "Racial Redemption," 770.

[117] Brown, "Chain of Belonging," 32; Stapley, *Power of Godliness*. On "patriarchal priesthood," see Ehat, "Mormon Succession," 28, and Flake, *Priestly Logic*, 22.

[118] On evangelical sanctification, see Grainger, *Church in the Wild*, 123.

[119] Notably, this preamble sets up Adam as writing portions of Genesis 1, thus answering a logical problem with the Mosaic Torah: how could Moses report on the creation he didn't witness? He didn't; Adam did.

A revelation on priesthood in September 1832 (D&C 84) framed subsequent teachings. The revelation includes a genealogy (84:6–18) explicitly focused on priesthood authority that simulates the biblical generations of Adam (Genesis 5:1) but in reverse. As opposed to the Bible, for Smith the line flows from Moses backward to Melchizedek, Abraham, Enoch, and Abel on the way to Adam. This priesthood makes "manifest" the "powers of godliness. And without the ordinances thereof, and the authority of the priesthood, the power of godliness is not manifest unto men in the flesh" (84:20–25). This priesthood thus augurs the proximity to divine things that bodily translation aimed for.

In the 1832 revelation, Smith reveals that those who are "faithful unto the obtaining" of priesthood will be "sanctified by the Spirit unto the renewing of their bodies." This new status is, precisely, a genealogical connection: "They become the sons of Moses and of Aaron and the seed of Abraham" (84:33–34). The connection between priesthood, genealogy, and the seed of Abraham is central to understanding what Smith was doing in his developing anthropology. He seems to have seen it as a mechanism for integrating his people into the family of God. He emphasized the genealogical priesthood more and more over the course of his career.

In an extended subsection of a composite 1831–1835 revelation setting up the priesthood hierarchy within the church (D&C 107:40–57), Joseph Smith retells the genealogies of Genesis 5. This time, instead of the endless "begats" at a specific age for each generation of patriarchs, the action documented at each turn of the generations is a priesthood ordination. Specifically, "the order of this priesthood was confirmed to be handed down from father to son, and rightly belongs to the literal descendants of the chosen seed, to whom the promises were made" (107:40). When Smith blessed his father, Joseph Sr., in September 1835, he granted that the elder Joseph would "hold the right of patriarchal priesthood." Furthermore, Smith placed his father within the Abrahamic covenant in that blessing, telling him, "I have set thee to be at the head: a multitude of nations shall come of thee, and thou art a Prince over them forever."[120]

In a December 1832 revelation (D&C 86), Smith revealed, "thus saith the Lord unto you with whom the priesthood hath continued through the lineage of your fathers, for ye are lawful heirs according to the flesh" (86:8–9).[121] Furthermore, "the Priesthood hath remained and must needs remain through you and your lineage untill the restoration of all things."[122] This wasn't just the Levites of ancient Judaism—it was a priesthood genealogy for all believers. The Saints were

---

[120] *JSPD4*, 488.
[121] *JSPD2*, 327.
[122] *JSPD2*, 327.

all lawful heirs to the transforming power of God. Smith's disciples became the human structure of a priesthood to organize all of history.

Smith's application of priesthood as organizing and constraining human generations targumized the spare biblical promise to Phinehas, son of Aaron, that "he shall have it, and his seed after him, even the covenant of an everlasting priesthood" (Numbers 25:13). For most modern interpreters, that promise explains why priests in Israel could only be drawn from certain family lines. In Smith's hands, though, the text was a cosmic infrastructure for communal salvation.

The theology of parental priesthood continued through the end of his life. In Smith's 1843 revelation on celestial marriage (D&C 132:29–33), he explicitly engages the Abrahamic promise as the infrastructure for the postmortal Chain of Belonging. The "works of Abraham" would stretch not only across all mortal human history but through the afterlife as well. Shortly after D&C 132, Smith preached that "Abrahams Patriarchal power" was "the greatest yet experienced in this church."[123] People needed to belong to each other, and the priesthood of Abraham and Sarah was the way.

The seed of Abraham was metaphysically potent. Where Jewish converts ritually acknowledged that they were receiving the status of Abraham's children, Smith understood that his people were being physically and metaphysically transformed. He by and large understood that the priesthood genealogy made his followers the literal offspring of Abraham. This genealogy was tied, with increasing regularity over time, to the patriarchal blessings modeled on Jacob's deathbed blessings of his children (Genesis 49) and administered as prayerful benedictions by either an ecclesiastical officer called "patriarch" or by the recipient's righteous father.[124] Thus Mariah Clark learned in her 1836 patriarchal blessing that she was "of the seed of Abraham"[125] and many others found themselves similarly tied to the sacred kindreds in their patriarchal blessings.[126]

In addition to patriarchal blessings, Smith also reread Galatians 3:29 to reveal that recipients of the priesthood in general "are sanctified by the spir[i]t unto the renewing of there bodies that they become the sons of Moses and of Aaron and the seed of Abraham" (D&C 84:33–34).[127] This was what he was interested in—a power that could remake his followers in their very essence.

Some people were Abrahamic by birth, while others were numbered among the Gentiles. In an 1839 sermon, Smith explained that "the affect of the Holy

---

[123] *WJS*, 245.

[124] The classic treatment is Bates and Smith, *Lost Legacy*. Ultimately patriarchal blessings routinely designated a recipient as belonging to a tribe, generally of Joseph. Mauss, *Abraham's Children*, 22, 34–35.

[125] *EPB*, 86.

[126] *EPB*, 12, 16, 71, 86, 87, 94, 95, 100, 128, 162, 163, 173; *T&S* 5:20 (November 1, 1844): 695.

[127] *JSPD2*, 297.

Ghost upon a gentile is to purge out the old blood & make him actually of the seed of Abram. That man that has none of the Blood of Abram (naturally) must have a new creation."[128] By teaching that his followers literally became the seed of Abraham, Smith became their claim to the Abrahamic covenant.[129] This was not the evangelicals' rebirth during emotional worship: this was a genetic reconfiguration of the worshiper. The genealogical priesthood force associated with Abraham and Sarah flowed through Church members' veins, part and parcel of their broader transfiguration.

Smith believed that his priesthood was a mechanism by which humans and gods could share their identity. True enough, they were all born into the species *Ahman*, but their developmental stages differed radically. He didn't believe that as mortals he and his followers had the same power, wisdom, and purity as God. That discrepancy was obvious. But over the long arc of eternity, he expected that through priesthood all would partake of the eternal identity with the gods.[130] This was the ultimate path that bodily translation pointed toward.

While he made these pronouncements in various sermons, an 1837 interaction with Mary Fielding in Kirtland exemplifies the basic point. She dreamed that Smith was wearing the "seamless garment" Jesus wore to the crucifixion. She found blood on the back, evidence that Christ had been stabbed there as part of the torture before his execution. When she told him the dream, he replied that "it was an evidence that he [Smith] wore the Priesthood of the Son of God and that he [Smith] would have to endure some of his [Christ's] strips."[131] This priesthood, tied to Christ, mediated the intense identity between Christ and Smith. That same identity also drove the future hopes of the Latter-day Saints.

The Saints weren't just becoming Abraham's children. By the 1840s, Smith was clearly teaching that human beings could be saviors to each other, thereby extending the transformative priesthood and human identity with Christ. As early as 1832, he had called followers "th[r]ough this Priesthood" to be "saviour[s] unto my people Israel."[132] The doctrine of human saviors is clearly present in the 1832 Olive Leaf, a point recognized by friends and foes alike.[133] In December 1834, he called his followers "to be saviors of men."[134] Lecture 7 in the Lectures on Faith continued to lay the conceptual groundwork in its discussion of salvation.[135] In an 1840 letter to Phelps, Smith remarked that he wanted

---

[128] *JSPD6*, 524.
[129] He may also have been interpreting Matthew 3:9.
[130] *WJS*, 340–62, 378–83, cf. Laub, "Journal," 18.
[131] Mary Fielding to "dear Sister & Brother," October 7, 1837, Kirtland, OH, MS 2779, folder 2, CHL, [3] (transcribed by Elizabeth Kuehn).
[132] *JSPD2*, 327.
[133] The debate between Parley Pratt and La Roy Sunderland is emblematic: Brown, *In Heaven*, 266. See also Pratt, *Voice of Warning*, 145; Harris, *Mormonism Portrayed*, 22–23; Caswall, *Prophet*, 95.
[134] *JSPD4*, 197, cf. D&C 103:9.
[135] *JSPR2*, 375–80.

to "be a savior of my fellow men."[136] In an October 1841 sermon, he was explicit that these secondary saviors were an exegesis of a spare phrase in Obadiah 1:21 (in the context of Isaiah 61:6 and Malachi 4:6), predicting that "saviours shall come up on mount Zion."[137] While most readers of the Bible saw a reference to biblical prophets or perhaps protectors of Israelite interests,[138] Smith saw an eschatological anthropology—believers could become saviors themselves—they could acquire "Power to Save all they Dead friends . . . and a grate Multitude of Others."[139] In 1844 he promised—only half joking—to carry his followers "on his back" "through the gates" of heaven.[140] What became more explicit in the 1840s was that the Abrahamic priesthood was the mechanism for this status that paralleled Christ. This was a power wielded by both men and women, as became clear in the Nauvoo temple liturgy. In a sermon to the Nauvoo Relief Society, Smith promised that righteous women "shall hereafter be crown'd a mother of those that shall prove faithful &c."[141]

As believers became secondary saviors to their dead, they joined Christ in wielding salvific power. In Smith's phrase in the 1840s, these "Saviours" were "in other words gods . . . come on mount Zion."[142] Just as typology functioned in scripture to transform and unite disparate human generations and their associated scriptural writings, so did a kind of metaphysical typology unite human with divine beings. In essence, Smith didn't just read typologically, he and his followers *lived* typologically, making possible a unity in transformation that connected the Saints to God through Jesus.[143]

Bringing the notion of human saviors into contact with contemporary Calvinism in 1841, Smith indicated, "All the election that can be found in the scripture is according to the flesh and pertaining to the priesthood."[144] By bringing believers into Abraham's sacred lineage, the Saints replaced election with this sacerdotal genealogy (with the caveat that they would be tested, as we saw earlier). In so doing, they became secondary saviors to the people connected to them as offspring, a sacerdotal variant of Paul's adoption theology.[145] These adoptive connections may have been strong enough to prevent the effect of backsliding, as the priesthood transformed recipients enough to guarantee

---

[136] *JSPD7*, 346.
[137] *JSPD7*, 434–40; Brown, "Adoption Theology," 44–47.
[138] For a typical Protestant view, see Clarke, *Holy Bible*, 4:698.
[139] Kingsbury, "Diary," 18, University of Utah Library. See also George Laub, "Journal," 2, 61–62, CHL.
[140] *JSPD8*, 358n404.
[141] Derr et al., *First Fifty Years*, 52.
[142] Laub, "Journal," 29, CHL.
[143] On the connection through Jesus, see Brown, *In Heaven*, 250–52.
[144] *WJS*, 74.
[145] Brown, "Adoption Theology" and Stapley, "Adoptive Sealing."

their salvation.[146] In an 1832 letter to Phelps, Smith reported that entire lineages could acquire or lose their salvation together, on the basis of the family being written into the "book of the Law of God."[147] This was heady stuff, extending beyond the confines of Pelagianism, and the Saints found it wholly persuasive and deeply biblical. The belief in their saving power was robust enough to elicit mockery from outsiders: Eliza R. Snow complained in 1838 that critics "say that the Mormons are so d—d sure of going to heaven, they had as lief die as not."[148]

Concerns about salvation, election, and the afterlife were common among American Christians. What was strange about the Restoration version was its vivid merger of physics and metaphysics, its genealogical nature, and its emphasis on human power. From the Protestant perspective, Smith and his disciples were playing out of bounds. As critics complained, and Church members periodically rediscovered, this power came with risks as well as new opportunities.

The Risks of Enchantment

Making themselves open to suprahuman agencies, especially the essence called priesthood, could be immensely reassuring. But porousness also involved ongoing threats to well-being. The same hazards to personal safety and integrity that haunted the ancients remained at play for many early Latter-day Saints. Their encounter with malevolent suprahuman agencies is in many respects typical of early modern folkways.[149] However much the churchmen and intellectuals pushed to disenchant, the majority of laypeople continued to believe in dark supernatural forces.[150]

People were often, perhaps always, at risk for invasion, whether as divine punishment for sins or the spiritual incursion of demons. Like most other Protestants, the Saints believed in afflicting providences. Smith and others viewed the 1834 cholera outbreak that broke up the Camp of Israel—an informal Church militia dispatched from Kirtland, Ohio, to protect the Saints in Independence, Missouri, from vigilantes—as divine punishment.[151] Many Saints believed that steamship explosions and similar aquatic perils came because the waters were cursed.[152] The destroying angel lurked about the lives of early Latter-day Saints; the kosher laws (discouraging coffee, tea, alcohol, and tobacco) encoded in the 1833 "Word

---

[146] Brown, *In Heaven*, 244–45.
[147] *JSPD2*, 319.
[148] Johnson, *Female Religiosity*, 57.
[149] Taysom, "Exorcism Rituals."
[150] See, e.g., Butler, *Sea of Faith*; Butler, "Disquieting History"; and Duffy, *Stripping the Altars*.
[151] Divett, "Cholera Epidemics," 10–12.
[152] *JSPD5*, 64.

of Wisdom" (D&C 89) existed in part to protect the faithful from the predations of that ominous figure.[153] More concretely, some experienced individual demonic possession.[154]

The Saints wielded an array of tools in their struggles with suprahuman agencies. They tried to be righteous to merit God's protection—obeying commandments, praying regularly, eating well, occasionally using apotropaic objects to control dark forces, and performing the occasional exorcism.[155]

In addition, they applied practical, Baconian logic to a supercharged version of the problem that other believers called "discernment," a spiritual gift that Smith assigned in equal measure to women and men[156] and had been talking about since at least 1834.[157] This gift relied on and illuminated Smith's theology of embodiment.

A revelation now known as D&C 129 is an 1856 amalgamation of several related instructions that Smith issued two decades earlier. In June 1839 Smith taught rules for differentiating devils from angels based on physical touch.[158] Smith highlighted the handshake, a basic greeting for Masons and a staple of Western social encounters for centuries.[159] Smith told his followers that when they encounter a supernatural visitor, they should "request him to shake hands with you" (according to the 1856 rendition). If the visitor tangibly took the person's hand, it was a bona fide angel. If the visitor demurred, it was an honest spirit—insubstantial and unable to attempt deception. If, however, the unknown visitor reached for the hand but left no tactile impression, then it was a devil pretending to be an angel. The willingness to deceive and the physical insubstantiality of demons gave them away.

With new resonances after the 1842 introduction of temple rites, Smith continued to speak about clasping hands as a key for differentiating devil from angel, with an eye to avoiding the devil appearing as the spirit of an old friend.[160] A coy hint in a letter of September 1842 suggested that the archangel Michael had helped Smith detect a devil disguised as an angel (D&C 128:20). He revisited the topic in 1843, distinguishing "resurrected personages" which have "bodies of flesh and bones" from "spirits of just men made perfect," who haven't been resurrected. Those just men made perfect are the ones who will demur from the request for a handshake.[161]

---

[153] Brown, "Destroying Angel."
[154] Hartley, *Joseph Knight*, 62–70.
[155] Taysom, "Exorcism Rituals."
[156] Smith explicitly assigned discernment to women "as well as to the Elders" in an 1842 sermon. Derr et al., *First Fifty Years*, 57. On discernment among, e.g., Methodists, see Juster, *Doomsayers*, 35.
[157] *JSPD4*, 165.
[158] *WWJ*, June 27, 1839.
[159] Albeit not without critics of its vulgar familiarity: Trollope, *Domestic Manners*, 94–95, 123.
[160] *JSPJ2*, 53, 257–58.
[161] *JSPD8*, 83, quoting the William Clayton journal of February 9, 1843.

To put this series of revelations into simple terms: Smith's followers hoped to shake hands with supernatural visitors as a hedge against their own acutely felt porousness. This discernment relied on the fact that humans and angels could only be whole when body and spirit combined. This vulnerability made the Saints a laughingstock in learned and more orthodox circles: for many Protestants, discerning demons was a superstitious remnant of an old worldview.[162]

Discussions about supernatural handshakes were part of a broader theological puzzle. In Smith's hands, the posited dualism of bodies and spirits was the context for a broader opposition between humans and demonic entities. In January 1841, he explains that "before foundation of the Earth in the Grand Counsel that the spirits of all *men* ware subject to opression & the express purpose of God in Giveing it a tabernicle was to arm it against the power of Darkness." He uses his marvelous literalism to motivate the explanation, citing Christ's use of the term "get thee behind me Satan" (Matthew 16:23 and Mark 8:33), to demonstrate that the embodied Christ could control demons. He also quotes James 4:7—"resist the devil, and he will flee from you" as equivalent evidence.[163] He thus inverts the Gnostic spirituality—without a body, spirits cannot repel the devil. Two months later, Smith added more explanation. "Satan cannot seduce us By his enticement unless we in our harts Consent & yeald—our organization [is] such that we can Resist the Devil If we were Not organized so we would Not be free agents."[164] The transcript is terse, but he seems to be suggesting that the premortal organization included development of physical bodies for spirits. Crucially, that physical organization was what distinguished humans from and gave them power over the spirits who had not been embodied, those who served Satan. Embodiment appears to have been the victor's spoils in the War in Heaven. A core purpose in life itself was the merger of bodies with spirits to defend against intrusions from the other world.

The other world wasn't the only locus of negotiation. The Saints were if anything more susceptible to other people in the present world.

This-Worldly Paths

Smith's followers were to be transformed through earthly interdependence as well as other-worldly processes. The most notable expressions came in the form of a sacred settlement called Zion and in a philosophy of "theodemocracy." These societies rejected the modern story about sharply distinct religious and political

---

[162] See, e.g., Fellows, *Exposition*, 85.
[163] *JSPD7*, 509.
[164] *JSPD8*, 75.

realms, which made possible deep communion but also created real danger as they hit up against American society. Part of what got the Saints in so much trouble was their scandalous unwillingness to agree that Lockean principles for government overall meant that religious communities had to be privatized. Such modern social forms seem to have struck Smith as still locked within the prison of individualism.

A Transgressive Zion

The limits to any modern buffering of the self were acutely visible in the Saints' sense of community power, invested with other-worldly sanctity. That communal holiness resided specially in a primordial city called Zion or the City of Enoch. A stray verse in the Hebrew Bible (Genesis 5:24) contains a fragment of an ancient textual tradition about a mysterious prophet named Enoch. The favored seventh-generation grandson of Adam, this Enoch spanned the space between heaven and earth by "walking with God" and then disappearing, presumably much as Elijah did in his flying chariot (2 Kings 2:10–12). The New Testament (Hebrews 11:5) amplified that tradition in a sentence in a subsermon on faith. "By faith Enoch was translated that he should not see death; and was not found, because God had translated him: for before his translation he had this testimony, that he pleased God." These bare mentions and their promise of the special power of translation were all the Bible had to say about this enigmatic figure.[165]

In Smith's hands, this ancient tradition about Enoch (merged with a reference to the restoration of Zion as the "city of righteousness" in Isaiah 1:26) became a way to talk about sacred communitarianism. He was interested in theocratic utopias from the beginning of his career. In the Book of Mormon (4 Nephi), a Christian Shangri-La arises after Jesus's personal visit to ancient America. The American community was similar to the Christian communitarian experiments recorded in Acts (2:44–46, 4:32) but encompassed an entire society rather than small cells within a larger society. The Christian utopia in ancient America lasted precisely two centuries before its "prosperity" failed when the wealthiest began wearing expensive clothing and abandoned communitarian ideals. Within a decade, this once-blessed society was as dysfunctional as antebellum America. Nephite society collapsed within two more centuries. The story of holy communitarianism was a tragedy as the Book of Mormon translation wrapped up in 1829.

---

[165] On Enoch see Blenkinsopp, *Creation*, esp. 1–2, 120, and Laurence, *Book of Enoch*.

In Smith's Prophecy of Enoch (now Moses 6–7) dictated the next year (see chapter 5), however, Smith described an earthly paradise that flourished so robustly as to share the fate of its eponymous founder: bodily translation to heaven. Where the early American communitarianism of the Book of Mormon failed, Enoch's city succeeded.

The Enoch of Smith's scripture is trained from the Edenic Book of Remembrance, which contained the pure language (see chapter 1). Echoing New Testament imagery of Christ, "the Spirit of God descended out of heaven, and abode upon" Enoch (Moses 6:26–30; cf. Luke 3:22, Matthew 3:16, and John 14:66). After a Mosaic-sounding admission of weakness, Enoch acquires seeric powers, including the power of miraculous speech (cf. Helaman 10 and Ether 12:20–27). This power comes when Enoch anoints his eyes with clay (resonant with Jesus's miracle in John 9:6), which allows him to witness panoramic visions of human history.[166] As a result of those visions, Enoch rehearses the Gospel of Christ and its intimate association with the Fall of Eve and Adam. As a consequence of his faith and seeric power, Enoch assembles a community separated from surrounding society. This group becomes "the City of Holiness, even Zion."[167] The city becomes corporately so righteous that it is "taken up into heaven" to dwell forever in God's "abode."[168]

This story of Enoch's heavenly city inverts the tower of Babel narrative, the bête noire of Smith's Restoration project. The first clue is Enoch's connection to the Edenic Books of Remembrance, the texts that resisted an early fall of language. United by the pure language and their righteous regard for others, the Zion community avoids destruction entirely. Enoch's story also provides a sideways look at the flood narrative. Noah and his family appeared to be the only "righteous before" God in their "generation" (Genesis 7:1). Smith, though, revealed an entire city so perfect that its inhabitants were translated straight to heaven. In other words, there were more ways than Noah's boat to avoid the uncreation of the flood, more ways than the Jaredites' barges to escape the curse of Babel. In the City of Enoch, Smith revealed such an alternative.[169]

Smith revealed other fragments of Enoch's story soon thereafter. In the 1832 Vision (D&C 76:57), Smith revealed that those who achieved the highest heaven would be part of the "order of Enoch," a merger of priesthood and the heaven to which Enoch and his followers had been translated. Smith clarified that

---

[166] On panoramic visions, see Brown, "Voice of God."
[167] The city is named the "City of Holiness" for God, who is named the "Man of Holiness." Moses 6:57, 7:19. The city thus bears the name of God.
[168] Note that the identical fate of Enoch and his eponymous city is itself an instance of the transformative synecdoche of correspondence.
[169] On flood as uncreation, see Blenkinsopp, *Creation*. On Enoch's Zion as inversion of the Fall, Flake, "Translating Time," 521.

membership in this order makes people "gods, even the sons of God" (76:58–59). Several months later (D&C 84), the Latter-day Saint priesthood is identified with its patriarchs in a sequential list of priests. This list integrates Enoch (and by extension his city) squarely into the genealogical priesthood: Enoch stands crucially between Noah and Abel/Adam (84:15–16).

A merger of two texts concerned with priesthood and ecclesiastical authority from November 1831 and April 1835 (D&C 107) bring Enoch into the Latter-day Saint present. In the transition from the 1835 material to the 1831 material, Smith recites details from Enoch's life and genealogy (107:48–49). Enoch was "before [God's] face continually" and was 430 years old at the time of his translation.[170] At the end of the patriarchal history, Smith reports that "these things were all written in the book of Enoch, and are to be testified of in due time" (107:57).

The Saints employed the exemplar of Enoch's city in support of earthly communitarian experiments, beginning with the conversion of the Morley Family commune outside Kirtland, Ohio.[171] With rare exceptions, Enoch's mythic city remained beyond their grasp, except in ritual. All of the experiments failed within a decade for all the expected reasons: jealousy, financial strain, and leadership disputes.[172] The Morley Family lasted only a few years as a commune.[173] The subsequent United Firm in Kirtland dissolved by 1834.[174] An ill-fated 1836–1837 attempt to use the banking system to support an integrated church economy failed miserably, almost destroying the Church.[175] In 1838, Smith had to flee Kirtland by dark of night amid large-scale, vocal disaffiliation and threats of violence.[176] The settlement they called Zion, in Jackson County, Missouri, led within a few years to a small-scale civil war, pitting the Saints against non-Mormon settlers. The Missouri conflict led to several fatalities, many defections, imprisonment of leadership, and the eradication of the Saints from the state.[177] When they regrouped in western Illinois at their official settlement of Nauvoo, the Church lasted little more than a half-decade before they were run out again at gunpoint, this time to northern Mexico. In each major settlement during Smith's life, the tensions at play in Latter-day Saint communities around religious authority and individual conscience are apparent.

Religious communitarianism seems to have led inevitably to tension and conflict. This happened both at the level of individual families and at societal scale.

---

[170] On D&C 107, see Smith, "Priesthood Revelations."
[171] Staker, *Historical Setting*, 45.
[172] Arrington, *City of God*, and DePillis, "Mormon Communitarianism."
[173] D&C 64:20 instructed the sale of the farm in September 1831.
[174] Parkin, "United Firm," 39.
[175] Staker, *Historical Setting*, 391–548; *JSPD5*, xxviii–xxxiii, 285–93, 363–66; Hill et al., "Kirtland Economy"; Walker, "Kirtland Safety Society."
[176] Bushman, *Rough Stone*, 332, 340.
[177] On the war, see Baugh, *Call to Arms*, and LeSueur, *Mormon War*.

Devotion to priesthood could create terrible rifts in biological families if some refused to convert, a struggle foreseen in the New Testament (Luke 14:26). For some Saints (as similarly true for many Protestant female preachers[178]), conversion meant the permanent disruption of their natal families. Phebe Crosby Peck explained in an 1832 letter to her sisters, "I often think of you while in my lonely meditation and sometimes it will cause a deep sigh to burst forth from my bosom thinking that perhaps I never shall see you again while in this world. and again when I think I have forsaken all for Christ, it brings consolation that surpasses the grief."[179] In an 1834 letter to her father, Rebecca Swain Williams Kimball wrote that "my heart morns for my relation acording to the flesh."[180] Many who made the sacrifice consoled themselves with the belief that their participation in the Kingdom consecrated that loneliness, creating new, more durable, and more sacred connections. But the tension never went away.

Societally, the Saints were trying to thread a needle whose eye got smaller the further they got from the Revolutionary era. Like many predecessors, they wanted to affirm individual rights but still enjoy the full authority of a religious community.[181] Church leadership attempted to explicate the appropriate balance in a letter from Kirtland in 1834. They wrote that "all men are created equal, and that all have the privilege of thinking for themselves upon all matters relative to conscience. Consequently, then, we are not disposed, had we the power, to deprive any one from exercising that free independence of mind which heaven has so graciously bestowed upon the human family as one of its choicest gifts."[182] Smith and his associates sought to leave space for temporal authority while maintaining the greater priority of heavenly mandates. "It is not our intention by these remarks," they disclaimed, "to attempt to place the law of man on a parallel with the law of heaven; because we do not consider that it is formed in that wisdom and propriety; neither do we consider that it is sufficient in itself to bestow any thing in comparison to the law of heaven."[183] In company with their commitment to individual liberty, they affirmed the superiority of God's way: "it is the law of heaven, which transcends the law of man, as far as eternal life is prefferable to temporal; and the blessings which God is able to give, greater than those which can be given by man!"[184] Recognizing the limitations of what is purely secular, they argued that "the law of man promises safety in temporal life; but the law of God promises that life which is eternal."[185] When it came to the

---

[178] Brekus, *Female Preaching*, 222.
[179] Johnson, *Female Religiosity*, 27.
[180] Johnson, *Female Religiosity*, 33.
[181] This had been a tension for centuries in the Atlantic Christian world: Wilken, *Religious Freedom*.
[182] *JSPD3*, 415.
[183] *JSPD3*, 416.
[184] *JSPD3*, 417.
[185] *JSPD3*, 417.

simple questions, in other words, of working and traveling, farming and animal husbandry, reading and writing, people should do what they wanted as individuals. When it came to the other world, higher laws had to prevail. And these laws would be administered by Church leaders. In practice, the lines were hard to draw, and earthly conflict shadowed other-worldly aspirations.

The story of attacks from outside is well known. Disaffections may show even more clearly the fissures between Latter-day Saint and American culture. The public disaffiliation and 1838 excommunication of Smith's former second-in-command, Oliver Cowdery—the most senior of the disaffected—exemplifies the tensions at play. Cowdery and other Church leaders disagreed about many things, including Church policy, Smith's private life, and Cowdery's management of Church affairs in Missouri. While the accusations brought against Cowdery were wide-ranging, Cowdery himself focused on specific problems in his rebuttal to the excommunication proceedings.

Leaders convened an April 1838 church disciplinary council in Far West, Missouri. Fourth among the long list of alleged infractions was "For virtually denying the faith by declaring that he would not be governed by any ecclesiastical authority nor Revelation whatever in his temporal affairs."[186] Cowdery responded to this accusation through a letter to Edward Partridge, claiming that he was, in essence, too modern for the Latter-day Saints when it comes to the separation of temporal and spiritual. His lengthy response tells a vivid story about the distance between the Zion community and Lockean principles.

> I will not be influenced, governed, or controlled, in my temporal interests by any ecclesiastical authority or pretended revelation what ever, contra[r]y to my own judgement . . . the three great principles of English liberty, as laid down in the books, are "the right of personal security; the right of personal liberty, and the right of private property" . . . they are so interwoven in my nature, have so long been inculcated into my mind by a liberal and intelligent ancestry, that I am wholly unwilling to exchange them for any thing less liberal, less benevolent, or less free. . . . the bare notice of those charges, over which you assume a right to decide, is, in my opinion, a direct attempt to make the secular power subservient to Church dictation. . . . This attempt to control me in my temporal interests, I conceive to be a disposition to take from me a portion of my Constitutional privileges and inherent rights.[187]

---

[186] *JSPD6*, 86.
[187] *JSPD6*, 88–89, punctuation modified for clarity.

Cowdery was sticking to his Lockean guns. He refused to return, as he saw it, to the era of ecclesiastical governance of secular affairs. Smith was, according to Cowdery, breaking the buffers necessary to modern selves.

Cowdery had made a similar complaint two months prior.[188] He seems publicly to have been willing to be led in strictly religious matters but would not allow religious leaders—especially those who, he believed, had bankrupted Kirtland—to manage his real estate transactions (deals that he himself often undertook on behalf of the religious community). In the explosive disagreement over the limits and shape of the individual and the community, he resigned his membership during the excommunication proceedings. He only rejoined the Church shortly after Smith's death and not long before his own. The acrimonious disaffiliation points out the modern rift. Tocqueville would have considered Cowdery typical of American individualism and the risks it posed to religious communities.[189]

But Cowdery was not the only one to employ Lockean rhetoric. In the aftermath of the Missouri War—marked by violence on both sides and during which the Saints experienced murder, rape, and the illegal seizure of land—a major focus of the Church and its leaders became pursuit of reparations from either the state or federal government for their losses of life and property during the Missouri War. Telling their story in that context required navigating treacherous cultural waterways.

In an 1840 letter to the editor, Smith and his lieutenants laid out a Lockean creed rather like what Cowdery had argued for during his church trial. "No goverment can exist in peace except such laws are framed and held inviolate as will secure to each individual the free exercise of consci[e]nce the right and control of property and the protection of life."[190] They argued for a sharp division between church and state. In addressing what power a religious community might exercise, they stuck to the standard requirement: all a religious body can do is excommunicate its members. It has no additional disciplinary authority. They did not mention the moral or spiritual authority a community might wield over temporal affairs.

When arguing the Saints' case against Missouri in Washington, Smith denied that his society had ever lived theocratic communalism.[191] This denial, as well as his inconsistent stance on the relationship of church and state, needn't necessarily be seen as dissembling. As many of his predecessors did, Smith seems to have struggled to find the right words to communicate how precisely his community would live in the contemporary legal-political system. He was trying to

---

[188] *JSPD6*, 16.
[189] Tocqueville, *Democracy in America*, 2:22, 28.
[190] *JSPD7*, 131.
[191] *JSPD7*, 131–33.

map a high anthropology and an otherworldly communalism onto contemporary political gridlines, and the fit was imperfect at best. The Saints saw themselves as truly living religious freedom, whatever their critics might say. They were operating within a different worldview.[192]

In Smith's eyes, what ruined Missouri and disrupted the Church community was good, old-fashioned priestcraft, a word he used to designate any hostile activity by professional clergy. He and his disciples had written a Motto for the church in 1838 that proclaimed "Exalt the standard of Democracy! Down with that of Priestcraft."[193] In an 1839 letter to George Tompkins from the jail in Liberty, Missouri, he complained that his imprisonment "was a religious persecution proscribing him in the liberty of consience which is garenteed to him by the Constitution of the United States and the State of Missouri."[194] He was careful even in his correspondence from jail to separate secular from religious activities and to maintain that rather than holding "military authority" he was instead "a religious teacher."[195] He just had an understanding of religious liberty that relied on alternative understandings of selves.

Smith's opponents would have none of it. They saw him as breaking all the rules of modern society. The advice from General John Clark in the immediate aftermath of the Missouri War is telling. This hostile militia general instructed the Saints to "scatter abroad" and "never again organize yourselves with Bishops, Presidents &c lest you excite the jealousies of the people."[196] In rough translation, Clark's instructions were not to try to build a religious community that was too robust. Religion had to be private. Zion could refer, as it did for many other Protestants, to worshipful gathering in churches, but it could not threaten societal order.[197] The Missouri War was a test of whether the Latter-day Saints could create a religious community able to manage its own community functions in a vigorous way, and it led to disaster.

A neologism from Smith's turn to national politics in the last years of his life—"theodemocracy"—exemplifies how uncomfortably the early Saints placed themselves in the streams of modern political thought. In a ghostwritten editorial, Smith called for a society that "emphatically, virtuously, and humanely" merged *vox populi* and *vox Dei*,[198] subverting the usual mantra that the "voice of the people" had displaced the "voice of God." In their theodemocracy, the Saints

---

[192] This is where the treatments of Winn, *Exiles*, and Hill, *Refuge*, break down. They don't appreciate the divergent social imaginaries at play for the Latter-day Saints.
[193] *JSPD6*, 45.
[194] *JSPD6*, 346.
[195] *JSPD6*, 348.
[196] "Letterbook 2," p. 1, *The Joseph Smith Papers*, accessed March 8, 2019, https://www.josephsmithpapers.org/paper-summary/letterbook-2/8.
[197] Peck and Lawton, *Historical Sketch*, 28, 31, 61, 87, 101, 119; Pitts, *Gospel Witness*, 10–14.
[198] *T&S* 5:8 (April 15, 1844): 510.

advocated a rule by God that embraced what was useful in democracy—the belief that all human beings matter and the desire to hobble political aristocracies. But they also seemed to be proposing a theocratic rejection of Lockean democratic principles. Smith had indeed described his powerful priesthood in 1843 as "a perfect law of Theocracy."[199]

But there's an important lexical point to make about Smith's theodemocracy. He didn't just add the divine particle *theos* to the populist *demos*. He also transformed *demos* itself. Scholarly work on theodemocracy hasn't sufficiently appreciated just what Smith meant by "the people."[200] Smith had in mind a communalizing metaphysics—that people can't fully exist separately from each other or from God—as he sought to triangulate his system within democratic principles. In the apt phrase of Americanist Jillian Sayre, "The physical space of the body . . . is not the site of individuation, but rather a space for congregation" within Smith's thought.[201]

Reading Smith's theodemocracy at face value may fail to appreciate what he was doing with and against modern political understandings. Married together in his neologism, God and humans ruled society together *because they were the same kind of being* and agreed with each other.[202] Whatever one thinks of the Latter-day Saint concept at a practical level (critics saw it as pure theocracy, proponents saw it as the truest democracy), theodemocracy was an ontological as well as political statement. It was an attempt to reduce the Enochian principles of community to the political exigencies of the early American Republic. Nauvoo theodemocracy rapidly flowed into the creation of the Council of Fifty, a secret committee that included high church leaders and a few loyal non-Mormons initially tasked with managing Smith's US presidential campaign. The Council of Fifty was meant to be the seat of government for a millennial kingdom preparing for Christ's Second Coming.[203] Following Smith's lead, Brigham Young stated at an April 1844 meeting of the Council, "No line can be drawn between the church and other governments, of the spiritual and temporal affairs of the church."[204]

For Smith, the point was that robust religious communities should exist, and people should be allowed to immerse themselves in those communities. This is one vision of religious plurality—one shared by many of the accidental architects of modernity[205]—but it's not the one ultimately chosen in the United States. Religion spanned the space between public and private as a communal

---

[199] *JSPJ3*, 86.
[200] Thus Mason, "Theodemocracy," and Park, "Mormon Challenge."
[201] Sayre, "Books Buried," 22.
[202] Thus *JSPAR*, 92.
[203] *JSPAR*, 40–42, 54, 81. On comparison to Enoch's government, see *JSPAR*, 102.
[204] *JSPAR*, 82.
[205] Wilken, *Religious Freedom*.

identity larger than the individual but smaller than the secular state. Once again, this Latter-day Saint sense that, ontologically, people were based in communities caused trouble for political doctrines that mandated exclusive individualism.

Conclusion

Early Latter-day Saint ideas about human identity were a complex mélange of ancient concepts about the interconnection of humanity and cosmos and rising sensibilities about human agency. Each time Smith and his early disciples start to look obviously modern or clearly premodern, the focus shifts and the view blurs. They saw humans as immensely powerful, and they were enamored of human agency. But for them, humans only really existed in the company of others. The Saints were excited about the potentialities of the nineteenth century, and they also understood themselves as the peers of ancients with extreme metaphysical power. They hovered between (or perhaps beyond) the porous selves of antiquity and the increasingly buffered selves of modernity. Restoration thought mapped poorly onto the oppositions required by the modern consensus. Borrowing Hegel's terminology, Latter-day Saints offered a synthesis between the thesis of porous and antithesis of buffered selves in early modernity. Neither style of human made sense in its own right, but together they pointed toward the vibrant interplay of community and individual, vulnerability and strength that could be achieved if one understood that humans were divine, together.

Smith's core notions—that the physical is intimately joined to the spiritual and individuals only really exist in community—belie his storied modern perfectionism. A rhetorical strategy employed by, e.g., the literary critic Harold Bloom[206] and the journalist Chris Lehmann[207] casts Smith as a modern American Gnostic. While this trope isn't wrong to emphasize Smith's interest in esoteric knowledge and human transformation, the catchphrase largely misses Smith's key inversion of Gnosticism.[208] In sharp contrast to Gnosticism, Smith loved and valorized physical bodies and the earth they inhabited. He saw physical matter not as a curse but as a necessary medium for eternal flourishing. The physical body was the source of power for the spirit, not, as the Gnostics would have it, a terrible prison.

---

[206] Bloom, *American Religion*, 22, 99, 112–14, 122–23.
[207] Lehmann, *Money Cult*, 24, 124–40, 152.
[208] Bloom does seem to recognize (e.g., *American Religion*, 32) that he uses "Gnosticism" as an idiosyncratic label that encompasses its opposite. McCarraher, "God and Mammon," 114, paints Bloom as inaccurate. On the other hand, Hanegraaff, *Esotericism*, 106, sees human deification as the core Gnostic heresy.

Latter-day Saints knew themselves best when they saw themselves, through priesthood, tied to the names, identities, and histories of those who came before. They looked forward to their own translation as humans into the direct physical presence of God. They knew that they were tasked with building, corporately, the kingdom of God, and that they would have to wield their hard-won agency to those shared ends.

For the early Saints, language, time, and human identity crackled with metaphysical power. Whatever cultural shifts might have already occurred, whatever starker changes came later, they staked their claims to a world thick with supernatural power that simultaneously acknowledged the dominion of human minds and the innovations of the political and technological worlds of modernity. Smith and his disciples brought to the reading, writing, and dictating of new scripture precisely these understandings of a world full of metaphysical power. To the corpus of textual translations, we now turn.

SECTION 2
TEXTS

In the first section, we worked through cultural contexts for Smith's translation. Language, time, and human identity are categories of central theological and practical importance to Joseph Smith and his disciples. Smith triangulated his religious teachings and communities within modern cultural sensibilities and with an eye to antique precedents. Nineteenth-century Latter-day Saints seemed to have been coming sideways at the polarities of modern secularity, drawing freely from both premodern and modern options. This context is necessary to understanding what Smith was doing with his translations.

This second section turns to the translation texts themselves. The sustained argument of the chapters in this section is that all of Smith's translations are biblical in nature. Smith produced three main collections of sacred texts, all of them English targums concerned with recovering the primordial Bible: the Book of Mormon, the New Translation of the Bible, and the Egyptian project. Put in alternate terms, Smith's translation corpus comprised an American Bible, sketches of a recovered Bible, and an Egyptian Bible. These texts deeply and—to critics, perversely—reread the Bible in a key that is noticeably indifferent to the ideological shifts we now associate with modern thought.

Smith's targums were not primarily written texts. They were, originally, speech acts. Usually but not always employing metaphysically charged objects (especially his interpreter stones), he dictated essentially all of his scriptures. In each case, Smith worked with assistants and amanuenses. He spoke aloud the English text, and these "scribes" recorded his words. In these chapters I take no position on how Smith translated. He provided little information regarding his subjective experience. A bit coyly, he only ever said that he used special stones and that his capacity to translate came through "the gift and power of God."[1]

On the basis of current evidence (depending on what one allows by way of possibilities about the structure and contexts of the universe), these texts were

---

[1] Brown, "Voice of God."

(1) largely products of Smith's literary-spiritual genius (a physicalist account) or (2) revealed through a divine encounter (a nonphysicalist account). Of course, those phrases raise more questions than they answer, as we have little substantial understanding of either genius or inspiration and we cannot know whether these two poles correctly identify the range of explanations that lie between them. Such intermediate positions might include the idea that (3) Smith was divinely inspired to set his vivid imagination on the intersections of the King James Bible and other ancient pasts, or (4) he believed himself inspired to do so. As is true for American religion generally, the role of human agency looms large in questions about mechanisms. No available model allows us to measure precisely the extent of Smith's agency in the translation process, even as that very agency feels important.

I will, however, comment that I don't see persuasive evidence for frank plagiarism, or intentional fraud. Smith really did seem to be having nonordinary experiences when he dictated the English texts that became scripture. Whether that nonordinary is hidden in the thickets of his distinctive neuroanatomy or derives from his contact with "gods really present," to borrow Robert Orsi's phrase, requires assumptions external to the historical record.[2]

Smith's scriptural productions are often seen as distinct projects, but understanding his metaphysics of translation makes clear the unity in his scriptures. Smith's three main scriptural projects represent interdependent aspects of the same fundamental project: to transform the Bible by wresting it free of its temporal and cultural bonds. By delving deeply into LDS scriptures themselves—their formal structure, their content, their aspirations—this section reveals the self-conceptions of the texts and the ways they might have helped readers reconcile the Bible to the new revelations that Smith was proclaiming.

The Book of Mormon wasn't intended to be an independent scripture, but instead to be integrated warp and woof with the Bible, which it in turn transformed. I consider its attempt to save the primordial Bible by destroying its Protestant version in chapter 4. I argue that Joseph Smith translated the Book of Mormon, and the Book of Mormon translated the Bible from one world to another, obliterating spatial and temporal separation. Smith became thereby a kind of time traveler, with scripture as his time machine.

Smith quickly followed his Book of Mormon with two intimately related phases of his broader scriptural project, one centering on the text of the King James Bible, the other focused on Egyptian hieroglyphs. In chapter 5, I propose that his New Translation extended the Book of Mormon project of rereading the Bible. Beyond simple textual repairs, the New Translation incorporated the

---

[2] Taves, *Revelatory Events*, proposes sympathetically physicalist models. On gods really present, see Orsi, *History and Presence*, Introduction.

recovery of lost texts like the Prophecy of Enoch and a preface to the Pentateuch called the Visions of Moses. The Bible that these texts recover is at once plural and time-bending.

Perhaps most controversially for his reputation as a translator, from 1835 to 1842 Smith studied and interpreted funeral papyri extracted from an armful of Theban mummies, a project that resulted in fragments of a scripture he called the Book of Abraham. While the English text bears no traditional linguistic relationship to the Egyptian glyphs on the papyri, the Book of Abraham is self-consciously a targum of the Primeval History and exemplifies Smith's dynamics of translation. I tell the story of this Egyptian Bible in chapter 6. In this latter effort, Smith made ever more explicit the close connection between language, translation, and humanity's location within the cosmos.

In the final chapter, I consider the temple rites that Smith brought to fruition in Nauvoo, Illinois, in the early 1840s. I argue that the Book of Abraham was a crucial ligament between Smith's targums and the suite of special rites—the endowment, sealings, and anointings—by which the Saints became capable of tolerating the divine presence. The temple rites provide a context for understanding the scriptures that preceded them. At the same time, these special ceremonies—both antique and modern—make better sense when understood in the context of Smith's ongoing concern with people and texts and their place in the cosmos.

4
The Task of the Book of Mormon
To Save the Bible, First You Must Kill It

The Book of Mormon opens around 600 BCE with the prophetic call of an otherwise unknown contemporary of Jeremiah, a wealthy visionary named Lehi. Immediately after Lehi sees a fire like Moses's burning bush, commanding him to prophesy imminent destruction to the people of Jerusalem, this founding patriarch of the Book of Mormon story experiences a dream-vision. That vision and his family's reactions to it are fraught with meanings for the book of scripture many contemporaries called America's Gold Bible and its creator called the Book of Mormon (Figure 4.1). (Mormon, Lehi's heir, edited the book a millennium after the story began.)

In Lehi's vision, Jesus and his twelve apostles descend from the clouds and hand the prophet what appears to be a version of the Old and New Testaments.[1] Shortly after this vision, Lehi learns that he must obtain a physical copy of the Old Testament.[2] But here's the catch: a dissolute cousin owns that copy, which is "engraven upon plates of brass."[3] When Lehi's oldest son attempts to secure the plates, this kinsman, Laban, accuses him of capital larceny. Nephi, the narrator and Lehi's righteous middle son, proposes that he and his brothers trade all their worldly possessions for the plates. Nephi explains that they need the brass Bible to preserve knowledge of ancient Hebrew, the sacred language of scripture. However, the greedy Laban robs them, leaving them penniless and, more important, still bereft of the culture-saving Bible. This situation can't persist.

So Nephi sneaks back into the compound and discovers Laban in a drunken stupor in a hallway. In an echo of David's encounter with Goliath,[4] this brief coma proves to be providential. God has bewitched Laban so that Nephi can commit a holy murder, impersonate his wicked cousin, and obtain the plates to take to the New World. Nephi assassinates Laban in order to save the Bible and his own kindred.

---

[1] The vision is in 1 Nephi 1.
[2] Those plates serve as a type for the gold plates of the overall record. The murder and theft of the plates is in 1 Nephi 3.
[3] Laban may have been named for Jacob's crafty, Syrian uncle-in-law (Genesis 24).
[4] McGuire, "Goliath."

THE BOOK OF MORMON:

AN ACCOUNT WRITTEN BY THE HAND OF MOR-
MON, UPON PLATES TAKEN FROM
THE PLATES OF NEPHI.

Wherefore it is an abridgment of the Record of the People of Nephi; and also of the Lamanites; written to the Lamanites, which are a remnant of the House of Israel; and also to Jew and Gentile; written by way of commandment, and also by the spirit of Prophesy and of Revelation. Written, and sealed up, and hid up unto the LORD, that they might not be destroyed; to come forth by the gift and power of GOD unto the interpretation thereof; sealed by the hand of Moroni, and hid up unto the LORD, to come forth in due time by the way of Gentile; the interpretation thereof by the gift of GOD; an abridgment taken from the Book of Ether.

Also, which is a Record of the People of Jared, which were scattered at the time the LORD confounded the language of the people when they were building a tower to get to Heaven; which is to shew unto the remnant of the House of Israel how great things the LORD hath done for their fathers; and that they may know the covenants of the LORD, that they are not cast off forever; and also to the convincing of the Jew and Gentile that JESUS is the CHRIST, the ETERNAL GOD, manifesting Himself unto all nations. And now if there be fault, it be the mistake of men; wherefore condemn not the things of GOD, that ye may be found spotless at the judgment seat of CHRIST.

BY JOSEPH SMITH, JUNIOR,
AUTHOR AND PROPRIETOR.

PALMYRA:

PRINTED BY E. B. GRANDIN, FOR THE AUTHOR.

1830.

Figure 4.1 Title page of the 1830 Book of Mormon, courtesy of the Church History Library, The Church of Jesus Christ of Latter-day Saints.

Armed with these two Bibles—one seen in vision only, the other consummately physical and worth killing for—Lehi and his family flee to a Promised Land in the Americas. There, we discover as the narrative proceeds, these Israelite refugees expand the Bible, both as specific new books from their own experience and fluid exegeses of the old books they have carried with them.

Note this fact: in the opening story of the Book of Mormon, a righteous family must steal a Bible from an unfit curator whom the righteous son murders, while receiving another Bible via a supernatural vision, in order to begin the stories that will create a companion American Bible. These narratives of Bibles rescued and unfit curators slain set the stage for the fraught relationship between the Book of Mormon and the Protestant Bible, what was in the early nineteenth century the King James translation.

The antagonistic relationship between the two scriptural anthologies draws on their similarity. The Book of Mormon borrows cadences, styles, and turns of phrase from the Bible and quotes extensively from Isaiah and the New Testament. It rejects and reworks centuries of Christian interpretation of Bible texts in plain language well suited to its American readers.

The American scripture's biblicism attracted many converts.[5] Moses Nickerson expressed exemplary gratitude in 1833 because "the scriptures have been opened to my view beyond account" by reading the Book of Mormon.[6] Similarly, Joseph Holbrook maintained that after having read the Book of Mormon, the Bible "was now a new book, having the seals broken, light and life and salvation on its pages."[7] Critics, on the other hand, saw the Book of Mormon as an inept plagiarism. These critics were right that the Book of Mormon is thoroughly biblical in its presentation, but they were incorrect to say that the book brought nothing new. Much of the work it did was paratextual, changing the grounds of reading even where the biblical words were unchanged.

In this chapter, I argue that the Book of Mormon saw one of its central roles as saving the primordial Bible by killing the corrupted Protestant one. Mormon's book lit the Bible on fire so that true scripture could be reborn from its ashes. Rather than being the "stunted stepchildren of the Bible," in Harold Bloom's dismissive epithet, Latter-day Saint scriptural texts were a *coup d'état* against an *ancien régime*.[8] Nor is the suggestion of the historian Seth Perry that "the text of the new scripture cites and improvises on the old" a sufficient characterization of the

---

[5] Harper, "Infallible Proofs"; Bushman, *Rough Stone*, 128; Frederick, *Allusivity*, xii; Hardy, *Reader's Guide*, 5–6.

[6] *JSPD3*, 355.

[7] Johnson, "People of the Books," 21, citing his ca. 1846 Autobiography. See also Gutjahr, "Golden Bible," 278–79.

[8] Bloom, *American Religion*, 72. More insightful reflections on this relationship are in Gutjahr, *American Bible*, 153, and Flanders, "Concept of Time," 112.

work the Book of Mormon was doing.⁹ The Book of Mormon was retranslating the Bible in a new key.

Shortly before he died, Joseph Smith announced to the outside world that he and his followers "believe the Bible to be the word of God as far as it is translated correctly." Many readers have seen this as a straightforward reference to Smith's New Translation (chapter 5), but the phrase also encompasses the Book of Mormon. He wasn't just suggesting, as many Protestants had, that the Bible could be mistranslated,¹⁰ or that reading in the ancient languages was better than reading in English, although he believed both to be true. He read the Bible in a fundamentally different way, as a precious trace of the ecstatic and visionary presence of God and a transtemporal conduit to communion with the ancient authors. Smith meant, I believe, that the physical Bible, especially if not exclusively the English Bible, was a limited, regional document, always in need of translation. This translation was more than merely linguistic. Scripture also needed a live prophet to traverse and transgress the constraints of time and location.¹¹

Among its other tasks, the Book of Mormon had to save the Bible, even if this salvation meant death first. It did so by taking the form of the Bible (in both its physical presentation and its content) as it transformed the older scripture. In this effort, Smith, an ardent anti-Protestant, pointed out and exploited apparent weaknesses in the Bible. In this chapter I describe the perceived problems with the Bible, including its lack of perspicuity, the limitations of human language, and the problems of evidential Christianity. I then discuss the ways in which the Book of Mormon addressed those failings. While I'm aware of other goals for the Book of Mormon—making converts, sacralizing Native pasts, and establishing covenant communities at a minimum—I draw attention here to its underappreciated role as the disruptive solution to the Bible's problems.

The Bible in Crisis

A fairly standard story about the crisis of the Bible focuses on the Protestant Reformation and its strenuous attempt to make the Bible bear the burden of the Catholic magisterium. The historian Jonathan Sheehan has articulated the problems of biblical authority after the Reformation.¹² In English and German scholarship, moral reform, and philosophical disputes, translations of the Bible

---

⁹ Perry, "Bible Culture," 6.
¹⁰ Sheehan, *Enlightenment Bible*, and Gutjahr, "Golden Bible."
¹¹ Brown, "Read the Round."
¹² Sheehan, *Enlightenment Bible*.

mediated many of the Bible's epistemic and interpretive crises. The American experience followed on the English and German precedents with specific New World twists and turns. While academic Bible criticism had flourished since the end of the seventeenth century in Europe, it was just arriving in America at the tail end of the Revolutionary period.[13] The Unitarian Joseph Buckminster (1784–1812) advocated German higher criticism in America in the 1810s, and his coreligionist Andrews Norton (1786–1853) held a chair in Bible criticism at Harvard by 1819.[14] This biblical criticism eroded the belief that Americans "could address Moses and Paul as contemporaries with whom they shared common assumptions and beliefs."[15] The more conservative scholar-theologian Moses Stuart (1780–1852) fought for a reactionary American Calvinist Bible criticism within the decade.[16] While these efforts probably reached commoners in somewhat limited ways, increasing numbers of Americans nevertheless approached the Bible more as a historical, moral, or cultural text than as the Word of God itself.[17] This was the Enlightenment Bible, to use Sheehan's term, and it was reasonably established in Europe and known in America.

In the European and American disputes of the seventeenth through nineteenth centuries, several issues mattered: the relationship between the Old and New Testament (often mixed with anti-Semitic vitriol), the unity of the biblical anthology, the question of whether the Bible should be seen as familiar or foreign, and anxieties about how the Bible affected claims of national authority. They also—although scholars have left this as an undercurrent rather than a main point—battled with the nature of individualism and the priority of detached reason. The modern world differed from the biblical world not just in its agricultural or technological aspects, but in how it reconceived individuals and their interrelationships, as we saw in chapter 3.

Joseph Smith saw Protestants as having lost the Bible entirely. In his view, Protestants didn't even believe the Bible they had. In the preface to the 1835 Doctrine and Covenants, Latter-day Saints rejected the accusation of "disbelieving the Bible."[18] In 1836 Smith maintained, "we believe the bible, and they [Protestants] do not."[19] In a demonstrative question and answer in the church newspaper in May 1838, Smith (or perhaps the editors on his behalf) responded to the question "Do you believe the b[i]ble?" with "If we do, we are the only people under heaven that does. For there are none of the religious sects of the day that

---

[13] Lee, *Biblical Certainty*.
[14] Conkin, *Uneasy Center*, 273; Norton, *A Statement of Reasons*, xv, engages German critics directly.
[15] Holland, *Sacred Borders*, 107.
[16] Conkin, *Uneasy Center*, 274–75; Gura, *Transcendentalism*, 35–36.
[17] Conkin, *Uneasy Center*, 268, and Lee, *Biblical Certainty*.
[18] *JSPD4*, 236.
[19] *JSPJ1*, 166.

do." "Wherein do you differ from others sects?" elicited a similarly dismissive answer: "Because we believe the bible, and all other sects profess to believe their interpretation of the bible, and their creeds."[20] Smith was thus incorporating a Catholic critique of the *sola scriptura* Bible while distinguishing between the primordial Bible and the modern one. He continued the same line in an 1839 letter to potential real estate collaborator and convert, Isaac Galland: "the difference between me and other religious teachers, is in the bible."[21] In an 1840 sermon in Washington, DC, a sympathetic outsider recorded Smith as preaching, "We teach nothing but what the Bible teaches. We believe nothing but what is to be found in this Book."[22] Similarly, "the Mormon Bible . . . contained nothing inconsistent or conflicting with the Christian Bible."[23] Converts to his church agreed: one wrote in 1845, "I took the Bible to see if it [Smith's Restoration] was true" and "found they were the only sect that kept to the Bible in all its purity."[24] Critics saw these claims as nonsense.[25] While biblicity was for many the truth criterion of the Book of Mormon, the new scripture sought to destroy the Protestant Bible in order to save its primordial antecedent.

The Gold Bible

In March 1830, the Grandin press in Palmyra, New York, produced a new book. Grandin printed five thousand copies, twice the size of a typical print run of the era.[26] Even the most casual reader of the book had to confront its biblicism. Observers called it a gold Bible, both in reference to Smith's gold plates and its overwhelming biblicity.[27] The octavo volume bound in leather looked like a small Bible from the American Bible Society,[28] and the language of the book—its cadences and commonplaces, its archaic word forms, its exegetical excerpting— was extravagantly biblical.[29] It was a modern targum.

---

[20] *EJ* 1:3 (July 1838): 42.
[21] *JSPD6*, 387.
[22] *JSPD7*, 177.
[23] *JSPD7*, 179.
[24] Young and Richards Family Meeting Minutes (CR 100 318), January 8, 1845, CHL, page 3.
[25] Thus, e.g., Bacheler, *Mormonism Exposed*.
[26] Daniell, *Bible in English*, 635.
[27] Thus *The Wayne Sentinel* in Palmyra, New York (June 26, 1829) indicates that the "Golden Bible" is "written in ancient characters, impossible to be interpreted by any to whom the special gift has not been imparted by inspiration."
[28] Daniell, *Bible in English*, 728.
[29] Gutjahr, *American Bible*, 152–53; Cohen, "Print Culture," 7–8; Smith, "Biblical Culture"; and Austin, "A Theory of Types." On archaisms, see Bowen, "Sounding Sacred."

Typical of many American Bibles, the Book of Mormon began with a formal preface.[30] Although Protestant Bibles had been versified since the sixteenth-century Geneva Bible, the Book of Mormon's large blocks of prose with minimal interruptions and limited versification was typical of older Bibles and some new ones.[31] Lucius Fenn described the Book of Mormon as a new Bible to a friend in 1830—"it is the same that our[s] is only there is an addition to it."[32] An 1830 editorial in the Rochester *Gem* described it as containing "the mysticisms of an unrevealed Bible!"[33] The Painesville *Telegraph* for its part reported that the Book of Mormon was "chiefly garbled from the Old and New Testaments, the Apocraphy having contributed its share."[34] Everyone who encountered it agreed that the Book of Mormon was fundamentally biblical.

The Book of Mormon explicitly embraces an intimate connection to the Bible. As Mormon wraps up his contributions, he reflects on the arc of the book's history. He addresses the remote offspring of the Lamanites (which early readers interpreted as nineteenth-century Native Americans) and Gentiles (white Protestants). He tells those nineteenth-century readers that the "record [the Bible] which shall come unto the Gentiles [American Protestants] from the Jews [of the Old World], which record shall come from the Gentiles unto you [Native Americans]. For behold, this [the Book of Mormon] is written for the intent that ye may believe that [the Bible]. And if ye believe that [the Bible], ye will believe this [the Book of Mormon] also" (Mormon 7:8–9). In that pointed summary, Mormon makes clear how interdependent the Bible and the Book of Mormon are, by design.

Early Latter-day Saints concurred with the prophet Mormon. The 1829 *Articles and Covenants*, one of the first guiding documents of the fledgling tradition, pronounced that the Book of Mormon proved "that the holy scriptures be true."[35] Phelps summarized the meaning of the Book of Mormon as Joseph Smith's legacy shortly after his 1844 assassination. He wrote, "its revelation is the very thing that produces an earthquake to this generation. It explains the bible;

---

[30] The reasonably standard preface was written by the Presbyterian divine, John Witherspoon. Daniell, *Bible in English*, 599–600. Perry, "Joseph Smith's Bibles," 762–63, argues that the purpose of the preface in the Book of Mormon was to increase its biblicity. Although the content of Smith's preface differs from traditional prefaces, I agree that its presence is a formal similarity. Smith's title page, however, is similar to Alexander Campbell's 1826 preface to the Gospels: Campbell, *Sacred Writings*, esp. 11–13.

[31] On the history of versification, Noll, *The Word*, 58–59. Note that Daniell, *Bible in English*, 728–29, incorrectly assumes that the late nineteenth-century versification of the Book of Mormon reflected early editions. The format of Bibles in America was various enough that any printing convention would likely have precedents by 1830. On a new translation with limited versification, see Thomas, *New Version*, 27.

[32] Welch, "Miraculous Translation," 171.
[33] Welch, "Miraculous Translation," 172.
[34] Welch, "Miraculous Translation," 177.
[35] *JSPD1*, 121 (D&C 20:11).

it opens the vision of the prophets."[36] Phelps was not alone. As the historian John Turner has correctly observed, "for many early converts, the very familiarity of the Book of Mormon's depiction of Jesus Christ bolstered its claims."[37]

Contemporary readers saw plainly what later scholars identified. Whatever else the Book of Mormon was for, it explicitly saw itself as a new Bible, destined to transform the existing Bible. In 1834, Eli Gilbert, a convert from Universalism, compared the Book of Mormon to the Bible "and found the two books mutually and reciprocally corroborate each other." The scriptures' interdependence was profound: as Gilbert said, "if I let go the Book of Mormon, the bible might also go down by the same rule."[38] Critics worried that this was true: one 1841 exposé admits that the Book of Mormon "corroborates and confirms the truth of holy writ."[39]

Such critics saw the Saints as biblical plagiarists; anything not stolen from the Bible wholesale was mere filigree. In the words of one Presbyterian critic, "only take away what their authors have manifestly stolen from the Bible, and there is nothing of moral truth remaining."[40] Opponents worried that people who had given themselves over to the Book of Mormon would not be able to go back to the Bible. By opening the Bible's flaws to scrutiny, conversion to Smith's church promised that believers would say, "we must be either Mormons or Deists."[41] These detractors may have been correct—in identifying (and in part creating) a crisis for the Bible that it alone could solve, the Book of Mormon raised the possibility that its converts could never return to the Protestant Bible. The critics weren't wrong—skeptics did sometimes use the presence of the Book of Mormon as evidence of a plurality that made Protestant belief problematic.[42]

Where the Bible was remote, the Book of Mormon was immediately relevant to the antebellum New York experience. The Book of Mormon expressed views on infant baptism, church and state, the providential role of the United States, and a dozen other timely issues. This immediacy came at a price: critics saw it as a vulnerability. Alexander Campbell made perhaps the most famous indictment of the Book of Mormon in his 1831 essay, "Delusions." There he argued that "this prophet Smith, through his stone spectacles, wrote on the plates of Nephi, in his Book of Mormon, every error and almost every truth discussed in N. York for the last ten years."[43] The Saints disagreed with Campbell, viewing the

---

[36] *T&S* 5:24 (January 1, 1845): 757.
[37] Turner, *Mormon Jesus*, 41.
[38] *M&A* 1:1 (October 1834): 9–10.
[39] Lee, *Knavery Exposed*, 7. The author also fumed (Ibid., 6) that the Saints claimed to "admit the truth and credibility of the sacred Scriptures, they profess to have obtained an additional revelation, by which new illumination is shed over every page of the sacred word."
[40] Turner, *Mormonism*, 130.
[41] Turner, *Mormonism*, 4, and Hunt, *Mormonism*, iv–v.
[42] Grasso, *American Faith*, 218.
[43] "Delusions," *Millennial Harbinger* 2:2 (February 7, 1831): 93.

antebellum relevance of the Book of Mormon as evidence that God could speak directly to their generation. The Protestant Bible famously lacked that capacity, even as various translations took linguistic liberties to improve its cultural relevance. But that is precisely what the Book of Mormon had to do. Thinking he had unearthed the fraud at the center of the Book of Mormon, Campbell—in the eyes of believers—had proved the book both true and relevant.[44]

The Problems of Language

Crucially, this new scripture delighted in, depended on, and attacked the failings of the Protestant Bible. It demonstrated what was broken and beyond repair in Christian scripture. The Book of Mormon set its sights on transforming the Bible into the texts it should always have been, which included criticism of the infidelity of language. We encountered the problems of language in Chapter 1. Here, a brief reminder will suffice: the Bible was written in ancient languages embedded within ancient cultures that were deeply foreign to antebellum Americans. Bible readers and believers had to span that gap to understand the Bible, which wasn't easy. Whatever its cultural dominance, Protestants quarreled over the King James text. The language was archaic, even in the nineteenth century. It smacked of Calvinism, at a time when Calvin was falling into disrepute. It was prone, according to Horace Bushnell, to support the machinations of "one-word professor[s]"—those who built complex theological structures on a single English word in the King James text.[45] The drift and imprecision of language thus appeared to contribute to sectarian strife.

Campbell, in the preface to his 1826 anti-Calvinist Bible translation, emphasized the troubles of language and its evolution. He reported that the death of Hebrew and Greek had preserved them from linguistic drift, but English evolved constantly, necessitating new translations every generation or two.[46] Many of Campbell's contemporaries felt similarly. Some tried to make up the distance with snippets of archaeology or maps of the ancient Holy Land, but the distance remained. If anything, the chasm widened in the early Republic as more and more voices called out the alienness of ancient Israel's scripture.[47] Andrews

---

[44] The defector James Hunt was perhaps more clear-eyed about this phenomenon than Campbell, realizing that the timeliness of the Book of Mormon content was in fact prime evidence for its inspiration. Hunt, *Mormonism*, 86–87.

[45] On one-word professors, see Bushnell, *God in Christ*, 46–50. On indictment of King James Bible as Calvinist, see, e.g., Campbell, *Sacred Writings*, 5–6.

[46] Campbell, *Sacred Writings*, 3–5.

[47] Gutjahr, *American Bible*, 64.

Norton relied on the constraints of human language to prove his point about the limits to the interpretation made by non-Unitarians in America.[48]

The Book of Mormon followed two parallel tracks in its consideration of the relationships between human language and scripture. First, it affirmed Smith's long-standing commitment to the sacred power of a pure language. Second, it acknowledged that human language, including the English of the King James Bible, was limited. There were many sacred things that could never live in a fallen human language, no matter how earnestly pro-Bible Protestants wished it were so.

As we saw in chapter 1, the Book of Mormon foregrounds the story of an ancient Mesopotamian tribe, the Jaredites. These Jaredites were saved from the curse of Babel through a miraculous dispensation made to their prophet, Moriancumer. In the Jaredite narrative within a narrative, we see the Book of Mormon as having a special connection to primordial language even as it acknowledged that human scripture was not written in that language. There was thus an ideal bar—the pure language of the primordial Bible—and the reality that human language always fell short of that ideal.

To that point, the Book of Mormon almost celebrates failures of language, suggesting that scripture will always be imperfect because it is written in human language. At times the book attributes the flaws to language itself: "there are many things which according to our language we are not able to write" (3 Nephi 5:18). The potshots it takes even extend to the language of prophets and scriptures.[49] The Book of Mormon disarms linguistic criticism by freely acknowledging its own errors. Justifying his approach to assembling the sacred texts, Nephi explains, "If I do err, even did they [the writers of the Bible] err of old" (1 Nephi 19:6). This confession contains a side swipe at the Bible, similarly riddled with errors.

The Book of Mormon freely admits what the Bible literalists could not confess—most important human experience, religious or otherwise, evades language. One could drown in the sheer volume of unwriteable things: Christ's physical ministry (3 Nephi 17:15, 26:18), Samuel the Lamanite's prophecies (Helaman 14:1), or those of his contemporary Nephi$_2$ (Helaman 8:3). Some concepts or experiences are utterly beyond language, whether spoken or written, especially Christ's teachings (3 Nephi 19:32–34). Sometimes the failing lies with the audience's understanding (3 Nephi 17:2), or the experience is just too large to be contained in a finite physical record (3 Nephi 7:17, 26:6–7). Nephi son of

---

[48] Lee, *Biblical Certainty*, 161.
[49] Richard Bushman lists the following as examples of such meditations on the failings of written scripture in the Book of Mormon: Jacob 3:13; 2 Nephi 31:1, 33:1; Words of Mormon 1:5; Alma 8:1, 13:31; Mosiah 8:1; 1 Nephi 6:3, 17:6; Jacob 4:1; 3 Nephi 5:8, 7:17, 17:15, 19:34, 26:6; Helaman 8:3,14:1; Moroni 9:19; Ether 12:25, 15:33. See also, e.g., 1 Nephi 19:2–3, 2 Nephi 11:1.

Lehi laments his "weakness" in language, his failure to be "mighty in writing." Moroni, the final writer, worries in an address to God that outsiders will "mock" the American scripture because "thou hast not made us mighty in writing."[50] He had reason to worry—some critics were mocking the Bible on precisely those grounds. Multiple prior translators had agonized over the same thing: the Adventist translator Nathan Whiting and Martin Luther himself had been concerned about: people taking "offence at the plain and simple manner of speech, which is written in the Bible."[51] But having miraculously inspired prophets endorse that approach within a scriptural text both pulled the carpet out from under the Bible (because it did not have prophets to interpret it) and set Smith's movement up for success (because it did have such prophets, both ancient and modern).

In its emphasis on the weakness of language, the Book of Mormon made a laughingstock of incipient inerrantism among Protestants. Nothing written in human language could ever be flawless, and anyone who claimed otherwise was lying. Such undercutting of the authority of the English language in which the Protestant Bible was written severely destabilized that once-authoritative text to make way for texts that were much more at peace with the infidelity of language.[52] In the process, once again, the Book of Mormon changed the grounds of reading the Bible. It also addressed the related problem of textual transmission.

Transmitting the Bible

The Protestant Bible was an attempt to capture in a single English form a tangle of textual variants across multiple languages and centuries in a diverse array of libraries and monasteries. These variants existed in large part because the Bible manuscripts had been hand-copied over many centuries. Just as DNA degrades over cycles of reproduction, so do manuscripts. Even if the earliest stable form of a given Bible text was clearly inspired, in other words, there was no guarantee that people many centuries later had received that actual text. Increasing evidence demonstrated that the original texts of the Bible, whatever their language, were uncertain. Erasmus in the sixteenth century cobbled together a Greek text driven by his collation of the Latin Vulgate. Over time, variations on the Erasmian text became the "received" text which, in Greek and for many readers, was considered the source text. The King James Bible was indebted to

---

[50] Similar examples multiply freely (e.g., 1 Nephi 19:6; 2 Nephi 33:1, 11; Jacob 4:1; Ether 12:23–24).
[51] Whiting, *Good News*, iv; on Whiting, see Gutjahr, *American Bible*, 106.
[52] Of course the Book of Mormon endured substantial criticism for its own weak language: Bacheler, *Mormonism Exposed*, 12–13.

this received text, but alternative versions continued to multiply. That multiplication itself multiplied when the German scholar Johann Jakob Griesbach (1745–1812) compiled a new Greek version that identified serious problems with the Erasmian text. Griesbach's Greek New Testament was published in America in 1809, generating substantial worry and controversy.[53] The multiplicity in ancient texts was mirrored by a similar multiplicity in English. By 1830, over seven hundred Bible editions circulated in America, among scores of denominations and religious associations.[54]

Depending on one's affect and inclinations, this proliferation of Bible versions could be seen as a wonderful puzzle with an ultimate clear solution, or a source of despair that no one would ever get the Bible text right. Those affective differences could lead to substantial disagreements. Skeptical critics saw the textual corruption resulting from centuries of transmission as a fatal flaw in the Bible. Buck's *Theological Dictionary* detailed the textual variants and competing translations of the Bible at great length,[55] and Thomas Paine was famous for his argument against the linguistic integrity of the Bible.[56] These and similar disputes forced the continuation of controversies about whether the Bible could be the word of God, and if so, which of the many editions correctly conveyed that word.[57]

To the appropriately primed critic, the multiplicity of texts and translations suggested defects in the whole Bible enterprise. The Bible imperfectly transmitted the Word of God from the presence of God to human minds. Joseph Smith and his scripture had a solution. The Book of Mormon came not as an avalanche of conflicting manuscripts spread across the monasteries and libraries of Europe but as an archaeological discovery made in one place by one man who then rendered it into divinely sanctioned English.

In clarifying where things had gone wrong, the Book of Mormon took great pains to clarify that there was a right way to transmit scripture and a wrong way. The Protestant Bible went about transmission the wrong way, through centuries of drifting, inaccurate manuscripts in multiple languages, an absence of prophetic authority to adjudicate translation and canon, and no clear link between the Bible and the church. The Book of Mormon, on the other hand, showed the right way forward. It could do the things the Bible couldn't. It contained, simultaneously, a devastating critique of the Bible and a radical solution.

---

[53] Lee, *Biblical Certainty*, 111–12.
[54] Daniell, *Bible in English*, 639.
[55] Buck, *Theological Dictionary*, 53–64, with contextualization in Holland, *Sacred Borders*, 113.
[56] Barlow, *Mormons and the Bible*, 50.
[57] Sheehan, *Enlightenment Bible*. See also, e.g., Gutjahr, *American Bible*, 93–95, 193; Stein, "America's Bibles," 180; Daniell, *Bible in English*, 633; Holland, *Sacred Borders*, 69–70; and Turner, *Mormon Jesus*, 50–51.

In the early revelations of 1 Nephi, in which Lehi and Nephi establish their bona fides based on their access to supernaturally pure Bibles, Nephi speaks with an angel (chapters 11–14) about his vision of the grand arc of human history, which tracks from the future birth of Jesus, through Lehite history, right up to the nineteenth century. The vision is concerned with prophecy, interpretation, and the Bible's future. The angel there tells Nephi that the Bible "proceeded forth from the mouth of a Jew; and when it proceeded forth from the mouth of a Jew it contained the fulness of the gospel" (13:24). Yet that original purity has been lost. Although the language isn't perfectly clear about which church in particular (or no specific church at all) is responsible for the gospel's deterioration, the angel is adamant that traditional Christianity has failed in its obligations to the Bible: "after the book hath gone forth through the hands of the great and abominable church, that there are many plain and precious things taken away from the book" (13:28).[58]

The Book of Mormon decries this textual pillaging. The narrator, Mormon, is angry with Protestants, whom he calls "Gentiles." He asks rhetorically, "Why have ye transfigured the holy word of God that ye might bring damnation upon your souls?" (Mormon 8:33). The word "transfigure" sounds a bit strange here, but the term alludes to the transfiguration of Christ. In the New Testament account, Jesus's countenance shines, he meets with angels, and a divine voice approves his calling (e.g., Matthew 17:1–8). Smith and others saw the transfiguration as a time when Christ was transformed.[59] The use of "transfiguration" in the Book of Mormon, linguistically, connects Mormon's observations to later pronouncements about failures of translation of the Bible. Little wonder Smith would need to translate the Bible for the salvation of souls. The mistranslated, mistransfigured Protestant Bible had become a vessel for damnation rather than salvation.

What's most impressive in 1 Nephi 13 is the sense that what has gone wrong is the loss of clarity in the biblical text. "Plain and precious" parts have been spilled like soldiers' blood over the millennia of the Bible's transmissions, a fact repeatedly emphasized in Nephi's encounter with the angel. What could have been perspicuous and authoritative has degenerated to the point that it is nothing of the sort. In the eyes of the Book of Mormon, the English Authorized Bible is a gutted shell of a once-holy book. In Jesus's own words, the Book of Mormon is intended

---

[58] That phrase "plain and precious" occurs almost a dozen times in 1 Nephi 13 and then recurs in 1 Nephi 14 and 1 Nephi 19. *Plain* in the related sense (albeit without *precious*) occurs at 2 Nephi 25:4; Moroni 7:15; 2 Nephi 9:47; 1 Nephi 16:29; 2 Nephi 32:7 (moral clarity); Alma 13:23; 2 Nephi 1:26 (moral clarity); 2 Nephi 26:33.

[59] Smith referred to Christ's transfiguration as a transmission of priesthood in an 1839 sermon—*JSPD6*, 543–44. He did not revise Matthew 17:1–8 substantially in *NewT*, 200.

from its origins in antiquity to provide the "plain and precious" truths that were missing from the Bible. According to Nephi's vision,

> behold, saith the Lamb: I will manifest myself unto thy seed, that they shall write many things which I shall minister unto them, which shall be plain and precious; and after thy seed shall be destroyed, and dwindle in unbelief, and also the seed of thy brethren, behold, these things shall be hid up, to come forth unto the Gentiles, by the gift and power of the Lamb. (1 Nephi 13:35)

When Jesus finally arrives in America for a whirlwind postresurrection tour, he explains that he has come in part to augment the ancient American proto-Bible with missing material (3 Nephi 26:2). To that end, he recites material from Isaiah, Micah, Matthew, and Malachi, self-consciously carrying the Bible to a people who lacked it. In retrospect, that first American Bible (the "brass plates" Nephi stole from Laban) exemplified the flaws in the Protestant Bible. That Bible had missing or mutilated texts that the direct presence of Christ would remedy. Its antitype, the King James Bible, was even more tattered. The Book of Mormon, on the contrary, was plain.

Jesus even points out an obvious flaw in the Book of Mormon. Reviewing the current draft of the book, he observes that he commissioned Samuel the Lamanite to prophesy that "there were many saints who should arise from the dead" at Christ's birth (Helaman 14:25). Sternly, Jesus asks, "Was it not so?" The chastened audience replies, "Yea, Lord, Samuel did prophesy according to thy words, and they were all fulfilled." One hears a slap of the forehead as Nephi$_2$ realizes that he has forgotten to record the specific fulfillment of prophecy. In response, "Jesus commands that it should be written." While more is going on here, as Jared Hickman has insightfully observed, it's notable that Jesus discovers that the American Bible has left out the fulfillment of an internal prophecy.[60] He forbids this violation of the standards of internal evidences. In these moments of Christ curating scripture, the Book of Mormon is indicating that the scriptural word of God is enfleshed imperfectly, and God is always fine-tuning that word, using Christ, angels, and prophets.

Smith's own practice of transmission was more complex. After lambasting the Bible for its failures of transmission, Smith oversaw shifts in the sacred texts he promulgated. The English text of the Book of Mormon has an important history. Smith cited worries about textual infidelity in his decision not to retranslate the first section of the Book of Mormon after his financier's wife stole it.[61] After that debacle, Smith safeguarded the original text carefully, doling out a few pages at

---

[60] Hickman, "Amerindian Apocalypse," 452.
[61] Bushman, *Rough Stone*, 66–68.

a time to the printer from a carefully reviewed (albeit occasionally inaccurate) printer's manuscript that Cowdery copied. He did not release the original manuscript to outsiders. But he also had no compunction about changing the text when he thought it should be improved. He supervised editions in 1830, 1837, and 1840.[62] They were largely consistent, but all had variations. Smith's model of scripture suggests that having a prophet who could write (and rewrite) scripture addressed the relevant problem—the correct text was the one the prophet validated. Smith's solution didn't satisfy all of his followers. At times, conflict about the extent to which he was allowed to revise scriptural texts erupted into public view, although in general, Latter-day Saints were glad for the flexibility and concreteness of a living prophet.[63]

Canon and Completeness

The Book of Mormon positions itself as a solution to the Protestant problems of canon, verbally assaulting the modern advocates of closed canon. The main thrust of this message comes in 2 Nephi 29, where Nephi is interpreting Isaiah for his people. Explaining the recovery of the Book of Mormon, God says, "because my words shall hiss forth [in fulfilment of Isaiah's prophecy], many of the Gentiles shall say, A Bible! a Bible! We have got a Bible, and there cannot be any more Bible" (29:3). Irritated with this posture, God growls, "I speak forth my words according to mine own pleasure. And because that I have spoken one word, ye need not suppose that I cannot speak another" (29:9–11).[64] The same message recurs in Jesus's mouth at his long-prophesied arrival. God's voice would not be stilled by any human canon.

Canonization is only obliquely discussed in the Bible; it is almost exclusively an extrabiblical activity (a point Smith made in 1833 to his uncle Silas, then a potential convert[65]). Not so with the Book of Mormon, which solves the problem directly and internally. Canonization is performed essentially by a single man, *within* the book itself.

A brief interlude called the Words of Mormon—which stitches together the two main sections of the Book of Mormon—exemplifies the process that occurs periodically throughout the book. The Words of Mormon are oddly placed—the narrative has just gotten underway, and already Mormon telescopes to the bitter

---

[62] For the changes, see, e.g., Larson, "Textual Variations."
[63] See Underwood, "Revisions"; *JSPD1*, xxviii; *JSPJ1*, 10fn17; *JSPD2*, 12. Smith protested when others attempted to revise his scriptures without approval: *JSPD1*, 118.
[64] This was a timely warning given the prominence of "Bible-onlyism" in the early Republic: Noll, *America's God*, 373.
[65] *JSPD3*, 303.

end of Lehite civilization. In view of the entire arc of ancient America's past, he personally "made an abridgment" and "searched among the records" available to him as the scriptural custodian. He describes his process for canonizing texts—"pleasing" material that "prophe[s]ies of the coming of Christ," especially those which are fulfilled within the text itself (1:3–4). This direct process of canonization happens "for a wise purpose" that is "whispere[d]" to him "according to the workings of the Spirit of the Lord." Crucially, "God worketh in me to do according to his will" (1:7). The Book of Mormon thus describes the necessary process for selecting and arranging scriptural texts, along with a clear chain of provenance. This is in implicit contrast to the Bible's tattered and unreliable canonization. Once again, in saving the Bible, the Book of Mormon killed it.

There's another layer to the Book of Mormon's assault on biblical canon, though. It positions canon itself as an illusion. Because it was tied to specific places and times, the Bible was a regional scripture, contingent rather than definitive. Smith undermined the possibility of a simple, single Bible. In the phrase of the media theorist John Durham Peters, Joseph Smith and his Book of Mormon were "turning the Bible back into *biblia*, many books, and relativizing it into the history of a particular region and people."[66] Peters is absolutely correct. The Book of Mormon's suggestion that the Bible was in fact merely one of many regional scriptures is central to its project of saving the Bible by killing it. Joseph Smith argued at length that scriptures were records of God's encounters with communities, and ancient Israel was one of many such communities. The Book of Mormon made two key claims in a sustained exegesis of John 10:16 (specifically its reference to "other sheep I have, which are not of this fold"): the Bible was itself a regional scripture, and the Book of Mormon was the vanguard of similar regional scriptures. Early Saints recognized this attribute and saw it as a benefit. When Smith's mother, Lucy Mack Smith, wrote to her brother Solomon, she indicated, "there are more nations than one and if God would not reveal himself alike unto all nations he would be a partial [God]."[67]

Early in the Book of Mormon (1 Nephi 19), Nephi offers an extended dismantling and reconstruction of the Bible's unique status. After calling out the Bible's lost plainness, Nephi portrays the Bible authors as mortals just like him (19:6). He adds that, crucially, there are many others like him who are also necessary to prove that the Old Testament actually testifies of Jesus (19:10). With that lede, Nephi presents the crucial act of destabilization. He reads the contents of the brass plates (the original Hebrew Bible) to his people because they need to "know concerning the doings of the Lord in other lands" (19:21–23). From the perspective of this plain-speaking, clear-seeing prophet and his followers,

---

[66] Peters, "Celestial Bookkeeping," 858.
[67] Johnson, *Female Religiosity*, 24.

the Bible tells only one of the important ethnic histories needing to be preserved and recounted. A few pages later (1 Nephi 22), Nephi testifies again that the Bible is "true" (22:30), while in the next breath (22:31) he makes it clear that he has recruited the Bible as another regional witness. "Ye need not suppose," he warns his audience, "that I and my father are the only ones that have testified." Returning to the key scripture of John 10:16, Nephi sneers at exegetes who cannot see that all scripture is regional. "Know ye not," he asks rhetorically, "that there are more nations than one?" (2 Nephi 29:6–7).

This regional destabilization entered broader conversations about the nature of canon. The Bible itself made respectful reference to scriptural texts nowhere to be found in the accepted canons. These "lost books" of the Bible were a high priority for Smith and others. According to the Book of Mormon, scriptural gaps arose because various peoples of God had their own history that wasn't known to others. Mormon is aware that the Bible can't contain his story: thinking back to the flight of the Lehites from Jerusalem, he comments that "no one knew it save it were [God] himself and those which he brought out of that land" (3 Nephi 5:20). In addition to the Lehites, the Book of Mormon introduces wholly unknown prophets such as Zenos, Zenock, Ezias (contextually not Isaiah himself), and others.[68]

When Jesus arrives to ancient America six centuries later, he again discusses John 10, performing a pointed exegesis (3 Nephi 15:21, 16:1) in which he tells the Lehites that they are the "other sheep." To avoid any unclarity, Jesus challenges readings of John 10 that claim the passage refers to Old World disciples. He dismisses that interpretation out of hand, "expound[ing] all the scriptures in one" (3 Nephi 23:14). This Book of Mormon—including exegetical expositions of Bible passages within the scripture itself—was the self-interpreting Bible the Protestant world wished for, but that very book stole from the Bible any claim to uniqueness.

The Book of Mormon advances many scriptural cousins to the Old World Bible. Jesus reports that "tribe" after "tribe" has been removed from Jerusalem by God, and these tribes—not the Gentiles, as most other Bible interpreters understood references to "tribes"—are the peoples whose regional Bibles will one day be united. Later in his preaching (3 Nephi 23:6–13), Jesus predicts additional regional scriptures: "other scriptures I would that ye should write that ye have not." When Joseph Smith received a revelation in 1829 about the Book of Mormon (D&C 10:59), he himself used John 10 to motivate the acceptance of the Book of Mormon as America's regional scripture.

---

[68] Zenos is referenced eight times, Zenock five, and Ezias once in the Book of Mormon.

Calling the Bible a regional scripture was not original to Smith. Such was a central claim of the Enlightenment Bible (including Locke's view[69]) and related sensibilities about the nature of scripture as fragmented and tied to specific cultures. Anglo-American Deists and Unitarians claimed that regionality as an article of faith.[70] The German theologian Johann Eichhorn (1752–1827) commented in an exemplary vein that "the New Testament was only 'of local and temporal character.'"[71] Joseph Buckminster made similar arguments that "like all other books," the New Testament was "composed for" and "adapted to" its original audience.[72]

Like the Deists, Smith and his followers were dismantling the Bible, but the Latter-day Saints' aim was to rebuild it in a way that resisted the dominion of modern detached reason. They claimed the Bible as a regional scripture not because it wasn't scripture in the traditional sense, as Enlightenment thinkers would have it, but because true scripture was always regional. God could enter all nations, times, and peoples directly, and these entrances were recorded in scripture. The contingency of scripture was not a mechanism of disenchantment or ultimate deauthorization, but the reality of all written revelation. In Smith's hands, such contingency was an attempt to expand the reach and power of scripture by liberating it from its verbal grave. No longer was scripture restricted to a small cross section of believers in and near Israel. Scripture could encompass many peoples all around the world.

The Acts of Translation

The Bible doesn't specifically engage the matter of its own translation. The miracle of Pentecost (Acts 2) suggested that the message of the Gospel would reach many different linguistic groups, but that was oral, charismatic preaching, not the scriptural text itself. The New Testament had often relied on the Greek Septuagint, and occasionally it explained specific Aramaic words that might have been unfamiliar to Greek speakers, but again, nothing was set in place about how and under what circumstances the scripture texts were themselves to be translated. For the Hebrew Bible, the oral Aramaic targums spanned the gap between worshipers and Biblical Hebrew. The status and reliability of such translations was always a cause for worry and controversy. When and under what circumstances could a translation have a status to match the text it was

---

[69] Gura, *Transcendentalism*, 25.
[70] Lee, *Biblical Certainty*, 22.
[71] Sheehan, *Enlightenment Bible*, 90, 119, 154.
[72] Lee, *Biblical Certainty*, 152.

translating? Occasionally, traditions arose to provide supernatural authorization for specific translations. Thus Philo of Alexandria said that the translators of the Septuagint had independently provided the identical translation, verbatim, as a result of a spiritual trance.[73] This story was important to establish that the Greek text of the Hebrew scriptures could in fact be trusted.

For more modern translations, some liked to depict Luther as working on his German translation under direct inspiration of the spirits of the original evangelists, and Luther himself maintained that his work of translation was an inspired act.[74] Although they could get squeamish about whether the translation itself had a status equal to the original (as might be implied by divine inspiration guiding the translator), many Protestants did hope that their translations were delivered by revelation. Some traditions maintained that the King James translators achieved their translation via a mechanism similar to Philo's account of the Septuagint.[75] Empirically, the King James Bible had obvious errors of translation, and no clear route to revelatory repair.[76] Translations were always provisional—as skeptics were prone to gloat[77]—but Protestant cessationism disallowed new revelation to fix those translations. The Bible thus struggled to speak once for all, especially for Protestants.

The Book of Mormon had a solution here as well—it modeled the right way to translate the Bible. The longest account of Book of Mormon translation comes in the presentation of the Jaredite gold plates, which Mosiah, then the possessor of the *Gazelem* stones that marked him as a seer, rendered from the pure pre-Babel language into Lehite Hebrew. We learn from this sequence that the Book of Ether was translated not by scholarship but by a supernatural act of seerhood. The rest of the Book of Mormon—and, by extension, all scripture—should be translated in precisely the same way. There is God, a prophet, and the instruments of seership.[78]

While they never backed away from the revelatory core, Smith and his followers could not quite wean themselves from at least some modern approaches. Smith was of two minds on the question, starting the Book of Mormon translation with an attempted consultation with outside scholars.[79] After that effort failed to elicit academic assistance (but confirmed for Smith and his followers that the Book of Mormon fulfilled prophecies in Isaiah), he transitioned to methods more

---

[73] Sheehan, *Enlightenment Bible*, 5.
[74] Sheehan, *Enlightenment Bible*, 6–7.
[75] Sheehan, *Enlightenment Bible*, 5–7, 67–68.
[76] Daniell, *Bible in English*, 625.
[77] Grasso, *American Faith*, 314.
[78] On the relevance of the Jaredite account to the overall Book of Mormon, see Brown, *In Heaven*, 78–81.
[79] Smith sent Martin Harris to consult with Samuel Mitchell and Charles Anthon, two prominent professors. See MacKay, "Translating the Characters."

consistent with the text's example, exercising a spiritual gift that modulated and mediated language in complex ways. Smith's subsequent followers have wanted the Book of Mormon translation process to be more modern and scholarly sounding, proposing a variety of mechanisms for translation that, while admitting supernatural assistance, look like a form of modern scholarship.[80]

Smith's account of the Book of Mormon translation was short on mechanistic details but long on the proclamation of the spirit of God. Clues from the Book of Mormon text suggest that hybrid translation approaches, dominated by spiritual gifts and perhaps relying on panoramic visions, were central mechanisms of the translation process.[81] Whatever the specifics, the process of translation was a miracle that served as an external evidence of Smith's Restoration. Even after a miraculous translation, though, one still had to make sense of the text. One had to know how to interpret the Bible correctly. There again, the Book of Mormon had some ideas.

Self-Interpreting Scripture

Whatever else may be true of the early nineteenth century, the old standard for deciding how to interpret scripture was in flux. It had become, in the words of one observer, a "sea of sectarian rivalries."[82] The pluralism of interpretation led at least one learned commenter to advocate "a simple, practical, common sense interpretation of the word of God" as "the only cure of religious insanity the world has ever seen."[83]

Many different churches existed in the antebellum United States, all derived from the same Bible. The multiplicity of denominations raised the question: How, exactly, do you found a religion on a Bible? The question hadn't been as hard to answer under Catholicism or even with Protestant establishments like Luther's Germany, Calvin's Geneva, or the Puritans' Massachusetts Bay. In older societies, if early sociology of religion is correct, one forged a church out of the social order that in turn perpetuated the church. By token of its establishment within society, such an institution could mitigate the schismatic effects of individual Bible reading. (Anti-establishment critics, of course, never agreed with that line of reasoning, and many undercut establishments through independent readings of the Bible long before formal disestablishment.[84]) As those establishments weakened, increasingly scholars like Johannes Michaelis wanted

---

[80] Many such accounts are presented in Welch, "Miraculous Translation."
[81] Brown, "Voice of God."
[82] A late reference to 1830s Illinois, quoted in Smith, "Hermeneutical Crisis," 88.
[83] Turner, *Mormonism*, 104.
[84] Noll, *The Word*.

their translations and commentaries "to introduce into the Bible *no religious system at all*."[85] This conceit depended on the central fiction that the Bible could interpret itself. In support of this notion, John Brown's eighteenth-century *Self-Interpreting Bible*, widely republished in the United States, served paradigmatically in its many editions and reprints to reassure readers that the Bible was in fact univocal.[86]

Critics pointed out that the scriptures were often opaque at best. American Protestantisms had no Catholic magisterium to rely on, just the pretense of transparency when one applied Common Sense theology to the text. For many, not even inspiration could be invoked to make sense of the Bible; the text had to be able to stand on its own.[87] But the diversity of common senses in America, motivating the great assortment of Christian churches, and the occasional infidels or Deists, represented a crisis of clarity from the perspective of Restorationist and similar critics.[88] While many Protestants believed that denominational differences did not threaten the integrity of the body of Christ, Restorationist critics saw this as a lie. They traced that lie to the Bible's obvious interpretive ambiguities.

The Book of Mormon repeatedly advertises its capacity to solve the Bible's problem of clear interpretation. It exhibits a near-obsession with plainness, identifying itself at times as a Bible with the obfuscation removed. In 2 Nephi 3:12, the book is said to have been created "unto the confounding of false doctrines and laying down of contentions." In its reuse of Isaiah texts (e.g., 2 Nephi 27:35), the Book of Mormon makes Isaiah the source of a prophecy that foretold the Book of Mormon's role in clearing up sectarian uncertainty: "they also that erred in spirit shall come to understanding, and they that murmured shall learn doctrine." Shortly thereafter, Nephi states that the "book shall be of great worth" in the future, precisely because it resolves sectarian controversy from within scripture itself. In Nephi's future (which was Joseph Smith's present) a multiplicity of "churches" will contend "one with another" (2 Nephi 28:2–4); the Book of Mormon will resolve that contention.

This determination to settle sectarian debates included central questions like the Unitarian/Deist critique of the divinity of Christ. Whatever the Bible may have failed to clarify by way of controversies about Christ's divinity, the Book of Mormon made plain. In the title page and 2 Nephi 26:12, the Book of Mormon carefully specifies that Jesus is "the Christ, the Eternal God." The book rejects the Socinians and related Unitarian skeptics who disputed the attribution of divinity

---

[85] Sheehan, *Enlightenment Bible*, 213.
[86] Daniell, *Bible in English*, 601; Perry, *Bible Culture*, 26.
[87] Thus, e.g., Moses Stuart: Lee, *Biblical Certainty*, 175.
[88] See Hughes and Allen, *Illusions of Innocence*.

to Jesus. Through the Book of Mormon, God sent a message across the millennia to rebuke thinkers like Thomas Jefferson and Joseph Priestly: Unitarianism and Deism were wrong.

The Book of Mormon incorporates hermeneutics directly into the scriptural text. Following the lead of the New Testament, it focuses interpretive attention on Isaiah.[89] The Book of Isaiah is often gnomic in Hebrew and is, if anything, even less scrutable in the King James translation. One of the most notoriously difficult books of the Hebrew Bible, it is the one most esteemed by Christians.[90] The love of Isaiah is as old as Christianity itself and relates to the apparent prophecies of Christ within it.[91] But, if Christians were honest, they had to acknowledge that the Old Testament text wasn't especially explicit. If Isaiah's internal use in the Christian Bible is remarkable, its importance in the Book of Mormon is even more so. Isaiah is the biblical book most quoted, revised, and interpreted within the Book of Mormon.[92] One could be forgiven for seeing within the Book of Mormon a midrash on Isaiah. If anyone had questions about how clearly Isaiah prefigured Christ, the Book of Mormon had the answer. But Isaiah is an obviously difficult text. Why would the Book of Mormon, with its thirst for plainness, include such lengthy excerpts from a notoriously abstruse book? It seems to me that the Book of Mormon was taming Isaiah, bringing it into clarity through new contextualization.

Take the Abinadi sequence of Mosiah 12 as an important example. Corrupt priests of King Noah mock this Christ-like prophet, urging him to explicate Isaiah 52. He in turn mocks them (and implicitly antebellum Americans) for not knowing how to interpret Isaiah, then spends several verses clarifying that the chapter is a prophecy of Christ. The Book of Mormon contains several similar episodes.[93]

Crucially, these acts of guided exegesis are themselves scriptural because they are contained within the Book of Mormon. While others had merged text and commentary much as the ancient Aramaic targums did—including a German mystic named Johann Kayser a little less than a century before Smith[94]—Smith placed the exegetical expansions in the mouths of authorized prophets. Others (including the original targum writers) tended to just

---

[89] This feature of the New Testament was well known in the early modern Atlantic. See, e.g., Wesley, *Old Testament*, 3:1947; and Clarke, *Holy Bible*, 3:481. The Geneva Bible and subsequent annotated editions frequently described Isaiah in deeply Christological terms. I thank Christopher Jones and John Turner for insights on this question.

[90] On Isaiah, see, e.g., Sawyer, *Fifth Gospel*.

[91] Blenkinsopp, *Creation*, 182, and Blenkinsopp, *Sealed Book*.

[92] See, e.g., 1 Nephi 10:7–8; 2 Nephi 12–24, 2–30; Jacob 5; 3 Nephi 20:39–40. I thank Joseph Spencer for guidance on this topic.

[93] See, e.g., Alma 40.

[94] Sheehan, *Enlightenment Bible*, 70–71.

merge text and interpretation, but Smith had those mergers performed in front of readers by prophetic authors with the same status as the original prophets.

In this respect, the Book of Mormon is like the New Testament, which scripturally reworked the Old Testament. But the Book of Mormon goes further, revising Old Testament, New Testament, and lost books (especially in Jacob 5) in a plain-spoken, nineteenth-century mode that is the very model of perspicuity.[95] Similarly, when the Book of Mormon reprints Isaiah 48:14–16 in 1 Nephi 20:14–16, it adds a line reassuring the reader that God will fulfill his prophecies.[96] While the Protestant Bible was lost in the brambles of the prophetic book that should have been its greatest ally in Christian belief, the Book of Mormon showed the way to domesticate Isaiah.

Whatever else it did, the Book of Mormon changed the grounds of reading the Bible. One twentieth-century line of scholarship counted sermons and their contents and argued that early Church members largely ignored the Book of Mormon, preferring the Bible.[97] But such tallies of sermons and proof-texting misunderstand the role that the Book of Mormon played in the early Restoration. The Bible Smith's disciples read had been transformed by the Book of Mormon. The Saints didn't quote the Book of Mormon in their recorded sermons as much as they quoted the Bible, true, but this accounting fails to appreciate that the Book of Mormon was reading the Bible. Even as they continued, by and large, to preach from the same King James Bible, Latter-day Saints encountered a vastly different Bible than their Protestant compatriots did, precisely because the Book of Mormon had transformed it.[98] In the phrase of one of Smith's lieutenants, "by that book [the Book of Mormon] I found a key to the holy prophets; and by that book began to unfold the mysteries of God."[99] While the Book of Mormon had its own distinct content (which is being mined in the last decade or two by literary scholars and theologians[100]), for faithful readers the book had meaning in large part because of the ways it transmuted the King James Bible.

---

[95] Spencer, *Vision of All*, considers Book of Mormon uses of Isaiah for a Latter-day Saint audience.
[96] Hardy, "Book of Mormon and Bible," 119.
[97] Reynolds, "Coming Forth," 8–9; Barlow, *Mormons and the Bible*, 47; Underwood, "Usage"; Merrill and Merrill, "Changing Thought."
[98] This likely explains some of the later Latter-day Saint resistance to using other Bible translations beyond the King James Version. These new translations ceded authority in interpretation to outsiders because the Saints only controlled the grounds of reading the King James Version.
[99] *M&A* 1:12 (September 1835): 178.
[100] See the essays in Fenton and Hickman, eds., *Americanist Approaches*.

Saving Evidential Christianity

Readers encounter the Bible in a context, and in the nineteenth century that context was shaped by the considerations of evidential Christianity, an outgrowth of Baconian empiricism and Scottish Common Sense realism. While we shouldn't overstate the degree of consensus, many American Protestants believed that their religion rested on a secure rational foundation of internal and external evidences.[101] "Internal" evidences were specific to the text itself: moral verities, special insights, the regenerating effect of the text on readers, and Old Testament prophecies fulfilled in the New Testament. "External" evidences were miracles that confirmed the status of the Bible, especially those reported in the New Testament.

The famed minister (and father to Harriet Beecher Stowe) Lyman Beecher (1775–1863) was close to a Protestant mainstream when he stated in 1829, "If I understand my own mode of philosophizing, it is the Baconian. Facts and the Bible are the extent of my philosophy."[102] Using the language of evidential Christianity, the Presbyterian Jonathan B. Turner similarly maintained that "no man should call on his fellows to embrace by faith a single item of religious doctrine, as such, until he can first furnish the full demonstration, the proof of its truth, either from nature or the word of God, or from both."[103] As Turner resisted what he considered fanaticisms (which, for Turner, applied to most of the popular religious expressions of the Second Great Awakening), he was "remonstrating against errors which do not and cannot exist in a land of light and bibles."[104] The light Turner referred to was the illumination of evidence, and the Bible he adduced was a rational one.

Evidentialist traditions within Christianity had existed independently for some time, especially but not exclusively as natural theology.[105] Evidences allowed believers to use contemporary methods and considerations while still maintaining support for aspects of traditional religion.[106] The marriage of faith and reason bore risks that some participants did not fully appreciate, not least the difficulty in getting the needed evidences to align precisely with common sense. Traditionalists struggled with certain logical inconsistencies. The external evidences associated with the Bible were visibly nowhere to be seen in the

---

[101] Holifield, *Theology in America*; Noll, *America's God*; Lee, *Biblical Certainty*.
[102] Noll, *America's God*, 292.
[103] Turner, *Mormonism*, 253.
[104] Turner, *Mormonism*, 254.
[105] On natural theology, see Holifield, *Theology in America*, esp. 180–81, cf. Buck, *Theological Dictionary*, 521–22.
[106] Rivett, *Science of the Soul*; Hindmarsh, *Early Evangelicalism*, 66, 107, 131.

contemporary landscape.[107] People weren't being raised from the dead; mountains weren't being torn down or rivers evaporated at a prophet's command. How could one accept miracles whose only attestations were shrouded in deep mystery and nowhere visible in the current environment? But allowing miracles in the contemporary world threatened the rational consensus and raised the specter of fanaticism. Miracles felt safer when relegated to the apostolic age, but that separation required a disjunction between what was possible in the present and what had been possible in the past, the doctrine of cessationism we encountered in chapter 2. Commonsense principles excluded such an option.

Mormon's scripture served as its own evidence in a way that the English Bible never could. Its very appearance in the world seems to reflect the Baconian worldview.[108] Following a stipulation inside the text (2 Nephi 27:13–14), Smith recruited eleven friends and family members as "witnesses" to sign testimonials or affidavits that they had personally handled the original gold plates.[109] The inclusion of the attestations of the witnesses in scripture wasn't an afterthought to shore up evidentialist claims as the type was getting set for final printing. The plans for the witness statements were explicit and clarified as anticessationist within the text of the Book of Mormon itself. The Book of Mormon prophesied that it would need affidavits from witnesses. That prophecy was the explicit sanction for the attachment of those affidavits to the scriptural text.

The use of the Book of Mormon as a miraculous evidence has been emphasized often, most extensively in recent years by the Latter-day Saint theological historian Terryl Givens.[110] He and others have correctly emphasized the Book of Mormon's importance as a miracle to authorize Smith's new religious movement, but they haven't drawn sufficient attention to the ways that in doing so the Book of Mormon was filling a void left by the Protestant Bible. The nineteenth-century Saints called attention to this fact. In an early essay lauding the evidential value of the Book of Mormon, Phelps makes clear that the Bible needed Mormon's scripture.

> Men generally believe upon testimony, and the rule is good. Now, as to the evidence of the truth of the bible, we have no eye witnesses to prove it, for they have been dead many hundred years, and the fashion of saying you believe it is true, because your father said so, will not amount to proof. . . . The Book of Mormon, besides the evidence of the Holy Spirit, showing that God is the same

---

[107] The Latter-day Saint John Corrill exemplifies this line of criticism when he said of the Book of Mormon that "it was as consistent to give credit to them as to credit the writings of the New Testament, when I had never seen the authors nor the original copy." *JSPD1*, 386.
[108] Hazen, *Village Enlightenment*, 155n41.
[109] Bushman, *Rough Stone*, 77–79.
[110] This is a central argument of Givens, *Hand of Mormon*.

yesterday, today, and forever, has the living witnesses to bear testimony that it is true.[111]

This statement grants the authority of external evidences and the role that human witnesses play in the authority of the Bible. That much was standard Christian evidentialism, as far as it went. Protestant readers would have been with Phelps fully to that point. But then he makes an implicit reference to the limitations of written language and Bible transmission that was the stuff of German higher criticism. The testimonies of the external evidences (Christ's miracles) were embedded within the very Bible they were meant to support: there were "no eye witnesses," only a "fashion" of inter-generational gossip. The Bible, according to Phelps, thus had to pull itself up by its own bootstraps. His reference to oral traditions passed from father to son sounds like a response to a rebuttal he had heard from interlocutors that the churches, whether Catholic, Protestant, or both, served as independent testimonies. Phelps relied on his readers to recognize that multigenerational hearsay did not meet evidentiary standards. Phelps wasn't really wrong about the problem—evidential Christianity and cessationism had logical flaws. Whether he was right about the solution is much more controversial. For Phelps's coreligionists, the obvious solution was the Book of Mormon, which featured living, breathing witnesses to the plates.

Persuasive proofs rooted in the Bible text were termed internal evidences.[112] For some this meant the moral grandeur of the teachings of Christ or the manifest societal power wielded by the Protestants who followed its precepts. It could even refer to the sense of inspiration one experienced when reading the book. The grand harmony of the Bible could be such an evidence. In the fulfillment of biblical prophecies, internal and external evidences came closest to each other.[113] For example, Isaiah prophesied of a suffering servant (53), and Christ was scourged and crucified. Or Joel prophesied of the Christian Pentecost (2:28), which occurred in Acts 2. According to this logic, the New Testament proved the Old Testament true by fulfilling it. Jonathan Edwards worked on a book he called the "Harmony" of the two testaments, in which he made the case for such internal evidences.[114]

Increasingly, however, critics argued that prophecy fulfillment was difficult to confirm. Enlightenment ideologies especially disrupted internal evidences.[115] It

---

[111] *EMS* 1:8 (January 1833): 59.
[112] Holifield, *Theology in America*, 186–90; and Lee, *Biblical Certainty*, 58.
[113] Some distinguished prophecy fulfillment from internal evidence, considering the scriptural harmony to lie in the realm of miracles. Thus, e.g., Jenyns, *Internal Evidence*.
[114] Lee, *Biblical Certainty*, 81–82.
[115] Sheehan, *Enlightenment Bible*, 151.

could never be crystal clear whether a specific event in the New Testament fulfilled a particular prophecy in the Old Testament.

The prophetic narrators of the Book of Mormon solve the internal evidences problem in several ways. First, the text explicitly describes the ways that the New Testament fulfilled the Old, especially regarding Christ. The religious historian Stephen Stein has argued that "The *Book of Mormon* is Christ-centered to a fault."[116] That Christocentrism is well known and widely commented by critics who see it as key evidence of the book's exclusively nineteenth-century provenance. But that fault was its self-proclaimed strength, one that gave it a leg up over the Protestant Bible. The book was designed to solve the Bible's manifest inability to acknowledge Christ explicitly in its Old Testament and to solve the problems posed by the figure of Christ in its New Testament, both central concerns of Unitarian criticism.

Christians had essentially always seen Christ in the Old Testament. Christ and the early apostles did so freely, most scandalously in his discussion (John 8: 56–58) about his relationship to Abraham and his apparent claim to have been Yahweh (Exodus 3:14–15). But these references were New Testament-specific. The Old Testament didn't name Jesus per se. The Book of Mormon solved that problem. For example, in the buildup to Christ's visit to America (Helaman 8), the prophet Helaman scolds his nineteenth-century readers for their blindness to the evidences of Christ. He lists prophets, both known and unknown. Mentioning Jeremiah, Helaman seems to remember the beginning of the Book of Mormon, in which Jeremiah's prophecy of the destruction of Jerusalem was demonstrated to be true. Then Helaman poses the rhetorical question, "Now we know that Jerusalem was destroyed according to the words of Jeremiah. O then why not the Son of God come, according to his prophecy?" (8:20). Although he's ostensibly talking to his peers, readers know that Jesus came. Helaman was talking to *both* his peers and a modern American audience. He wanted them to know that the true Old Testament testified explicitly of Christ.

In considering his purpose as a scriptural narrator, Nephi proclaims (2 Nephi 11:4), "My soul delighteth in proving unto my people the truth of the coming of Christ." According to their then-current timeline, he's speaking at roughly the same time as Jeremiah and Ezekiel. But in place of the cryptic Christology of those Bible books, Nephi offers a transparent account of Jesus. He's far more specific than the Bible. A few chapters later (1 Nephi 22:20), Moses is explicitly prophesying of Jesus. Shortly thereafter (2 Nephi 26), Nephi describes good people and bad people. The good ones exhibit "steadfastness for the signs" of the coming of Christ, signs Nephi believes are obvious to all. No murky metaphors

---

[116] Stein, "America's Bibles," 172.

here: Nephi says explicitly, "the Son of Righteousness shall appear unto them; and he shall heal them, and they shall have peace with him, until three generations shall have passed away, and many of the fourth generation shall have passed away in righteousness."

A second way the Book of Mormon resolves problems of internal evidence is to routinely create evidences internal to itself—prophecies of future events whose fulfillment is also attested. In the Words of Mormon we learn that "the things which are upon these plates pleasing me, because of the prophecies of the coming of Christ; and my fathers knowing that many of them have been fulfilled; yea, and I also know that as many things as have been prophesied concerning us down to this day have been fulfilled, and as many as go beyond this day must surely come to pass" (1:4). Here Mormon testifies that the past, present, and future of the ancient biblical prophecies is fulfilled *within* the Book of Mormon narrative. This is a clear, scriptural endorsement of the mechanics of internal evidences of prophecies. Once again, the Book of Mormon had saved the primordial Bible (and its capacity to map itself onto evidential Christianity) by exploiting weakness of its Protestant version.

The Book of Mormon famously injects the New Testament into the Old Testament, repeatedly.[117] Readers have wondered why so much of the New Testament (600 phrases, by one count[118]) is present in this record of émigrés from Jerusalem six centuries before Christ. For Smith, true scripture depends on its harmony across the ages, and the Book of Mormon displays such harmony at length. Whether these anachronisms are seen as ultimately problematic, they shouldn't be understood as accidental. David Wright, for example, complains that Alma reuses language from Hebrews,[119] but that complaint is grounded in a misapprehension of the work the Book of Mormon considers itself to be doing. Having the New Testament in the Old, explicitly, is critical to the project of saving the Bible and its internal evidences.

A third way the Book of Mormon deals with internal evidences is that it calls people to be transformed through the "plainness" of its language, a plainness that describes both convicting moral clarity and textual perspicuity. In a sermon delivered to a group considering conversion from an iniquitous society, a prophet reports an experiential solution to an epistemological problem. If the hearers are to find the proto-Christian Gospel true, they must themselves be true to it (Alma 32). Modern readers are meant to be listening over the shoulders of these ancients as they are called to "experiment" on Mormon's message. As the word transforms readers' lives, they will see that it is true. Word and humans

---

[117] See Barlow, *Mormons and the Bible*, 36–40.
[118] Frederick, "Redaction," 46.
[119] Wright, "Transformation of Hebrews."

intermingle then and now, according to the Book of Mormon. The book thus self-consciously argues that its internal evidences are valid because the book regenerates its readers. The same basic epistemology is at play in a call for potential converts to use prayer to determine the truth of the Book of Mormon (Moroni 10). The point here is that internal evidences included not just fulfilled prophecies but the effect that scripture had on the reader: The Book of Mormon put the Bible's demure attitude to shame, explicitly and self-consciously forcing a spiritual transformation on its readers.

Evidence in a Modern Age: The Problem of Miracles

As early Latter-day Saints looked for continuity between the Old and New Testaments, and the Book of Mormon, they also sought continuity between the biblical world and their own. How could the world of the New Testament be packed full of miracles while contemporary Christian life was devoid of such marvels?[120] The Saints cried foul: if miracles were ever true, they argued, they also had to be true now.[121] The disjunction between past and present to accommodate ancient miracles (cessationism) ran afoul of the philosophical requirements of experimental science that the laws of nature not change.

Many Christians understood that the miracles of the New Testament were the external evidences necessary to prove the Bible, and they were applicable once, for all.[122] It was one thing to find Jesus in Isaiah or the European colonization of America in the biblical Exodus from Egypt, or to see the converting effect of the word of God on individual readers. It was another thing entirely to raise the dead or move a mountain. However much people wanted miracles in their own lives, the truth or falsity of scripture and religion didn't depend on such extraordinary events for most Protestants. But Enlightenment principles mandated that what was once true would always be true. The Bible itself never indicated that supernaturalism would be superseded; it promised instead that miraculous signs would follow those who believed. How, then, critics wondered, had miracles ceased? The Book of Mormon took on that criticism with palpable glee.

The Book of Mormon is steeped in miraculous tales and periodically gloats over how much better these external evidences function there than they do in the Bible. Where the fiery furnace of Babylon happened once in Daniel, the Book of Mormon offers its own version of that miracle "thrice." Where Daniel survived the lion's den once, the Book of Mormon offers its version of that miracle

---

[120] See Shaw, *Enlightenment England*, and Mullin, *Modern Religious Imagination*.
[121] See *EMS* 1:1 (June 1832): 3, Pratt, *Voice of Warning*, and *T&S* 2:14 (May 15, 1841): 409–11.
[122] Turner, *Mormonism*, 112.

"twice." In this case, the miracle workers are not Daniel and other Jews detained in Babylon, but rather the mysterious Three Nephites, who were among Jesus's twelve New World disciples during their mortal lives. The three were granted their wish of continuing their ministry on earth beyond a natural life span, so they were translated. These Nephite disciples thus personally carry the age of miracles from antiquity to the present by token of their translated immortality (3 Nephi 28).[123]

The Book of Mormon modeled its anticessationist message in practice. For example, in the turbulent lead-up to Christ's visit to America, the text describes unbelieving Nephites persecuting the people of God. The persecution hinges on whether prophecies of Christ's coming—to which righteous Christians have held fast—will come to fruition. Skeptics threaten these American proto-Christians with death if the prophecies of Christ's coming aren't fulfilled.[124] In this setting, a faithful prophet, $Nephi_2$, announces that the chief judge will be found murdered. Skeptics run to the judgment seat to confirm the judge's death because "if this thing which he has said concerning the chief judge be true, that he be dead, then will we believe that the other words which he has spoken are true" (Helaman 9:1–2). It couldn't be clearer in this encounter: if the prophet truly exhibited the marvelous clairvoyance required to know the judge was dead, then the scriptural prophecies he revealed were true also. $Nephi_2$'s clairvoyance proves correct, but the skeptics immediately change their tune, accusing $Nephi_2$ of being an accomplice to the murderers (9:16–17). Although the Book of Mormon preaches a strong anticessationist message, it also acknowledges that even the most impressive miracles may not, ultimately, persuade.

Along these same lines, various Book of Mormon characters routinely resist even the most powerful external evidences. Nephi's older brothers see an angel and then shortly thereafter rebel, causing Nephi to complain that they were "past feeling" (1 Nephi 17:45). In the lead-up to Christ's arrival (Helaman 16:23), the narrator wearily comments that "notwithstanding the signs and the wonders which were wrought . . . Satan did get great hold upon the hearts of the people." According to Moroni, what makes people fail to believe is their reliance on the incipient language of Enlightenment: they begin "to depend upon their own strength and upon their own wisdom, saying: Some things they may have guessed right among so many" (Helaman 16:15–16). Elsewhere the Book of Mormon claims that the failure of these miraculous events to convince others reflects the influence of Satan, the author of cessationist doctrines (3 Nephi 1:22).

---

[123] The furnace is 28:21, and the "den of wild beasts" is 28:22, cf. Daniel 3:15–27, 6:16–22.

[124] The first round of threatened killings is called off when the miracles associated with Christ's birth occur. However, new violence arises, including secret executions, when the resurrected Christ is due to appear. Compare 3 Nephi 1:5–16 and 3 Nephi 6:20–30.

The Book of Mormon is aware of the risks to external evidences and takes preventive measures to defuse criticism. In a nested sermon on faith and divine power (Ether 12:6ff), Ether explains that faith has to precede the miracle. Both the miracles *and* a willingness to see them are required. Again, the Book of Mormon is teaching antebellum readers how to use and understand external evidences. God was giving them permission to know that only hard-hearted observers would reject external evidences in the modern age. This was the opposite of what most Christians heard in Sunday sermons, and for many converts, the end of cessationism was exhilarating.

Inside the book, various episodes indicate how external evidences are to be deployed. Nephi berates his brothers for their infidelity, suggesting that they have no excuse—they have already had many evidences of the truth of the Gospel (1 Nephi 7:8–15). At least once, the Book of Mormon tackles the evidence problem head-on by resolving an apparent scientific misstep within the Bible (Helaman 12:14–15). Explaining references to the sun standing still (Joshua 10:12–13 and Habakkuk 3:11), the speaker explains, "according to his word the earth goeth back, and it appeareth unto man that the sun standeth still; yea, and behold, this is so; for surely it is the earth that moveth and not the sun." Problem solved.

Parley Pratt made the argument about evidence explicit in 1840: "Do away the principle of direct Revelation then, and we do away the religion of the Bible, and have nothing left but atheism."[125] No system without active revelation could, in Pratt's terms, be considered biblical because the Bible itself so obviously depended on it. One hears Pratt gently nodding toward the Deist critics who had done cessationism one better: not only were there no miracles now, there were no miracles ever. Pratt thus positioned the Book of Mormon as the only possible theist response to Deist criticism. Once again, the Saints were kicking the chair out from under the Protestant Bible in the interests of making space for their primordial replacement.

Across all the major domains of evidential Christianity, the Book of Mormon outcompeted the Protestant Bible. For external evidences, the Saints were working miracles themselves. Saints like Zina Huntington and her mother Zina Baker or her friend Elizabeth Ann Whitney exercised gifts of healing, tongues, and visions; Zina Baker even famously (and transiently) raised a man from the dead.[126] Many elders were healing converts and exorcising demons. In addition, the Saints had affidavits from living witnesses, both foreseen within and published with their scripture. For internal evidences, they had vastly more coherent, explicit engagement of scriptural prophecies as well as a scriptural epistemology founded in the transformation of the reader. The Book of Mormon

---

[125] Pratt, *Plain Facts*, 2.
[126] Brown, *In Heaven*, 47.

seemed to implement intentional strategies in a targeted way. It could even clear the path to a church.

Getting from Bible to Church

The problem of mapping the Bible onto a church was a smoldering crisis for Protestants. Within a few generations of the Reformation, the increasing distance between civic authority and denominational structures made actual the theoretical question of how to build a church. But the Bible had precious little to say explicitly about how to build and operate a church. Reliance on the Bible alone, in fact, led to a proliferation of denominations.[127]

While most Protestant denominations were confident enough of biblical warrant for their ecclesial distinctions, some internal critics became emphatic about the need to build a church exclusively on the basis of explicit Bible instructions. Alexander Campbell was the most famous of nineteenth-century Protestant critics of this stripe. He actively resisted all church structures that differed, to his eye, from that described in the Book of Acts.[128] He believed that the solution to questions of ecclesiastical authority was to read the Greek New Testament as a blueprint for a recovered church. To make that point abundantly clear, Campbell's followers named their churches after Jesus rather than using national (e.g., Anglican), governmental (e.g., Presbyterian), or ritual (e.g., Baptist) distinctions.[129] In retrospect, Campbell's campaign was doomed from the beginning, as Smith saw clearly. The New Testament has little to say about the specifics of church structure: there are a few names for disciples, vague and tantalizing hints about Eucharist and baptism and, in the late epistles, some mention of various offices (e.g., 1 Timothy 3, Titus 1). But the New Testament didn't even actually specify how to name a church, only that outsiders called Christ's followers "Christians" (Acts 11:26). Campbell had to make that argument on his own.

The Book of Mormon, however, provided explicit instructions to early Americans hoping to restore the primitive church, exposing the inadequacies of the Protestant Bible as it repaired them. 3 Nephi, for example, explicitly addresses key matters of ecclesiology. In Christ's visit to the new world, he quickly solves the problem of naming a church by proclaiming that it has to be the "church of Christ" (3 Nephi 26:21). This was the name Smith and his followers first adopted. The Book of Mormon named the new church, even as it lambasted those who

---

[127] Gregory, *Unintended Reformation*, 100; Noll, *The Word*, 290–96.
[128] Campbell, *Sacred Writings*, 10, and discussion in Benson, *Restorationists*.
[129] On Campbell, see, e.g., Hughes and Allen, *Illusions of Innocence*, and Thomas, *Alexander Campbell*.

dared to misname a denomination, indicting the Catholics and almost all Protestants in a breathless condemnation (27:3–8). Elsewhere in 3 Nephi we find more explicit discussions of ecclesiology, including a baptismal prayer (11:25, where the prayer is patterned somewhat differently than in Mosiah 18:13, with both complying with Christian standards for universal baptismal prayers).

The precedent of the Book of Mormon was strong enough that when Smith and colleagues renamed the Church in 1834 to clarify that they were the "Latter Day Saints" as complement to the former days of the ancients, it generated controversy.[130] A schismatic church in Kirtland reverted to the original Book of Mormon name.[131] In a June 1838 letter to Wilford Woodruff, Smith explained, "They did not understand, that by taking upon them the name of Latter day Saints, did not do away that of the Church of Christ. Neither did they consider, that the ancient church, was the Church of Christ, and that they were Saints." He then drew attention to multiple references to the people of God as Saints in the Bible.[132] In other words, by calling themselves Saints, Smith's disciples became antitypes of the prophesied saints of the Bible (especially Daniel 7:18, 27). Thus even the transition into the church's new name was driven by Smith's integration of his followers into the Bible.[133] In that move, though, he was doing the same thing Campbell had done—namely, arguments from first principles. Because ultimately, as biblical as he was, scripture was dead for Joseph Smith without a live prophet.[134]

Near the end of the Book of Mormon, Moroni discovers that he has more time to write than he'd anticipated. Hoping that he will be useful to the Lamanites' descendants and their Gentile peers in the far-distant day when the Book of Mormon is presented in English (Moroni 1), he catalogs materials for recreating the church, with an eye to rituals and governance. There, in rapid sequence, he outlines the rite to confer the Holy Ghost (Moroni 2), inserts the priesthood ordination prayer (Moroni 3), and records the prayers for the Lord's Supper (Moroni 4–5). He even specifies the church's meeting schedule (Moroni 6). Again (assuming that one believes church governance should be specified in canonized scripture), the Book of Mormon appears to succeed where the Bible has manifestly failed. In a sense, the Book of Mormon thus incorporates its own Book of Common Prayer into scripture, avoiding the distance between canonized texts and practiced liturgy that affected many Protestants.

---

[130] *EJ* 1:3 (July 1838): 37.
[131] *JSPD5*, 442.
[132] *JSPD6*, 156.
[133] Clarke, *Holy Bible*, 4:596–97, indicates that those references to saints in Daniel indicated that Christians rather than Jews would take over the world in the end times.
[134] Brown, "Read the Round."

Latter-day Saints modeled many of their early rituals on those Book of Mormon precedents.[135] When Oliver Cowdery set out to establish the norms for early Church governance in 1829 in the "Articles of the Church of Christ," he quoted from those sections of the Book of Mormon. Smith stayed true to that direction when he amplified Cowdery's document slightly as the *Articles and Covenants* of the Church as well as when he dictated the Laws of the Church shortly thereafter.[136] The Book of Mormon's liturgical and ecclesiastical instructions were thus written immediately and explicitly into the bylaws of the new church. The book's liturgical texts had an important rhetorical role to play. Emphasizing the implications for ecclesiology of the Book of Mormon's appropriation of the Bible, Phelps maintained that the Book of Mormon "cuts the Gordian knot of priestcraft."[137] "Priestcraft" was the Latter-day Saint code word for illegitimate religion—both Catholicism and the ever-multiplying Protestant sects. Where Protestants were forced under the lights of scripture alone to determine which Catholic patterns to retain and what innovations to accept, the Saints could turn confidently to their American Bible and find all the direction they needed. For Smith's followers at least, the conundrum of how to get a church from a Bible had apparently been solved. Their access to a plainer Bible—through which they could recover the primordial Bible beyond—addressed for the Latter-day Saints the multiplicity problem.

Conclusion

Smith's first scripture, his Book of Mormon, was an expansion and revision of the Protestant Bible that told America's primeval history. The Book solved many of the key problems of the Bible. Where the Bible's original documents were long lost, Joseph Smith possessed the original manuscripts of the Book of Mormon and affidavits of authenticity from living eyewitnesses. Where the Bible's meanings were often murky, Book of Mormon language was intentionally "plain," sometimes to the point of dullness. The Bible's transmission and translation had occurred anonymously over many centuries, but the Book of Mormon was transmitted and translated in a few months in 1829 by a single prophet working individually with a few scribes. Smith's competitors, the Campbellites, complained that most churches ignored the New Testament's blueprint for the true church, but the Bible was inaccessibly remote from the nineteenth century.

---

[135] Stapley, *Power of Godliness*, 16.
[136] *JSPD1*, 369–73.
[137] *T&S* 5:24 (January 1, 1845): 757.

The Book of Mormon, on the other hand, contained explicit, timely advice relevant to the creation of the true church in the last days.

Latter-day Saints understood that in its audacious rereading, the Book of Mormon gave them control over the Protestant Bible. The American scripture solved the Bible's mysteries even as it placed the Bible as a regional scripture alongside others of the past, present, and future. It was as American as Jonny Appleseed's hard apple cider, but it provided for Smith and his followers a vista onto the pure Bible beyond human meddling. Mormon's book was both modern and ancient.

Smith and his followers dismantled the Bible in order to rebuild it in a more robust and spiritually charged form. The contingency of scripture was not a mechanism to disenchant or deauthorize the Bible, but to expand its reach and power. *Every* people could experience the direct presence of God and the creation of scripture. Smith seems to have seen scriptural plurality not as a route to abandoning Christianity but as its most normal form of flourishing.

The lessons of the Book of Mormon stayed with Joseph Smith throughout his career. A year before his assassination, he preached that a dead Bible couldn't stand against the living spirit. "I will turn linguist," he proclaimed. "[There are] ma[n]y things in the bible. whi[c]h do not. as th[e]y now stand. accord with the revelati[o]n of the holy Gho[s]t to me."[138] A month later he said that there was "No Salvation between the two lids of the bible without a legal administrator."[139] Here he was making an ecclesiastical argument about the inability of the Bible to support sacraments or church infrastructure. But he always had in mind the reality that it wasn't as simple as words on a page. The Latter-day Saints reserved the right to read the Bible, such as it was, according to the lights of their prophetic power.

In retrospect, the Book of Mormon was important for miraculously initiating a tradition of prophetic reworking of Bible texts. A more formal prophetic repair of the Bible itself immediately followed.

---

[138] *JSPJ3*, 33.
[139] *JSPJ3*, 67.

5
Rereading the Bible
Joseph Smith's New Translation

As the Book of Mormon made its way off the Grandin press in Palmyra in March 1830, Smith turned his attention even more directly to the King James Bible and its flaws. Beginning with a pair of visionary texts with a subsequent move to textual corrections and emendations, Smith worked on a "New Translation" to supplant the "Old Translation" of the King James Version.[1] This New Translation project continued the work of the Book of Mormon in a natural progression, moving from America's lost scriptures to the missing texts of the ancient Near East to the garbled remnants contained in the King James Bible. We saw in chapter 4 that the Book of Mormon was concerned with repairing the King James Bible via both direct and indirect means. The Book of Mormon acknowledged that it was insufficient, though. More would be required to finally heal the Bible. In this chapter, I consider the work of rereading that followed the Book of Mormon, in which Smith recovered other lost texts and then worked with Sidney Rigdon on an autodidact effort to repair the extant Protestant Bible.

This New Translation was only continuing a project initiated by the Book of Mormon. 1 Nephi 13 had made explicit that the Protestant Bible was in tatters. The Book of Mormon not only diagnosed the problem but also explained how the primeval Bible would be restored. In his introduction to Ether (Ether 1:1– 5), Moroni leaves out key Old Testament texts. "They [the details] are had upon the [brass] plates," he states, and then indicates that Joseph Smith will recover those Bible elements Moroni left out of his abridgment. "Whoso findeth them, the same will have power that he may get the full account." This power to obtain "full account" is an authorizing prophecy for Smith.[2] He would continue to unearth the primordial Bible even after the Book of Mormon was published. The Book of Mormon had killed the old Protestant Bible, but there it still sat on shelves across America. To the extent that the Bible continued to command attention, Smith would need to do surgery on it directly. Phelps for his part was explicit that this next phase of translation was a vital step in perfecting

---

[1] Parley Pratt uses the terminology explicitly in *MS* 3: 3 (July 1, 1842): 46.
[2] I also agree with Perry, "Joseph Smith's Bibles," 766, that the Isaiah excerpts in the Book of Mormon are a point of continuity between the Book of Mormon and the New Translation.

scripture: "This is a sufficient reason for the Lord to give command to have it translated a new: Notwithstanding King James' translators did very well, all knowing that they had only the common faculties of men and literature, without the spirit of Revelation."[3] While at first glance, the project was simple and discrete, in point of fact, Smith's new translation was a complex, multifaceted project.

Taxonomy of Smith's Bible Translations

Scholars and believers have made multiple attempts to define the scope of Smith's formal translation of the Bible—what the Utah Church has called the "Joseph Smith Translation," members of the Community of Christ (formerly the RLDS Church) have regarded as the "Inspired Version," and the earliest Saints, including Joseph Smith and Sidney Rigdon, referred to as the "New Translation." Some recent observers have favored describing the New Translation as a "revision," "redaction," or "correction."[4] I believe those characterizations sell the project short by mistaking one aspect of the project for the whole. For their part the early Saints understood even the work now called redaction as containing "great and glorious things" that were being "revealed."[5] Accounts of the New Translation should engage that early reception history. In addition, few have recognized how plural Smith's New Translation was or its place among other Bible reading traditions. Similarly few have appreciated the continuities between Smith's new Bible and his other scriptural products, all of which are sustained rereadings of the Bible. Indeed, Smith's engagement of the Bible ran the gamut from visionary revelations of missing books (including a new preface to the Torah), to esoteric etymologizing about specific words, to visionary exegeses of John's Revelation, to what he specifically called his New Translation of the Bible and hoped one day to publish.

Before engaging these various texts, I recall the central arguments of *Joseph Smith's Translation*: (1) most of Smith's translated, revelatory, and scriptural corpus rereads the Bible, and (2) the relevant classification for most of Smith's rereadings was the ancient targum, an oral vernacular translation that itself became a kind of scripture. Smith was never not rereading the Bible, never not struggling to define its meaning, to make it flesh in his world. By emphasizing the term "rereading," I'm intentionally echoing, for rhetorical rather than

---

[3] *EMS* 1:1 (June 1832): 3.
[4] Flake, "Translating Time," 509–11, 513–14, calls it "redaction." The Joseph Smith Papers editors have settled on "inspired revision": *JSPMRB*, xxiii.
[5] *JSPD2*, 267.

philological reasons, a traditional etymology of the term "religion" as close and repeated reading.[6]

Joseph Smith used the same language to describe the genesis of his New Translation as he had for the Book of Mormon. In the preface to the New Translation, he indicated that it was "translated by the power of God."[7] Smith's followers similarly understood that an inspired translation was required. A January 1833 revelation maintained that Smith was "do[ing] the work of translation for the Salvation of Souls."[8] This reference to the New Translation is suggesting that the broken Bible, despite the Book of Mormon's work of reform, was still leading people away from Jesus and his salvation. Smith's calling was to make sure that the Bible could speak purely.

Smith's readings were often esoteric, a formal term to designate the pursuit of hidden meanings invisible to the casual or uninitiated reader. More anciently, a similar style might have been "allegorical" or "anagogical."[9] An esoteric reader isn't bound tightly to the simplest interpretation of texts as they are written. This was a style of reading that fits less and less well in the modern world, but it was Smith's polestar.

This esoteric approach was justified by the fact that the English Bible was imperfect and the primordial Bible stood, inaccessible, behind it. Smith had practiced esoteric reading his whole career, and in the 1840s became both more confident and more public about it. In 1843 his German tutor Alexander Neibaur, a convert from Judaism and dabbler in Jewish mysticism, was endorsing Kabbalah in the Church newspaper,[10] while Smith was practicing esoteric reading. In May 1843 he reported that there were "3 grand secrets lying in this chapter [2 Peter 1] which no man can dig out, which unlocks the whole chapter. What is written are only hints of things which ex[is]ted in the proph[e]ts mind which are not written. Concer[n]ing eternal glory."[11] Such talk of keys and locks and the unwritten contents of the minds of the Bible's original authors is typical of Smith's esoteric approach to Bible reading. He'd been calling out the imperfections of the written Bible since at least 1829. The Bible was mostly shadows and fleeting impressions. But it pointed a prophet's mind in the right direction.

Smith understood his Bible rereading as revelation from God that superseded as necessary the printed word. This prophetic spirit animated the dry bones of the Bible's texts. In January 1843, he preached that "old. & new Testame[n]t is

---

[6] Smith, *Relating Religion*, 179–96, deemphasizes the traditional etymology.
[7] *NewT*, 159.
[8] MS 782, folder 0001, CHL (dated incorrectly there as 1834). Smith, "Priesthood," 16–17.
[9] Buck, *Theological Dictionary*, 21; Kugel, *Read the Bible*, 22–25.
[10] *T&S* 4:14 (June 1, 1843): 220–22, continued in *T&S* 4:15 (June 15, 1843): 233–34. On Neibaur, see Woods, "Still a Jew." See also Bloom, *American Religion*, 77–128.
[11] *JSPJ3*, 20.

not the gospel.—as a map is not the country it represents. It tells what the gospel is."[12] Maps contain errors and even when perfectly accurate are not actually the territory they depict. Access to the territory required something more than just a map. In April 1843, Smith preached plainly that "God may correct the scriptur by me if he choose."[13] In October of that year he taught that five minutes of direct vision of heaven would teach the believer more than "read[ing] all that ever was writt[e]n on the subject," including all published scripture.[14] Discussing Bible translation in a major sermon in April 1844, Smith said, "I thank God for the old Book but more for the Holy Ghost."[15] He positioned himself as a prophet guided by the Holy Ghost who could see what other readers, including clergy and learned interpreters, couldn't.

Contemporary critics understood Smith's mode of Bible translation but cast it in an entirely different light. The anti-Mormon agitator Origen Bacheler, for example, complained, "this Mormon alteration of the Bible is not made by means of a critical examination of the original, according to the established rules of language; but by Smith's inspiration. No regard is paid to the original; Smith tells, not what it *is,* but what it *ought* to be. The Mormon edition of the Bible, therefore, is not a new translation, but a new revelation—another gospel."[16] Bacheler was right, as far as he went: Smith did not understand himself to be bound by the English text of the Protestant Bible. There was more to scripture in his view than all that.

Smith believed that the extra meaning hidden in the Bible text in antiquity was carried into the present by the spirit and power of God. A prophet/seer was the individual who recovered access to it.

Smith's Bible Timeline, 1829–1833

The choice of a starting point for Smith's Bible will be arbitrary, but I believe, if only for heuristic purposes, that a vision Smith had in 1829 is the moment when the New Translation budded off the Book of Mormon project. As Smith and Cowdery were pondering the fate of John as the author of Revelation, Smith had a vision of a lost papyrus of (part of) John's original Revelation that quickly solved the mystery of the ancient apostle's fate—he had, it turns out, chosen a transformation that allowed him to abide on earth as an immortal for the centuries until

---

[12] *JSPJ2,* 208–209.
[13] *JSPJ2,* 354.
[14] *JSPJ3,* 109.
[15] *WJS,* 345.
[16] Bacheler, *Mormonism Exposed,* 23–24.

Christ's return.[17] Recall that the Book of Mormon started with the prophet Lehi seeing a vision of a temporally dislocated Bible; in Smith's 1829 vision of John's Revelation, the Book of Mormon had formally reproduced its mechanisms for rereading the Bible into the nineteenth century. Smith, like Lehi, was reading a visionary Bible torn from its original time. Within just a few months of the publication of the Book of Mormon, Smith began in earnest to fulfill Moroni's prophecy in Ether 1 of a seeric translation.

Additional material came quickly. In June 1830 Smith dictated a visionary prologue to the canonized Book of Genesis (perhaps as an amplification of Numbers 12:8[18]). The inner circle soon called this prologue the "Visions of Moses," and that title is probably the best of the available options. The revelation engages the familiar text of Genesis (and in places the New Testament), but more than anything, we witness Moses experiencing the grand, panoramic visions of Moriancumer, Lehi, and Nephi. The kindred Prophecy of Enoch appears to have been dictated six months later, in November–December 1830.

The official Joseph Smith History reported the genesis of the Prophecy of Enoch. "Much conjecture and conversation frequently occurred among the saints, concerning the books mentioned and referred to, in various places in the old and new testaments, which were now nowhere to be found. The common remark was, they are 'lost books'; but it seems the apostolic churches had some of these writings, as Jude mentions or quotes the prophecy of Enoch the seventh from Adam. To the joy of the little flock, which in all, from Colesville to Canandaigua, numbered about seventy members, did the Lord reveal the following doings of olden time from the prophecy of Enoch."[19] According to an outside observer, the texts contained "a more particular description of the creation of the world, and a history of Adam and his family, and othe[r] sketches of the antediluvian world, which Moses neglected to record."[20] That outside account was a reasonable summary. These two texts, focused on the primeval history, were the core of a new book of scripture.

These early visions were meant to define the shape of the overall project—John Whitmer labeled his copy of the translation manuscript, "The Book of the Generations of Adam," an allusion to Genesis 5:1 and the Books of Remembrance.[21] The new project, like the rest of Smith's work, was concerned with interconnecting generations across time and assuring that God's voice was not stilled.

---

[17] *JSPMRB*, 15–16. The visionary parchment of D&C 7 does not explicitly identify itself as a portion of John's Revelation, but that is its most straightforward interpretation.
[18] Givens, *Greatest Price*, 37.
[19] Joseph Smith History, vol. A-1, 80–81, CHL.
[20] *JSPD1*, 359, quoting *Painesville Telegraph* 2 (January 18, 1831).
[21] *JSPD1*, 359.

This New Translation continued the work of the Book of Mormon to transform the Bible. Contemporary observers recognized this fact. A Baptist reported of Smith's New Translation: "The Gospels too, we are given by them to understand, are so mutilated and altered as to convey little of the instruction which they should convey. . . . Our present Bible is to be altered and restored to its primitive purity, by Smith, the present prophet of the Lord, and some books to be added of great importance, which have been lost."[22] This was how the early Saints perceived their mandate; Smith and his collaborators saw their work as a necessary mark of modern revelation, which they counterposed to the hopeless Protestant task of relying on Bible interpreters. In 1834, Cowdery called out the absurdity in his view of trying to save the Bible without revelation. Bible interpreters, he said, admit that "no man can understand, because they are all metaphors and types, and the Author of them long since ceased to speak to men; and the whole must remain at last as it was in the beginning!"[23] Even Bible interpretation was fruitless without modern revelation. This was a need the New Translation could meet.

The formal Bible project seems to have moved in a different direction when Sidney Rigdon joined it in late 1830. Rigdon converted in November 1830, arriving to Smith's side on December 10, after the Visions of Moses and at least half of the Prophecy of Enoch had already been dictated.[24] Smith rapidly put this learned convert to work. Rigdon's charge to assist in the translation came in December 1830, as a "38th Commandment" subtitled "Sidneys call to writing for Joseph &c."[25] Speaking in the name of Christ, Smith calls for his auditors to "become the sons of God," a promise that echoes Moses 6:68 (the midpoint in the Prophecy of Enoch, suggesting that Rigdon joined the effort sometime after the first half of the Prophecy of Enoch).[26] Smith then acknowledges Rigdon's famous agitation on behalf of spiritual gifts, explicitly calling Rigdon an Elijah who had prepared the way for the Latter-day Saint Restoration. Protestants are reprimanded for "their folly & their abominations shall be made manifest, in the eyes of all People."[27] In place of the cessationist Protestant ministers, God will use "the weak things of the world"—the "unlearned" and "dispised"—to initiate Christ's return.[28] The revelation then reminds Rigdon that God had "sent forth

---

[22] Gutjahr, *American Bible*, 153, citing Mulder and Mortensen, *Among the Mormons*, 74.
[23] *EMS* 2:18 (March 1834): 141.
[24] Jackson, *Book of Moses*, 1–52. John Whitmer's recollection that Rigdon joined the effort before the start of the Prophecy of Enoch (*JSPH2*, 15–17; *T&S* 4:22 [October 1, 1843]: 336) appears incorrect.
[25] *JSPR1*, 63.
[26] I'm unpersuaded by suggestions (e.g., Cirillo, "Enochic Tradition") that Rigdon drove the content for the Prophecy of Enoch. He didn't arrive at Smith's side until it was half completed, his imprint on the later project was in the vein of Campbell's *Sacred Writings*, and the content comports well with the Visions of Moses, which was completed before Rigdon's arrival.
[27] *JSPR1*, 63.
[28] *JSPR1*, 65.

the fullness of my Gospel by the hand of my servent Joseph," a probable reference to the Book of Mormon. The crucial next step is a charge for the Bible translation that God had given to Smith: Rigdon and his prophet will receive "the Keys of the mystery of those things which have been sealed, even things which were from the foundation of the world."[29] The authorizing revelation thus approved of esoteric reading as a mainstay of the translation effort. Contextually the Prophecy of Enoch was one of those promised keys for sealed things.

Rigdon learns that the Holy Ghost/Comforter will direct them if Smith stayed steady: "the comforter, the Holy Ghost, that knoweth all things" will provide the revelation they needed for their joint projects. With that preamble, the revelation then states, "the scriptures shall be given even as they are in mine own bosom, to the salvation of mine own elect for th[e]y will hear my voice, & shall see me, & shall not be asleep, & shall abide the day of my coming, for they shall be purified, even as I am pure."[30] These clauses lay out Smith's vision for the New Translation in clear terms. The Bible translation was to transport primordial scripture (that which resides in God's "bosom") to the present. When that primordial word arrived at human ears, it was for their "salvation," which entails a purification to make them capable of abiding God's presence. In other words, Smith's transformation of scripture would transform human beings. God's word—translated through Restoration scripture—had the power to save.

The revelation then proposes another task for Rigdon, which draws on his theological knowledge and training. Rigdon is to preach and "call on the Holy Prophets to prove his words, as they shall be given him."[31] As was typical for Smith, this project and its two leaders would serve two purposes: (1) an objective appeal to evidential Christianity—proving doctrines from the Bible—and (2) a metaphysically abundant scripture. It would be facile to maintain a strict division of labor, claiming that Rigdon directed the first purpose and Smith the second. But the general spirit of the distinction is probably true.

Rigdon and Smith took seriously the mandate to justify Restoration claims in the controversies with other Protestants. Under Rigdon's influence, the project became more a task of fine-tuning the English text to solve its obvious problems, albeit with intermittent glimmers of Smith's esoteric readings.

Rigdon continued to play an important, perhaps dominant, role through 1833. When announcing the completion of the first full pass through the Bible, Rigdon used the first person plural to indicate that he and Smith had "finished the translating of the Scriptures for which we returned gratitude to our heavenly father," at a time when Frederick Williams was in fact serving as the primary

---

[29] *JSPR1*, 65.
[30] *JSPR1*, 65.
[31] *JSPR1*, 67.

scribe.[32] Similarly, Rigdon was the one in June 1833 to report that they had not recently found any lost books of the Bible in their work on the New Translation.[33] Rigdon clearly saw himself as jointly responsible for the New Translation once he began working on it.

Some debate whether Smith finished his New Translation of the Bible. The complete text was never published in his lifetime and only exists in an attempt at a fair copy. One interpretive line noticed emendations on the manuscripts, assumed they were Smith's, and inferred that Smith continued to modify that fair copy until the end of his life. Later scholarship suggested that, on the contrary, the manuscript revisions were written by individuals whose timing of participation ruled out dates after 1833. This later scholarship has also observed that Smith was seeking to publish rather than continue the translation after 1833.[34] Smith spent substantial rhetorical energy seeking support for publication, trying to settle problems of what format it would be published in, and what scriptures it would be united with (especially the Book of Mormon).[35] He wanted to be the one to control its final format, which may have impeded publication.[36]

The idea that Smith's Bible translation was complete may have served to support the hopes of some Latter-day Saint scholars to consider the New Translation canonical.[37] The reality, though, is that Smith was always revising. He edited most of his scriptures even after publication.[38] In addition, in 1835 Smith quoted an aspect of the Prophecy of Enoch (relating to corporeal resurrection) that is missing from extant texts.[39] More importantly, though, Smith spent his entire career retranslating the Bible. He was not alone in the attempt.

Context and Competition

Smith joined a growing chorus of Bible translators. By the last few decades of the nineteenth century, there were thirty-five new translations published to compete with the King James Bible, thirty-one of which were by Americans.[40] Almost all reused prior work, with varying degrees of attribution. These new translators all understood that the English Bible was imperfect and hoped to improve its

---

[32] *JSPD3*, 166, with a similar claim shortly thereafter: *JSPD3*, 167. See also *JSPD3*, 5.
[33] *JSPD3*, 149.
[34] Jackson, "Genesis."
[35] *JSPD3*, 68.
[36] *JSPD2*, 267, and *JSPD3*, 154.
[37] Thus *NewT*, vii, 7–10, 13, and Jackson, "Genesis."
[38] Smith revised multiple revelations both for the 1833 Book of Commandments and 1835 Doctrine and Covenants. Although less extensive, Smith revised the text of the Book of Mormon in places for the second and third editions.
[39] *JSPD5*, 55.
[40] Gutjahr, *American Bible*, 91.

doctrinal clarity and relevance to America's nineteenth century. Many, perhaps most, of the Bible translations in America involved preexisting English texts—often but not always the King James. Few of the creators had the time, energy, and skill to undertake a full retranslation; most thought King James was in the ballpark, even as they loved to criticize it.

Most relevant to the Saints was Alexander Campbell, whose own "New Translation"—intended to advance New Testamentism in place of the sectarianisms of early America—was the most direct competitor to Smith's and Rigdon's project.[41] Smith and Campbell fought publicly for most of Smith's career.[42] Campbell relied on translations from the Griesbach text by Scottish divines. His own changes were, in his phrase from the title page, "various emendations," albeit with a sarcastic assault on the notorious italics of the King James translators, changes in key theological words, and a preface and appendix.[43]

After Rigdon joined, Smith's New Translation became more self-consciously a direct competitor to Campbell's popular New Testament edition. Rigdon and Smith began to mirror fairly consistently Campbell's technique of making minor adjustments to preexisting translations, albeit with King James as the base text, rather than Campbell's mélange of recent scholarly translations.

While ultimately differentiable, the projects of Campbell and Smith/Rigdon are importantly similar. Both attempted to wrest control of the Bible from mainstream Protestant churches. Both were intensely primordialist, seeking to free the Christian world from the theological tyrannies of the King James Bible. Campbell had only one base text—the Griesbach New Testament—available to him, and he approached it with all the learning and iconoclastic defiance he could muster. Smith, on the other hand, cracked the canon wide open, inserting several new parabiblical works and seeing in spare English words and phrases a primordial vastness.

The Methodist founder John Wesley (1703–1791) published his *Explanatory Notes upon the New Testament* in 1755, which combined "small alteration[s]" of the King James text with extensive commentary for "plain unlettered men."[44] Adam Clarke, in the form of a commentary derived from Wesley, offered textual corrections in the apparatus. Noah Webster did his part to make the Bible more readable. Webster felt that cleaning up the basic English would vastly improve intelligibility and decrease sectarian confusion, independent of any primary connection to the ancient Greek or Hebrew

---

[41] "The New Translation," *The Christian Baptist*, 7 vols. in 1 (Cincinnati: D.S. Burnett, 1835): 326–27. See discussion in Perry, "Joseph Smith's Bibles," 766–67.
[42] See, e.g., *JSPD4*, 169–70.
[43] Campbell, *Sacred Writings*; Daniell, *Bible in English*, 648–49.
[44] Sheehan, *Enlightenment Bible*, 94. The quoted terms come from Wesley's preface.

texts. Thomas Belsham, an English Unitarian, published an "Improved Version" of the Bible in 1808, with an American edition in 1809.[45] Even Benjamin Franklin had an offering in the genre.[46] Some language reformers even believed that reprinting the Bible in a new, simpler alphabet would resolve ignorance about its contents.[47]

Farther outside the mainstream, the Shakers worked at reforming the scriptures, although they primarily did so through the merger of Word and Spirit in Ann Lee (with the exception of a transient flash of support for a newly revealed Shaker Bible in the 1840s[48]). A generation or so before Joseph Smith, Richard Brothers of New York published a millenarian reinterpretation of the Bible that included various minor emendations and revisions to the text of the English Bible. According to Brothers, "The alteration I have made in copying some of the prophecies, is by the direction and command of the Lord God."[49] Brothers was clear that there had been additions and subtractions from the original Bible, which he was repairing. Brothers wanted people to "place him at the head of a reconstituted Hebrew nation as king and high priest."[50] He wasn't so terribly different from Smith in both his primordialism and his emphasis on current revelation.

Nathaniel Whiting, a New York Baptist-turned-Millerite, published *The Good News of Our Lord Jesus, the Anointed* in 1849 with an Adventist publisher. His approach, rather like Smith's, was to use the King James as the base text and then amend it where it was unclear or where words were more Latinate than Anglo-Saxon. Like Campbell, Whiting picked certain words to highlight in his translation for anti-Catholic or anti-traditionalist ends, especially *baptizo* as "immerse."[51]

Smith and Rigdon thus participated in a culture of Bible translation that was primarily concerned with solving interdenominational conflicts without appearing to be doctrinal or extrabiblical. Smith was as happy as the next sectarian to pull the carpet out from under Presbyterian ministers or Congregationalist divines. But Smith had a much grander project in mind, one that would involve rereading and rewriting the Bible for the rest of his life.

---

[45] Lee, *Biblical Certainty*, 136.
[46] Holland, *Sacred Borders*, 69–70.
[47] Barton, *Something New*, 15, 23–28. Barton saw his "perfect" alphabet as a solution to many social problems.
[48] Stein, "America's Bibles," 173–74.
[49] Brothers, *Revealed Knowledge*, 47. I thank Don Bradley for this source.
[50] Juster, *Doomsayers*, 156.
[51] Gutjahr, *American Bible*, 106, and Paul, *Bible Translators*, 250–51. The text is Whiting, *Good News*.

Expanding Smith's Bible Translation

Like many of his contemporaries, Smith was concerned with excavating God's voice from beneath the rubble of centuries of human confusion and linguistic drift. In his biblical revisions and in the Book of Mormon, he used the language of translation to describe the work of overwriting, revising, salvaging, and looking beyond the King James Bible. Smith's focus was on moving past the English text.

Under the New Translation rubric, I consider the Visions of Moses, the Prophecy of Enoch, and Smith's revisions, annotations, and brief expansions of the King James text to be part of the New Translation. Contrary to precedent, I also include significant elements of his primary revelations. In doing so I am mindful of the fluidity of the precedent Smith himself set. He often sought to distinguish among his various projects, although he never did so definitively. In a March 1833 meeting, he distinguished "the translating of the prophets" from his work to "receive revelations to unfold the mysteries of the Kingdom."[52] And yet he used his translating room as his general revelation room, employed similar methods to reveal texts, and tied many of his texts explicitly and persistently to the Bible. While there likely are subtle differences that may be important, these juxtapositions at a minimum suggest the importance of broadening the scope of what we classify as Smith's New Translation of the Bible.

A variety of documents beyond the fair copy of the Smith-Rigdon project clearly belong with the New Translation. Interwoven through the formal Bible project came other revelations that were similar in format and content. In my view, large portions of the collection of prophetic texts Smith revealed belong with the New Translation. Exemplary texts include the already mentioned D&C 7 (1829) as well as D&C 42 (February 1831), D&C 45–46 (March 1831), D&C 76 (February 1832), D&C 84:77–85 (September 1832), D&C 86 (December 1832), D&C 88 (December 1832–January 1833), D&C 93:7–17 (May 1833), and D&C 113:1–6 (March 1838). In all of these texts Smith repurposed, reformed, and reread Bible texts in the same ways he did in the formal New Translation project. His creative targums extended across his scriptural corpus.

Smith and his church collected his primary religious texts for publication as *The Book of Commandments* in 1833, but anti-Mormon vigilantes destroyed the press and type. Two years later, operating from the relative stronghold of Kirtland rather than the disputed outpost in Missouri, the Saints tried again. The new scripture was called the Doctrine and Covenants. This volume was to be the modern Latter-day Saint Bible, "the word of the Lord,"[53] or the "faith articles and covinants of the Latter Day Saints."[54]

---

[52] *JSPD3*, 42.
[53] *JSPD4*, 218.
[54] *JSPD4*, 393.

The "doctrine" in the title replaced the earlier *Articles* in the church's first governing statement from 1831. The committee tasked with the project hoped to provide "a perfect understanding of the doctrine believed by this society."[55] Smith preferred doctrines to creeds—even if it's not always clear what the difference is—and the new title emphasized that preference.[56]

Among the doctrines presented in this new scripture were the *Lectures on Faith*. Chosen in part because they "embrac[ed] the important doctrine of salvation,"[57] the *Lectures on Faith* read like an exegetical mimesis of the New Testament Letter to the Hebrews, wrestled into the idioms of Common Sense theology. The *Lectures* often grappled with the meaning of Bible texts, especially the cryptic language about faith and priesthood in Hebrews. The *Lectures* appear to be cowritten by Smith and Rigdon and may have been their next major project after the New Translation collaboration. A twentieth-century campaign to decanonize the *Lectures on Faith* emphasized Rigdon's heavy hand,[58] but Smith's radical theology is spread throughout the texts.

The term "covenants" in the title Doctrine and Covenants pointed to the meanings of Restoration scripture. Although the tradition in English Bibles was to render the Greek term *diatheke* as "testament," the term was also appropriately translated *covenant*, as it connoted an ongoing relationship between God and humans. A variety of commenters, including Alexander Campbell, acknowledged the difficulties of rendering *diatheke* into English.[59] Smith's choice of the term covenant—while perhaps echoing Puritan covenant theology[60]—also identified this new book of scripture with the structure of the Bible.

There would be, in other words, an Old Testament, a New Testament, and a Latter-day Testament. Further textual evidence suggests that Smith intended his book as another new American Bible. Between The Book of Commandments and the 1835 Doctrine and Covenants, Smith and his associates changed the name for discrete texts from "chapter" to "section," a designation that has persisted to the present day. In this terminological approach they may have been following Campbell's practice in his *Sacred Writings*. Campbell divided the text into logical "sections," independent of the established chapter divisions. Smith and Rigdon also changed "Gospel" to "Testimony" in the titles for the Gospels, presumably

---

[55] *JSPD4*, 235.
[56] In the preface to the 1835 Doctrine and Covenants, they described "articles of religious faith," even as they worried about potential backlash against such articles. *JSPD4*, 236.
[57] *JSPD4*, 459.
[58] Van Wagoner et al., "Decanonization."
[59] Thus Campbell, *Sacred Writings*, 470 (page 68 of the Appendix) and Buck, *Theological Dictionary*, 569.
[60] Givens, *Feeding the Flock*.

in deference to Campbell.[61] If true, this again marks the competition between Smith's and Campbell's projects of Bible translation.

Smith's covenants included a wide array of documentary objects. There were texts dictated in the name of God (e.g., sections 1, 42, 133; much as the Book of Mormon was dictated in the name of ancient American prophets), individualized instructions (e.g., sections 25, 34, 36, 39) or rebukes (e.g., sections 3, 9, 56), and notes jotted during an oracular Question and Answer session (e.g., sections 77, 78, 131). Most of these texts are biblical in form, word choice, syntax, and aspiration. As with the Book of Mormon, scriptural clauses and images were the building blocks of the verbal revelations contained in the Doctrine and Covenants. Where the Book of Mormon focused disproportionately on Isaiah, the Doctrine and Covenants emphasized the Gospel of John and the Apocalypse ("Revelation") of John. Taxonomically, substantial swaths of the Doctrine and Covenants are part of Smith's project of Bible translation. Smith's revelatory and translation texts should be understood in community with each other.[62]

One theologically pregnant Bible revision came in an 1838 description of an 1823 encounter (later canonized as D&C 2). In Smith's account, Moroni had retranslated the book of Malachi in the encounters between the angel and the prophet leading up to the receipt of the gold plates. Moroni adds to Malachi 4 the promise that Elijah will "reveal unto you the Priesthood."[63] This revision referred forward (and perhaps backward, given its late date of composition) to an 1836 experience with Elijah in Kirtland, also canonized (D&C 110). Smith reported that Elijah brought him the temple priesthood in fulfillment of Malachi's expanded prophecy. The generations of time—the hearts of children and fathers—were thus interconnected.

The 1832 Vision (D&C 76) is another spiritual experience that belongs with the New Translation. Smith and Rigdon reported—much like the panoramic visions of Enoch and Moses—a simultaneously hierarchical and universalist glimpse of the afterlife. This new vision of hierarchical afterlife glories, most of which are internal to the traditional Christian heaven, is a targum of John 5:29 that also engages John 14:2, 1 Corinthians 15, and several other passages. The Olive Leaf revelation (D&C 88), given several months later as an expansion and reinforcement of the themes introduced in the Vision, continues the approach. In the Olive Leaf, Smith reconceives the Parable of the Laborers (Matthew 20) in a staggering reinterpretation of human potential—he reports that the prize given the laborers no matter when they begin their work in the vineyard is "equality"

---

[61] Thus Campbell, *Sacred Writings*, 52, 54, 56, 60, et passim. On "testimony," see Barney, "Ancient Texts," 88.

[62] The claim of, e.g., *JSPD3*, 83, that D&C 93 is distinct from the New Translation, for example, seems obviously wrong.

[63] *JSPH1*, 222, 224 (Draft 2).

with Christ. Smith was not just proposing a new path to Calvinist salvation, he was expanding the notion of salvation itself. The 1833 True Light revelation (D&C 93, esp. 7–17) constitutes a visionary preface—largely in the name of Christ—to the Prologue of John that plays with Christian Platonic imagery. The Gospel of John spoke about a "light of men" that "shineth in darkness," a "true Light, which lighteth every man." In Smith's hands, the "light and the Redeemer of the world; the Spirit of truth . . . came into the world, because the world was made by him," and then explains how the light and humans interacted: "Man was also in the beginning with God. Intelligence, or the light of truth, was not created or made, neither indeed can be." Once again, Smith's revelations reconfigured Bible texts in support of a distinctive theology.[64]

Smith often used his Bible rereadings for exigent circumstance, applying the hermeneutic strategy of his Book of Mormon prophet Nephi to "liken the scriptures" to the readers. This is of course a common way to read the Bible in many communities. In Smith's hands, this practice created new scripture. On March 8, 1831, Smith issued a revelation (D&C 46) that confronted the problems of decorum. Kirtland contained multiple varieties of Latter-day Saints, and some of them practiced an especially charismatic form of worship—trances and frenzies, speaking in tongues, healings, and visions to rival the wildest camp meeting.[65] As part of this revelation, Smith revisits 1 Corinthians 12, a chapter that the Book of Mormon had already reread (Moroni 10:10–18). When Smith and Rigdon approached the passage in Corinthians in the formal New Translation, they only altered 12:31, to eliminate Paul's disparagement of the spiritual gifts he had just enumerated. Instead of Paul praising the gifts but then pointing toward a "more excellent way" beyond those gifts, the revision made clear that the return of spiritual gifts through the Restoration was in fact that "more excellent way."[66] In D&C 46, the enumeration of gifts occurs without much commentary, but in place of Paul's equivocations in favor of community (he recognized that the charismatic gifts threatened to break apart the church at Corinth), the text (46:26) simply indicates that "all these gifts come from God, for the benefit of the children of God." This 1831 revelation is an especially clear example of the integration of the New Translation project with Smith's other scripture in the early 1830s.

Similarly, Smith and Cowdery were attempting in 1831 to map out a set of rules for the church, a replacement for the Methodist *Discipline* that many converts would have known.[67] Making their church both ancient and modern,

---

[64] Brown, "Materialists," 16–19. Notably, Smith's true light theology resonates with contemporary Protestant "vitalist" theologies—Grainger, *Church in the Wild*, 8, 98.
[65] Staker, *Historical Setting*.
[66] *NewT*, 507.
[67] Stapley, *Power of Godliness*, 5–6.

Smith and Cowdery inserted an updated Decalogue into the *Laws of the Church*, this time adding consequences to the prohibited sins. By way of example, the new text specifies that murder cannot be forgiven and supplements the prohibition against adultery with New Testament language.[68]

The always hazy boundary between new scripture and exegesis is engaged directly in D&C 86, an 1832 revelation that came in the midst of the New Translation. Smith characterizes it as "a Revelation explaining the Parable [of] the wheat and the tears."[69] The passage in Matthew shares a series of agricultural parables and an interpretation that contrasts crops and weeds and comments on the difficulty of separating young plants before the harvest. Smith moves through the parable item by item to explain its images—the field is the world, for example, and the sowers are the original apostles. He clarifies that the sowing of tares was the apostasy that his Restoration overturned. He then speaks of the lineal priesthood (chapter 3), an ever-important topic in his theology. Smith makes scripture directly relevant to his people, adds some basic interpretation, and stamps his approval. In the hands of a Protestant minister, this might have been a Sunday sermon. For Smith, though, it was a revelation that brought the Bible into the Latter-day Saint magisterium. Notably this was a case where the New Testament itself offered a clarification (Matthew 13:18–23): Smith was doing the Bible one better.[70]

How to classify a given text isn't always clear. How much Bible material, reworked how extensively, and in what company constitutes a translation for Smith? He was continuously reading, reworking, and repurposing the Bible in all of his revelatory work. Take the single verse of D&C 29:13, for example: "For a trump shall sound both long and loud, even as upon Mount Sinai, and all the earth shall quake, and they shall come forth—yea, even the dead which died in me, to receive a crown of righteousness, and to be clothed upon, even as I am, to be with me, that we may be one." The verse begins its eschatological exploration with reference to a "long and loud" trumpet as on Mount Sinai, an allusion to Exodus 19:17–20 that frames the human resurrection as a typological recapitulation of God's sacred encounter with the Hebrews as they wandered the deserts after leaving Egypt. That early Hebrew encounter with God prefigures the experience of resurrecting the Saints at the end times. The next clause comes from Matthew 27:51–53, the resurrection of the dead at Christ's death. Then Smith visits 2 Timothy 4:8 for his reference to the crown of righteousness; and he appropriates the term "clothed upon" from 2 Corinthians 5:2 to refer to resurrection as the assumption of a heavenly body, mimicking the resurrected body

---

[68] *JSPD1*, 251.
[69] *JSPD2*, 324.
[70] Matthew 13:6–43; 3–8 is one parable, 18–23 interpretive language, and 24–30 another parable.

of Christ. Smith then includes an echo of John 17:11 to bring humans into unity with God in the resurrection. Smith thus weaves together Moses, Yahweh, Jesus, and unity in resurrection figured by the Matthean text.[71] In one long sentence, Smith retools at least five separate Bible tropes.

We could protest that Smith is using scriptural commonplaces as building blocks for texts. That is certainly true in certain passages. But this specific example raises the question of how much textual manipulation is required to constitute a translation and when the repurposing of tropes might itself constitute translation. The divisions are blurrier than they might appear at first blush. This fluidity and overlap need to stay in mind as we consider the other texts of the New Translation.

The Old Made New Again

In this section I inspect a specific example of prolonged and intricate exegesis that exemplifies what Smith was doing in his New Translation. Ever concerned with the Bible's primeval history, he transformed Genesis 3, the story of human exile from the garden orchard at Eden.

In the Hebrew text, immediately after God creates the woman, the narrator comments that the humans are naked but unashamed. The text appears, then, to explain how it is that humans came to wear clothing: they ate fruit from a tree that changed their understandings of primal nudity. But this isn't a simple etiological tale—other things are afoot in the Garden. Humans eat the fruit because a trickster snake misrepresents God's instructions. Eve counters with another misrepresentation of God's commands, and then she realizes aloud that the forbidden fruit is actually palatable, so she shares it with Adam. Once God discovers their disobedience, he curses the snake (humans will hate and murder snakes), the woman (child-bearing and/or rearing will be painful), and the man (agricultural work will be difficult). As part of this general cursing, God decrees that humankind will return to the earth (i.e., die) because they are after all, of the soil—the word "human," in its Latinate forms and in Hebrew, has reference to the earth or earthiness, as opposed to heavenly beings. The humans are banished, and angelic sentries with immolating swords prevent their reentry into the sacred orchard. That's the Hebrew story, more or less.

---

[71] The textual issues are often complex. Some commentators have misunderstood, for example, Smith's reference to the curse for the wicked in Ezekiel, maintaining that it should be seen as a reference to Zechariah 14:12 (*JSPD1*, 180, cf. Brown, *In Heaven*, 36–37), when in fact Smith was invoking the image of devouring fire from Ezekiel 15 (esp. 4). Smith was arguing, as he always did, for the unity of the biblical texts by maintaining that Zechariah and Ezekiel tell the same story.

Smith's radical rereading of Genesis 3 began in the Book of Mormon. There the founding patriarch Lehi gathers his family around his deathbed. He tells them the stories that matter most as he prepares to depart. He wants them to understand the story of the Garden of Eden, which he retells as one of tragic trade-offs and ultimate blessings. (We encountered parts of this sermon in chapter 3.) Lehi doesn't quote directly from Genesis, but he coins a memorable reinterpretation of the Fall as a step toward bliss: "Adam fell that men might be; men are that they might have joy" (2 Nephi 2:25). Beyond this sermon, the Book of Mormon sticks to the notion of a Fall that sets into motion God's plan for human salvation.[72]

When Joseph Smith first began his New Translation, his Visions of Moses retold the Genesis 3 story with a long and important addition that is now Moses 4. In Smith's new revelation, we learn that Satan was not actually the snake—contrary to Christian typological readings—but he was the inspiration for the snake's behaviors. Second, as we saw in chapter 3, Satan's plan from the beginning has been to block the human exercise of moral agency, or the freedom to act for themselves. Satan "sought to destroy the agency of man," and his rebellion caused him to "bec[o]me Satan, yea even the devil" (4:3–4). Having become a fallen angel, Satan converts the devilish snake to be one of his minions (4: 5–6). The story as recounted in Moses then ends with the expulsion of Eve and Adam from the Garden of Eden.

A parenthetical remark at the end of Moses 4 then indicates something of the mechanisms of translation both anciently and modernly. God explains to Joseph Smith (who was dictating to an assistant) that "these are the words which I spake unto my servant Moses . . . and I have spoken them unto you." Then comes an injunction to secrecy that is reminiscent of the secrecy by which Smith regulated access to the gold plates. These special revelations of the first humans were to be shown only "to them that believe." The Moses writings are thus doubly esoteric—they are pregnant with ancient meaning, and they are to be kept secret from the probing eyes of unbelievers.

Smith returns to the point a few verses later (5:10–11) to make the point even clearer and to tie the illuminations of the New Translation back to the Book of Mormon sermon. In Lehi's narration, Adam and Eve both turn to the reader to disclose their newly acquired revelatory understanding of the reasons for their fortunate Fall. They see that the only agency-preserving path forward was to fall into moral capability and culpability, to have and love offspring, and to choose to be obedient to God's law. This comment in Moses extended Lehi's observation that moral agency can only function in the presence of opposition (2 Nephi 2:10–13). The perfect peace of Eden was an infantile fantasy. There is no meaningful

---

[72] 2 Nephi 9:6, Mosiah 4:7, Alma 12:22–33.

life without tension, turmoil, and heartache. This conflict appears to be a feature of the universe. Satan is cast as a bumbling enabler in a master plan that required human confrontation with evil. Only in opposition could anything truly good arise.

These texts are making a practical argument tied to the justice of God. As Lehi's family wonders why exactly they are cursed to wander through the desert wastes rather than stay in their comfortable homes in Jerusalem, Lehi responds that their luxury in the capital was a false security much like Eden before the Fall. This was both a practical and a metaphysical claim. Eve and Adam discovered what Lehi's family learned—the hollowness at the center of Eden's innocence, and the need to escape it.

This exegesis of the Fall spills over into an independent revelation text, another reminder that Smith's rereading of the Bible doesn't divide neatly into distinct projects. The 1830 revelation (D&C 29) that we encountered earlier demonstrates this overlap. Its first half is tied to Isaiah, Malachi, and John's Apocalypse and the Millennial reign of peace, which is explicitly modeled on the idylls of Eden. Then the revelation transitions back into the first times. In verses 35 and 36, we encounter the concepts of Moses 4, signaling that the end times are a return to the beginning. Smith argues that the Fall signals the entry into mortality, which will end in the eschaton with Christ's millennial reign.

In a partial chiasmus (29:32) on a theme introduced the verse prior—"First spiritual, secondly temporal, which is the beginning of my work; and again, first temporal, and secondly spiritual, which is the last of my work"—Smith argues that the spiritual precedes the temporal and then the temporal precedes the spiritual. What Smith has in mind here takes some careful reading, but the symmetry between beginning and ending appears to be the interpretive key. The first spiritual and temporal is his account of the dual creation accounts of Genesis. While the existence of two creation narratives is a famous problem in Bible criticism, for Smith they were a marker of abundant reality. The "beginning" in the chiastic couplet of D&C 29 refers to the creation of the world: God creates the world in spiritual form before creating it in temporal/physical form. Eve and Adam exist in a species of infantile physicality before bursting into full-fledged temporal life with the Fall. Following the precedent of Alma 12, the crux of the miniature chiasmus is human mortality, while the resolution of that chiasmus points to the death foretold as the consequence of human mortality created by the Fall. Temporal in the second half ("the last of my work") refers to mortal death, and spiritual refers to the resurrection into the millennium into a postmortal paradise. But this time the people in Eden have been transformed by their transient temporality. They have fallen heaven-ward, through mortality. This time when they approach the Edenic paradise, they do so as transfigured beings rather than raw potentialiaty. Smith's rereading of the Bible's etiology story for human mortality—extending across the Book of Mormon, Doctrine and Covenants, and New Translation—proposes a revised Fall that sees deep meaning in human mortality.[73]

There are other markers of continuity between the Book of Mormon and the New Translation of the Bible, including Smith's ongoing commitment to cyclical dispensationalism. The scriptural timelines remained jumbled up, with the future often intruding on the past. In Smith's version of Genesis 15:9–12, for example, Abraham has explicit knowledge of the coming of Christ, just as the ancient Lehites had. Similarly, Smith's revisions of Exodus 34:1–2 indicate the ways in which what came to be called the Mosaic Law—so often damned with faint praise in the Book of Mormon[74]—arose because ancient Israel was not qualified for the entire Gospel system that had been revealed in and immediately after Eden.

Two key themes predominate: first, the Fall as a story about human deification through the infusion of divine essence and human choice, exercised with the protection of Jesus as Savior; and second, the temporal admixture in Smith's dispensationalism. They are twin components of his ongoing struggle to overcome the rent in the cosmos. The former is an ontological separation overcome, the latter a temporal separation spanned. Another key narrative within the New Translation project combines those two aspects in the mysterious figure of Enoch.

The Man-God Enoch

We encountered Enoch in chapter 3 as the patron of a heavenly community, the exemplar of human transformation, and a connection between humanity and God. We won't revisit those important concepts here. Instead, we'll consider what Joseph Smith's "Extracts from the Prophecy of Enoch" has to show about the nature of scriptural translation.

Enoch and his city were translated instead of dying, drawn bodily to heaven as they were transformed by the voyage through space. Enoch (alongside Elijah) represents the ontological purification of humanity.[75] In his body and life story we see a microcosm of the grand human narrative initiated by the Fall as humans are remade ontologically over the course of their mortal lives.

The Prophecy of Enoch portrays several interactions between Enoch and God. Enoch experiences an ascension with an associated panoramic vision in which space and time are obliterated. In it, he is caught up to a high mountain where he

---

[73] Smith continued to affirm this fortunate Fall narrative in an 1841 sermon: *JSPD8*, 30.
[74] See, e.g., 2 Nephi 11:4–5; Mosiah 13:30–31; 2 Nephi 25:24; Alma 25:15–16, 34:13–15.
[75] See, e.g., Nibley, *Enoch*.

and God together confront the vast scope of human history. And they weep. In those tears we see the reason why the Fall is bittersweet rather than simply fortunate. Mortality is a time for the exercise of human agency in the presence of evil that gradually and painfully transfigures the children of God. However grand the ultimate outcome, it still hurts to watch. Enoch is thus blessed with the fraught awareness of the sum total of humanity and its difficult plight. The solution is implicit in the vision and explicit in the story of Enoch's city. It is human beings' act of coming together in the shadow of God that builds them into deity and transfigures them in preparation for the return to Eden.

Formal considerations also matter for this text. Specifically, the Prophecy of Enoch displays impressive integration with Smith's other scriptural texts, especially the Book of Mormon. First, the story of Enoch's city being saved in the buildup to the Noachian flood precisely mirrors the main narrative of the Book of Mormon about a righteous remnant being preserved from universal destruction. On this analogy, Enoch is Lehi, the world is Jerusalem, and the flood is the Babylonian invasion of Jerusalem. While the Enoch story ends with the righteous flight from the wicked world, that is where the Book of Mormon begins.

The Prophecy of Enoch is also deeply concerned with the power of language, which is another connection to the Book of Mormon. The Enoch narrative mirrors the stories about Moriancumer, the great seer possessed of divine language (and $Nephi_2$, who shares in Moriancumer's power). Enoch is similarly mighty in speech—"all nations feared greatly, so powerful was the word of Enoch, and so great was the power of the language which God had given him" (Moses 7:13). Earlier in the Prophecy of Enoch (6:8–9), Smith revises Genesis 5:1–2. He repurposes this brief summary of the work of human creation to read "in the day that God created man in the likeness of God made he him in the image of his own body."[76] Thus the Book of Mormon and the Prophecy of Enoch had the same thing to say about divine embodiment.

The connection to language persisted into the reception of the text. On February 27, 1833, Church members (perhaps David Patten) sang a Song of Zion (an early genre of glossolalia) about the Prophecy of Enoch.[77] The content is a lyrical retelling of Enoch, perhaps by Sidney Rigdon, and the form is important. The genre is named for the sacred city of Enoch, and it was a glossolalic performance subsequently rendered into English. These worshipers thus participated in a process perhaps similar to that by which Smith generated the text, demonstrating the ongoing fecundity of metaphysical scripture. It was not the first time Smith had linked his nineteenth-century followers to the ancient prophet

---

[76] *NewT*, 97.
[77] *JSPMRB*, 508–11, cf. EMS 1:12 (May 1833): 96. On glossolalic Songs of Zion, see *JSPD4*, 271, 405; Howe, *Mormonism Unvailed*, 135.

Enoch. In a December 1830 letter to the Church in Colesville, Smith reported that "Enoch, the seventh from Adam beheld our day and rejoiced."[78] This comment tied the current believers to their precedent in the Hebrew Bible. This was the kind of ongoing connection that Smith hoped to create with his scriptures.

In March 1831, Smith returned to the topic in D&C 45:11–14. There he revealed that God "received [Enoch] unto myself" as an act tied to the long-promised day of millennial peace. Implicitly, the Saints had their path lighted by this shimmery figure from mythic past and future. As he further worked through the nature of this physical translation (45:16–17), Smith revealed that the Enochians didn't have to suffer through separation of spirit and body, a fate perhaps available to the believers who happened to be alive at the time of Christ's return. Those events of past, present, and future are then joined together in his reworking (45:18–20) of the Olivet discourse (Matt 24–25, Mark 13, and Luke 21). Of note for the arguments for continuity in the various translation projects, Smith also signals his move from pure visionary reports into translation of the Bible (45:15–16).

In the 1835 revelation on priesthood (D&C 107), Enoch returns again, as we saw in chapter 3. Here I draw attention to the fact that this 1835 scripture reminds us that the New Translation is constantly spilling from one scriptural project to another, all of them concerned with rereading the Bible. Recognizing the unities in this sprawling textual corpus motivates a careful consideration of what Smith and others understood the broader project of rereading the Bible to be about.

Interpretation

What exactly was Smith doing with his New Translation? Some Latter-day Saints have understood him to be seeing ancient protomanuscripts, perhaps in Hebrew, Aramaic, or Greek, and filling in lacunae in the modern text. Others have felt that he was merely addressing nineteenth-century theological controversies by giving himself control over the text of the Bible.[79] Still others have seen him as trying to enter the literature of the biblical concordance, mapping out the interconnections of the ancient corpus of texts as he pursued possible resonances throughout scripture.[80] For example, the Latter-day Saint classicist Thomas Wayment argues that when Smith retranslated a particular verse in his New Translation, he commonly did so by bringing in verbiage from other scriptural

---

[78] *JSPD1*, 216.
[79] Huggins, "Romans 7."
[80] Perry, "Joseph Smith's Bibles," 766, argues that Smith and Rigdon probably used Scott's Bible to make concordance-style substitutions into the text.

verses. His project was thus to harmonize all of scripture, drawing the Bible into one.[81] In that effort, Smith and Rigdon used Clarke's Methodist Bible commentary for filling in gaps in understanding, thus connecting aspects of their work to prior reading traditions.[82]

There's an element of truth in all of these accounts, but they strike me as incomplete. They don't seem to get at the ways that Smith was inhabiting scripture. He was being both esoteric and exoteric, learned and visionary. He was bringing all available resources to the project of healing the rift (as Barlow has aptly suggested[83]) at the center of creation. We don't have to see Smith as a pure-blooded Kabbalist to realize that he was participating in a long and widespread tradition. He stayed connected to metaphysically rich currents of Bible reading.

Smith for his part tended to think in terms of the effect he hoped to have on readers and the relationship he bore to the fulness that attended the primordial Bible. Smith explicitly saw what he was doing as "translating the fulness of the Scriptures."[84] He anticipated that his New Translation would unlock the secrets of the Bible *and* exegesis. An 1831 revelation (D&C 45) reported, "I say unto you it shall not be given unto you to know any farther then this until the New Testament be translated & in it all things shall be made known Wherefore I give unto you that ye may now Translate it that ye may be prepared for the things to come."[85]

Occasionally Smith's New Translation is straightforward about its commitment to metaphysical correspondence. In the Christological reflections of Moses 6, Jesus indicates, "And behold, all things have their likeness, and all things are created and made to bear record of me, both things which are temporal, and things which are spiritual; things which are in the heavens above, and things which are on the earth, and things which are in the earth, and things which are under the earth, both above and beneath: all things bear record of me" (6:63). This Neoplatonic-sounding aside makes clear to readers the deep infrastructure of the typology and likening that occurs throughout Smith's scripture.

Kabbalists thought that particular words, and even their individual letters, could contain meanings well beyond themselves. They could be portals into a life beyond. John Durham Peters comments, "Kabbalah is in part the reading of intent in things where no meaning was intended," riffing on Walter Benjamin's old aphorism about "read[ing] what was never written."[86] Smith would, I suspect,

---

[81] Wayment, "Joseph Smith Translation."

[82] While partial reliance on Clarke has been acknowledged for decades (e.g., Huggins, "Contemporary Source"), Wayment and Lemmon, "Smith's Bible," provides a more thorough treatment.

[83] Barlow, "Fractured Reality."

[84] *JSPD2*, 85.

[85] *JSPD1*, 279.

[86] Peters, *Speaking into the Air*, 204.

have protested that his esoteric reading was discovering primordial intent rather than inventing meaning from whole cloth. He understood himself to be making contact with the original authors through vision, visitation, and inspiration. He might have also noted that the modern resistance to such abundance in text (the possibility that intent can be metaphysically present) was part of the problem he was addressing with scripture. And Smith would have resisted the notion that his reading was purely mystical. It was also studious, even scholarly, and it was openly in discussion and disputation with Protestant peers, including Methodists and Baptists like Clarke and Campbell.

As was common in his intellectual and spiritual life, Smith was cutting orthogonally across the plane of modernity. He was, to put it more colloquially, ranging all over the map. The deeply metaphysical and extremely practical mode of his Bible rereading also spilled over into his more episodic acts of exegesis. He couldn't stop himself from constant, imaginative rereadings.

Marvelous Literalism and the Metaphysics of Reading

Shortly before he died, Smith employed a nearly Kabbalistic exegesis to decode the first sentence of the Hebrew Bible: God oversaw an entire council of Gods who tamed an unruly world that predated them. That Hebrew sentence (*Bereshit bara Elohim et hashamayim ve'et ha'aretz*) is even now a bit cryptic, but current scholarship suggests that it should read something like, "As God [a majestic plural] began to create heaven and earth." Smith disagreed. He saw the reference to beginnings (*bereshit*) as a nod to the "head" of a divine council. The verb translated *create* (*bara*) Smith saw as organization of preexisting matter, in open defiance of the standard Christian teaching of creation from nothing.[87]

We can see the imaginative path of association from the Hebrew words to Smith's exegesis, even while we acknowledge that modern scholars wouldn't agree with him.[88] This exegesis—as many another of his textual improvisations—tied his divine anthropology directly to the Bible text.[89] Smith wasn't aiming to agree with Protestant clerics or align with academic consensus. He was happy to use occasional tools of scholarship as additional portals into the world of his vivid exegesis. The New Translation never ended.

I have elsewhere labeled this approach "marvelous literalism."[90] I was quibbling with other proposed terms—"selective literalism" or "creative

---

[87] In that latter respect, Smith—whether he knew it or not—was following Plutarch's reading of Plato's *Timaeus*. Brague, *Wisdom of the World*, 136. Seixas transliterated *bara* as *baurau*.
[88] Barney, "Genesis 1:1."
[89] Some of Smith's disciples took the baton and ran with it. See, e.g., Brown, "'Paracletes.'"
[90] Brown, *In Heaven*, 11, 124, 245, 260, 262, 271.

literalism"[91]—and trying to suggest that something different was going on than the usual sense of literal inerrancy that became prominent in Protestantism in the later nineteenth century. Smith was using idiosyncratically literal readings to support metaphysical transformations. He sometimes exploded tiny snippets of Bible text into vast new stories. I did not do enough then to explain what I meant by "marvelous literalism," which perceptive critics noticed.[92] In this section I take up the charge to explain and explore marvelous literalism as an extension of Smith's formal work on the New Translation.

I chose "marvelous" because Smith's disciples saw his literalistic exegeses as the products of a spiritual gift. And the content of these "literal" readings was anything but literal in the sense that Protestant readers would have understood the term. But he did attend closely to the words on the pages of the King James Bible (and sometimes words in more ancient texts). He did not attend to every verse or even every book of scripture. He trained his miracle-making eye on specific turns of phrase or rhetorical structures. The content Smith called into life from the Bible was miraculous, powerful, and supernatural. More than anything, this marvelous literalism reflected the application of the same approach to metaphysical correspondence that undergirded his entire scriptural project. He was in this respect a modern practitioner of the ancient principle of allegorical reading, although his allegories created new scripture.

Often Smith took oddities of the King James Bible and made of them something special. In Nicholas Frederick's insightful phrase, he "had a keen sense for finding the 'holes' or 'knots' present in the scriptures, those places where a writer makes a statement" that "taunt[s the reader] with ambiguity."[93] Those ambiguous places Smith could read as if the surface words were simply and straightforwardly true even as he saw that they pointed well beyond themselves. Was language fallen? Yes, as we saw in chapter 1. But that fallen language contained fragments of the truth that could beckon to the prophetic reader and the interpretive community. The verbal clues triggered the recovery of deep truth from the ancient texts.

In a September 1838 letter to disciple Stephen Post, Smith presented an exegesis of Ezekiel 37:15–20, especially the reference to "The Stick of Joseph in the hand of Ephraim." Positioning the Book of Mormon as the stick of Joseph and Post as an Ephraimite (as the Latter-day Saints were, in their adoption into the house of Israel), Smith argued that every time a Church member held a Book of

---

[91] On selective literalism, see Barlow, *Mormons and the Bible*, 33–40. On creative literalism, see Cummings, "Quintessential Mormonism."
[92] *Mormon Studies Review* 3 (2016): 170–73.
[93] Frederick, *Allusivity*, 81.

Mormon in his hand, he was fulfilling an Old Testament prophecy. "Solve this mistery and se[e]," he urged Post.[94]

In 1843, Smith performed one of his signature exegeses on Luke 3:22. He reported that the "Holy Gh[o]st is a personage in the form of a personage.—does not confine itself to form of a dove.—but in sign of a dove." Note that he's struggling here with his own teaching that the Holy Ghost is anthropomorphic. If he is in human form, then how could the Bible refer to the Holy Ghost as having been "in a bodily shape like a dove"? The wrong kind of literalism would mandate that the Holy Ghost was a shape-shifter or even existed permanently as a bird. Smith's literalism here induced the flexibility necessary to preserve anthropomorphism for the Holy Ghost. In this specific case, rather than positing a shapeshifting Holy Ghost, he understood the text to be referring to the "sign" of the dove, presumably indicating that the Holy Ghost was not bodily present in the account, whatever the nature of the King James use of the confounding word "bodily." As if justifying himself against those who would criticize this flexibility, he then explained, "No man holds the book more sacred than I do." He instructed his audience, "when you have heard go & read your bible. if the things are not verily true."[95] He was supremely confident that the Bible was an authority on which his teachings rested.

In another example of his marvelous literalism, Smith revealed a hierarchy of prophets, priests, and kings in Genesis, which became important to the Nauvoo temple liturgy (chapter 7). He noted that Abraham is a prophet who owes obeisance to Melchizedek, who is denominated as both a priest and a king (Hebrews 7:1–3).[96] The spare and jumbled references to these various offices proved custom-made for the priestly hierarchy that Smith had created within the Church. In retrospect, the King James Version had contained the fragments necessary to understand sacerdotal hierarchies. Smith's marvelous literalism had just reassembled the fragments as he believed they had needed to be all along.

Smith also made real the ancient Hebrew metaphor of sexual infidelity to describe human unfaithfulness to God. When the New Testament invokes the infidelity trope to indicate that people who seek signs are unfaithful to God, Smith reports that this act somehow ramifies physically in their bodies. Those who seek signs are, quite literally, adulterers. In a July 1839 sermon, he indicated "whenever you see a man seeking after a Sign you may set it down that he is an adulterous man."[97] He returned to the theme in 1843.[98] Note again that this reading speaks to a metaphysical correspondence, a metaphor made real in the world. It

---

[94] *JSPD6*, 244.
[95] *JSPJ2*, 251.
[96] *JSPJ3*, 66.
[97] *JSPD6*, 521.
[98] *JSPJ2*, 258.

highlighted his resistance to separating the world of transcendent order from the world of human beings.

When he turned to Revelation 20:12 in a September 1842 sermon, Smith wondered why it referred first to books and then to the book of life when it came time for the final judgment. The Book of Life made sense—Smith had even written one of his own, and plenty of Christians believed that the Book of Life contained the heavenly record of the merit of humans' mortal lives. Smith thus understood a multiplicity of books to exist—the plural books were connected to the singular Book. "The books spoken of, must be the books which contained the record of their works, and refers to the Records which are kept on the earth." In that stroke, he espied dense interconnection between his own rituals and the records of the rituals and the ultimate Book of Life. Smith said, "in all your recordings it may be recorded in heaven." "Or in other words, taking a different view of the translation, whatsoever you record on earth shall be recorded in heaven."[99] Once again, Smith's marvelous literalism was creating connections between the earthly and heavenly realms. As above, so below.

Yet another instance of marvelous literalism played off the deep correspondences between heaven and earth. Luke 20 records a mocking thought experiment by Sadducees hoping to prove that Jesus's belief in an afterlife was irrational. They considered what would happen if the levirate marriage custom were followed by a woman, serially marrying seven brothers. Would each of those marriages persist in the afterlife? Such persistence might create bizarre permutations. Jesus responds that "neither do they marry nor are given in marriage" in the afterlife, so the question of marriage versus singleness made no sense in heaven. Or at least that is how most Christians have interpreted the passage.

Smith, however, reported that the key to the problem was that marriages had to span both heaven and earth to amount to anything. Marriage, Smith revealed, needed to be ritually performed on earth in order to be real in heaven. Jesus wasn't saying that no one would be married in heaven, just that there couldn't be any weddings that occurred *only* in heaven. Heaven and earth were interconnected permanently by the metaphysical priesthood.[100]

Some critics viewed Smith's brand of exegesis as superstitious divination or proof-texting. The defector William Hunt saw Smith's marvelous literalism as little more than divining tea dregs: "these self-complacent conjurors can all handle the mystic symbols of Isaiah, Ezekiel, and St. John, with the same ease and grace that a well-bred lady does her tea-pot."[101] But Smith's marvelous literalism was more than that. He was creating a kind of living scripture. As was true with

---

[99] *JSPJ2*, 146.
[100] Brown, "Levirate Widow."
[101] Hunt, *Mormonism*, 77.

all of his scriptures, there was no separation based on time. The whole Bible was available to him.

In a late sermon, Smith achieved a high point as an interpreter. He announced, "I will still go on & shew you proof on proof. all the Bible is as equal one part as another."[102] The equality of the Bible allowed him to reject the learned individuals who wanted to make the Bible coherent by downplaying particular odd sections of text. For a prophet, the entire Bible could be a textual playground. When he described his hermeneutic approach, he both stuck with the standard of perspicuity and laid out his hunger to inhabit the minds of the people within scripture. In a January 1843 sermon, Smith said "Elders in this church preach.—no rule of interpretation.—what is the rule of interpretati[o]n? Just no interpretati[o]n at all. understand precisely as it read.—I have Key by whi[c]h I understa[n]d the scripture—I enqire what was the question whi[c]h drew out the answer."[103] While this work of contextualization wasn't his only approach, his desire to understand the minds and persons of the ancients was clearly an operative principle in his Bible interpretation.

By the end of his life, Smith was confident in his episodic translations. In the revelation on baptism for the dead (D&C 128), he grapples with 1 Corinthians 15:29 (an obscure reference to Christians who "baptize for the dead") at length, tying it to Revelation 20:12, which evokes the final judgment as God reading from sacred books, including the "book of life." In verse 8, he says he is "taking a different view of the translation" before merging Revelation 20:12 with Christ's bestowal of a binding power on his disciples (Matthew 18:18) that Smith calls "priesthood." The priesthood proves to be the mechanism by which the Church's temple records of baptisms for the dead become the books of judgment.[104] Typically for Smith he is surfacing hidden connections among verses to draw them toward a meaning relevant to his sacramental and sacerdotal theologies. As he moves further along his elaborate exegesis, he indicates, "I might have rendered a plainer translation to this, but it is sufficiently plain to suit my purpose as it stands." In those spare terms, Smith showed himself to be a man who feels extremely confident of his mastery of scripture and its use in his new world. He had mastered the Bible.

Smith was also busy writing himself and his followers into the Bible. They weren't just reading, they were writing, aggressively. Smith wrote several of his letters as if they were epistles from the New Testament. In an 1839 letter addressed to Edward Partridge and the church, Smith echoed Paul by identifying himself as a "prisoner for the Lord Jesus Christ's sake" who sends greetings

---

[102] *WJS*, 382.
[103] *JSPJ2*, 251–52, underscore in original.
[104] *JSPJ2*, 146–47.

and prays for grace on the recipients.[105] A holograph letter to his wife that same year he called an "Epistole," seeing himself as writing a new New Testament.[106] Smith's revelation in December 1833 (D&C 101) includes a parable of his own, involving the planting of twelve olive trees. In 1839 he generated another parable, this time from Luke 13:19, depicting the Chain of Belonging and the close interconnection between the living Saints and the angelic dead.[107] While critics may not find much to look at in those parables, for the Saints this was clear evidence that Smith was creating a new Bible before their eyes. They were entering the Bible directly.[108] This was after all what the Doctrine and Covenants was for, as we saw earlier.

Similarly, a question and answer session in the spring of 1838 (D&C 113:1–6) is part of the New Translation of Isaiah 11 and Isaiah 52.[109] Here, Smith writes himself into scripture alongside Christ. The Bible comes to describe a man "of the house of Joseph, on whome thare is Laid much power."[110] This is meant to be interpreted as Smith himself, of that there can be no doubt. Months later when Smith thought about the call to Zion in the fall of 1838, he included in a letter to a disciple the encouragement to "come up to Zion with songs of everlasting joy" (Isaiah 35:10).[111] His followers attempting to get to Missouri, the Latter-day Saint Zion, were thus fulfilling and participating in the Old Testament.

To the ongoing question of what aspects of the biblical text Smith was recovering, he was clear that the scriptural communion he offered went well beyond any specific written text. He was finding the revelation that may not even have made it into the original written form of scripture. It was the deep intent hovering beyond language, like the spirit of God brooding over the abyss in Genesis 1.

Conclusion

Smith seized on problems in the King James Version and made of them something grand, believing that fallen language still contained fragments of the truth that a prophetic reader could recover. He spent his career working through multiple channels to recover the primordial Bible. While he was not alone in this quest in the nineteenth century, he went about it differently than his Protestant contemporaries. Smith's peers tended to read the Bible as if it were either a

---

[105] *JSPD6*, 360.
[106] *JSPD6*, 375. (Wilford Woodruff similarly labeled his journal, "The First Book of Wilford": Ulrich, "Early Diaries," 273.)
[107] *JSPD6*, 545.
[108] *JSPD3*, 393.
[109] *JSPD6*, 50.
[110] *JSPD6*, 53.
[111] *JSPD6*, 244.

facilitator of inner discovery (the Word of God capable of regenerating the believer, whether in an established service in a Congregational church or in the wild fervor of a camp meeting) or as a historical-cultural document for rational study. Smith, by contrast, needed the Bible to come alive, to bring the past into the present. He animated that Bible with metaphysically potent language.

From the Book of Mormon to his last public sermons, Smith was hard at work changing the grounds of reading the Bible. His Bible was vaster than any available to his Protestant compatriots, and his approach to it both changed the understanding of the Bible and brought it into full life. That life was deeply dependent on the principle of metaphysical correspondence, as he was hoping to unite heaven and earth. His particular approach to the tensions inherent to religious thought and practice in the early nineteenth century created a variety of potential problems and mysteries for his followers. Those would be put to a special test when Smith encountered a collection of Egyptian papyri midway through his career.

6
The Egyptian Bible and the Cosmic Order

In 1966, the University of Utah Coptologist Aziz Atiya (1898–1988) learned that the New York Metropolitan Museum of Art owned several funerary papyri from Ptolemaic Egypt, artifacts whose appropriate disposition had vexed the museum for decades.[1] The distinctively American provenance for these documents drew curators to show them to Atiya. The fragments in question came from a collection that Joseph Smith Jr. had purchased in Kirtland, Ohio in 1835.

The afterlife journey of those papyri was in some respects as elaborate as the voyage such documents anticipated for the spirits of the deceased. Interred in Thebes around 200 BCE, the papyri were appropriated around 1820 by the Italian adventurer Antonio Lebolo, then ended up in the collection of Michael Chandler, an itinerant showman largely lost to history. Chandler made it from Philadelphia to Cleveland, thence to the nearby folk expert in hieroglyphs, Joseph Smith, then residing in the Latter-day Saint town of Kirtland. The prophet, in collaboration with trusted colleagues, used the papyri to draft a collection of philological documents and publish a new book of scripture, carrying the papyri and their sacred products from Kirtland to Missouri to the new Latter-day Saint capital at Nauvoo, Illinois.

Joseph's mother, Lucy Mack Smith, displayed the artifacts in a makeshift frontier museum in the early 1840s (some evidence suggests that the Smiths hoped to integrate the museum into the Nauvoo temple[2]). After Smith died, his family retained the papyri. His widow Emma Hale Smith and her second husband sold them to a collector, Abel Combs, who sold most of them to another collector, who in turn housed them in the St. Louis Museum, from which they were sold to Wood's Museum in Chicago. Most of the papyri were likely destroyed in the Chicago fire of 1871, but Combs's housekeeper inherited a few. Those latter papyri ultimately made their way to the Metropolitan Museum, by way of her grandson.[3]

Such are the peregrinations of the Joseph Smith papyri. What early Latter-day Saints did with these ancient documents is also a fascinating story with many unexpected turns. Smith's encounter with the papyri resulted in a collection of

---

[1] Gee, "Puzzles," 115–16.
[2] McBride, *Nauvoo Temple*, 3.
[3] Todd, *Book of Abraham*, and Peterson, *Book of Abraham*.

manuscripts, some of which were published in 1842 as the Book of Abraham. The published texts of the Book of Abraham—sparsely commented by Joseph Smith himself—entered the scriptural canon forty years later. (The associated grammatical texts were less complete, harder to categorize, misplaced for decades, and never canonized.) The published manuscripts positioned themselves as a biblical lost book retelling the Genesis story in the name of Abraham. This Egyptian Bible returned again to the Hebrew Bible's primeval history; revealed, confirmed, or expanded several distinctive Latter-day Saint doctrines; and—most controversially—demonstrated to Smith's followers his mastery of hieroglyphs.

The Book of Abraham did all that and more for believers for over a century-and-a-half. It did nothing of the sort for critics. As Egyptology shifted toward a modern professional discipline, it became increasingly clear that the product of Smith's encounter with the hieroglyphs looked nothing like an academic translation. No professional non-Mormon Egyptologist would ever endorse the English text of Smith's Egyptian project as containing straightforward linguistic translations.[4]

Though the disconnect between the modern interpretation of the papyri and Smith's English-language documents had been noted since at least the 1860s,[5] the recovery from the Metropolitan Museum of papyrus fragments among the remnants of the Joseph Smith collection—a *Breathing Permit* and *Book of Going Out by Day*, both ritual texts to guide the newly deceased in the afterlife—resulted in a flash of controversy.[6] Following Joseph Smith's lead, Latter-day Saints had traditionally understood the papyri as coded references to their scriptures and cosmology, a view fundamentally at odds with academic Egyptian interpretations. The leading Church classicist of the day, Hugh Nibley, imaginatively identified the funerary papyri as an early Egyptian version of the Nauvoo temple liturgy, while critics framed the recovered papyri as proof of Smith's deceit.[7] Some Latter-day Saints separated from their church in the aftermath of the publicity about the papyri; the topic still figures in many popular works by and for disaffiliating Church members.[8]

---

[4] By "Egyptian project," I mean all of Smith's work relating to hieroglyphs and the papyri. See Brown, "Chain of Belonging," 12.

[5] The French Egyptologist Theodule Deveria analyzed the facsimiles in Remy and Brenchley, *Great-Salt-Lake City*, 2: 540–46. F. S. Spalding, *Joseph Smith*, collected scholarly responses to the facsimiles.

[6] See, e.g., Wilson, "Summary Report"; Stephen Thompson, "Egyptology"; and Ritner, "Breathing Permit."

[7] Contrast, for example, Nibley, *Joseph Smith Papyri*, with Larson, *Joseph Smith Papyri*, and the counterpolemic in Gee, "Tragedy of Errors."

[8] The "Book of Abraham problem" figures, for example, in the pastiche of anti-Mormon tropes published as http://cesletter.com/Letter-to-a-CES-Director.pdf (accessed August 16, 2016), with one Latter-day Saint response at http://debunking-cesletter.com (accessed February 2, 2018). As an emblem of the tension, a counterculture press published an antagonistic rendering of the text of the Smith papyri by an Egyptologist (Robert Ritner) who had been the academic advisor of a Latter-day

The Egyptian papyri, their antebellum American context, Smith's translations, and the debates about their nature and significance have generated many decades of controversy within and around the early Church. These stories—and the cultural contexts and implications that the polemics on both sides have consistently missed—are the work of this chapter. For ease of exposition, I briefly review the historical context, consider the relevant documents on their own terms, and then tie Smith's Egyptian project back to questions of his complex dance with modernity. With a special eye to its relevance to the nature of time, self, and scripture, I argue that Smith was revealing an Egyptian Bible saturated by the metaphysics of hieroglyphs.[9] This special Bible played an important role in the elaboration of Smith's replacement for the Chain of Being, what I call the Chain of Belonging. In this treatment, I am especially interested in understanding what the texts were for, what they did, and what they had to say about themselves.

We begin with context.

Egypt in America

Two core sets of traditions mediated Smith's encounter with Egypt, one mainstream and the other esoteric (admitting that the two are closer than many observers have been comfortable acknowledging). In the nineteenth century, most thinkers were drawn to the antiquity of Egypt and its pictographic language. Egypt contained origins and archetypes as well as the promise of mysteries lost to the Bible when the Hebrews fled their captivity for the promised land. The pictograms held the key to recovering those secrets.

The after story of ancient Egypt is reasonably well known. Although its long period of political domination ended long since (while the timing is debated, the Egyptian empire was clearly waning by the seventh to sixth centuries BCE), Egypt continued to wield substantial cultural power.[10] Egyptian civilization was already visibly ancient in classical antiquity.[11] In the early nineteenth century, Egypt returned to prominence in the aftermath of Napoleon's invasion and looting of artifacts (1798–1801), including Egypt's mummified dead.[12] This new

---

Saint (John Gee) who has argued that Smith's translation was in fact Egyptologically accurate (albeit of missing papyri). The edition bristles with swipes at Smith and Gee. See Ritner, *Joseph Smith Papyri*, versus Gee, *Introduction*.

[9] I charted early thoughts on several of these themes in "(Smith) in Egypt."
[10] See, e.g., Russell, *Ancient Egypt*; Trafton, *Egypt Land*; Irwin, *American Hieroglyphics*, 72; Albanese, *Republic of Mind and Spirit*, 38, 125; and Day, *Mummymania*.
[11] Take the exemplary account in Plato's *Timaeus* 22b–e explaining how the Nile protected Egypt from cyclical loss of history with each ecological devastation. Cooper, *Plato*, 1230.
[12] Day, *Mummymania*, 3, and sources therein cited. Trafton, *Egypt Land* explores the complex paradoxes of America's situation of itself within ancient history.

physical availability of Egypt triggered resurgent interest. Egyptiana figured in political rhetoric, sermons, museums, and traveling displays as well as American cemeteries.[13] People even saw themselves as consuming mummies in the form of medicinal teas.[14] Outside the mainstream, Egypt was a foundation for hermeticism, a mostly Christian esoteric wisdom tradition that was important to Renaissance neoclassicism and early modern philosophy.[15] Egypt loomed large as history, power, and mystery.

In defense of such conventional beliefs, Egypt likely was one of the earliest human cultures to develop a complex society. Its religion is perhaps the oldest known in any substantial detail, and it was probably important to the development of monotheism.[16] Supported by the fertility of the Nile within an arid wilderness, the early Egyptians achieved substantial, durable feats of engineering. And, in contrast to other ancient civilizations, enough of Egypt remained through late antiquity (the period before Europe's "Middle Ages") to impart a sense of continuous presence. This presence came largely through biblical rhetoric and esoteric traditions that persisted well into modernity.

For Smith, Egypt was the promise of primeval culture, power, and wisdom. For an ardent primordialist like him, perhaps no relics could be more important than objects from Egypt. Such physical articles could serve as portals to the ancient world. In Smith's hands they opened an Egyptian window onto the primordial Bible, the texts his translation work had always been trying to restore.

Without Napoleon, Smith would never have laid eyes on either mummy or papyrus. In the networks of early Atlantic culture, the European expropriation of Egyptian artifacts meant that within a few decades of the French invasion a small collection of Ptolemaic-era mummies from Thebes had made their way into Smith's translation room. When Michael Chandler came to Kirtland with his road-weary "posthumous travelers," he found fertile ground. Smith rallied donors and purchased the collection for a hefty sum.[17]

---

[13] Buck, *Theological Dictionary*, 194; Davies, *Culture of Salvation*, 101–102; Farrell, *American Way of Death*, 170.

[14] The material from which the teas were brewed was often called "mummia"; drinking it dated at least to medieval Europe. On Egyptomania, see Day, *Mummymania*, and MacDonald and Rice, *Ancient Egypt*.

[15] On Hermetism, see, e.g., Ebeling, *Hermeticism*, and Brooke, *Refiner's Fire*. Russell, *Ancient Egypt*, 194–95 provides a contemporary situation of Hermes in theories of ancient Egypt. Rollin, *Ancient History*, an eighteenth-century reference Smith donated to the Nauvoo Library, also mentions Hermes in these terms (1844 edition, 65, 79, 119). On Hermes and early modern philosophy, see Gillespie, *Theological Origins*, 82–83, 175.

[16] Assmann, *Moses the Egyptian*.

[17] See Brown, "(Smith) in Egypt," 26–27. The rough equivalent in 2018 dollars may have been around $60,000: http://www.in2013dollars.com/1835-dollars-in-2018?amount=2400, accessed March 6, 2018.

Immediate Contexts and Continuities

The mummies arrived in Kirtland at an important moment for Smith. He was working to establish his church's infrastructure and was a couple of years into creating the Kirtland Temple rites (see chapter 7). On the translation front, work had fallen quiet. He wanted to continue translating and urged his followers to support him. The once visionary New Translation of 1830 had largely morphed into a competition with Campbell and had mostly wrapped up by summer 1833 (although, as we've seen, he continued his novel Bible rereadings). The Book of Mormon was established and circulating. Of the gold plates only a few transcripts of hieroglyphs (the "Caractors" documents) remained.[18] Smith's targumizing project had stalled, at least in terms of major scriptures. In addition, by 1835 he had spent at least six years episodically on the trail of prelapsarian pictograms (see chapter 1). As of 1835, he still had nothing that could prove his hieroglyphic mastery publicly and incontrovertibly.

That situation changed in summer 1835, with the arrival of Chandler's mummies and their papyri. In Chandler's papyri Smith at last owned what all agreed were Egyptian hieroglyphs. The glyphic game was on.

Smith's key collaborator in this endeavor was W. W. Phelps, his trusted advisor in linguistics and scholarly arcana for years. While Phelps had arrived too late to help with the Book of Mormon, he was with Smith for most of the key innovations in the quest for pure language. Ghostwriting in the 1840s for Smith, Phelps summarized their encounter with the corpses in public correspondence with a New York newspaperman, claiming that "although dead, the papyrus which has lived in their bosoms, unharmed, speaks for them in language like the sound of an earthquake. *Ecce veritas*! *Ecce cadaveros*! Behold the truth! Behold the mummies!"[19] This seismic call issued from the long-stilled throats of the Theban mummies and promised to reveal the deep mysteries lurking behind the sectarian King James Bible. Smith had hoped that another assistant, Warren Parrish, could play an important role, even promising Parrish that as part of the work on the Egyptian Bible he would "know of hid[d]en things" and "be endowed with a knowledge of hid[d]en languages."[20] His lieutenant and confidant Frederick G. Williams was also transiently involved. Oliver Cowdery hoped to stay central to this new project, even embellishing his 1833 patriarchal

---

[18] MacKay et al., "'Caractors' Document." See also *JSPD1*, 361–64. The document had been made into placards by 1844 as a celebration of Smith's abilities as a translator of hieroglyphs: Kimball, "Anthon Transcript."

[19] *T&S* 4:24 (November 1, 1843): 374.

[20] *JSPD5*, 52–53.

blessing in 1835 to prophesy that he would still "be an instrument in the hands of his God, with his brother Joseph, of translating and bringing forth to the house of Israel."[21] In the event, Parrish and Cowdery proved durably unfaithful, while Phelps (other than a hiatus associated with a falling out during the Missouri War) persevered.

Importantly, many of the Saints saw the Egyptian papyri as linguistically and metaphysically connected to their Book of Mormon.[22] The Book of Mormon script was Reformed Egyptian, and it emphasized the sacred continuities between Smith and the biblical patriarch Joseph of Egypt, a connection Smith himself emphasized by occasionally assuming Joseph's Egyptian title—*Zaphnathpaaneah*—as a pseudonym.[23] Cowdery also emphasized the continuity between the missing Reformed Egyptian of the Book of Mormon and the apparently Unreformed script of the papyri. He maintained that some Book of Mormon "characters" were "like those of the writings" on the papyri. Phelps confirmed this interpretation in an 1835 letter to his wife, arguing that the papyri would "make a good witness for the Book of Mormon."[24] Smith reportedly showed the Caractors document to Chandler during the negotiations over the papyri.[25] Similarly, when Lucy Mack Smith described her son's encounter with the Book of Mormon plates, she said that he "transcribe[d] the Egyptian alphabet" from them.[26]

What I call Smith's Egyptian Bible—a suite of interrelated documents— follows and expands on the work initiated in the Book of Mormon and the New Translation: the recovery of the primordial Bible.[27] Complementary to the visions of Moses and Enoch, within his Egyptian Bible, Smith brought the primeval history of Genesis to its sequel: the rise and career of Abraham. To understand the import of Smith's Egyptian Bible requires knowledge of the texts themselves, to which we now turn.

---

[21] *JSPD5*, 512. An 1829 revelation promised Cowdery that "other records have I, that I will give unto you power that you may assist to translate" (D&C 9:2).

[22] *JSPR4*, xiv–xv, correctly calls out continuities among these scriptural projects.

[23] 2 Nephi 3:14–20, with expansion of the theme in *EMS* 1:6 (November 1832): 41. The pseudonym is used in *Nauvoo Neighbor* 1:9 (June 28, 1843).

[24] *M&A*, 2:3 (December 1835): 235; Phelps's letter of July 19–20, 1835, was reprinted in Van Orden, "Kirtland Letters," 556.

[25] *JSPJ1*, 67, 105.

[26] *JSPD1*, 355.

[27] The suggestion by the twentieth-century Latter-day Saint thinker Sidney Sperry that Abraham 3 is an Ur-text for Genesis 12 exemplifies this sense of continuity between the New Translation and the Egyptian Bible. *Deseret News*, April 6, 1935, 1.

Overview of the Texts

The Saints' encounter with mummies and papyri resulted in several manuscripts, none of which appears to be in final form.[28] Smith's Egyptian Bible contains four collections of documents: (1) the Ptolemaic-era papyri; (2) the hieroglyphic grammar documents; (3) the Book of Abraham, existing in manuscript and published forms; and (4) the facsimile interpretations (metaphysical interpretations of vignettes within the papyri). The fact that the texts are not complete introduces some caution into interpretation. Still, the available documents integrate well into Smith's overall scriptural project. Emblematically, Cowdery announced that the papyri represented "an inestimable acquisition to our present scriptures."[29] He was more correct than he knew.

The funerary papyri, largely written in hieratic script (a cursive form of hieroglyphs), were illustrated with a variety of vignettes—special type scenes relevant to the ritual function of the texts, sometimes but not always illuminating the associated text. They are fairly typical religious texts of the Ptolemaic era and are generally concerned with the afterlife status of the decedent to whom they were attached.[30] Both Latter-day Saints and their critics have seen these documents' status as paramount: some practicing Church members maintain that the Book of Abraham is a scholarly, linguistic translation (albeit of no longer extant papyri), while their critics counter that the papyri bear no linguistic connection to the Book of Abraham. Unfortunately, most such discussions of the documents generate more heat than light. What matters for our discussion here is the fact—undisputed by all—that these papyri contain ritual stories for and about the dead in a script that was for millennia associated with sacred pictography.

The Grammar Documents

By and large, the hieroglyphic grammar documents cluster around a projected interpretive lexicon of Egyptian hieroglyphics.[31] These grammar documents,

---

[28] Smith's request for funding to support his ongoing Egyptian translations even after the serialization of the first sections of Abraham supports the view that the current Book of Abraham is an unfinished work. See *The Wasp* 1:37 (January 14, 1843): 3.

[29] M&A, 2:3 (December 1835): 236.

[30] These papyri have been analyzed at length. A full translation is presented in Ritner, *Complete Edition*. On the Latter-day Saint side, see Rhodes, *Books of the Dead*, and Rhodes, *Book of Breathings*.

[31] I use the term "grammar" following their precedent to reflect what they considered themselves to be doing. By way of potentially relevant precedent for the name and structure of *GAEL*, Moses Stuart's 1832 *Grammar of the Hebrew Language* (a text the Kirtland Saints purchased to help with the Egyptian and Hebrew projects) includes an important chart on page 2, labeled "Ancient Hebrew Alphabet," which is structurally similar to *GAEL*.

patterned on scholarly reference works, sought to wrestle sacred glyphs into the realm of common sense and the science of grammar while expressing a belief in Egyptian writing as the linguistic expression of metaphysical correspondence. In this way, the hieroglyphic grammar documents represented the same basic impulse as Smith's New Translation of the Bible. Even as they contain inchoate and sometimes inconsistent notions, the grammar documents remain informative. The philological exercises provide an important window into Smith's religious and social vision and the broader context of hieroglyphic culture in which they operated. Without the grammar documents, the themes and aspirations of the canonized Book of Abraham can be only partly understood.

The bulk of the work on the hieroglyphic grammars seems to have stretched from the summer of 1835 to early 1836. After Joshua Seixas arrived in Kirtland in January 1836, the documentary evidence suggests that Smith and his collaborators turned to Hebrew language and grammar to solve the mysteries of the papyri, likely sensing that they had taken Egyptian grammar as far as they could. The Latter-day Saint Bible scholar Matthew Grey thus appears correct in his suggestion that the Kirtland Hebrew School was part of the Egyptian project.[32] By April 1836 (shortly after the temple dedication and pivotal solemn assembly, as described in chapter 7), Phelps had left Kirtland, and all work on the hieroglyphic grammar documents ceased.[33] Despite Smith's desire to return to this work, there's no clear evidence for any further labors on the hieroglyphic grammars, even in 1842, when Smith and Phelps briefly returned to the Egyptian materials to ornament several political documents.[34] Some portions of the Book of Abraham, especially the beginning of its opening chapter, may rely on the grammar documents, but overall the hieroglyphic grammars do not dominate the published scripture. Instead, the grammars flesh out the conceptual context.

Incomplete, unpublished, and impressionistically organized, the Egyptian grammar documents were once called the "Kirtland Egyptian Papers," although that initial name hasn't held up. The collection includes two notebooks, three loose-leaf documents, a hand-drawn copy of a hypocephalus, *Egyptian Alphabet* documents, an "Egyptian Counting" manuscript, and a ledger book called the *Grammar and Alphabet of the Egyptian Language* (hereafter *GAEL*; Figure 6.1).[35]

The names for the documents suggest what several early Latter-day Saints hoped they would represent—their mastery of ancient languages and the science

---

[32] Grey, "Word of the Lord," extended in "Egyptian Papyri." The fact that Smith sought the Hebrew Lexicon to interpret the Kinderhook plates in 1843 confirms this notion: *JSPJ3*, 13.

[33] On the date of Phelps's departure, see Van Orden, "Kirtland Letters," 548.

[34] Brown, "Ghostwriter," 44–45, 59–61. In 1838, gossip in Jackson County had it that Smith was still planning to work on the hieroglyphic grammar: Swartzell, *Mormonism Exposed*, 25.

[35] I follow *JSPR4* in this taxonomy. The title page of *GAEL* includes a pedestrian spelling error that I do not reproduce here.

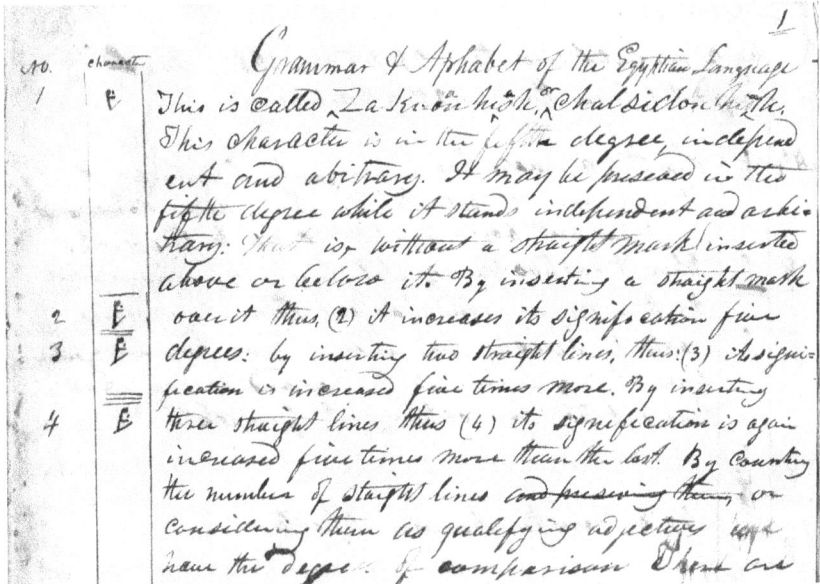

Figure 6.1 Title page of the Grammar and Alphabet of the Egyptian Language. Image courtesy of the Church History Library, The Church of Jesus Christ of Latter-day Saints.

of grammar. While multiple scribes had a hand in various documents (including occasional holographs of Smith), the handwriting of Phelps dominates the *GAEL*. Phelps played a prominent intellectual role in the hieroglyphic grammars,[36] even if the earliest documents appear to derive from Smith's dictation.[37] In parallel, Cowdery and Williams made an abortive attempt to create grammatical documents for the Reformed Egyptian of the Book of Mormon as part of the 1835 work on the papyri. Their translation of snippets of the book of Jacob into glossolalic Hebrew-like syllables parallels the form and content of the Egyptian grammar documents.[38]

---

[36] Brown, "Ghostwriter," explores these topics at some length, inspecting the long-term relationship between Smith and Phelps, in which Smith relied on Phelps's reported mastery of foreign languages and secular learning.

[37] This is suggested by the various phonetic rendering of given glyphic names in the loose leaf "Egyptian Alphabet" texts. See *JSPR4*, 53–110.

[38] *JSPD1*, 361–64, with some discussion in Grey, "Word of the Lord," 254. The texts are Jacob 5:13, 7:27. The Williams version contains more glyphs that do not appear to match any of the extant Book of Mormon Caractors documents or the Egyptian grammar documents. Some but not all of Williams's glyphs look vaguely Ethiopic (as was printed in small snippets as part of the 1821 Laurence translation of the Book of Enoch), but there is no clean connection between the two.

The grammar documents strained toward an ultimate grammar book, an aspiration that the historian Ken Cmiel has associated with humanistic learning in the late eighteenth and early nineteenth centuries.[39] If we can judge by the extant documents, Smith's grammar would fit somewhere between primers for school use and the ancient mystical lexicon of Horapollo, with perhaps a hint of those most notorious grammars of Atlantic culture, the *grimoires* (spell books).[40]

The major grammar document is the *GAEL*, which is an early sketch of the projected reference work.[41] While *GAEL* remains an unfinished draft, it's the most mature of the grammar documents, containing thirty-four pages of reasonably coherent written content within a large ledger. It is clearly drawn from the *Egyptian Alphabet* documents. *GAEL* reads like a glossary of ancient runes. Each entry includes a hieratic character (or portion thereof, or other glyphic material), its pronunciation in an English transliteration, and impressionistic sentences explaining the underlying meaning. The entries are arranged in two "parts" (about fourteen pages in length), each of which is divided into five "degrees" (two to three pages in length). The first part seems, more or less, to deal with humans, whereas the second part is more concerned with angels and stars.[42] What the authors mean linguistically by "degrees"—a formal term of art within the grammar documents—isn't entirely clear, but it has to do with multiplication, reproduction, and ramification for a given glyph. The idea sounds somewhat like conjugations in Latin or Greek or the varied meanings of Hebrew roots.[43] For example, a given hieratic character might be transliterated as *Zool*. In the first degree of the first part, *Zool* means "From any fixed period of time back to the beginning."[44] The scope and content of the definition increase with each passing degree. By the time *GAEL* reaches the fifth degree of the second part for *Zool*, the definition is seventy-four words long and connects Abraham, Noah, and the genealogical priesthood to the scope of time stretching from the present to the primordium.[45]

The grammar documents are a hieroglyphic puzzling through the esoteric traditions of signs. I think of these transliterations of glyphs' names as "graphic glossolalia," a written version of the sacred singing in unknown syllables that is the more familiar version of the glossolalia we encountered in chapter 1.

---

[39] Cmiel, *Democratic Eloquence*, 32, 37, 48.

[40] On Horapollo, see Young, "Egypt," and Cory, *Horapollo*, with modern commentary in Iversen, *Myth of Egypt*, 47. On grimoires, see Davies, *Grimoires*, and Dillinger, *Treasure Hunting*, 92–93.

[41] Hauglid, "Egyptian," 492–95.

[42] The parts may also correspond to the layout of glyphs on the papyri. See Tvedtnes, "Critics," 73–74.

[43] If the *GAEL* did draw on knowledge of Semitic radicals, that might suggest an 1836 date for the *GAEL* for which there is otherwise little good evidence. I doubt that in fact Phelps and Smith were drawing on that specific grammatical concept.

[44] *JSPR4*, 158–59.

[45] *JSPR4*, 128–29.

Glossolalia is fundamentally concerned with spiritual contact with concepts (or agencies) beyond human language. The syllables uttered by the person engaging in glossolalia—whatever the specific resonances may be—are beyond human language. The sacred syllables are a point of contact between the world of human language and the world beyond. An observer must then render those unknown syllables into a familiar human language, a process called interpretation. Such are the well-established mechanics of glossolalia. Rarely if ever are the glossolalic syllables themselves written, unless perhaps by outside observers in an anthropological vein.[46] Most often glossolalic syllables are sung, in rapid succession, leaving no graphic trace of that ecstatic encounter with primal language.

In the case of the hieroglyphic grammar documents, something similar is happening. Sacred glyphs deeply connected to a world beyond mere human language are rendered into syllables that do not belong to any known human language. Those glossolalic syllables are then rendered into human language, in this case English. Instead of a glossolalic singer and a separate interpreter in a sustained oral performance, though, in the case of the grammar documents, the process occurs deliberately on paper, in the format of a lexicon. To put it too simply, Phelps and Smith wrestled the raw spiritual act of glossolalia into the earthly science of grammar. This is what I mean by graphic glossolalia: the inscription of syllables beyond human language with an accompanying interpretation into English.[47]

Polemical arguments have wrangled over the details of the interrelationships of the documents of the Egyptian project.[48] The grammar documents are obviously kindred with Smith's decoding of the vignettes into his facsimiles. They integrate thoroughly into the work to discover the primordial language of Eden. Smith and Phelps may have employed the grammar documents in the creation of some portions of the Book of Abraham, but they are clearly not the sole or even primary textual source of the published scripture.[49] We can't solve minute

---

[46] See, e.g., Lamson, *Shakers*, 78–79.

[47] There may be a subtle, nongenetic, association between Smith's merger of visionary experience and text here and Ellen Harmon's (founder of Seventh-Day Adventism) mergers of vision and text. See Perry, *Bible Culture*, 40–41. Alphabetic mysticism (especially but not exclusively in Gnostic writings) is similar. See, e.g., *Pistis Sophia* 4, 142; *Gospel of the Egyptians* 44 and 46; and *Zostrianos* 127, with discussion in Johnson, *Religious Experience*. See also Ebeling, *Hermes Trismegistus*, 17, and Davies, *Popular Magic*, 110, 147, 153. The Hellenic Egyptian spells brim with alphabetic mysticism: Betz, *Greek Magical Papyri*. Finally, the Oxford mystic John Hutchinson (1674–1737) may be another nongenetic antecedent, in his work on glyphic, unpointed Hebrew: Hindmarsh, *Early Evangelicalism*, 118–19; Buck, *Theological Dictionary*, 228–29.

[48] See, e.g., Larson, "Joseph Smith Papyri," 88–99; Ritner, Joseph Smith Papyri, 29–44; Smith, "Dependence," versus Nibley, "Kirtland Egyptian Papers"; and Gee, *Introduction to Book of Abraham*, 32–39. I thank Brian Hauglid for help with these sources.

[49] Large amounts of published material are absent from the grammar documents. Even at the barest grammatical level, at least five words are in the published Book of Abraham but absent from the grammar documents: *shagreel, olishem, kahleenos, shulem,* and *olimlah*.

questions of textual interrelationships on the basis of current historical evidence. Here, I'm interested in what the entire collection of documents communicated about the nature of early Restoration thought and its triangulation within modern intellectual and spiritual currents.

The Book of Abraham

The Book of Abraham exists in several partial manuscript copies and a version published sequentially in the church newspaper in spring 1842. The manuscript versions, primarily in the hand of Warren Parrish and Willard Richards,[50] are generally similar, with some subtle and occasionally important differences. The best evidence suggests that Smith dictated the text, with textual revisions to the Richards manuscript near the time of printing.[51] Abraham 1:1–2:18 appears to be largely contemporaneous with the grammar documents.[52] Given their obvious dependence on the Seixas grammar and relevance to the temple liturgy, Abraham 4–5 were probably dictated in early 1842. Abraham 3 is of less certain dating, perhaps a collation of material dictated from approximately 1838 to 1842, with final dictation likely in 1842.[53]

To the question of dating Abraham 3, Smith sought funding to publish the Book of Abraham in 1837.[54] He was using content from the Book of Abraham in the summer of 1838, suggesting that it was on his mind then, although there's no clear evidence of translating per se in 1838.[55] He publicly discussed key content for Abraham 3 in the spring and summer of 1839.[56] A letter from Elizabeth Haven Barlow to her sister in October 1839 suggests Smith may have been working on Abraham 3 at that time.[57] He returned to the themes in a May 1840

---

[50] For more thoughts on Phelps's role, see Brown, "Ghostwriter," 37–38.

[51] After Warren Parrish was excommunicated, he told the Painesville *Republican* that he "penned down the translation of the Egyptian Hieroglyphicks as [Smith] claimed to receive it by direct inspiration from Heaven." *JSPD5*, 74.

[52] All the known Kirtland-era manuscripts cease at 2:18, and that is the text for the initial installment of the Book of Abraham publication in *T&S* 3:9 (March 1, 1842): 704–706.

[53] Based on Smith's report that he was busy performing new translation work in 1842, I think it most likely that he was dictating Abraham 4–5 (and possibly Abraham 3 in its published form) at that point. His announcement that he had solved Egyptian astronomy in October 1835 could represent his translation of the hypocephalus (Facsimile 2). On Abraham 4–5, see Grey, "Use of Hebrew."

[54] *JSPD5*, 77.

[55] Thus Smith's May 6, 1838, discourse: "He also instructed the Church, in the misteries of the Kingdom of God; giving them a history of the Plannets &c. and of Abrahams writings upon the Plannettary System &c." See also his July 1838 preaching: "Is there not room enough upon the mountains of Adamondi awman, or upon the plains of Olea Shinihah, or the land where Adam dwelt." See *JSPD6*, 134, 193.

[56] *JSPD6*, 369–70, 543. See also *JSPD3*, 85.

[57] Haven reported that Smith preached a sermon on "the kingdom before the foundation of the world." He "said he would feed the church with meat, Explained some passage of Scripture which is not translated right and which have even been a stumbling block to the world. He also related some

letter to missionaries headed to Israel.[58] A January 1841 sermon similarly alluded to Abraham 3,[59] while he sought resources to "attend to the business of translating" in August 1841.[60] Smith discussed content from Abraham 3 at Wilford Woodruff's 35th birthday party on 1 March 1842.[61] Smith's March 1842 journal mentions new translation work right after the publication of the first installment of the Book of Abraham; the extant manuscript drafts from which printing occurred date to 1842 and include apparently last-minute adjustments to the language at the time they went to press.[62] Currently available evidence can't distinguish (1) Smith dictating in a new form material he'd been working with for three or four years from (2) Smith revising previously dictated material in 1842. In other words, the second half of Abraham probably belongs somewhere between 1838 and 1842, with important activity focused in the first half of March 1842.

Even so, the published Book of Abraham is obviously unfinished. Smith admitted as much—he anticipated and perhaps dictated additional material from Abraham as well as a projected Book of Joseph of Egypt.[63] I suspect that the temple liturgy and its emphasis on mystically powerful language and the sacred primordium (chapter 7) provided the impetus for publication in 1842: the timing and content—including explicit callouts to the temple in the facsimile interpretations—strongly suggest such a relationship.

The published Book of Abraham reads like a collection of related texts by the same author(s), albeit in an artificial order. In the discussion that follows, I hew to the chronology of the text, beginning in the time before the world was and ending with Abraham's life and times. The Book of Abraham is presented in four distinct parts (arranged here in narrative-chronological order, to match the flow of Smith's primordial Bible): (1) a cosmological prequel to Genesis 1 (Abraham 3) that introduces the Chain of Belonging, (2) a targum of Genesis 1–2 that incorporates themes and material from other places (Abraham 4–5), (3) a hieroglyphic introduction to Abraham's life (Abraham 1:1–4), and (4) a targum of Genesis 12–20 (Abraham 1:5–2:25).

---

very interesting facts which he has lately translated from the records which came with the Mummies." Elizabeth Haven Barlow, Quincy, IL, to Elizabeth H. Bullard, Holliston, MA, September 21, 1839, Barlow Family Collection, MS 941, bx. 1, fd. 1, CHL.

[58] Smith and colleagues told Orson Hyde and John Page that they were on a mission that "is worthy of those inteligences who surround the throne of Jehovah to be ingaged in." *JSPD7*, 281–82.
[59] "At the first organization in heaven we were all present and saw the Savior chosen and appointed." *JSPD7*, 495.
[60] *JSPD8*, 228.
[61] *JSPJ2*, 39.
[62] *JSPJ2*, 42: Smith "Commenced Translating from the Book of Abraham."
[63] In February 1843, Smith advertised that there was more of the Book of Abraham to come: *JSPD5*, 77.

According to its narrative chronology, the Book of Abraham begins before the world was, before even the spirit of God began to brood over the waters of chaos in Genesis 1. In retrospect the early visions of Moses and Enoch were incomplete. Abraham was to tell more of the cosmic prequel that had begun to sketch out. Abraham 3 contains an explosion of cosmological narratives tied to the implements of translation, the *Urim* and *Thummim* (perhaps exploiting *Urim* as the plural of the hometown, *Ur*, from which Abraham was fleeing). As part of this cosmogony, chapter 3 outlines the divine secrets of astronomy, in what appears to be an expansive meditation on Job 38:1–7. In the Hebrew Bible account, God asks Job, rhetorically, whether Job was present at the founding of the world, "when the morning stars sang together, and all the sons of God shouted for joy." This Jobian text was a favorite biblical anchor for the belief in stars as angels and a placement of human intelligence at the beginning of the cosmos.[64] This mysterious allusion in Job may also have anchored the stories that happened before Genesis 1. The connection between the Bible's primeval history, cosmology, and astronomy was secure for many other Christians. Adam Clarke's Bible commentary included tables of celestial bodies in his treatment of Genesis.[65]

In Abraham 3's prequel to Genesis, Abraham experiences a panoramic vision. Instead of picturing humans, though, as many other prophets had,[66] Abraham sees human-like stars. He discovers Smith's Chain of Belonging as a principle of cosmic order and hierarchy. He also refines the account of the process by which Jesus became Savior during cosmic prehistory—a council of angels and humans was called, a plan was presented, Jesus and Satan proposed approaches to implementation that differed primarily in the priority of human agency (as we saw in chapter 3), and God chose (apparently as an exegesis of Isaiah 6:8) Jesus as the leader for the implementation of what Latter-day Saints called the "plan of salvation" (Abraham 3:22–28). With this new information, the creation saga of Genesis 1–3 makes more sense. The 1842 components of the Book of Abraham—especially the prequel and creation saga—returned to the primeval history in support of the temple liturgy. After the prequel, the Abraham text transitions into its targum of the first chapters of Genesis.

Abraham 4–5 (a unitary block) picks up from chapter 3, rereading Genesis 1 in a distinctively Latter-day Saint way. There Abraham emphasizes that the creators of the earth were a divine team who "organized" the earth. Among other modifications, this retelling of Genesis 1 makes explicit that God is the plural *Elohim*, the Gods—a change from the still singular "God" of the visions of Moses and Enoch in 1830. The text also clarifies the odd King James syntax of "morning

---

[64] See, e.g., Clarke, *Holy Bible*, 3:168, and Givens, *Souls Had Wings*, 16.
[65] Clarke, *Holy Bible*, 1: 28–29.
[66] Brown, "Read the Round."

and evening," and the use of "time" in place of "day" to refer to epochs of creation. This connection to "set times"—one mechanism by which Smith's celestial bodies affected human beings—binds Abraham 3 more clearly to Smith's rereading of Genesis 1 and the grammar documents.[67] As Matthew Grey has pointed out, much of the lexical work of Abraham 4–5 depends on the Hebrew training materials from 1836.[68] We shouldn't, though, be too distracted by the use of the Seixas material. Abraham 4 and 5 are not merely the result of an autodidact ornamenting Genesis with gems from the Seixas grammar. There's a theological as well as linguistic infrastructure for the theology presented, and Smith reengages prior revelations (e.g., D&C 88:17–25) in this work.[69] Smith's targums in Abraham 4–5 are grappling with notions of the sacred hierarchy in the Chain of Belonging, the astronomical hierarchy of time, and the role of humans in the creation.

That Smith includes targums of the primeval history in his Book of Abraham underscores the early belief in the identity of sacred, ancient languages and Smith's constant rereading of the Bible. Contemporary observers noted this fact: Charlotte Haven, on hearing Lucy Mack Smith read from Abraham in Nauvoo, thought "it sounded very much like passages from the Old Testament."[70] An Illinois newspaper made a similar point in 1852.[71] But the merger of Hebrew scripture with Egyptian papyri speaks to the unity of pictographic language and the need to tell and retell those first stories. In an excavation of the primal language of humanity, the pure language of scripture necessarily plays a central role.[72]

Abraham 4–5 targumizes the dual creation narratives of Genesis 1–3. The initial creation account (understood as a spiritual creation) is completed within the first three verses, and then the Abraham text runs through the implementation of that creation. The astral creation accounts (Genesis 1:3–5, 14–18)

---

[67] Abraham 3 explicates the language of Genesis 1:14–16, explaining both what is involved in regulating "seasons" and "days" and "years" and what it means for a particular light to "rule the day," thereby recurring to a prior engagement of that text in the Olive Leaf—D&C 88:42–45.

[68] Grey, "Use of Hebrew," which follows Walton, "Seixas," and Muhlestein and Hansen, "Work of Translating."

[69] Abraham 4–5 substitutes obedience for the traditional declaration that the creation is good. The passage in the Olive Leaf indicates that "abid[ing] the law" is what allows an object to fill the "measure of its creation," culminating in the declaration that the earth itself (the object of creation) abides a law to fill its creation. The Seixas grammar doesn't indicate a substitution of obedience for the declaration of goodness.

[70] Haven, "Letters from Nauvoo," 624.

[71] Hauglid, *Textual History*, 223.

[72] Abraham 4–5 may have also been sensitive to the troubled status of italicized words in the King James Bible. While this analysis is merely suggestive, of the 37 italicized words in the targumized sections of the Bible, 26 (70%) were modified in the corresponding sections of the Book of Abraham. I thank Brady Winslow for performing this analysis of Genesis 1:1–31; 2:1–10, 15–25; 11:28–29; 12:1–13. When more than one sequential word was in italics, e.g., "it is," we treated them as a single italicized word.

recur in Abraham (4:3–5, 13–18). The verb "organize" occurs four times in three verses, intentionally recalling the organization of human spirits in Abraham 3:22 and Smith's interpretation of the Hebrew word *bara*, which we encountered in chapter 5.

The Abraham narrative seeks to resolve several potential problems with the received Genesis text, beginning with the problem of the Fall. Specifically, instead of the "day" of the Genesis account, Abraham explains that Adam would die in the "time" as measured according to the star Kolob (see what follows) that he ate the forbidden fruit, rather than on the same earth day (Abraham 5:13). This aside self-consciously resolves an apparent inconsistency in the Bible text: Adam lived for many centuries after eating the fruit.

The narrative flow is then interrupted to solve another textual problem in the Genesis account—herbs were originally said to grow before the arrival of rain to nourish and humans to cultivate them. The Abraham version of the story explains that the mist (4:6) took care of the need for precipitation before humans were created (4:7) and placed into a garden where they could then grow herbs.[73] And in yet another act important to orienting sacred hierarchies, the Book of Abraham reorders the naming sequence and the creation of Eve, assuring that Eve gets her name ("Woman") before the animals get theirs (4:17–21). The Abraham targums thus continue the work performed by the Book of Mormon and the New Translation, recovering primordial clarity from the remnants in the Protestant Bible.

After the creation, the Book of Abraham transitions chronologically into a targum of Genesis 12 that introduces the character of Abraham. This is in fact where the published Book of Abraham begins. The first portion of Chapter 1 is a concatenation of images and clauses in three verses, from an original manuscript in Phelps's hand. This brief section could represent a kind of warmup exercise for the ultimate scripture, much as the grammar documents may have been. It is stylistically different from what follows, and much of the content—although not the order—can be mapped to entries within the *GAEL*.[74] This introduction may, in other words, bridge some of the space between the grammar documents and the published work, a segue from the grammatical explorations steeped in hieroglyphic culture to the intense targumizing at the core of the Book of Abraham. It is also possible, however, that the *GAEL* entries were back-formed from the dictated introductory text.[75]

---

[73] Judging by Noah Webster's 1828 *Dictionary*, "herb" in antebellum America was similar to its late twentieth-century meaning.

[74] This is the argument of Smith, "Dependence," which is more evocative than persuasive, although some textual aspects may corroborate his claim: *JSPD5*, 77.

[75] This is the argument of McLellan, "Abraham 1:1–3."

The stylized preface adverts to Smith's priesthood based in parenthood, a genealogical chain of power, the nature of authority, and esoteric knowledge. Those themes persist through the Book of Abraham. Essentially, then, those first four verses encapsulate much of what is to come. The extant manuscripts transition into Abraham 1:5–2:18, likely dictated in the fall of 1835 as a targum of Genesis 12. (While the available manuscripts stop at 2:18, the flow of the published text continues through the end of chapter 2.) After a transitional verse (1:4), the narrative echoes the call of Lehi (1:5; cf. 1 Nephi 1, esp. 18–20, echoing Luke 4:24 and John 4:44) at the beginning of the Book of Mormon, when he found himself rejected by his countrymen for speaking the truth with prophetic authority. Abraham 1:8–12 shows Abraham's countrymen to be committed to the worship of false gods, including even human sacrifice.[76] The narrative about human sacrifice is tethered to a vignette (Facsimile 1) by the abrupt phrase "I will refer you to the representation at the commencement of this record" (1:12). This vignette typifies all pictograms, as the text then announces that *Kahleenos* is the "Chaldean" word for "hieroglyphics" (1:14).[77] After this aside to demonstrate the textual basis of the human sacrifice narrative, Jehovah rescues Abraham—a textual anticipation of the subsequent rescue of Isaac from Abraham later in life in Genesis 22. This deeply intertextual aside, which confirms the text's authenticity and clearly situates Abraham within the prophets of scripture, then gives way to the main narrative—the lineal priesthood of cosmic power.

The published Book of Abraham thus fuses a variety of themes and ideas within an overall structure of a targum. While it's not directly based on the grammar documents (with small possible exceptions), these documents are part of the same quest. The primordial Bible and its pure language are allowed to glimmer forth through the drab confines of the English Protestant Bible. They were joined by another form of hieroglyphs come to life, esoteric interpretations of several of the images that adorned the hieratic texts.

The Facsimiles

Smith included stylized vignette interpretations with the published Book of Abraham as "Fac-similes." Employing an interpretive approach familiar from the grammar documents, the facsimiles circulated as siblings to the anticipated Egyptian Grammar and complements to the published scripture. These

---

[76] While Josephus, *Antiquities of the Jews*, 1:7:1, suggests that Abraham had to flee the Chaldeans because of their worship of chthonic deities, and Cowdery was apparently reading Josephus during this period, the Book of Abraham doesn't seem to follow Josephus.

[77] The canonical *Rahleenos* is probably an error—the Kirtland manuscripts use *Kahleenos*. See *JSPR4*, 197, 209, 223, 291.

"figures at the beginning" of the Book of Abraham were the very definition of hieroglyphs, pictures telling ancient stories.[78] The Latter-day Saints publicly delighted in the facsimiles, even as they battled with skeptical critics.[79]

Facsimile 1 ties itself to the textual material relating to human sacrifice, based on what most Egyptologists consider a depiction of resurrection from a platform called a lion couch, in Abraham 1.[80] Facsimile 1 also incorporates material relevant to the Nauvoo temple liturgy.

Facsimile 2 is a hypocephalus, a circular text intended to be placed under the decedent's head. The facsimile 2 interpretation relies heavily on words in the *GAEL* and is closely connected to the material in Abraham 3 and the Masonic terminology of the temple liturgy (including explicit reference to "grand Keywords").[81] In a coy preterition that points to temple mysteries, many of the symbols are left shrouded in mystery, teasing the reader with new material yet to be revealed. Between the manuscript and the published versions, the phrase "cannot now be revealed" transitions to "cannot be revealed" to outsiders, suggesting that the depicted secrets had in fact been revealed in the temple liturgy.

Facsimile 3 is another, less convoluted extension of the Abraham 3 astronomical material, which confirms that Abraham taught his intensely sacerdotal and genealogical astronomy at pharaoh's court.[82] Facsimile 3 is based on a vignette that modern Egyptologists term an Osiris throne scene, from the *Book of Breathings*, in which the god Osiris receives offerings and perhaps the decedent.[83]

The facsimiles thus appear to be important connections between the grammar documents and the main scripture, and the Egyptian Bible and the temple liturgy. They exemplify the interpretive approach Smith and his collaborators took to the encounter with hieroglyphs. They also fit well into the category of graphic glossolalia, filling a similar role in the lives of believers.

So much for the texts themselves. The themes they explore are what now draw our attention. The content focuses closely on Smith's transformation of the

---

[78] Abraham 1:14. The facsimiles are published in *T&S* 3:9 (March 1, 1842): 703; 3:10 (March 15, 1842): 722a; 3:14 (May 16, 1842): 783–84. Some words are found in both the vignettes and the grammar documents but with varying meaning (e.g., Oliblish, Enish-go-on-dosh, Kae-e-vanrash, Jah-oheh, Flo-eese).

[79] See *T&S* 3:14 (May 16, 1842): 790, and a reprint from the New York *Herald* in *T&S* 3:13 (May 2, 1842): 773–74. See also *The Wasp* 1:2 (April 23, 1842): 3, in which William Smith (Joseph's erratic brother) responded to allegations that the facsimiles unmasked Latter-day Saint intentions to perform human sacrifice. Kidder, *Mormonism*, 335, parodied the facsimile as "Illustration of Mormonism, No. 1."

[80] On this resurrection scene, see Baer, "Breathing Permit," 118.

[81] See discussion in Ehat, "Mormon Succession," 43–4.

[82] As a lens onto the early interpretive plurality, *M&A*, 2:3 (December 1835): 236, argues that the vignette is a scene of the last judgment rather than a reference to Abraham teaching in Pharaoh's court.

[83] On the motif of Osiris on his throne, see Coenen, "Document of Breathing," 40–41.

traditional Chain of Being into his genealogical Chain of Belonging as a conceptual infrastructure for a communalistic heaven.

Themes of the Egyptian Bible

Smith's Egyptian project explores, in complementary ways, themes at the center of early Latter-day Saint thought. The documents ground these ideas in the Abrahamic hinge point between the primeval history and the rest of the Bible. These thematic explorations help to clarify the contexts and themes of the early Restoration. I see three main motifs at play in Smith's Egyptian Bible. First, the documents present sacred pictography as constituting metaphysically correspondent language, which united ancient languages in one. Second, the Egyptian project provides imagery of female power, which is part of its notion of priesthood grounded in parenthood. Third and relatedly, these documents elaborate at length Smith's Chain of Belonging, which extends the interconnections among human microcosm and stellar macrocosm and leads back to the earth's primordium in Eden.

In this Egyptian Bible, we get a glimpse of Smith's project: to interconnect humanity across time and space through an expansive metaphysics. As he does so, he resists the sharp boundary markers increasingly imposed by proponents of modernity.

The Metaphysics of Pictography

The Egyptian Bible project extended work on the recovery of the pure language, including the modification of Smith's Sample of Pure Language in May 1835, discussed in chapter 1. In that "specimen" of pure language, Phelps used Hebrew-sounding transcriptions for some characters, much as the subsequent grammar documents did. Importantly, although Phelps seems to have included Masonic ciphers (which relied on a 1:1 correlation between code letter and real letter) in his specimen, he interpreted the ciphers as pictograms rather than letter equivalents.[84]

The bulk of the attention to the power of pictograms comes in the grammar documents and the facsimiles, although the canonized Book of Abraham

---

[84] W. W. Phelps to Sally Phelps, May 26, 1835, HBLL. Will Schryver identified the Masonic cipher, although he has not yet published his observations. The transliterations sound like the Hebrew letters *zayin* and *ayin*, although the associated characters are not similar to the Hebrew letters. For sample Masonic ciphers, see Bernard, *Light on Masonry*, 143, 248, 251.

also reflects these concerns, foregrounding its discovery of the pure name for pictograms. These texts provide a crucial connection to the hieroglyphic quest that predated them. The documents treat glyphs as pictograms charged with metaphysical power. These pictograms connected to both literal referents and expanded semantic targets in a cascading reference.

Many if not most of the grammar interpretations are pictographic. A dot, like the pupil of an eye, is *Iota*, "the eye or to see or sight," a visual leitmotif in the documents. One "compound" of *Iota* appears to be an eye with a horizontal eyelash.[85] The pictograms could also be geographical, such as a curved line like a horizon interpreted as "the whole earth" or "the whole of anything." When the curve is inverted, it takes on an antipodal meaning—"under the sun; under heaven; downward . . . going down into the grave; going down into misery = even Hell").[86]

Smith, Phelps, and Cowdery practiced a combinative pictography: several important glyphs are composites. A character associated with Abraham's origins is "shown dissected" by treating its individual strokes as distinct characters.[87] Similarly, a stick figure (*Ho hah oop*) represents Jesus, an "intercessor." This figure's left leg is the glyph for delegation (*Jah-ni-hah*), anticipating the Abraham 3 account of a savior, Jesus, chosen as God's legate to earth in the premortal drama.[88] The glyph for *Kiahbroam* combines the character for *Zub Zool oan* ("first man or father of fathers") with an eye (*ki*) and a figure that seems to trace the horizon.[89] The composite glyph means "a father of many nations," a novel deconstruction of the patriarch's name. Implicit within this gloss is the image of Abraham seeing his posterity and thereby comprehending the earth.[90] These pictograms held the story of Abraham's covenant: his offspring would extend to the visible horizon and beyond.

The glyph interpretations often merged physical and metaphorical meanings. The glyph *Zi* (an upside-down "T") means both "upright" and "modest and chaste being taught most perfectly."[91] The same glyph is later transcribed as *Zub*, now described as vertical ascent: "leading up or to: the time for going up to the altar to worship; going up before the Lord[;] being caught up."[92]

The grammar documents, among other aspects of the Egyptian project, confirm the early Latter-day Saint belief that sacred languages could be united. In

---

[85] *JSPR4*, 56–57, 118–19. *JSPR4*, 355, displays all variants of *Iota*.
[86] *JSPR4*, 124–25.
[87] *JSPR4*, 120–21.
[88] *JSPR4*, 180–81. *Jah-ni-hah* represented "one who was the second person in authority." Cf. Abraham 3:24.
[89] More than one glyph and name was associated with vision or the eye.
[90] *JSPR4*, 120–21, 124–25.
[91] *JSPR4*, 122–23, 131–32.
[92] *JSPR4*, 126–27.

a statement later attributed to Smith, Cowdery claimed that "many characters or letters [on the papyri are] exactly like the present, (though probably not quite so square,) form of the Hebrew without points."[93] In other words, Hebrew and Egyptian scripts were kindred. The Book of Mormon (1 Nephi 1:2) set the stage for such a merger, as the Nephites wrote a language "which consists of the learning of the Jews and the language of the Egyptians." In his own engagement of the Book of Mormon characters, Cowdery labeled the ancient language underlying them as "Hebrew."[94] These sentiments partook of Egyptological traditions. Thus, the French writer Pierre Lacour reported in a widely circulated 1821 essay that the language of ancient Egypt was Hebrew, including the script.[95] It's unlikely that Smith and Phelps read Lacour's *Essai sur les hieroglyphes*, but they participated in ancient and widely disseminated traditions about the unity of sacred languages. We ought not to be surprised that the early Saints soon turned to their Hebrew teacher to help them solve their Egyptian problem. If he could only teach them Hebrew, they seem to have believed, they would be one crucial step closer to mastering Egyptian hieroglyphs.

Many of the transcriptions in the grammar documents sound Hebrew; Hebrew letter names are invoked for certain glyphs, including *aleph, beth,* and *gimel*.[96] The interpretations of those names at least once play off the traditional pictographic accounts of the origin of those Hebrew letters (e.g., *beth* as house). The name for Egypt (*Ah meh strah*) seems to be a modification of the name of Ham's son Mizraim, perhaps via Josephus, with the divine particle (*ah*) prepended.[97] In essence, *ah-meh-strah* may be equivalent to *ah-miz-ra*, with the *-im* at the end of *Mizraim* dropped because it appeared to be a grammatical plural.

The focus on the deep unity of sacred languages likely also explains why Smith included obviously Hebrew or Hebrew-derived words as Egyptian terms in the Book of Abraham and the facsimile interpretations. Among the Hebrew words (often using the Seixas transcription scheme) are Raukeeyang (i.e., *raqia*, "firmament"; facsimiles 1 and 2), Elkenah (1 Samuel 1:1), ha-kokobeam (*ha-kokabim*,

---

[93] *M&A*, 2:3 (December 1835): 234. Cowdery appears to have based this assessment on Moses Stuart, *Grammar of Hebrew*, 12, which told the story of Hebrew script, including the "present *square* form of the Hebrew letters." Cowdery had purchased the Stuart grammar during a trip to New York to purchase reference works for translation in October–November 1835.

[94] *JSPD1*, 361–64.

[95] Iversen, *Myth of Egypt*, 131.

[96] *Aleph* (*JSPR4*, 176–77) is the top half of the Hebrew letter and means "in the beginning with God, the son, or first born"; *Ba eth* (*JSPR4*, 168–69) is somewhat stylized but recognizable as *beth*, while the glyph named *Beth* (*JSPR4*, 160–61) is a hatched single line meaning "residence." *Gah mel* (*JSPR4*, 180–81) appears to be a *gimel* laid on its side and refers to a "promising situation." These might suggest that the Stuart grammar was used in constructing parts of the grammar documents. This use of Hebrew letters does not, however, require the arrival of Seixas, as Cowdery had brought Hebrew reference works back to Kirtland by November 1835.

[97] *JSPR4*, 126–27. Smith, "Dependence," 46, suggests that Josephus's rendering (*Antiquities* 1:6:2) as *Mestre* affected the phrasing in *GAEL*.

"the stars"; facsimile 2), and shammau/shaumahyeem (*shamaim*, "expanse," facimile 1). In the case of the firmament and the heavens, Smith openly equated *raqia* and *shamaim*, seeing the facsimile as an opportunity to perform an exegesis of the Hebrew of Genesis 1. He clearly knew that he was engaging Hebrew in this targum; he just saw the Hebrew Bible as deeply connected to Egyptian.[98]

The unity of ancient sacred languages encompassed all the languages of sacred writ. New Testament Greek terms and phrases also appear in the grammar documents. *Alpha* and *Omega* combine (perhaps under the influence of Smith's Edenic word for God, *Ahman*) as *Ahmeos*, a symbol similar to the capital Greek *alpha* that means "God without beginning or end."[99] *Hades* appears in several permutations involving *Hahdees*, a glyph like the lowercase Greek *lambda* referring to the "kingdom of wickedness." Even Arabic numerals joined the fray, in a document in Phelps's hand matching essentially all the numbers from one to nine to Egyptian characters.[100]

Phelps and Smith recognized Hebrew and Greek letters and words: the intermixing of ancient languages in the Egyptian project was unlikely to be accidental. The merger reflected instead their belief in the unity of scriptural languages at their pictographic beginnings. In the language beyond languages in which God spoke the world into existence, the sacred languages could have a shared origin. What is often seen as a novice mistake in the Egyptian project is evidence of Smith's and Phelps's deep belief that sacred languages retained at least some fragments of the deep unity in the original language.[101]

In 1843, Phelps and Smith proposed an etymology of the word "Mormon" that confirmed their ongoing belief in the continuity of ancient languages. The etymology positions *mon* as the Egyptian equivalent of the Hebrew word *tob* or the Greek term *kalos*. By combining *mon* with the English word "more," the polyglot portmanteau *Mormon* therefore meant "more good."[102] In their autodidactic way, Phelps and Smith were continuing to position Egyptian hieroglyphs as a solution to Babel's plurality.

Sacred pictography and the intermixing of scriptural languages once again point to the pervasive influence of metaphysical correspondence in early Latter-day Saint scripture. Pictograms were morsels of language that bound objects and concepts in space. The sacred overlap of Hebrew, Egyptian, and Greek represented times (and textual spaces) when languages were deeply,

---

[98] In this respect, Smith mirrored the promiscuous intermixing of languages in some antique magic papyri. Betz, *Greek Magical Papyri*. Many of these syncretic spells include names of deities or other incantations in an array of non-Egyptian languages.

[99] On *Ahmeos*, see *JSPR4*, 180–81, and *JSPR4*, 56–57. For context, see Webster, *American Dictionary*, s.v. "A"; and D&C 95:17.

[100] Brown, "(Smith) in Egypt," 55–56.

[101] Walton, "Professor Seixas."

[102] Brown, "(Smith) in Egypt," 56.

even constitutively, interconnected. A formal grammatical construct within the grammar documents had a similar role to play in expressing the power of metaphysical correspondence. A horizontal line interpreted as a visual marker to specify the degrees was itself intimately tied to reproduction and genealogy.[103] Those connections mediated by the notion of degree are intimately tied to lineage and reproduction, a model of priesthood that had an easy and sustained connection to the power of women.

The Priestess and the Multiplication of Power

In addition to sacred pictography, another important theme in the grammar documents is the divinity of women. Given the centrality of Eve to the Garden of Eden story and the intimate ties—mediated through Abraham and Sarah—between priesthood and reproduction, we should not be surprised to see images of female power in the Egyptian Bible. In fact, the Egyptian materials, especially the grammar documents, abound with accounts of women's sacred authority.

The gender association may have benefited from the depiction of several female figures in the papyri themselves. For Cowdery, the most noteworthy was a picture of Eve speaking with a legged snake, thus confirming the Genesis account of Eve's temptation. "The serpent, represented as walking, or formed in a manner to be able to walk, standing in front of, and near a female figure, is to me, one of the greatest representations I have ever seen."[104] In that drawing, Cowdery saw an external evidence for the Bible. Smith, happy enough with such evidence, had other things in mind for the figure of Eve. Eve permeated the grammar documents both directly and through her female offspring. Notably, Eve was the one God instructed to multiply and replenish the earth (Genesis 1:28) in the Bible account. That sense of multiplication, kindred to the notion of semantic ramification, played an important role in Smith's Egyptian targum and its engagement of the priestess.

Especially as it connected with the recreation of the world in the aftermath of the flood—when Noah and his wives received the same commandment as Eve, to multiply and replenish the earth (Genesis 9:1)—Smith's Egyptian project contains accounts of female priestly power spread across multiple figures and scenes. This female sacerdotal power, tied to reproduction, is in many respects a prequel to the full flowering of Smith's parental system of priesthood in the

---

[103] Brown, "(Smith) in Egypt," 59–61.
[104] M&A, 2:3 (December 1835): 236, describing a vignette on Joseph Smith Papyrus 4. William Appleby confirmed that interpretation in a reminiscent account in his Autobiography and Journal, 1848–1856, 72–73, CHL.

Nauvoo temple (chapter 7), in which women were formally ordained as queens and priestesses.[105]

The priestess theme in Smith's Egyptian Bible encompasses two main aspects. The first concerns the discovery of Egypt by a woman who is the eponym for the Egyptian nation. The story of the special women who were both named Egypt (in fact, a mother-daughter pair) is present in Smith's Egyptian project as a suggestive hint rather than a sustained narrative. In Josephus and other sources, Egyptus was understood to be the male eponym for Egypt. The identification of a woman with Egyptus appears to be novel with Smith and Phelps.[106] In the published Book of Abraham, the relevant material reads, "The land of Egypt being first discovered by a woman, who was the daughter of Ham, and the daughter of Egyptus, which, in the Chaldean, signifies Egypt, which signifies, that which is forbidden; when this woman discovered the land it was under water" (Abraham 1:23–24).[107] This brief account appears to be filling in the otherwise obscure action of Genesis 8:16, in which Noah's sons and daughters-in-law must explore the newly dry earth as the flood waters recede.[108] In the earliest manuscripts, *Zeptah* is Ham's wife, her name drawn from the glyphs for *Zip* and *Tah*. Her daughter with Ham was named Egyptus. The name Egyptus likely spread from daughter to mother as an inadvertent merger of the two names within the manuscripts.[109]

The association between the enigmatic woman and the discovery of Egypt is present in the grammar documents as well, and it appears to derive from an image on Fragment of Book of the Dead for Semminis, in which a woman is rowing a boat as she perhaps looks into the distance under the shade of her right hand (Figure 6.2).[110]

Presumably, she espies a land just discovered under the water on which she floats. Importantly for this argument, just beneath her vessel is the character that is identified in *GAEL* as *Iota taues Zip Zi*, decoded as "The land of Egypt which was first discovered by a woman."[111] This composite glyph combines *Zip Zi* (woman), *Iota* (sight), and *taues* (being under water). Beneath that character is the horizontal line that the grammar documents define as the ramifying "degree" (Figure 6.3).

---

[105] On queens and priestesses, see, e.g., England, "Nauvoo Journal," 164, and Lewis, *Proceedings of the Mormons*, 8.
[106] Josephus, *Works*, 584.
[107] The name of Ham's wife is not attested in the Bible. The Apocryphal Book of Jubilees identifies it as Neelatamauk; other sources propose other names. None that I can locate proposes Egyptus.
[108] Egypt was thought to have been founded "soon after the deluge." *M&A* 3:6 (March 1837): 471.
[109] Metcalfe, "Wife of Ham."
[110] She appears to me to be holding the upper section of her oar; I'm following what I suspect was the interpretation of Phelps and Smith. For the full papyrus, see *JSPR4*, 16–17.
[111] *JSPR4*, 124–25.

Figure 6.2 Image from Fragment of Book of the Dead for Semminis—C, a possible textual anchor for the Egyptus tradition in Smith's Egyptian Bible. Image courtesy of the Church History Library, The Church of Jesus Christ of Latter-day Saints.

Figure 6.3 Magnified image of the character for woman/degree in the bottom left of the image in Figure 6.2. Image courtesy of the Church History Library, The Church of Jesus Christ of Latter-day Saints.

Even beyond the highly suggestive characters adjacent to the vignette of the woman apparently discovering something from her boat, the grammar documents generally support this line of interpretation. A woman is the eponym for Egypt, and the discovery of Egypt is connected to water. Beyond the image of a woman rowing, the connection to Ham (it is his wife and daughter, after all, who are named Egyptus) is fundamentally a connection to Ham's father Noah and the repopulation of the world after the flood in Genesis 8–9. (Ham is associated with Egypt in the Bible and parabiblical traditions, generally through his son Mizraim.[112])

Phelps and Smith seem to have seen the female figure in the boat, known that Ham was associated with Egypt, and understood that the female figure—surely a daughter-in-law to Noah from Genesis 8:16—was associated with the discovery of Egypt as the floodwaters receded. To understand the metaphysical basis for this claim requires the papyrus and its vignette, Smith's commitment to sacred pictography, and biblical traditions about Ham and the flood in the context of the Noachide recapitulation of the world's first peopling. This confluence of inputs speaks to the sense in which Smith's project was precisely a targum and the papyri were the infrastructure for the pictographic connections that made the targum possible.

If the first point about female authority in the Egyptian project is Smith's novel assertion that Egypt was discovered by a woman, the second is his connection between women, priesthood power, and the generations of time. The specific female figure—the eponymous matriarchal founder of Egypt—joined others in wielding female power in the expression of matriarchal authority over later generations. The small and generative glyph *Zip* does work throughout the grammar documents. Not only does it figure in the name *Zeptah* that morphed into *Egyptus*, it is also a term consistently associated with women. *Zip Zi* in the fourth degree of the first part is "all women" and is explicitly tied to multiplication and numerals.

Throughout the grammar documents, humans and their relationships are inter-convertible with language, generally through this equivalence of biological and grammatical multiplication.[113] The hieratic glyph that is transliterated *Zip Zi* appears to be the underscore mark, the horizontal line that marks the ramification of semantic degrees, as we discussed earlier. This dual use of a single glyph as a grammatical construct and as a name for women implicitly argues that female power is tied to the ramifications and interconnections of hieroglyphic language. *Zip Zi* as the name for a glyph shows up in several other locations,

---

[112] Psalms 78:51, 105:23–27, 106:22. On Mizraim, see Creighton, *Sacred and Profane History*, 1:127–28. See also discussion in Fleming, *Scripture Gazetteer*, 1:441.
[113] *JSPR4*, 134–35.

generally representing a variant of women or in one definition "a tittle or dignity conferred upon women." Other semantically similar glyphs are taken to indicate the "crown of a princess or queen." Repeatedly, then, glyphs for women represented royal power and authority. Commonly in early Restoration thought, such invocations of royal power were tied to priesthood.[114] The Egyptian project and its predecessors thus saw titles, dignities, and royalty as synonymous with priesthood.

Beyond but related to *Egyptus* and *Zip Zi*, we encounter another royal-priestly female figure in the story of the pharaonic princess whom Smith seems to have identified among the mummies.[115] We can trace this figure, *Katumin*, through the grammatical degrees of the *GAEL*. A series of glyphs follows her, an archetypal princess, through a process of maturation from a young virgin to an established mother. In other words, the grammatical degrees track her ascent along a reproductive hierarchy that parallels the extension of priestly power.[116] The grammatical degrees of reference run alongside the expansion of a genealogical priesthood power through marriage and reproduction in Katumin's life.

Early in the grammar documents, a compressed ellipse is the character associated with Katumin. The association between that character and women may derive from Fragment of Book of the Dead for Semminis, in which a female figure appears to be pouring water onto a tree. The water droplets look like the character interpreted as Katumin, recalling especially the tie to the receding flood waters associated with Egyptian women in the *Egyptus* narrative (Figure 6.4).

Furthermore, Katumin is defined as "a lineage with whom a record of the fathers was intrusted by tradition of Ham, and according to the tradition of their elders, by whom also the tradition of the art of embalming was kept."[117] This seems to be a reference to the fact that the mummies held the papyri in their arms, but it also connected back to the persistent themes of genealogy, priesthood, and scripture. Remember that genealogical records are, among other things, concerned with the transmission of priestly authority in Smith's exegesis of Ezra 2 (see chapter 1). Elsewhere, Katumin is tied to "the name of the royal

---

[114] The suggestion of a royal priesthood underlying the equivalence of kings and priests seems to be an exegesis of Revelation 1:6 and 5:10, which Smith understood to be using the term "kings and priests" as a synonymous couplet rather than a list of separate statuses. Smith used that imagery in his 1832 Vision (D&C 76:56–58), journal entries in 1843 (*JSPJ3*, 66, 86), and sermons in 1844 (Historian's Office, General Church Minutes, April 7 and April 8, 1844, CR 100 318, bx. 1, fd. 19, CHL). See also *JSPAR*, 95–96, 278, and Willard Richards, Nauvoo, IL, to Brigham Young, New York City, NY, July 18–19, 1843, Brigham Young Office Files, CR 1234 1, bx. 41, fd. 28, CHL. I thank Brady Winslow for these sources.

[115] On the possibility that Katumin was one of the mummies Smith purchased, see Brown, "(Smith) in Egypt," 61n150.

[116] This maturation progresses in parallel in the definitions of *Ho oop hah*. See discussion in Brown, "(Smith) in Egypt," 60–61.

[117] *JSPR4*, 120–23, 156–57.

Figure 6.4 Image from Fragment of Book of the Dead for Semminis—C, suggesting a comparison between water droplets and the glyph (inset at the bottom drawn from GAEL) associated with Princess Katumin in Smith's Egyptian Bible. Image courtesy of the Church History Library, The Church of Jesus Christ of Latter-day Saints.

family in the female line."[118] One other stray hint suggests that Katumin may have been associated with Solomon's Temple, when Cowdery used the Bishop Ussher chronology to indicate that the Egyptian princess was born in *Anno Mundi* 2992, the year of Solomon's Temple.[119]

To recap, a princess named Katumin, bearing specially charged records, represents a lineage and exemplifies the idea of grammatical and reproductive degrees as fulfillment of the biblical mandates to multiply. Consistent with Smith's other teachings (and as was true for men also), this priestly power of

---

[118] *JSPR4*, 56–57.

[119] *JSPR4*, 31, Cowdery's "Valuable Discovery" document. The "2962" in the text is an error, as Cowdery indicates that she lived twenty-eight years and died in Anno Mundi (AM) 3020. Her birth year was thus AM 2992. According to the standard Ussher chronology, that is the year of Solomon's temple and the conclusion of the Abrahamic period. Ussher reported that the world was created in 4004 BCE.

women appears to be tied to parenthood, procreation, and the cycle of generations. In other words, women are central priestly participants in the realization of the Abrahamic blessing in the world.[120] There's even a hint that *Katumin* may be a reference to a type (i.e., an archetypal princess) in her "descent from her by whom Egypt was discovered while it was under water."[121] In other words, Katumin came from Egypt. They partook of the same royal line. By extension, so will the women who follow.

Within the canonized Book of Abraham, the main reflexes of princess Katumin's story are a brief reference to priestly virgins sacrificed by pagan priests (Abraham 1:11) and the ongoing emphasis on genealogy and reproduction. While the Book of Abraham doesn't make this point explicit, this merger of reproduction and priesthood power suggests that the instructions to Eve and Adam to "multiply and replenish the earth" (Genesis 1:28), mirrored in the parallel instructions to Noah and his family (Genesis 8), were in fact priesthood callings.

According to the Egyptian project, men exist with power parallel to that of women. One glyph for a powerful patriarch describes the "extension of power by marriage or by ordination,"[122] suggesting the ongoing interconnection of marital and priestly power. This reference again ties the priesthood that Smith associated with both Egypt and his temple to parenthood, a physical and metaphysical force in which both men and women participated. The Book of Abraham's treatment of this genealogical priesthood hovered between engaging the problems with Egypts's offspring (because of Ham's curse, which separated him from Abraham's covenanted blessings) and the power that inheres in the genealogical priesthood.[123]

The twin concepts of genealogy and priesthood seem to represent, in these hieroglyphic stories about Abraham, two sides of the same coin. In the published scripture, God tells Abraham that he and his seed are, by definition, "Priesthood" (Abraham 2:11). In fact, this brief sequence of verses (2:9–11) reinterprets Genesis 17:6–8 in a way that exemplifies the conceptual work that Smith's targums did. In place of the relatively simple announcement of Abraham's covenant in Genesis, Smith's Abraham offered an expansive reframing in terms of a priesthood that could interconnect all of humanity.[124] As opposed to the terse promise of plentiful offspring in Genesis, the Book of Abraham reveals that Abraham's

---

[120] Hovorka, "Sarah and Hagar" suggests that women are involved in the Abrahamic covenants in the Bible. Hovorka probably did not go far enough in her appreciation of the power attributed to women in Smith's Egyptian project. Stapley, *Power of Godliness*, does emphasize the role of women in that early notion of priesthood.

[121] *JSPR4*, 140–41.

[122] *JSPR4*, 132–33; Brown, "(Smith) in Egypt," 57–63.

[123] See, e.g., Abraham 1: 2–4, 18, 24; 2:10–11.

[124] I thank Kathleen Flake for bringing this juxtaposition to my awareness.

progeny "shall bear this ministry and Priesthood unto all nations." The ministry is the evangelism of strangers into Abraham's family—"as many as receive this gospel shall be called after thy name and shall be accounted thy seed." The Book of Abraham hammered home the deep and necessary dependence of priesthood (the power that converted believers and organized them in the church) on parenthood (biological multiplication), specifically that of Abraham and Sarah. Priesthood was thus explicitly the power by which Abraham's and Sarah's sacred parenthood could unfold across the globe. This notion of Abrahamic priesthood had deep roots in Smith's revelations, and through the Egyptian project the necessary incorporation of women into that priesthood became somewhat clearer.

The promise of priestly power for women was exciting for many participants, even as it unfolded in the context of assumptions about the nature of gender that have not weathered the interceding decades well. Smith and Phelps were endorsing neither late modern gender equality nor Victorian sexual norms. The priestess theology of the Egyptian Bible engaged the intersection of heavenly and earthly powers as they concerned genealogy and reproduction.[125]

In Smith's Abrahamic system (especially as manifest in the Egyptian Bible and the accompanying temple liturgy), women were sources of power, although their power could only be wielded in company with men. This was true throughout the early Restoration—women had striking power, which they could not wield in isolation. The hierarchy of men over women—a connection between the classical Chain of Being and Smith's genealogical revision as the Chain of Belonging—is apparent in the grammar documents. Another interpretation of the glyph *Zip Zi* (third degree) reads "under or beneeath, second in right or in authority or Government, a fruitful place or fruitful vine."[126] This was the combination consistently present in Smith's thought—women had vast cosmic powers that they wielded with men who stood higher in an ontic hierarchy.[127]

Smith's Egyptian Bible highlights aspects of a female priesthood—centered in the fulfillment of the Genesis command to multiply and replenish the earth—that came to fruition over the course of the Egyptian project as it became the Nauvoo temple liturgy. While in the temple that female priesthood became formally codified and implemented, the textual tributaries appear in Smith's Egyptian Bible. Women's connection to life, mediated through the first mother Eve, makes the human family possible. Smith's Egyptian Bible, with its focus on parenthood-based priesthood, brings women directly into the royal line.

---

[125] This is a major argument of Stapley, *Power of Godliness*, who charts the persistence of this "cosmological" model through approximately 1890.
[126] *JSPR4*, 140–41.
[127] Kathleen Flake (e.g., "Priestly Logic") has written insightfully on these themes.

Women thus stand at the center of the Chain of Belonging, another major theme within the Egyptian project.

The Chain of Belonging, Human and Astral

Smith tied his notions of interlaced priesthood and parenthood to a radical reinterpretation of the ancient scientific construct of the Chain of Being, which was an ontological hierarchy encompassing the entire universe in which all classes of beings differ from each other in their essence. This foundation of a lineal priesthood was central to Smith's strategy to advance a genealogical Chain of Belonging in which humans, angels, and Gods were genetically interconnected. The new hierarchy was genealogical rather than ontological.

Smith's approach to humans' mutual embeddedness placed him in the crosscurrents of several of the ideological shifts later associated with secularity, as we saw in chapter 3. When it came to questions of extrahuman biology, he seemed comfortable with the Chain of Being, as manifested by a reference to the "scale of nature" and a straightforward endorsement in an 1832 revelation (D&C 77:3). For example, he saw in the beasts of Revelation representatives of the various "classes of beings in their destined order or sphere of creation." But when it came to rigid ontological or aristocratic hierarchies, he largely rejected the Chain of Being.[128] Instead of the gradations in ontology from the classic Chain of Being, Smith argued that human beings were interconnected in a vast family tree. The hierarchy was parental, genealogical; the power that interconnected humanity was called priesthood. Smith's genealogical Chain made it all the way to (and perhaps through) God. The God of the Bible was in his view not the wholly transcendent creator of the Chain of Being, but the oldest progenitor of the genealogical Chain of Belonging.

Smith's revelations in 1832 and 1833 paved the way for this revised understanding, with the introduction of hierarchies in heaven in the Vision and the Olive Leaf. The Vision saw a reference to "many mansions" (John 14:2) as indicating a hierarchy of afterlife kingdoms, while the Olive Leaf tied this to the possibility of human perfection. Those prior revelations are a template for the astronomical observations in Abraham. Smith's April 1836 vision indicated the connection between an Elias/Elijah figure and Abraham: "Elias appeared and committed the dispensation of the gospel of Abraham, saying, that in them and their seed all generations after them should be blessed."[129] This notion that

---

[128] For contemporary discussions of the Chain of Being, see *M&A* 1:8 (May 1835): 113; *M&A* 1:7 (April 1835): 108;, and William Phelps, Letter to Sally Phelps, May 26, 1835, HBLL.
[129] *JSPD5*, 228.

one's seed would be blessed as Latter-day Saints participated in the Abrahamic promise was ubiquitous. Believers incorporated these images further into their writings and revelations. Lorenzo Barnes received a blessing telling him that "all the powers of the priesthood we seal upon thy head & upon thy sead forever."[130] Priesthood and offspring were consistently interrelated.

The Book of Abraham makes clear that God had spoken with Abraham "face to face," the same as he had with Moses (Abraham 3:11), and provides a panoramic vision. This new vision starts with God revealing the sacred names of celestial bodies, apparently to complement Abraham's knowledge of their set times. (These special names may be the astral equivalents of the new names of the temple; see chapter 7.)

Immediately the Book of Abraham relates the conversation in which God tells Abraham that he will have unlimited progeny (an anticipation of the earthly Abrahamic covenant of Genesis 15 and 17) by assuring that the reader knows that the vision occurred at night, when the stars would be visible (Abraham 3:14, cf. Genesis 22:17). The text then reiterates the principle of hierarchy and places God at the head of the Chain of Belonging (3:18–19).

Shortly thereafter begins a famous account (3:22–28) of the preexistent "intelligences" among whom Christ predominates. The Book of Abraham sketches out (3:27) the backstory of the cosmic theomachy and an account of God's leadership of a team of demiurges (a term I borrow from Plato's *Timaeus* for the "craftsman" who made the cosmos from an ideal divine template) who craft an earth for humans to inhabit and be tested, while deploying an obscure reference to the "first estate" lost by certain angels in Jude 6.[131] Abraham 3 thus pulls together disparate biblical materials to extend the primeval history into a time before time. It thereby establishes the original infrastructure of the Chain of Belonging, which simultaneously integrates celestial bodies into the family of angels, gods, and humans.

One particularly expansive glyph interpretation in the grammar documents points out what Smith was doing with his Chain of Belonging. The glyph for the celestial kingdom recapitulated the Vision (D&C 76) and anticipated the celestial marriage revelation (D&C 132). This glyph combines four simpler glyphs: *Lish* (God), *Zi* (woman or queen), *ho e oop* (prince), and *Iota* (sight/eye). This composite glyph is glossed as "one glory above all other glories, as the [sun] excels the moon in light, this glory excels being filled with the same glory equally." In other words, the glyph reiterated the astral hierarchy of glories described in the

---

[130] *JSPD5*, 135.
[131] The theomachy is also described in Moses 4 and Revelation 12. The reference to the council of demiurges also contains a vague but intriguing evocation of the Gnostic contest and perhaps an echo of Job's famous trial, which begins in Job 1:7–12.

1832 Vision in a way that emphasized the familial unity of the highest echelon of the celestial Chain. When the Egyptian pictogram placed a man and a woman together in the presence of God, Smith subsumed the traditional Chain of Being into the human family, whose "many parts" were thereby "united."[132] This was his Chain of Belonging. Several other glyphs similarly describe the "degrees and parts" of the many afterlife kingdoms described in the 1832 Vision.[133] These interpretations and the revelations they draw on together get at the possibilities of harmonies among human beings in heaven and on earth.

Smith emphasized the association between the funerary papyri and "the system of astronomy" that "was unfolded" through them, with a special focus on "the formation of the planetary System."[134] Though it is tempting to situate the astrophysical speculations of Smith's Egyptian Bible within established astronomies—Ptolemaic, Copernican, or otherwise—early Latter-day Saint ideas about stars aren't fundamentally concerned with the concepts of formal astronomy.[135] They cared much more about the overlapping hierarchies of humans, stars, and gods.[136] They were, in other words, fleshing out their Chain of Belonging in its human and astral aspects.

These stars wove themselves into human souls and societies, existing in hierarchies that paralleled and sustained human genealogy. These hierarchies touched human lives in part through the control of time by celestial bodies. Within the grammar documents, Smith, Phelps, and Cowdery wove together an exegesis of the Hebrew astrogony (cf. Genesis 1:14–18, with its emphasis on stars as ruling and determining), a literal reading of 2 Peter 3:8 ("one day is with the Lord as a thousand years"), and the commonplace view, confirmed by Buck's *Theological Dictionary*, that time is a "mode of duration marked by certain periods, chiefly by the motion and revolution of the sun."[137] Smith, Phelps, and Cowdery suggested that celestial bodies determined their *gravitas* on the basis of the time signaled by the length of their orbit.

People had long known from astronomy that days were defined by movement through space. The transition on earth from light to dark and back again happened because the earth spun on its axis as it hurtled through space, and the years, marked by the transitions of seasons, occurred because the earth made its way around the sun. That was all clear enough. A few months before the papyri

---

[132] *JSPR4*, 160–61.
[133] *JSPR4*, 160–61, 180–81.
[134] *JSPJ1*, 67, 124.
[135] Bushman, *Rough Stone*, 454–55; Vogel and Metcalfe, "Scriptural Cosmology"; Gee, "Geocentric Astronomy."
[136] Thus William Warburton reports that in ancient hieroglyphs a star "denoted or expressed the idea of the DEITY." *Divine Legation*, 2:295.
[137] Buck, *Theological Dictionary*, 573. Webster's 1828 dictionary contained a similar description of "relative time."

arrived, Oliver Cowdery had conscientiously referred to "a few days, measured by this present sun."[138] In an editorial shortly after the publication of the Book of Abraham, Smith and his colleagues argued that human "spirits are governed by the same priesthood that Abraham, Melchizedec, and the apostles were" and that "they are organized according to that priesthood which is everlasting." Tying human genealogies to cosmic hierarchy, as the Book of Abraham does consistently, the editorial indicated that these human spirits "all move in their respective spheres, and are governed by the law of God."[139]

The hieroglyphs provided an instrument for clarification of the nature of astral time. To solidify their biblical foundation, Smith and Phelps employed cubits as an astronomical metric.[140] In heaven "the measurement according to Celestial time" was held to "signif[y] one day to a cubit, which day is equal to a thousand years according to the measurement of this earth."[141] These cubits (one quarter of "the leng[th] from the end of the longest finger to the end of the other when the arms are extended," or approximately twenty-one inches) measured the arc length of an orbit, thus the amount of time required to revolve around a center place.[142] Smith and Phelps apparently employed the notion that a span called a cubit subtended one degree of the sun's orbit around the earth.[143] (Neither Phelps nor Smith was so obtuse as to believe that a star's orbit was less than two feet.) Their method therefore described a celestial orbit from the perspective of an individual on a subservient planet, watching the dominant celestial body. The measure of that movement was both bodily (defined in terms of an individual's limbs) and sacred (it was a measurement in the Hebrew Bible). These sacred cubits also connected back to the first human body. In the phrase of one popular lecturer, such measurements were "coeval with [the] hand of our first father Adam!"[144] In this early Latter-day Saint view, cubits emphasized the close association between humans and the cosmos in sacred astronomy. Just as orbits measured human lives, so did human bodies measure orbits. These concepts are not precisely the zodiacal body of folk religion, though they draw on the same conceptual framework of metaphysical correspondence.[145] The published Book of

---

[138] M&A 1:7 (April 1835): 108.

[139] T&S 3:11 (April 1, 1842): 745.

[140] These cubits also appear in Facsimile 2.

[141] JSPR4, 166–67. Cubits are generally defined as 21 to 27 inches and reflect the length of a forearm from elbow to fingertip. Clarke, Holy Bible, 2:261, described various definitions of "cubit" in his exegesis of 1 Samuel 17:4. Buck, Theological Dictionary, 31 defined a cubit as 21.8 inches, within the range Phelps and Smith proposed.

[142] JSPR4, 178–79.

[143] Such is the persuasive argument of the emeritus astronomer Johnson "One Day." See also, e.g., Seymer, Ancient Egypt, 1:252, and Narrien, Astronomy, 77. While Seymer's and Narrien's books are admittedly British publications, British books commonly circulated in the United States, and they suggest the presence of traditions relevant to the use of a cubit of arc length to describe an orbit.

[144] T&S 5:5 (March 1, 1844): 462.

[145] On the zodiacal body, see Butler, Sea of Faith, 80.

Abraham confirms the material from the grammar documents in its description of a gradation of "set times" for stars leading "unto the throne of God" (Abraham 3:10, 4:15–6).

Smith and Phelps may have drawn some inspiration for their human-like astronomy from a story about Smith's biblical namesake. In an 1832 editorial, Phelps invoked a famous dream of the Hebrew Bible in which "the sun and moon, and the eleven stars made obeisance to" Joseph of Egypt (Genesis 37:1–9) as evidence of Joseph Smith's authority and holy lineage.[146] The power of the biblical Joseph over his brothers, the tribes of Israel, served as a potent image for Smith and Phelps, with astral valences.

Within the Egyptian Bible, Smith proposed a hierarchy of celestial bodies based on light (rather than just astral time), recalling his 1832 revelation "on priesthood" (D&C 84) and the True Light revelation of 1833 (D&C 93), while slightly modifying the temporal framing of the Olive Leaf (D&C 88). A distinctive targum of Genesis 1:14–18 appears to be the biblical basis for the hierarchy of light among celestial bodies. It didn't require much of a stretch. Light was the medium by which stars reached human awareness, the power that separated stars from the inky blackness of the night sky. Within the grammar documents, the glyph *Flos isis* (possibly a compound of the Greek *phos*—light—and the Egyptian goddess *Isis*) signifies (fifth degree) "the highest degree of life, because its component parts are light. . . . the light of the grand governi[n]g of 15 fixed stars centre there."[147] Starlight confirmed the hierarchies that ordered and linked space and time; bodies with more central orbits possessed greater light. In the second degree, *Flos isis* is "the King of day or the central moving planet, from which the other governing moving planets receive their light . . . slow in its motion."[148] A derivative glyph, *Kli flosis* (fifth degree), "signifies Kolob in its motion, which is swifter than the rest of the twelve fixed stars; going before, being first in motion."[149] This motion connected Kolob back to the questions of how time binds human beings and their experience.

Egypt was often associated in nineteenth-century America with sacred astronomy, and astronomy with sacred history.[150] The Bible joined traditional

---

[146] *EMS* 1:6 (November 1832): 41.
[147] *JSPR4*, 164–65. Isis figured prominently in some American metaphysical traditions, including as a representation of the twelve stars. Heavlin, *Mysteries of Isis*, 15, 234.
[148] *JSPR4*, 178–79, 182–83.
[149] *JSPR4*, 164–65. "Kli" seems to be an abbreviated *Kolob* prepended to a contracted *flos isis*.
[150] Bellamy, *All Religions*, 27, explained that Egyptians "have long had the honor of the mention of the constellations." See also Commentary on Genesis 41:8 and Daniel 2:10, in Clarke, *Holy Bible*, 1:231 and 4:568, and Josephus, *Antiquities of the Jews*, I.7.1–2, see also *M&A* 2:3 (December 1835): 236. Cowdery had framed Smith's discovery of his golden plates within traditions from Josephus two months earlier: *M&A* 2:1 (October 1835): 196. See also the series "The Wonders of Ancient Egypt," *Nauvoo Neighbor* 1:31 (November 29, 1843); 1:32 (December 6, 1843); 1:33 (December 9, 1843); 1:34 (December 20, 1843).

scholarship and folk wisdom with narratives about magicians and divines who saw truth in the skies, prophets who could make the sun stop moving, or a God who marked the birth of his Messiah-son by positioning a star over the baby's crib.[151] Connections between stars and God are very old. The Leonid meteor shower of November 1833 impressed many, including the Saints, and celestial marvels played a central role in the wonder lore that defined for many the imminence of Christ's return.[152] Stars have always mattered, and not just to astrologers.

The connection between celestial and human bodies is exemplified in the story of the star Kolob. This Kolob narrative incorporates a sustained exegesis of Job and Genesis, a religious astronomy, and (probably) a gentle modification of the Hebrew word for star (*kokab*).[153] Within the grammar documents, *Kolob* grounded the celestial Chain of Belonging. In the Book of Abraham, it is the governing star nearest to God: "These are the governing ones; and the name of the great one is Kolob, because it is near unto me, for I am the Lord thy God: I have set this one to govern" (3:3). That special Kolob was the star by which God told time (3:4), which solved a logical problem in the text, as discussed earlier.

The grammar documents dramatically expand the modest discussions of the special star in the Book of Abraham. *Kolob* represents "the first creation . . . nearer to the Celestial, or the residence of God."[154] This star was the "first in government, the last pertaining to the measurement of time."[155] Kolob was the pinnacle of the celestial bodies known as *hah kokaubeam*.[156] It was (second degree) the "eldest of all the Stars, the greatest body of the heavenly bodies."[157] Kolob signified the "first beginning to the bodies of this creation . . . having been appointed for the last time the last or the eldest."[158] The fact that this Kolob is both first and last according to time seems an obvious echo of the Alpha and Omega designation by which Christ is known in the New Testament.

In the grammar documents, each star has its own *kairos*, or "set time," and Abraham receives the right to know each of these stars and set times. To know a celestial body's *kairos* is to discern its name and its power.[159] The binding of times was parallel to the genealogical priesthood of the human hierarchies. As the

---

[151] Matthew 2 and Joshua 10.

[152] On the meteor shower, see Van Wagenen, "Singular Phenomena." On wonder lore in America, see, e.g., Marsden, *Edwards*, 69, 121.

[153] Zucker, "Student of Hebrew," 51, proposes this minor deformation of *kokab*, but misses the emphasis on proximity to God in Abraham 3:3, 9.

[154] *JSPR4*, 166–67.

[155] *JSPR4*, 166–67, 178–79.

[156] This transliteration of the Hebrew *ha'kokabim* (the stars) follows Seixas's Sephardic system.

[157] *JSPR4*, 166–67, 178–79.

[158] *JSPR4*, 170–71.

[159] Abraham 3:6–7, 10. I'm aware that I'm using *kairos* in an idiosyncratic way. My analogy here relies on the notion that being bound by the set time of a planet instates a propitious relationship.

eldest hierarch, Kolob received a priesthood scope over other celestial bodies—*GAEL* defines it in its third degree as "the highest degree of power in government, pertaining to heavenly bodies."[160]

This Kolob, which was the brightest star with the most central orbit, is the most familiar of the celestial bodies described in the Egyptian project. The interdependence of starlight and habitation may be a targum of Job 38:19–20, in which God speaks from a whirlwind to Job, with a probing question: "Where is the way where light dwelleth? and as for darkness, where is the place thereof, / That thou shouldest take it to the bound thereof, and that thou shouldest know the paths to the house thereof?" God was asking Job whether he was present at the primordial creation when light was separated from darkness. But in those spare words, it appears that Smith and Phelps saw hints of the interrelationships among stars, lights, and the passage of time. Consistent with Smith's practice, these interpretations and extensions were translations that saw the vast truths lurking in muddled sections of the King James Bible.

The special star Kolob rapidly made its way into Latter-day Saint ritual, discourse, hymnody, and cosmology. It figured especially prominently in aspirations to move through space bodily, as we saw in chapter 3. Through this especially bright star with a divinely central orbit, Smith showed his followers the way to heaven.

The Egyptian Bible used sprawling targums of the primeval history to situate believers within the Chain of Belonging. Given the centrality of integration into that Chain within the Nauvoo temple liturgy, it's little wonder that the Egyptian Bible is so intensely tied to the temple liturgy. Before treating the temple specifically in the next chapter, it's worth considering what the Egyptian project might say about the triangulation of Smith and his disciples within the currents of modern culture.

Secularity and the Egyptian Bible

Though Jean-François Champollion had definitively identified the phonetic nature of Egyptian hieroglyphs by about 1822, the phonetic interpretation was discordant with prior traditions. Relatively few listeners were immediately interested in abandoning the understanding of hieroglyphs as pictographic codes.

Champollion is a useful inflection point in the disenchantment of Egyptian language and culture. The mysterious hieroglyphs turned out to be a syllabary

[160] *JSPR4*, 174–75.

(a writing system that encodes syllables rather than letters) based on the rebus (visual puns, as when a picture of an *eye* is used to represent the first-person pronoun *I*), rather than pictograms per se. Hieratic script proved to be a simplified cursive variant of hieroglyphs.[161] According to Champollion and his heirs, Egyptians didn't have any special mysteries hidden in the language itself, however many spells and incantations might have been preserved in magic papyri and funerary texts.[162] Scholars could understand all they needed to know by treating Egyptian like any other human language. Once the Egyptian language had been stripped of its metaphysical power, it became more difficult to maintain that, for example, Thoth/Hermes was the god of language or to imagine that glyphs provided access to a world beyond the merely physical. Within a few generations, Egyptology resembled an established, secularized mode of understanding one early culture among many in the antique Mediterranean.

Yet many nonspecialists, particularly those most resistant to Enlightenment-style traditions of reproduction and verification, continued to see Egypt as a major source of wisdom and mystery. Popular writers continue to the present day to wonder about the technological marvels of the Egyptian funerary monuments. Many still see hieroglyphs as infused with great meaning.[163] These individuals have resisted the elite and academic disenchantment. So where do the Saints belong within these modern Egyptian currents? Theirs is a complex collage of old and new.

To rehearse my basic point in the interest of clarity, when Smith encountered mummies and their funeral papyri in 1835, he employed hieroglyphs as mystical correspondences—abundant linguistic objects of real divine presence—to expose primordial truths from the Hebrew Bible's history. This pictographic project in an Egyptian key revealed aspects of Smith's divine anthropology, primarily as a targum of the Genesis creation accounts. He integrated those principles with his repurposed Chain of Belonging while fixing logical problems in the King James text along the way.

Even as they sought deep metaphysical reality, Smith and his colleagues were still enmeshed in the modern world. The papyri were standard religious texts from Ptolemaic-era Thebes; they were written in standard hieratic script. Smith and his lieutenants were prone at times to understand them in plain terms, as when Brigham Young and Willard Richards wrote from England asking whether Smith wanted them to transcribe glyphs from the British Museum to send to him for review.[164] But the Egyptian documents were something else too, and

---

[161] Powell, *Writing*, esp. 85–127.
[162] On Egyptian magic, see, e.g., Pinch, *Magic in Ancient Egypt*, and Meyer, *Ancient Christian Magic*.
[163] On the broader history of Egyptology, see Thompson, *Wonderful Things*, vols. 1–3.
[164] *JSPD7*, 394.

that is what Smith and his associates also saw. The papyri contained hieroglyphic portals into the pure language of the primeval Bible and the words, authority, and person of Abraham. They called forth an experience probably best considered graphic glossolalia.

Form and content merged in this project, which exemplified the metaphysical aspirations of hieroglyphs. Smith worked to make the cosmic presence actual in the world through his engagement of hieroglyphs. As he did so, he reiterated the key positions he had taken in opposition to rising sensibilities about the nature of time and human selves.

Conclusion

Smith communed with ancient Egypt through the papyri, mummies, and glyphs. Smith's Egyptian Bible was also concerned with the nature of time itself, as measured by the celestial bodies. This time was deeply personalized and heterogeneous. Time was measured not in seconds or days but in parent-child relationships. It was not counted with watches or calendars but by human-like stars. The use of astronomy for the calculation of time spans two modes of thinking about scientific observation and measurement. The notion that certain times could be dominated by certain planets was classic zodiacal astrology. At the same time, it reflected an astronomical consensus. When Smith weighed in, he did so in a way that biblicized astrology. Time was wrapped up in the special star Kolob, which corresponded to Jesus.

Smith also had something important to say about the nature of human selves in his Egyptian Bible. Selves could not exist independently, and they were not well buffered. Parents could affect children and vice versa. Celestial bodies mirrored and influenced human bodies and society. Selves were suspended in a relational medium he called priesthood. This priesthood extended through both women and men to bind the generations of time together.

Once again, Smith and his followers drew on trappings of modern culture to make peace with the exigencies of their environment, but their project was a fundamentally enchanted one. Caught between the two worlds, such as they were, the early Saints wanted to wield all that was good in both. Whether they were blissfully unaware or defiantly resistant—I suspect the latter—they lived in a world that didn't fit into the channels of modernity and its discontents.

Smith's work to transform the Chain of Being is exemplary here. While Locke and others eliminated the Chain of Being by abandoning hierarchy and, later, materializing people, Smith saw the Chain of Being as the promise of a vastly humanized system of harmony. This harmony, his Chain of Belonging, integrated divinized human beings into the fabric of the cosmos. That was his goal. One key instrument in that work was a special kind of scripture that was both human and textual and was intimately concerned with mediating and obliterating spatial and temporal distance. This mode of scripture culminated in the sacred rituals of the Nauvoo temple.

7
The Transcendent Immanent Temple

In 1846, the Illinois anti-Mormon editor Thomas Sharp, a member of the vigilante mob that had murdered Joseph Smith in June 1844, gleefully reported gossip from two seceding Church members who were horrified by the "obscene rites" being practiced in the Nauvoo temple. "The Saints have endeavored to keep the ceremony of the endowment perfectly quiet; but some of them have let the cat out of the bag and disclosed all," Sharp began his breathless denunciation of his Latter-day Saint neighbors. He claimed that men and women moved through the ritual system in naked pairs ("If a male cannot find a female to take the endowment with him, the heads of the church provide one") as part of an elaborate bathing ceremony. The scandalous bath was then followed by an "oil[ing] with perfumed sweet oil." The nude couple were then left alone "as long as they see proper," the newspaperman noted with a lascivious wink and a nudge. While he admitted that the "really deluded amongst the Saints consider this ceremony sacred," Sharp believed that the rites were actually a vehicle for the "gratif[ication]" of church leaders' "brutal lusts."[1] Other critics agreed, on similarly weak evidence, that the Nauvoo temple liturgy was a sacralized orgy.[2] As best we can tell, participants were in fact transiently naked—albeit segregated by gender and thus without the lascivious undercurrents critics loved to hate—as part of the bathing of their bodies in preparation for ritual investiture in the temple. After this preparatory cleansing, they made their way through the liturgy fully clothed. Contrary to Sharp's hopes for titillation, there's no reliable evidence for temple sex among the Nauvoo Saints.

Nudity wasn't the only cause for scandal, though. Smith and his followers also outraged their Masonic peers, with whom they had formed a temporary fraternity. Masonic complaints emphasized irregularities and modifications to their traditional rituals by Joseph Smith and his band of believers. He was not only advancing people too quickly through the three Masonic degrees but also claiming that modern Masons were apostate from their ancient antecedents. The temple rites sharply divided the core of the Church from outsiders.

The Saints saw the Nauvoo temple endowment as both a continuation of the original, more limited Kirtland temple rites and a vista onto the vast power of a

---

[1] "Ceremony of the Endowment," *Warsaw [IL] Signal* (February 18, 1846): 2.
[2] One sees hints of this in Bennett's accounts of harems in his *History of the Saints*, 217–25, 272–78.

special priesthood that would unite the entire human family. They understood themselves as participating in primordial rituals that had been part of humanity since the beginning. They located authority and power in the persons of Eve and Adam in Eden.

The Latter-day Saints understood the temple as a sacred place in which the physical could be invested with the metaphysical, as participants acted out Smith's targums of the primeval history. The notorious nudity—as odd as it seemed to outsiders—recapitulated the primal undress of Eve and Adam in their first home in Eden. The temple brought to fruition an intense primordialism and identification with holy ancestors. These Latter-day Saints were no Victorians. But their defiance of Victorian norms wasn't about free love, social atomism, and the rupture of obligations. Their rebellion was about rewriting human DNA from ancient and sacred templates.

The temple is embedded in stories of time, language, and human identity—the three primary themes we explored in the first section of this book. In this chapter we return to those themes and show how images of human and linguistic translation come together within Smith's temple liturgy. The stories of the Nauvoo temple have been told many times in varied venues, with differing levels of adherence to the traditional taboo against discussion of its core ritual elements.[3] I take a middle road here.[4]

While I introduce the temple history to provide relevant context, I don't intend to retread well-worn ground. What is most important for our purposes is that Smith's lifelong effort to translate the Hebrew Bible's primeval history came to fruition in his 1840s temple rites. While his followers had witnessed scripture being written about them and for them from the beginning, in the temple liturgy they stepped directly into those texts. They violated barriers of time and space, integrating themselves directly into the cosmos and its most ancient stories. They did so bodily, in and with the very flesh and bones that they prayed would one day be translated into the presence of God. In this mix of bodies and scriptures they participated in the fluid identity of metaphysical correspondence.

In this chapter, I highlight the fact that the temple is the location (in time and space) that brings together the twin senses of human and linguistic translation. It does so within an infrastructure of transcendent immanence, what I take to

---

[3] McBride, *Nauvoo Temple*. Treatments of the endowment include Brown, *In Heaven*, 145–202; Ehat, "Mormon Succession"; Buerger, "Mormon Temple"; and Anderson and Bergera, *Quorum of the Anointed*.

[4] I'm aware of and glad to honor ritual prescriptions against discussions of certain aspects of the Nauvoo temple liturgy. Lest readers uninitiated in Latter-day Saint temple worship should worry, the relevant stories can be told in insightful and rigorous ways while honoring those traditional proscriptions. In addition, the taboos have a story to tell: I discuss this secrecy that isn't quite apophasis in its own section of this chapter.

be Smith's blurry dualism that sees the transcendent and immanent realms as deeply interdigitated. The Latter-day Saint temple is a physical structure bursting with metaphysical presence. In that special building, worshipers themselves might become vessels of abundance, tight coilings of the transcendent and the immanent. Believers acted out in ritual the goal Smith had been pursuing with his translations. Using scriptural language, they connected with the dead in a temporal jumble of past, present, and future. As they performed those rituals they physically recreated places they connected with the center of the Universe—Eden and heaven. Along the way, they reconstituted the universe in permanent interconnections of human beings.

A Brief History of Temples

Smith's temple system is a tree with an extensive root structure in the soil of his biblical primordialism. The initial mentions of a temple come in his first scripture: the Book of Mormon's refugees from Jerusalem built one shortly after they arrived in America. They erected that temple according to the precedent of Solomon (2 Nephi 5:16), although the text had little to say about it afterward. The temple continued to play an important, if underspecified, role in the life of America's ancient Hebrews. They occasionally preached from its steps (e.g., Mosiah 2 and 7 or Jacob 1–2). God once wrote on the temple's walls, although the account is only secondhand (Alma 10; cf. Daniel 5). The book of Alma manifests a more generic notion of temples as one among many places of worship, used almost figuratively rather than in the weighty sense reserved for the Temple of Solomon (e.g., Alma 16:13, 26:29). No temple liturgy of any sort is mentioned in the Book of Mormon, but the temple still had a foothold in ancient America. More relevant to the focus of the American scripture, the temple is where Jesus came after his resurrection (3 Nephi 11). The building seems, more or less, to be the special location where worshipers gather and to which God can come.

However vague the Book of Mormon was about whatever rituals might have been observed in ancient American temples, Smith moved to create a modern temple within a year or two of its publication. Some of the impetus to do so appears to derive from Malachi 3:1—"I will send my messenger, and he shall prepare the way before me: and the Lord, whom ye seek, shall suddenly *come to his temple*" (emphasis added). Smith seems to have understood this as a requirement for having a functional temple at the time of Christ's Second Coming. Preparations for the millennium thus had to include such a physical structure. This understanding of the role of the temple, couched explicitly as an exegesis of Malachi 3, is present in the 1831 *Laws of the Church* (D&C 42:36). Latter-day Saints continued to use this language to describe the purpose and role of the temple, including Eliza R. Snow's 1841 celebratory poem, "The Temple of God."[5] The temple was to be a part of the grand transformation of believers and of the earth they inhabited at the time of Christ's return. These early texts emphasized the fact of the temple as a millenarian object, but nothing of its internal features.

This millenarian temple belonged in the New Jerusalem, the American city Christ would visit. Smith identified Jackson County, Missouri, among the "remnant of Jacob" (American Indians) as that New World Jerusalem, and immediately directed settlement there. Unfortunately, the existing residents of the county seat at Independence objected to Latter-day Saint occupation. Impatient with the ongoing violent disagreements with locals in Jackson County, Smith appeared willing to consider a temple in every major Latter-day Saint settlement while they awaited the main temple in Jackson County. The first real work on a temple thus came in Kirtland, Ohio, where Smith lived in the 1830s.

The context for the Kirtland temple was an attempt to assemble the Saints' first group of trained ministers. Using a colorful and contemporary biblical term for a seminary, Smith related that he was founding "schools of the prophets" (or "schools of the elders").[6] Those frontier seminaries aspired to train a lay clergy, imparting a knowledge and authority that, they hoped, would be recognized by their peers, neighbors, and critics. The Saints were preparing to evangelize the world in anticipation of Christ's return. The seminary (through global evangelism) and the temple (through exegesis of Malachi) were both key aspects of preparation for the Second Coming.

The Olive Leaf (D&C 88) outfitted these threadbare seminaries with an ultimate goal and the early strands of a liturgy. That liturgy was specific and limited—at first it involved *pedilavium* (foot washing patterned on John 13) and a ritual greeting that constituted commitment to the group.[7] "Art thou a brother or brethren?" they asked within what was at the time an all-male fraternity, responding that they were devoted to each other in a "determination that is fixed, immovable, and unchangeable" (88:133).

The revelation added momentum to anticipation that believers would individually see Jesus, in their own personal anticipation of his millennial return: "The days come, that you shall see him, for he will, unveil his face unto you, and it shall be in his own time, and in his own way, and according, to his own will" (88:68).[8] The Olive Leaf also began the public discussion about human deification. The two main threads of Smith's ultimate liturgy—ritual community and

---

[5] *T&S* 2:19 (August 2, 1841): 493–94.

[6] While the main one was associated with the temple in Kirtland, Smith had Parley Pratt lead another similar seminary in Missouri (*JSPD3*, 200). This use of the term seems to have come mostly from the precedent of Samuel, Elijah, and Elisha—1 Samuel 19:18–24 and 2 Kings 2, 4:38–44.

[7] On the introduction of pedilavium, see *JSPD5*, 49.

[8] *JSPD2*, 341.

Figure 7.1 The Kirtland Temple. Image courtesy of the Church History Library, The Church of Jesus Christ of Latter-day Saints.

human deification—were thus woven together from the beginning, just as they had been in the story of Enoch's sacred city (chapter 3). These individual and corporate transformations of human beings strained toward the great translation of all believers at Christ's return, although at this point the aspects were relatively undifferentiated.

As the Kirtland nucleus grew and matured, the Saints prepared together for the erection of the Kirtland Temple, their "stone chapel" (Figure 7.1).[9] The temple had to be constructed, the church organization solidified, the global missionary effort orchestrated, and the town of Kirtland built up. The Kirtland Temple was to be the cornerstone of all those efforts.[10] Alongside practical considerations, Smith and his close disciples further developed the liturgy to include two innovations—patriarchal blessings, which extended beyond the core male priesthood officers to encompass all Latter-day Saints, and anointing rituals that extended the pedilavium of 1832–1833.

[9] See, e.g., *EJ* 1:1 (Oct 1837): 16, and *JSPD5*, 143.
[10] Howlett, *Kirtland Temple*, chapter 2.

As we saw in chapter 3, patriarchal blessings adopted recipients into Israel (bringing to life Paul's promise in Romans 8–9 that believers in Christ were adopted into the house of Israel, while simultaneously allowing Latter-day Saints to imagine themselves as Father Jacob's children receiving his deathbed blessing) and initiated the themes of sacerdotal genealogy that ramified dramatically in Nauvoo.[11] Playing at the interface between celestial parenthood and ecclesiastical priesthood, these blessings formally integrated recipients—women and men—into the nation of Israel and prepared them for evangelism and Christ's millennial reign.[12]

The *pedilavium* practiced among priesthood officers moved from the washing of feet alone to the washing and anointing of other parts of the body with a mix of cinnamon-infused whiskey and olive oil. The use of oil largely followed Hebrew Bible precedents for kingly and priestly anointing. Up to this point, the rituals looked like charismatic primordialism—some other groups were practicing pedilavium and/or chrisms, although mainstream Protestants were squeamish about such rituals.[13]

After the blessings, washings, and anointings came the "enduement of power," which meant several different things, mostly tied to preparing elders for global evangelism.[14] The most important phase of the enduement was the spiritual outpouring of spring 1836, tied to the temple dedication and the "solemn assembly" that followed a few days later. Here, male elders were called to take the power of Pentecost—the ancient antidote to Babel—and use it to convert the world. These men were going to be the new apostles to match the original Christian apostles of former days. For that work, they needed the spiritual power to work miracles. The enduement (often called by the term that later predominated, "endowment") was an outpouring of spiritual power that gave them what they needed. This Kirtland endowment was more charismatic than structured, even if its preparations were ritually organized and tied to an increasingly concrete priesthood hierarchy.[15]

While participants and leaders had their eyes set on the ancient Near East, the Kirtland Temple endowment season also drew on the precedent of Presbyterian holy seasons (the precursors to American camp meetings). During these events, participants engaged in songs, prayers, extended sermonizing, festive meals, and participation in the Eucharist, among other spiritual experiences intended to kindle faith and commitment. Revivals were designed to regenerate believers within a community of believers—the early enduement belongs in that context, which combined personal Gospel witnesses with a social infrastructure.

[11] See *JSPD6*, 526, and Brown, *In Heaven*, 126, 148, 213–18.
[12] Thus, e.g., EPB, 69, 70, 89, 105, 124, 128, 169, 188, 192.
[13] Brown, *In Heaven*, 154–55; Brekus, *Female Preaching*, 65, 156.
[14] Stapley, *Power of Godliness*, 14–15, 82–85.
[15] Bushman, *Rough Stone*, 315–16; Corrill, *Brief History*, 23.

Latter-day Saint Kirtland in late 1835 and early 1836 had many of the trappings of such a holy season, and that season bound together the Saints in worship and love. Once again, another familiar Protestant notion became metaphysically charged and primordialized.[16]

Along with the general pursuit of spiritual power to evangelize, the quest to see the face of Jesus intensified as the Kirtland temple rose on its foundation.[17] At the solemn assembly celebrated in the newly dedicated Kirtland Temple, the early Saints received, in spades, what they sought.[18] Lyman Wight reported after a blessing from Smith, "I now see God and Jesus Christ at his right hand let them kill me I should not feel death as I am now." The minutes of the March 30, 1836, Solemn Assembly emphasized that the prophecies were fulfilled: "the Saviour made his appearance to some."[19] A few days after the solemn assembly, Joseph Smith and Oliver Cowdery reported that they "saw the Lord standing upon the breastwork of the pulpit" (D&C 110:1–8). Multiple other accounts confirm receipt of the promised vision.[20] Giddy with power, elders set off to prepare the world for Christ's return.

Believers hoped to recapitulate the holy season each year in order to support new crops of evangelists, but after another Kirtland endowment in 1837, the abandonment of Kirtland (due to an economic scandal in the aftermath of the national Panic of 1837), followed by the Missouri Mormon War and its aftermath, led to sustained interruption of the Kirtland liturgy. Only in Nauvoo would it be revisited as it was transformed.

The Kirtland temple liturgy, however compelling at the time, was in retrospect incomplete. Most significantly, it barred women from several of the rituals, however much they participated in the overall spiritual energy of the holy season. On the other hand, other aspects of the Kirtland temple worship, especially those tied to gifts like glossolalia, centered on women. Mary Fielding, a Canadian convert who soon married Hyrum Smith, reported such an event in 1837: "some of the Sisters while engaged in conversing in tounges their countenances beaming with joy, clasped each others hands & kissed in the most affectina[te] manner. they were describing in this way the love and felicity of the Celestial World . . . I believe as do many others that Angles were present with us."[21] Her promise

---

[16] The standard treatment of Presbyterian holy seasons is Schmidt, *Holy Fairs*, with application to Latter-day Saint Kirtland in Brown, *In Heaven*, 161–63.
[17] See, e.g., *JSPJ1*, 26; Arrington, "Cowdery's Sketchbook," 417, 420.
[18] Staker, *Historical Setting* and Bushman, *Rough Stone*, 305–21.
[19] *JSPD5*, 221. See also *JSPD5*, 158.
[20] See, e.g., *JSPJ1*, 170, 174–75, 215–16; Harper, "Pentecost Continued," 17, 21. Zina Diantha Huntington was blessed by her father to see the face of her "Redeemer": blessing 1319, CHL, copy in author's possession.
[21] Mary Fielding to Mercy Fielding, July 8, 1837, Kirtland, OH, MS 2779, folder 2, CHL, [1]–[2] (transcribed by Elizabeth Kuehn). While Fielding doesn't say, it seems most likely that the kissing was an extension of the "holy kiss" tradition of Moravians and other groups, patterned on references in Paul's letters to a kiss of holy love, also called the "kiss of peace."

of celestial felicity and the community of angels, along with the intensity of female interconnection, stood at the core of temple worship and would persist throughout temple history.

Such moments of charismatic community notwithstanding, women were excluded from several of the Kirtland priesthood rituals. Joseph Smith's cousin George later commented that the women were "right huffy about" their exclusion from most preparatory rites—the pedilavium, washing and anointing, ritual greetings in the School of the Prophets, and a variety of blessings and sealings performed within priesthood meetings. Admittedly, women's memoirs and recollections focused more on the power they did experience—such as in Mary Fielding's account of the solemn assemblies—than the rituals from which they were excluded.[22] Many apparently chose silence over protest. Some may also have felt that the specific Kirtland rituals were for the men and their priesthood, while women were busy experiencing the direct presence of God to different ends. Those caveats notwithstanding, I suspect that George Smith was remembering correctly that some Kirtland women were upset at being denied certain rituals. Whatever the inner mental states of the Latter-day Saint women of Kirtland, the rituals of the 1830s—tied as they were to specific evangelistic roles that Church leaders, along with most Americans, associated with men[23]—were by and for men. Men would evangelize the world, and the temple was necessary to support that evangelism.

The temple's male focus changed dramatically in the 1840s, as the system took on an overwhelmingly familial aspect.[24] Within the Nauvoo Female Relief Society under the leadership of Emma and Joseph Smith, women emerged as priestly figures. Smith's March 30, 1842, lecture to the Relief Society urged that "the Society should move according to the ancient Priesthood, hence there should be a select Society separate from all the evils of the world, choice, virtuous[s] and holy—Said he was going to make of this Society a kingdom of priests a[s] in Enoch's day—as in Pauls day."[25] He continued the theme in April, explaining that "the Sisters would come in possession of the priviliges & blessings & gifts of the priesthood—& that the signs should follow them."[26] This closing quotation of Jesus's commissioning of the disciples in Mark 16:14–18 shifted away from the Kirtland focus on male evangelists and onto the broader sense of adoption into the priesthood family. Both women and men would exercise the temple priesthood.

---

[22] Ulrich, *Plural Marriage*, 7–8.
[23] Brekus, *Female Preaching*.
[24] Some have noted that this familialization was reminiscent of Puritan covenantalism. Cooper, *Covenant Organization*, esp. 35, 76–77.
[25] Derr et al., *First Fifty Years*, 43, cf. 31.
[26] *JSPJ2*, 52.

This extended liturgy grounded in family relationships incorporated new connections to the ancient past that extended the biblical foundations of Latter-day Saint worship. In the magnified Nauvoo temple system, Smith deployed his targums of the primeval history, especially the New Translation and the Book of Abraham, as part of the infrastructure of a ritual return to the first times.

The first step into the Nauvoo liturgy was a new rite that extended baptism and the patriarchal blessings and furthered Smith's ongoing need to unite the living and the dead. Smith formally introduced baptism for the dead in a sermon in 1840, solving what some call Christianity's "scandal of particularity."[27] To the question, What happens after death to the countless millions who never heard the true Christian message during their lives? the Saints' answer was now: We'll baptize them by proxy. Phebe Woodruff described the announcement as an "interesting sermon" where the biblical and logical case for baptism of the living for the dead was "made so plain that none could dispute it reasonably."[28] In a contemporary letter to her husband, Vilate Kimball called it "a new and glorious subject" which "caused quite a revival in the church." Since the revelation, she said, "the waters [of the Mississippi River] have been continually troubled" (an allusion to the healing pool at Bethsaida in John 5:4).[29]

Initially performing these rites in the Mississippi River, the Saints soon built a pool based on the "brass laver" of Solomon's temple in which they could save their dead through sacramental identity.[30] They did so as part of the extension of Smith's familial priesthood and the interconnection of the living and the dead. As a mark of that connection, Smith indicated that guardian angels would be involved in the process: believers should be baptized for family but not their "acquaintances unless they [the deceased] send a ministering spirit to their friends on earth."[31] Vilate Kimball clarified that such alerting by ministering spirits was required only where a genetic bond was not present: one was sufficiently connected to one's blood ancestors to be baptized for them without separate intervention.[32] This ritual innovation fulfilled Smith's hopeful promise of 1830, that God through him would "gather together in one all things both which are in heaven and which are on earth" (D&C 27:13).[33]

Baptism for the dead is perhaps the clearest example of metaphysical correspondence in Latter-day Saint liturgy.[34] One of the central arguments Smith

---

[27] McDermott, *Edwards*, 17–25.
[28] Phebe Woodruff to Wilford Woodruff, October 6, 1840, MS 19509, CHL.
[29] Vilate Kimball to Heber C. Kimball, October 11, 1840, MS 18732, CHL.
[30] The first baptisms occurred in the Mississippi on September 13, 1840: *JSPD7*, 460n205.
[31] *JSPD7*, 419.
[32] Vilate Kimball to Heber C. Kimball, October 11, 1840, CHL.
[33] *JSPD4*, 411–12.
[34] When he introduced baptism for the dead, the living were corresponding with the ancient but as-yet-unredeemed dead. The font had to be a literal grave, below the earth: "that which is earthly conforming to that which is heavenly." See Peters, "Celestial Bookkeeping," 854.

made in favor of baptism for the dead was that since believer baptism is a burial in water it *is* a unity with the dead—"The ordinance of baptism by water, to be immersed therein in order to answer to the likeness of the dead, that one principle might accord with the other," generalizing to the hope "that all things may have their likeness, and that they may accord one with another" (D&C 128:12–13). The language of "likeness" and "accord" are classic terms of metaphysical correspondence. In fact, the Saints were called to such direct correspondence that their own bodies became objects of real presence for the salvation of the dead.[35]

On the backbone of the baptisms for the dead and with a hint of new ceremonies for the endowment, Smith pushed for the building of the Nauvoo temple in earnest (Figure 7.2). In a church-wide proclamation of January 15, 1841, he and colleagues indicated that the Nauvoo temple would "enable all the functions of the priesthood to be duly exercised."[36] That priesthood was concerned with helping the disciples to "strive to emulate the actions of the ancient covenant fathers, and patriarchs."[37] A revelation a few days later stated that God would reveal to Smith "all things pertaining to this house and the priesthood thereof" (D&C 124:42).[38]

As the temple building grew, Smith introduced his second liturgical innovation: a new endowment that drew on and transformed important strands in Western esotericism. The most proximate contact with those ancient traditions came through the fraternal order of Freemasonry. Smith had been around Freemasonry for much of his life; several people in his extended family were Masons. Snippets of Masonic lore circulated broadly in antebellum America, albeit modulated profoundly in the dustup after the 1829 William Morgan murder.[39] In the 1840s he engaged Masonic traditions in earnest, especially in his temple liturgy and the associated, sacerdotal transformation of the Nauvoo Female Relief Society.[40]

Freemasonry wasn't the only access point in nineteenth-century America to Western esoteric traditions; nor was Smith an empty vessel for Freemasonry. It would be a facile interpretive mistake to think that the Nauvoo temple liturgy is best explained as a plagiarism of Freemasonry. Just as he had when he encountered the Bible, Smith took to the texts and ritual enactments of Freemasonry

---

[35] On baptism for the dead more generally, see Tobler, "Mormon Sacramentalism," and Brown, *In Heaven*, 219–22.
[36] *JSPD7*, 502.
[37] *JSPD7*, 502.
[38] *JSPD7*, 518.
[39] For general scholarly introductions to Freemasonry, see Bullock, *Revolutionary Brotherhood*; Hackett, *Freemasonry*; Stevenson, *Origins*; and Jacob, *Radical Enlightenment*.
[40] On Relief Society, Derr et al., *First Fifty Years*, 43.

Figure 7.2 The Nauvoo Temple, ca. 1847. Image courtesy of the Church History Library, The Church of Jesus Christ of Latter-day Saints.

with the confidence of a prophet wielding a sharp knife and a well-inked pen.[41] He was ready to transform both text and context for the traditions made

---

[41] Thus Heber Kimball to Parley Pratt (June 17, 1842, CHL): "thare is a similarity of preast Hood in masonary. Bro Joseph Ses Masonary was taken from preasthood but has become degenrated, but menny things are perfect."

accessible in Freemasonry. As with his other projects, he applied his marvelously literal rationalism and his penchant for metaphysical translation of both texts and peoples to his encounter with Freemasonic rituals.

Beyond his liturgical work, Smith briefly found a comfortable home in Freemasonry. Yet he and his followers were banned from Freemasonry within two years. To official complaints that he had corrupted the order's "ancient landmarks," Smith contended that he had instead restored them to their primal purity.[42] In other words, he'd done to Freemasonry what he did to the King James Bible: he had destroyed it in order to remake it as a vessel for primordial truth. That was how the early Latter-day Saints, familiar with both Smith's temple liturgy and its Masonic antecedents, understood the interaction: Smith had recovered ancient truth from its corrupted modern form in Freemasonry.[43]

Smith introduced his new temple endowment in the spring of 1842, within a few weeks of his induction into Freemasonry. He did so in the upper room of his brick store, where he "kept the sacred writings, translated ancient records, and received revelations."[44] Smith never conducted his endowment ritual in the temple itself, which was only completed the year after his death, but the liturgy sanctified the temporary locations where he did so. The Nauvoo liturgy combined the Kirtland precedents, Smith's targums of first times, and his translation of Freemasonic rites. He situated these multiple strands within his divine anthropology.

The introduction of the temple endowment shifted the locus of theology and practice. In 1841, Smith had famously claimed that the Book of Mormon was the "keystone" of his religion. While that may have been true in the 1830s, and the Book of Mormon was generally important to the early Saints, by the 1840s, the endowment more obviously played that role. Recall that a keystone drops into an arch at the end of construction, connecting the two sides and bearing the force exerted by the columns of the arch. The temple liturgy brought together Smith's anthropology, scriptural theology, hermeneutic esotericism, ritual, aspirations for human transformation, marriage, primordialism, respect for the dead, and hunger to know that nothing could interfere with human communion.

The endowment drama placed believers in the Garden at Eden, where they imagined themselves as their first parents grappling with the theologically pregnant events of the earliest chapters of the primeval history, the stories Smith had been rereading his whole career. Participants then simulated the arc of their lives (and the lives of their sacred ancestors) from Eden through exile and the

---

[42] On Masonic criticism, see Homer, "Freemasonry and Mormonism," 30–33.
[43] Brown, *In Heaven*, 185–86.
[44] Joseph Smith History, draft notes, May 4, 1842, CR 100 92, CHL; see also Joseph Smith, History, May 4, 1842, vol. C-1, CR 100 102, p. 1328, CHL.

probationary suffering of mortality. The path drew to a close with the worshiper's personal return to the heavenly precincts. They structured their ritualized mortal walk toward heaven on promises to God and each other within the context of the familialized priesthood. The endowment completed as their lives did, with the promise of heavenly security, love, and family in heaven. As they made their way through the endowment, participants demonstrated their fidelity to priesthood patterns, with tests performed by individuals representing angelic guards like the *cherubim* protecting postlapsarian Eden in Genesis 3:24. Brigham Young, trying to persuade Smith's mother to join with the main body of the Church, described the temple as a "house unto the Most High" that made it possible to "bring back again the Children of Adam & Eve, Abraham & Sarah, Joseph & Lucy into the presence of the Most High God, even the places that they were destined for from before the foundation of the world."[45] In an 1853 sermon, Young preached that the endowment prepared believers to pass "the angels who stand as sentinels, being enabled to give them the key words, the signs and tokens, pertaining to the Holy Priesthood, and gain your eternal exaltation."[46]

The Nauvoo liturgy was intensely communal, concerned with women and men as parents and partners. In these interdependent roles, the Saints became divine. Their new liturgy was self-consciously integrated into a church, heavily Christianized, and concerned with reformulations of priesthood as a kind of parenthood. The Nauvoo endowment focused on reifying priesthood and training participants in how to navigate their postmortal journey into heaven. In the phrasing of Smith's ghostwritten diary, male and female participants

> attend[ed] to washings & anointings, & endowments, and the communications of keys, pertaining to the Aaronic Priesthood, and so on to the highest order of the Melchisedec Priesthood, setting forth the order pertaining to the Ancient of days & all those plans & principles by which any one is enabled to secure the fullness of those blessings which has been prepared for the church of the firstborn, and come up and abide in the presence of Eloheim in the eternal worlds.[47]

This dense paragraph evokes the role of Smith's familial priesthood and its keys in securing salvation and moving believers from death into postmortal glory.

In the language of one observer, the Nauvoo temple rites were "the Turms of Admission into the Kingdom in Order."[48] These rites, in other words, were a priesthood-based portal to heaven, and the terms of admission were special

---

[45] Brigham Young to Lucy Smith, April 4, 1847, CHL.
[46] *Journal of Discourses* (Liverpool, 1853), 2:31.
[47] Joseph Smith History, draft notes, May 4, 1842, CR 100 92, CHL, cf. Joseph Smith, History, May 4, 1842, vol. C-1, CR 100 102, p. 1328, CHL. The present form of the entry was written in April 1845.
[48] Ehat, "Mormon Succession," 210, citing Joseph Fielding's "Nauvoo Journal," 153–54.

words spoken in ritual contexts and conjoined to specific movements of the body, all occurring within the context of reciting Smith's targums of the primeval history. The temple ceremonies were the place where Smith sought to translate his human followers. The linguistic and human sense of translation merged in the Nauvoo liturgy as followers translated ancient words, which in turn translated the speakers themselves. Through the temple liturgy, they came to be placed into the cosmos.

The Harmony of the Cosmos

Smith's temple worshipers made their way through a simulated Garden of Eden, progressing through the different phases of the earth's deep history while they physically moved through rooms decorated to symbolize the grand journey. These movements within the temple liturgy were ritualized fulfillments of the power of sacred movement promised to the Saints in the 1830s (see chapter 3).

The work Smith's disciples did to locate themselves within the cosmos places them within a long-standing history of such attempts. Remi Brague has elegantly described the cosmic order and its relation to humanity from antiquity to the early modern period.[49] Brague observed the consistent ancient notion that what we moderns call "the universe" was a unity called "cosmos." That cosmos contained an order, and that order made demands on humans and their societies. More to the point here, no sense could be made of a human life without recourse to that cosmic order, which both stood above humans and permeated their society.

In the endowment, worshipers participated in the cosmic order as it stretched through time. Smith had been talking to people about living in Eden since the 1830s. He'd been trying to settle his people in the section of Missouri that he associated geographically with Eden itself. The Saints sang about and worshiped near the great valley (Adam-ondi-Ahman) where they believed Adam had gathered his offspring for a deathbed farewell. Now in the temple rites, believers stepped into a ritual recapitulation of that Eden. They did so as part of their integration into the ancient cosmos. They did so in a way that both effected and affected that cosmic order. The order stood over them, but they also helped shape it.

Where metaphysical correspondence generally represented a divine/cosmic influx controlling human lives, for Smith correspondence allowed his followers, as they exercised the familial priesthood that encompassed both women and men, to etch their lives onto heaven. More than anywhere else, Smith's temple

---

[49] Brague, *Human Experience*.

rituals made clear how bidirectional correspondence had become—that fact stands at the core of Smithian translation. He permuted the antique principle of correspondence to create a heavenly family not even God could disrupt. This is the sense of his late sermon in which he called his followers to be "crafty" and assure that they had sealed their beloveds to them in a priesthood so potent that those relationships could not be overturned.[50] Increasingly over time, he indicated that this priesthood was both intensely familial and concerned to do the work of human translation—to prepare believers to stand in the presence of God.

In a sermon in the summer of 1839, Smith made the association explicit. There he taught that the familial priesthood was the order established by Adam in the aftermath of the Fall. This was the order sealed by Adam's deathbed sermon and related blessings at Adam-ondi-Ahman, events that Smith had been preaching about since the early 1830s. Notably, the familial priesthood preceded the earth and the garden. It was truly primeval. In Smith's phrase, "The Priesthood was. first given To Adam: he obtained the first Presidency & held the Keys of it, from gen[e]ration to Generation; he obtained it in the creation before the world was formed as in Gen. I, 26:28,—he had dominion given him over every living Creature. He is Michael, the Archangel."[51] Although the transcript of the sermon is spare, the key elements are clear. In the time before mortal life Adam, in the guise of his angelic alter ego Michael, obtained the priesthood that would transfer from generation to generation. That priesthood organized the Chain of Belonging on earth.

Smith continued, "The Priesthood is an everlasting principle & Existed with God from Eternity & will to Eternity, without beginning of days or end of years," a phrase that placed priesthood into his overall schema of eternal self-existence while also interpreting Hebrews 7:3.[52] Priesthood had existed as long as God and humanity, forever. He then puzzled over the juxtaposition of the eternity of priesthood and its instability among mortals. Why, for example, had human beings lost the full priesthood at various points along the genealogical path from Adam through Abraham to Moses? The familial priesthood should have prevented apostasy. How then, Smith seemed to ask, could Jesus and Paul apparently decry the Law of Moses when Moses was visibly a prophet and recipient of priesthood?[53] Smith indicated that "Moses Sought to bring the children of Israel into the presence of God. through the power of the Priesthood, but he could not."[54] Recalling that Smith saw translation as the movement of human

---

[50] Brown, "Chain of Belonging," 1.
[51] *JSPD6*, 542.
[52] *JSPD6*, 543–44.
[53] The historical relationship between Jesus and Moses is complex. Smith was operating within an interpretive tradition that saw Moses and "law" as synonymous and inconsistent with the higher Christian grace.
[54] *JSPD6*, 544.

beings into the presence of God, he is thinking here of translation as an act that expresses the eternal priesthood. He then transitions to an explicit connection between translation and the person of Enoch. According to Smith, the early Hebrews "tried to restore these very glories but did not obtain them. but Enoch did for himself & those that were with Him, but not for the world."[55] By obtaining priesthood, in other words, Enoch restored the primordial glories, which allowed his city of believers to make its way to heaven through the process of translation. His people were not for this world.

Those who followed after Enoch in the quest to be translated out of the world would find themselves similarly transformed. They would discover that they were in fact gods.

Divine Anthropology in the Temple Endowment

The Bible's primeval history is awash with first things—the origins of the world and humanity. In Smith's hands the earliest texts of the Bible were also an account of the creation of the gods. In the technical jargon, the creation of gods is a *theogony*, but since for the Saints it was the theological entry into his divine anthropology (see chapter 3), I'll continue to refer to the concept as divine anthropology here. The temple liturgy became the place where worshipers used specially embodied reflexes of sacred language to be transformed into gods. This transformation occurred within the ritual drama of the Bible's primeval history. The temple endowment placed Joseph Smith's followers inside this history.[56] The Nauvoo liturgy played out the chiasmus of D&C 29, revolving around the movement from spiritual to temporal and back.[57] In a church building, using their bodies, the worshipers immersed themselves in the heavens. They were at once both mortal and immortal.

The scriptural-liturgical nexus of the temple brought Smith's divine anthropology into clear view. What's most relevant about the Nauvoo temple liturgy is its integration with the familial priesthood, which began in Kirtland. The Kirtland temple was architecturally arranged according to church hierarchy. Entire walls and suites of pulpits were associated with given offices in the nascent priesthood. As the priesthood became familialized, so did the temple. That priesthood became the basis for the temple's divine anthropology. In his Egyptian

---

[55] *JSPD6*, 544.

[56] This is where Seth Perry's notion of "performative biblicism" (Perry, *Bible Culture*, 67–68) is too weak to bear the weight of incarnating the Bible for ardent primordialists. There's more at play in these ancient lives than "performance."

[57] Recall from prior chapters that this 1830 text espied the secret of human life in the dance between spiritual and temporal framed within the Bible's two creation accounts.

project, Smith introduced the infrastructure of priesthood as the mechanism by which an obvious plurality of gods could exist. Just like planets, humans were a family of celestial bodies imbued with divine essence. They would exist in the divine priesthood power that had made Adam Adam and Christ Christ.

Smith suggested that one key aspect of the priesthood he was describing was that it was a cosmic power to transform humans into the kind of beings that could withstand the unmediated presence of God. As we saw in chapter 3, he revealed in 1831 that "without this [priesthood] no man can see the face of God even the father and live." With Smith's early disciples, later readers are left to puzzle over the mechanisms by which human beings could tolerate the presence of God without being destroyed. For this transformation, the temple rites became crucial: Smith elaborated later that the priesthood that mattered most for these purposes was the Nauvoo temple priesthood, which anointed and sealed worshipers to the relevant status. This capacity to mediate physical and ontological distance through transformation was, more or less, translation.

We should not overstate the consistency of the trajectory of humans into gods in Smith's thought. His ideas came in fits and starts, with suggestive foretastes and occasional backpedaling. Even admitting such disclaimers and equivocations, though, these threads in his thought are undeniable. He was proposing a divine plurality—his followers, transformed within the liturgies of the church, would be gods without number. Instead of being a process that wraps up before the creation of humanity, as was typical for theogonies, Smith's divine anthropology had never started and would never end. It was always in process—tethered, through translations both textual and human, to the time before time when God organized the world. The ongoing birth of the gods recurs perpetually within the temple endowment.

In a sermon delivered at the time he was introducing the temple liturgy in spring 1842, Smith made a connection that ties the endowment to divine anthropology and sacred movement through the cosmos. He preached, "if you wish to go whare God is you must be like God."[58] Both aspects of the statement involve translation—the first is a sense of translation through space, the other of translation as transformation. That month, in that place, Smith's reference could only have been to the temple ceremonies. Within temple worship the early Saints were trying to go where God was, and they realized they would need to be transformed to undertake that journey. Their prophet was giving them the guidance they needed.

The summer 1843 revelation used to support polygamy (D&C 132) came within a temple setting, used temple language, and described polygamy within

[58] *WWJ*, 2:169.

the infrastructure of the temple's Chain of Belonging. Within that context, Smith emphasized the association between the temple rites and human deification. "The new and everlasting covenant . . . was instituted for the fulness of my glory." Those who obey the covenant's dictates "receiveth the fulness thereof" (132:6). Failing to enter the Chain of Belonging meant that those who fall short "are not gods, but are angels of God forever and ever" (132:17). Similarly, failure to participate in the necessary rites, means that people "cannot . . . inherit my glory" (132:18). The righteous who participate appropriately "shall pass by the angels, and the gods, which are set there, to their exaltation and glory in all things, as hath been sealed upon their heads, which glory shall be a fulness and a continuation of the seeds forever and ever. Then they shall be gods, because they have no end" (132:19–20). Smith's June 1843 sermon said much the same thing: "gods have an ascenden[c]y over the angels angels remain angels.—some are resurrected to become gods by such revelations as god gives in the most holy place.—in his temple."[59] George Laub, a disciple who reconstructed some of Smith's sermons shortly after his death, recalled the teaching of godhood in familial terms—the temple made "a man to be a god to his family for this is the order and organization of heaven."[60] The output from the temple rites was, in the end, divine beings.

There's something ontological at play here. The charged nature of human participants in the Nauvoo temple rites extends some recent proposals in religious studies. The religious studies scholar Robert Orsi has told the story of battles between Protestants and Catholics over the real presence of God in the Eucharist—a microcosm of broader arguments about God's presence in the world.[61] These are locations where the ostensibly solid barrier between immanent and transcendent realms visibly leaks. Orsi and others recommend that we consider the adjective "abundant" to describe the incursions of "gods really present" into the immanent world.[62] For many Catholics, the world abounded with objects beyond the Eucharist—relics, holy water, shrines, saints' artifacts, and so on. The restriction of abundant objects was a central mark of Protestant modernity where it occurred. Smith and his followers still, complexly, inhabited a world of abundant objects.[63]

In the Nauvoo temple liturgy, worshipers themselves became objects of divine presence. The rite of baptism for the dead exemplifies the process by which believers became such objects. As we've just seen, this rite was a key part of the Nauvoo temple development that solved the scandal of particularity. It supported

---

[59] *JSPJ3*, 34.
[60] Laub, "Journal," 72.
[61] Orsi, *History and Presence*.
[62] See the useful summary and minor quibbles with applications of the technique in the context of Mormon studies in Taysom, "Abundant Events," esp. 5–6.
[63] Brown, "Objects."

the Chain of Belonging by making Church members into vicars of their ancestors. The Saints were baptized as if they were the ancestors, offering up their bodies to the departed because the dead lacked viable bodies of their own. Thus, in their bodies Smith's followers called the dead into eternal life. Through Smith's vicariousness, in other words, human beings themselves became sacraments.[64] The dead inhabited the living sufficiently that the baptism could permanently bind the two together. The Saints and their dead inhabited supercharged bodies, flitting between states of existence and shared identities.[65]

Beyond vicariousness, baptism for the dead used human bodies for other cosmic purposes. Smith was working to locate his people within space and time, but also to define space and time in terms of his people. This circularity would not have bothered him: he spent his religious career searching for the "one eternal round" that was God's ambit.[66] Smith was working within this circularity to sacralize time through its connection to human and divine priesthood. In an echo of Old Testament genealogies, time for Smith was measured in parental bonds: what mattered was not how many years had elapsed but how many generations had intervened. The sacred human bonds at the base of time were both the tie between God and humanity and the connections among specific humans. As we saw in chapter 3, the Saints used the language of sealing and adoption to describe this process, which constituted a theology of secondary saviors.

The sense of creating communities and interactions among humans, gods, and angels was central to the Nauvoo temple infrastructure. Recall that worshipers made their way through a series of tests of knowledge and ritual practice that bound them by covenants to other beings. Participants were entering into a fraternity of angels and gods. The Church leaders who ritually welcomed lay worshipers into that sociality were acting as angels and gods. In his final, temple-drenched Sermon in the Grove, Smith taught, "You have got to learn how to be Gods yourselves; to be kings and priests to God, the same as all Gods have done; by going from a small degree to another, from grace to grace, from exaltation to exaltation, until you are able to sit in glory as doth those who sit enthroned in everlasting power."[67] The language of kings and priests (interpreting Revelation 1:6 and 5:10)[68] began as early as the 1832 Vision, which reported that those with the highest degree of afterlife glory were "priests and kings, who have received of

---

[64] Smith made clear that this was an expression of correspondence in June 1843: *JSPJ3*, 33.
[65] The basic story of the later extension of proxy work is told in Bennett, "'Endowments,'" with context in Stapley, *Power of Godliness*, chapter 2.
[66] On the phrase "one eternal round," see 1 Nephi 10:19; Alma 7:20, 37:12; and D&C 3:2, 35:1. The phrase was common, including in hymns by Isaac Watts. However, Smith does not seem to have used it in the familiar providentialist sense.
[67] *T&S* 5:15 (August 15, 1844): 614; cf. *WJS*, 350.
[68] Freemasons (Bernard, *Light on Masonry*, 331) and a recent British sect (Buck, *Theological Dictionary*, 523) used similar language.

his fulness, and of his glory" (D&C 76:56). The same language figured in 1830s hymnody.[69] By 1844, references to king and priests (or the queens and priestesses who ruled with them) was an explicit invocation of the rituals of the temple, in which anointings and sealings to that status took place. Those rites launched the Saints on the path to deification.

As the endowment came into greater clarity immediately after Smith's death, this language persisted and amplified. Brigham Young preached on New Year's Eve 1844 "upon Priesthood, the Godhed, the dutes of Male & Female, there exaltations &c."[70] Orson Hyde reported the next year, "We have been anointing And ordaining Kings And Priest unto God. I have been Anointed A king & Priest unto God."[71]

That central attribute of the Nauvoo temple liturgy ought not to be forgotten. Ritualistically, in the temple rites the Latter-day Saints were acting out the broader journey their lives were meant to take. The journey was spatial within the endowment, but it was also ontological. The worshipers were moving into heaven as they were becoming the kinds of beings who could physically tolerate the actual divine presence. The ritual was Smith's ongoing creation. It was the promise that people were more than they appeared to be.

The Right Name of Things

At the interface of language and identity, the temple rites put worshipers into certain types of relations. A core component of this identity and its power lay in the knowledge and exercise of sacred names—both the hidden name of God, and the ritual name of each worshiper. These new names were integral to the Nauvoo temple liturgy.

Smith's interest in names was wide-ranging and long-standing. Since the early 1830s, he had wanted to know ancient names. This was part of his quest to understand the language in which names had deep meaning. For Smith, one crucial facet of this quest was the desire to identify and be able to voice the true, hidden name of God. When Smith revealed the Nauvoo temple liturgy, he emphasized the importance of "grand key words," a term he borrowed from Freemasonry. Just weeks before he died, he "spake concerning key words. The [grand] key word was the first word Adam spoke and is a word of supplication. He found the word by the Urim & Thummim—It is that key word to which the heavens is opened."[72]

---

[69] Smith, *Sacred Hymns*, 10.
[70] Beecher, "Nauvoo Diary," 300.
[71] *WWJ*, 3:43–44.
[72] *JSPJ3*, 334.

A year before he introduced the Nauvoo endowment, Smith preached, "Great God has a Name By wich he will be Called Which is Ahman." He'd been teaching that special term as God's name since 1832, as we saw in chapter 1. In the 1841 sermon he added, "in asking have Referance to a personage Like Adam for God made Adam Just in his own Image Now this a key for you to know how to ask & obtain."[73] Here Smith was suggesting an Adamic identity with God— and claiming that people needed to know the divine name to make requests of God. We could be forgiven for hearing echoes of the powerful language of ancient theurgy or ritual magic. Such traditions foregrounded the importance of names both for knowledge and for gaining power—a fairy can be summoned, and forced to heed, by uttering its name; foreign gods can grow in strength when their names are spoken aloud (e.g., Exodus 23:13). An individual who could voice the true name of God would be an individual endowed with great power. In the Nauvoo liturgy worshipers implemented such theurgic naming in special prayers of supplication.[74]

Another facet of Smith's quest for true names involved his worshipers' own sacred, veiled names. In the temple endowment, Smith recurred to the Edenic language, both in ritual snippets of that language uttered aloud and in the assignment of sacred names to worshipers. As part of the service and complementary to Masonic practice, after completing the endowment, followers bore a name beyond the one their parents had bestowed on them. The temple names had at least two main purposes—they were part of enchanted acts of supplication, and they confirmed Smith's teaching that human beings were fundamentally and deeply spiritual.[75] The second, heavenly name existed in conjunction with the other, earthly name. In a sense, the temple name was analogous to the individual spirit. Just as the spirit mirrors the body in the other realm, so does the new name mirror the mortal name. Smith taught that spirit and body were the soul of humans—in the temple he seems to have revealed that conjoined names were the name of that soul.

Smith situated the temple names within the Bible in at least two ways. First, in John's Revelation (2:17), God promised to the believer "a white stone, and in the stone a new name written, which no man knoweth saving he that receiveth it."[76] This is the clearest and most direct connection to the Bible and indicates the connection to visionary prayer mediated by special stones that the Saints called Urim and Thummim (recall Smith's imagery of resurrected worlds as Urim and Thummim in chapter 3). Other Christians had different views of Revelation

---

[73] William P. McIntire, Notebook, pp. [14]–[15], MS 1014, CHL.
[74] Quinn, "Prayer Circles"; Bernard, *Light on Masonry*, 272.
[75] See Brown, *In Heaven*, 191–95, for preliminary thoughts on temple names.
[76] Masons interpreted this scripture similarly: Bernard, *Light on Masonry*, 331.

2:17, mostly relating to spiritual regeneration and the transformed sense of identity believers experienced with Christ. Adam Clarke, for example, followed the precedent of ancient Roman *tesserae*, stones in which an individual's name was inscribed to indicate special benefits that would accrue to the individual or his heirs. Using the tesserae, the new name is "the name of *child of God*." The secrecy that Smith connected to the temple rituals was, in Clarke's interpretation, mentioned because "this name of child of God, *no man can know* or understand but he who has received the tessera, or Divine witness."[77]

Second, Smith's belief in the power of sacred names seems to have fit well with ancient views about the nature of names. When Moses encountered God, he asked him what name of address to use (Exodus 3:13–22). In a cryptic phrase, God replied, "I am that I am." That disclosure of the divine name had immense conceptual power in ancient Hebrew religion, which sought to protect the sacred name of the Lord (YHWH, the tetragrammaton, from the Greek for "four letters"). While the specific injunctions against the use of YHWH (and its traditional pronunciation as "Adonai" or Lord rather than Yahweh, the proper name) are not spelled out in the Hebrew Bible itself, various passages make clear that at least some of God's power derived from his name. This name may have been seen as a distinguishable aspect of God's divine power.[78] God's true name may have been so separable that it could enter into a special messenger or angelic representative (Exodus 23:20–21). This interest in the power of the name of God extends across multiple related religious movements in the ancient Near East and is present in both canonical and parabiblical texts.[79] Smith wasn't so terribly far from ancient biblical beliefs when he endorsed the power of otherworldly names.

To recap, God gave believers a special private name, and names had religious power. Within the context of a theology that claimed Gods and humans shared the same species identity, this meant that humans themselves would have a divine name not so unlike the Hebrew tetragrammaton. They would participate directly in the power of Eden's language. In a sense, they were receiving their names the way all creation had in Genesis 2:19–20, in Eden's language in the presence of Adam.

As was true of Smith generally, the spirit names sounded Gnostic in their commitment to deep and sacred truths from the other realm but anti-Gnostic in their embrace of physicality. The temple names didn't indicate the dissolution of the immanent into the transcendent. On the contrary, the early Saints had names in both worlds. One's birth name was immanent. It was a part of this regular world.

---

[77] Clarke, *New Testament*, 499–500.
[78] Daniel McClellan discusses (albeit from within the controversial discipline of "cognitive science of religion") the Hebrew divine name in "Early Christology," 658–61.
[79] Fossum, *Name of God*, sees the mobility of this name as a Jewish source for the Gnostic doctrine of the demiurge.

The temple name was a part of another world, the world of spirits and the cosmic past. In the temple ceremonies, worshipers hovered between the two realms.

Smith was far from alone in his beliefs that names disclosed their recipients. Different names might apply at different phases of existence, and names held power. These powerful names recalled (and perhaps instantiated) the mystically pure language of the primordium.

Worshipers' temple names had echoes in Masonic liturgy, although the parallels are incomplete. Masons (through the Royal Arch traditions) were in pursuit of the secret name of God (the "grand omnific word") and other special passphrases, including the names of handgrips and passkeys.[80] The first degree initiates also received a shared name urging them toward "caution" in possible discussions of Masonic secrets.[81] Occasionally Masons would address each other by the names of the liturgy, for example *Jachin*.[82] Special names were therefore employed as pass-codes in the liturgy and occasionally had a role in esoteric enlightenment not dissimilar to Smith's theurgic impulse.[83] Mark Master initiates received their own version of the stone from Revelation, which contained an abbreviation for an extended epithet for Hiram Abiff.[84] Admitting that Smith tied the names to Revelation 2:9 doesn't mean there wasn't material for him to reshape in the Masonic rites. Even as they retained aspects of the Masonic password, the names for Smith were more clearly participating in the divine anthropology. The most straightforward sense of Masonic usage was not the Latter-day Saint sense of discovering the individual's angelic-divine name, it was about forging bonds and protecting the fraternity from outsiders. The Masonic names had been transposed into a Latter-day Saint key—Smith had translated them.

In his final months, Smith tied the notion of knowing the true names of people back to the problem of Bible translation in a way that recalled the ancient power of language. In his 1844 King Follett sermon, Smith questioned the King James Bible for rendering *Yakov* (Jacob) as James. He believed that he could see through that muddled translation to the truth of things. He then indicated that no wisdom could come to a worshiper who addressed a patriarch by the wrong name, saying, "if Jacob had the keys you might talk about James and never get the keys."[85] The overlap of language, text, and humans is palpable. Part of what Smith brought to

---

[80] Brown, *In Heaven*, 181–82; Bernard, *Light on Masonry*, 132, 258, 267. On passphrases, see, e.g., ibid., 59.

[81] Bernard, *Light on Masonry*, 34.

[82] Bernard, *Light on Masonry*, 46. Jachin was the name for one of the pillars in Solomon's temple: 1 Kings 7:21.

[83] Thus Bernard, *Light on Masonry*, 288: "I have still the name of Adam to teach me, that from the most low I must go to the most high."

[84] Bernard, *Light on Masonry*, 99—"H. T. W. S. S. T. K. S. ·Hiram Tyran, Widow's Son, sent to King Solomon."

[85] *WJS*, 351.

the world by nature of his approach to translation was the capacity to see through the obfuscations of mortal reality to the deep truth shimmering beyond it. In translating the Bible (freeing it from its misleading names), he was pointing toward the translation of his followers, whom he similarly liberated from their false names. Able to address the ancestors by their true names, the worshiper gained access to power and community. Once again, translation encompassed linguistic and human transformation within the temple rituals.

The power of the capacity to know a true name was exciting, even perhaps dangerous. It was not to be taken lightly, a lesson Freemasons emphasized and even (rarely) protected with violence. Certain words could never be pronounced in specific places (or, more to the point, outside specific places). For Latter-day Saints, certain words and actions could take place only in special, sacred physical contexts, always with an eye toward the physical temple. Consistent with ancient and contemporary antecedents, the temple system required a sacred secrecy.

That Which Must Not Be Spoken

The secrecy of the temple liturgy did not arrive suddenly in 1842 with Smith's induction into Freemasonry. He had been concerned about the risks of disclosure of Gospel mysteries (and anti-individualistic economic practices) from the beginning of the Church. In the *Laws of the Church* (D&C 42), Smith instructed his colleagues to "keep the mysteries of the Kingdom unto thy Self for it is not given unto the world to know the mysteries."[86] Similarly, an 1829 revelation (D&C 19:21–22) encouraged early disciples to "show not" their more radical doctrines "unto the world." He wrote to church leaders in Missouri in August 1833, "o be wise and not let the knowledge I give unto you be known abroad for your sak[e]s."[87] According to Wilford Woodruff's account, when Smith announced his grand plans for Kirtland, he indicated that "many glorious things not now to be named would be bestowed upon the Saints, but all these things are better imagined than spoken by the Children of Jacob."[88] Mary Fielding in letters to siblings in 1837 emphasized the practical side of secrecy—the "seen of confusion" as church leaders fought over allegations and innuendo, the "great number of Persons" pressing "to know the real state of the case, and her accompanying worry that disaffected Saints would kill Smith based on information disclosures—as the Kirtland Church collapsed.[89]

---

[86] *JSPD1*, 255, cf. D&C 42:65.
[87] *JSPD3*, 268.
[88] *JSPD5*, 378.
[89] MS 2779, folder 2, CHL.

Smith's penchant for secrecy was notorious, especially as it relates to his scandalous marital practices and his theocratic aspirations for the Kingdom of God.[90] Smith was working so far outside the realm of normal society that, as a practical matter, he likely had to keep some things secret if he was to achieve his aims. Theocracy and polygamy violated core tenets of contemporary American culture. The early Latter-day Saints were not playing by the rules of modern liberal democracy. They were trying to live what they saw as a consummately biblical life instead, which to them required theocracy, as we saw in chapter 3.

Even before he introduced the temple, he had determined that certain mysteries had to be kept secret from outsiders. His general tendency toward avoiding publicity intensified as he became initiated into Freemasonry and its specific system for managing the dissemination of lodge rituals.[91]

Masons not only swore strict oaths not to divulge the contents of the rituals, but in the rites themselves they "effac[ed] the ineffable word" to "hinder its being exposed to the profane."[92] The fraternity practiced and treasured its secrecy, and Smith agreed with them. In a sermon in October 1843, he taught that "the secrets of masonry. is to keep a secret."[93] Similarly, a special letter to the Relief Society in the spring of 1842 instructed, "Let this Epistle be had as a private matter in your Society, and then we shall learn whether you are good masons."[94] William Clayton for his part referred to the participants in the temple liturgy as belonging to "the secret priesthood."[95]

Not all of Smith's secrecy was to protect scandalous practices.[96] Some were liturgical secrets, mysteries in the ancient Mediterranean sense.[97] The temple was the focal point for this sacred secrecy. Both internal and external to the ceremonies, the Latter-day Saints understood that more was going on in the temple than could be said out loud anywhere else. Silence was a way to keep open the portal between immanent and transcendent realms by designating spaces and words apart from the purely immanent.

Sacred quiet wasn't new to American Christianity. Early modern Quakers saw silence as a way to avoid the misleading multiplication of words. Their famous plain speaking rejected such prolixity. In moving beyond plainness to entire

---

[90] *JSPAR*, and Park, "Council of Fifty."
[91] In May 1842 he told the Relief Society that "It is necessary to hold an influence in the world and thus spare ourselves an extermination; and also accomplish our end in spreading the gospel or holiness in the earth": Derr et al., *First Fifty Years*, 70.
[92] Bernard, *Light on Masonry*, 275.
[93] "President Joseph Smith's Journal," 134 (October 15, 1843), CHL.
[94] Derr et al., *First Fifty Years*, 99.
[95] Smith, *Intimate Chronicle*, 105.
[96] Fluhman, *Peculiar People*.
[97] On the mysteries, see Meyer, *Ancient Mysteries*; Smith, *Drudgery Divine*; Ustinova, "Mystery Rites"; and Van Den Berg, "Eleusinian Mysteries."

silence, Quakers sacrificed their voices to their community.[98] This Quaker sensibility seems to be missing, by and large, from Joseph Smith's writings and practice. However much he worried over the limits of language, he was not one to fall silent. Instead, his temple silence seems more intended as an enclave from the press of temporal and immanent concerns.

Ideas about secrecy weave in and out of Smith's scriptures in both positive and negative ways. The Book of Mormon despises secret societies that seek to hide their criminal acts.[99] Some have seen the book as an anti-Masonic manifesto, primarily on the basis of its indictment of those criminal gangs.[100] At the same time, many Book of Mormon prophets and Jesus himself had things to say that they could not say, according to the text, as we saw in chapter 4.

During the succession crisis after the murder of Joseph and Hyrum Smith, problems of secrecy dominated the course of the beleaguered church. Sidney Rigdon, who had fallen out of the inner circle in Nauvoo, had been an influential leader for most of early Restoration history. But Rigdon was systematically excluded from the temple rites. After Smith's death, he attempted to seize control of the church back from the Twelve Apostles. That bid for power, among other complexities, led to an 1844 trial for his membership. During that trial, the apostles indicated that they were Smith's rightful successors because they had participated in the temple rites. In arguing his own defense, Rigdon returned to church charters and articles. He tried to argue for a continuity that he could superintend, by returning the church to its 1830s roots.

The apostles responded that "He [Rigdon] don[']t know all the ordinations, nor he won[']t till he knows something more than the written word." His critics continued, "there are keys that the written word never spoke of, nor never will."[101] They sharply distinguished between traditional articles of faith or practice and the unwritten, esoteric world of the temple. Rigdon was assuming that the Church would run the way a Protestant church ought to, with a modern emphasis on the stability of the written word. The apostles represented a competing vision in which much that mattered about both the world and the Church would evade the neat systematization and routinization that comes from written language. In other words, Rigdon's exclusion from temple secrets meant that he could never belong in the post-Smithian church, let alone run it. In the event, Rigdon left Nauvoo, founding his own sect in Pennsylvania.[102]

---

[98] Bauman, *Speaking and Silence*, 22.
[99] See, e.g., 2 Nephi 9:9; Alma 37:21–32; Helaman 2:3–11, 6:17–31; and Ether 8:9–22, 11:22.
[100] Not exclusively, of course. Some have also seen similarities between Enoch's gold triangles and the gold plates. The Gadianton sequence is the most potentially relevant of the adduced evidence. Vogel, "Anti-Masonick Bible."
[101] *T&S* 5:17 (September 15, 1844): 666–67.
[102] Rigdon's story is told in the outdated but never superseded Wagoner, *Sidney Rigdon*.

The sacred secrecy of the temple was in some respects apophatic, or "negative"—the idea being that we approximate what is true by admitting that we can only describe with certainty what isn't true. Sacred mysteries are beyond mere human language. But temple secrecy was also expressly concerned with creating a space in-between words and the worlds to which they pointed. This space could be visited but not wholly described, though the experiences beyond such description were nevertheless tethered to a specific place and time. The secrecy also generated opportunities to create a wholly oral canon, free from the incursions of literality, because the Saints not only couldn't speak about it outside the temple, they couldn't write it down for later perusal.[103] In essence, temple secrecy was an agreement that certain things were so intrinsically ineffable that one mustn't even try to contaminate them with immanent language. In Kathleen Flake's classic argument, this allows for a fluidity that looks like fixity. They are playing at the interface of textuality and orality. There are things that can't be spoken, and the temple is the place for many of them.

The anthropologist Brad Kramer, in some elegant work comparing the Utah Latter-day Saints with the Cutlerite sect (a tiny Midwestern group that still practices aspects of the Nauvoo temple liturgy), has suggested that secrecy plays an important role in the establishment and maintenance of community.[104] Extending Flake's argument on ritual, Kramer sees the multiple levels of temple secrecy as providing room for Latter-day Saints of various levels of ideational commitment to situate themselves along a spectrum of orthodoxy. By not talking about specific details, practicing Latter-day Saints don't have to spar over areas of disagreement. The lack of discussion about many aspects of the temple creates a kind of ritual unity among people who may not share identical views about what it all means.

In addition, silence has the power to increase the nature of sacredness. It divides off certain conceptual structures from the everyday. By putting the temple into a separate place in the world, silence thus increases the sanctity and importance of its liturgy. Admitting the potential relevance of Kramer's analysis for current Latter-day Saints, we may not have the answer for the 1840s. But secrecy did seem to have a role in establishing and maintaining sanctity. That which is secret can in fact be more sacred than it would otherwise be.

Temple secrecy is another instance of language mandating that language itself be embodied in a holy way. The temple allowed people to speak in a pure language even though they appeared to be speaking English. Outside the temple, the same words that brought believers into the presence of God were merely

---

[103] Flake, "Oral Canon." The modern temple rites are actually written to allow for training and standardization, but those written copies are carefully restricted to the temple itself.
[104] Kramer, "Structured Silence."

profane. It's not just the flexibility that Flake espies nor the cohesion in the face of heterodoxy that Kramer describes. It's also about control of the sacred, which allows it to be brought into contact with the profane without dissipating.

Living the Temple

The Nauvoo liturgy was pretty heady stuff. I've considered at length the theological and conceptual infrastructure of the ritual system. But these theologies also came to life in the persons of Smith's disciples who participated in them. How did these participants actually understand what they were doing? Contemporary accounts from devoted participants are rare. It was mostly those scandalized by the rituals who left contemporary documentation.[105] The general sense of secrecy around the temple foreclosed much record-keeping from those who remained within the fold. Still, some participants made occasional comments that can help triangulate the experience of this strange temple.[106]

For most participants, the Nauvoo temple liturgy was so wrapped up in the systemic shock of polygamy that they couldn't disentangle the experiences from each other. The temple included preparation for evangelism, proxy baptism, anointings, an initiation ceremony, and celestial marriage (with celestial marriage divided into marriage per se and a royal anointing called the anointing for burial or Second Anointing). Celestial marriage encompassed the eternity of family ties, the postmortal durability of community, and the plurality of wives. We can't blame participants for being distracted by polygamy—plural marriage was a huge pill to swallow for most people.

We should also remember that only the elite participated in Smith's live temple liturgy; the vast majority of Latter-day Saints only participated in temple rites after Smith's death, as Brigham Young prepared his people to abandon the United States in 1845–1846. Most Saints encountered the rites under Young's hand in the almost-finished Nauvoo temple. This Nauvoo endowment by and large happened in an incredible rush of ceaseless rituals. It was like an industrial machine, churning out ceremonies almost around the clock. On a historical note, most faithful members' memories were affected by their later experiences in Utah with the endowment as it existed in that period. With those caveats, though, several participants gave a flavor for how they experienced the Nauvoo temple rites.

---

[105] The two best-known accounts are Van Dusens, *Positively True*, and Lewis, *Proceedings of the Mormons*.

[106] I thank Jenny Reeder for help with these sources.

Sarah Dearmon Pea Rich remembered her experience several decades later. She felt a strong need to justify polygamy, but she also had found a way to remain deeply committed to her faith for fifty years by the time of her reminiscence. In her account, what the temple brought above all else was a confidence about salvation and family. "We ware his chosen people and had embraced his gospel," she reported. For four straight months, she had a sister wife watch her children while she and her husband labored in the temple from seven in the morning to just before midnight. "Many ware the blessings we had received in the House of the Lord which has caused us joy and comfort in the midst of all our sorrows and enabled us to have faith in God." She continued, "if it had not been for the faith and knowledge that was bestowed upon us in that temple by the influence and help of the Spirit of the Lord our journey would have been like one taking a leap in the dark." In this latter respect, she was following Young's lead. He, too, had understood the priesthood organization made possible within the temple as necessary to reorganize the church in anticipation of its exodus out of the United States. The special secrets of the temple contained a set of ritual knowledge and an approach to the holy that bound Church members together as they abandoned the United States. Rich continued to think through the meanings of the temple, explaining, "As the gospel with all its fullness had been restord to the earth through the Prophet Joseph Smith of course all the former ordenences were restord. Allso among other things celestial marriage was restord and the ordenences there onto ware performed in the temple just eluded to." Reflecting and responding to the close relationship for participants between temple and polygamy, she explained, "I could not have [accepted polygamy] if I had not believed it to be right in the sight of God and believed it to be one principal of his gospel once again restored to the earth that those holding the preasthood of heaven might by obeying this order attain to a higher glory in the eternal world and by our obedience to that order we ware blessed and the Lord sustained us in the same for through obedience to that order my dear husband has left on this earth a numers posterity like the ancient Apostles and Servents of God."[107] In this account, Rich is working through polygamy and the Chain of Belonging simultaneously. Admitting that she's writing in reminiscence, she says that she found in the temple a powerful reassurance that Smith's Chain of Belonging made genealogy and salvation synonymous. One can see the threads coupling the different phases of the temple, especially its connection to marriage, reproduction, and the Abrahamic promise. Priesthood was tied to heaven, which was in turn tied to one's offspring. The temple was about building a heavenly family modeled on that of Abraham and Sarah. Rich seems to have understood well what was at

---

[107] Madsen, *Journey to Zion*, 173–75, quoting an autobiography, ca. 1890.

stake. The "higher glory" she refers to is a part of the deification of human beings effected within the Chain of Belonging.

Mercy Fielding Thompson also essentially lived in the temple during its early operation. She was one of the few who received her endowment under Smith's direction, in this case guided through the rituals by Smith's first wife Emma. Of that initial endowment, she recalled primarily that Smith told her that the endowment ceremony "will bring you out of darkness into marvelous light."[108] In this reference, he was retooling 1 Peter 2:9. Although other Christians wouldn't read the passage that way, notably for his purposes, the verse starts with a reference to "a chosen generation, a royal priesthood, an holy nation." For Smith the juxtaposition of generations, priesthood, royalty, and statehood seemed relevant to the promise of enlightenment associated with the temple rites. It was specifically the temple's union of the various components that made its promise of enlightenment so portentous. He saw himself as expanding minds, translating bodies, and creating kingdoms.

Mercy's brother Joseph Fielding noted in his nearly contemporary diary regarding the Nauvoo temple, "I entered it for the first time, and I truly felt as though I had gotten out of the world."[109] Similarly, Heber C. Kimball, an early apostle, reflected the cosmic scope of temple worship for many participants as part of his testimony during the Rigdon trial. "I have handled with my hands, and have heard with my ears, the things of eternal reality," he said, cryptically but emphatically excluding Rigdon from the Church's inner circle.[110] That mention of eternal reality was a pointed reference to the transcendent realm made accessible to worshipers in the temple.

Phelps, reflecting shortly after Smith's death on the prophet's scriptural legacy—especially as it regards the Egyptian Bible, which played an important role in the Nauvoo temple—counterposed Smith's revelations to the claims of "deists, geologists, and others." The distance between the two was so great, in Phelps's mind, "it almost tempts the flesh to fly to God, or muster faith like Enoch to be translated and see and know as we are seen and known!"[111] Phelps thus associated translation with obtaining knowledge. And not just any knowledge, but knowledge of the truths about human identity in the temple.

After the Saints arrived in Utah and had a little more time to attend to and process the temple experience, some waxed more eloquent about its meaning. A woman writing under a pseudonym described the practice of saving the dead in the temple. She wrote, "not only are men favored with these great and sacred

---

[108] *Juvenile Instructor* 27 (July 1, 1892): 400.
[109] McBride, *Nauvoo Temple*, 13, citing Ehat, "Joseph Fielding," 158–59.
[110] *T&S* 5:17 (September 15, 1844): 664.
[111] *T&S* 5:24 (January 1, 1845): 758.

blessings but women also are saviors of women. There is no inequality even in ministering for the dead. Woman acts in her sphere as man in his. Therefore is man not without the woman, nor the woman without the man in the Lord. The work of performing the ceremonies requires as much labor and falls with as much dignity upon woman as man. Therein is the goodness of our Father to His daughters made manifest. Holy women now minister in the Temple of God."[112] In this account, the writer drew attention to both the priestly power of women within the temple and a complex variant of the notion of complementary gender spheres. She maintained that the language of Paul (1 Corinthians 11:11) indicated that both men and women would work together within the temple. For participants, the temple had a great deal to say about the structure of the world and their prospects for power both in this world and afterward. There was in that a sense of movement between spheres. God too would straddle the spheres.

The Immanent-Transcendent God

As we saw in the discussion of Smith's anthropology in chapter 3, Smith rejected the binaries he inherited from his modern predecessors and peers. In the debates about dualism versus monism, Smith took a middle position that affirmed dualism within a harmonious unity. Spirit and body—both material but of different sorts—merged as soul. Temporal and spiritual existed in an interwoven cosmic structure of interdependence. In parallel debates about transcendence and immanence, Smith suggested that the transcendent suffused the immanent without being exhausted in that suffusion. The two realms were interlaced. Bringing it to the personal level, humans weren't what they seemed to be, but neither was the God of the Bible. Smith pushed to unravel the curtain separating realms and construct a cohesive harmony. Neither monism nor dualism was adequate in his view to the task of describing the relationships between the two realms.

Smith was hoping to provide for himself and his followers access to the harmonies of the transcendent immanent, this state of being both within and beyond the world envisioned by the systems that others proposed and advocated. Like many other critics, he believed that the Calvinists cared too much about the transcendent realm and its separateness. Theologically, the Calvinists denigrated human potential while emphasizing the vast chasm that existed between humans and God. At a practical level, Smith despised the learned and restrained clergy who couldn't tolerate his earthiness. He wanted more attention paid to the present world. He couldn't stop building utopias, as if he were a mystical cousin

---

[112] *Woman's Exponent* 6:11 (November 1, 1877): 83.

to the skeptical utopianist Robert Owen (1771–1858). Smith used his temples as the infrastructure for his cities, with each city planned around a central temple; the original plan for the City Zion was built around twenty-four temples.[113] He was, however, uninterested in walking the course associated with contemporary skeptics, socialists, and liberal Unitarians. He had no interest in an exclusive focus on the immanent as the most appropriate (or only) cause for care in the world. The truth hovered for Smith and his followers between the extremes.

The attempt to make the immanent transcendent and vice versa is visible in Smith's erecting expensive church buildings in Kirtland and Nauvoo, according to inspired blueprints, that were to serve as God's foothold on earth. This commingling of transcendent and immanent is why the Saints understood themselves to be anointed as celestial royalty in the Nauvoo temple. They were taking wood, stone, iron, fabric, and their own bodies, and they were investing those objects with divinity. In doing so, they entered a supercharged world beyond dualism through the temple as they inhabited the scriptural past. In a sense, the melding of people and epochs was also the merger of ostensible monism into blurry dualism.[114] In the temple the established binaries—past and present, human and divine, spirit and body—merged in anticipation of the utter transformation of human beings. The constituents continued to exist in their own right even as they were melded together.

In all this, Smith was defying the split between immanent and transcendent. He wasn't a monist, he just refused a dualism that divorced the two realms. Smith's believers were still embodied humans even as they were divine beings. They continued to live on earth even as they grew into a single transpersonal entity, the Chain of Belonging. They continued to be individuals even as they were known corporately. The Latter-day Saints were called to a kind of ontological-metaphysical dance. We might wonder whether the merger of the translations of Enoch and Elijah speak to the dance between individual and corporate. Enoch was translated as a city, while Elijah was always just a single man aboard a fiery chariot. The former is a corporate model, the latter an individual one. The early Saints were called to both of those translations simultaneously.[115]

A metaphor borrowed from the legal theorist Jeremy Waldron may help to illuminate what I mean by this notion that Smith was calling his followers to live actively among two worlds at the same time. I've misappropriated the term "scintillation" from Waldron's engagement of general humanity and specific human lives as the basis for grounding human equality. Waldron argues that

---

[113] *JSPD3*, 243–58.
[114] Smith was not so unlike other Enlightened villagers for whom "the blurring of worlds seemed to make the world they lived in perfectly clear": Hazen, *Village Enlightenment*, 149.
[115] I thank Jana Riess for this illustrative contrast.

a valid account of human dignity and equality must *scintillate* between the general and the specific. We cannot, in Waldron's terms, see humans merely as ideal types or exclusively as their single selves. They are both, and the effective establishment of grounds for human equality requires an ability to flit between the two, constantly.[116] As I've sought to communicate how Smith understood the relationships among the immanent and transcendent (the dualist and the monist, the divine and the human, the spiritual and the temporal), I see scintillation as precisely the right term. Smith proposed a dynamic merger of both poles of traditional dualism. In the temple, his followers scintillated ritually as they had been called to do for years.

This metaphor of scintillation brings us back to one of the core connections that drew me to write *Joseph Smith's Translation* in the first place. It seems to me that Smith saw translation as the mechanism by which human beings might scintillate between transcendent and immanent realms. That is, I think, the plain sense of his understanding of translation as human transformation, which was always about how mortal beings could bear the divine presence. Enoch, Elijah, Moses, Alma, and the Latter-day Saints in their temple were all tasked with taking mere physical human beings and placing them into the unmediated presence of God. They were called to translate, to scintillate between the two realms or states of being. Smith was advocating that his followers understand themselves as capable of being human and divine, immanent and transcendent—though not necessarily at the same time. They would have to flit between the two.

Smith's desire to enjoy the weaving of transcendence and immanence in and out of each other seems to have driven his belief that what other Christians called God was ineluctably plural. That plurality of gods was central to his preaching, especially near the end of his life. It was perhaps his most radical theological legacy.

A God Split in Two (or More)

Divine plurality is among Smith's wildest heresies and the idea least at home in Protestantism.[117] Not even Swedenborg went as far as Smith did in this respect.[118] Allowing for the ontological equivalence of humans and God along with the afterlife persistence of human identity—as the temple and other sacred texts obviously did—necessarily meant that Smith was teaching that what Protestants

---

[116] Waldron, *Human Equality*, chapter 4.
[117] See also Brown, *In Heaven*, 271–74.
[118] Swedenborg taught, in his popular *Concerning Heaven and Its Wonders, and Concerning Hell*, that *Maximus Homo* (the composite of the planet-based angels) was something like a God, but his approach to divine plurality was different from Smith's.

called God was fundamentally plural. There was no logical way around it—every deified human added to the number of gods. In addition he found biblical evidence for his strain of Christian polytheism. Here again the story of Smith's divine plurality is more complicated than prior depictions would suggest.[119]

Incidentally, many later biblical scholars have suggested that Smith was in the ballpark of correct about divine plurality, given evidence for a Council of Gods in early Hebrew and other West Semitic religious traditions, including textual hints in the Hebrew Bible itself—most famously Psalm 82. The Israelites were ultimately (mostly) monotheists, but lesser gods worked in close cooperation with the head God, ultimately Yahweh (himself probably merged with the Canaanite head God El in the biblical text). Many scholars view monotheism as a relatively late phenomenon in Israelite religion.[120]

Smith's characterization of divine plurality varied from sermon to sermon, with increasing boldness over time. Sometimes he had in mind simply the plurality of the species *Ahman* without greater specification. Other times he had in mind specific deities. Rarely did he endorse the pure unity of the God of traditional Christian creeds, at least not under that name.

It seems clear that Smith's plural God included, at a minimum, God the Father, God the Mother, Jesus, and a premortal Adam as the Archangel Michael. It may also have included Eve, although her role wasn't spelled out. Divine plurality could also extend beyond that small core; often it encompassed the entire human and angelic family of *Ahman*. If Phelps in 1845 is a reliable witness, and I believe that he is, then that plural God, subsumed into its head God (who was presumably the figure named *Elohim*), encompassed the entire Chain of Belonging.[121] Every deified human, on this influential interpretation, was an aspect of the plural God.

Smith probably became aware of *Elohim* as a grammatical plural in 1836 as part of his studies in the Kirtland Hebrew School.[122] In addition to that fraught kernel of Hebrew grammar, Smith also espied plurality in superlative biblical phrases. When God was described as "God of Gods" or "Lord of Lords," this suggested to Smith that God was one among other deities. He recurred to that theme in an 1839 homiletic letter, with further intensification over the 1840s.[123]

Smith's strongest statement for divine plurality came as he was attacked by seceding disciples in 1844, in what proved in retrospect to be a harbinger of his imminent assassination. The seceders accused their former leader of heresy,

---

[119] Alexander, "Mormon Doctrine"; Beckwith and Parrish, *Mormon Concept*.
[120] See, e.g., Smith, *Biblical Monotheism*; White, *Yahweh's Council*; and Day, *Gods and Goddesses*. See also Dever, *Folk Religion*.
[121] On Phelps's 1845 witness, see Brown, "Paracletes."
[122] Zucker, "Hebrew," and Grey, "Word of the Lord."
[123] *JSPD6*, 370.

theocracy, and polygamy in terms that called for his arrest and perhaps execution. As his critics got angrier, Smith seems to have become more public in elaborating his heresies.

By 1844, Smith's language about divine plurality had focused into an exegesis of stray terms suggesting that God may have had a father. Thus Revelation 1:6 reports that worshipers are made "kings and priests" (which Smith expanded in his familial way to include "queens and priestesses") unto "God and his Father." Smith begins his final sermon, the June 1844 "Sermon in the Grove," with that precise text. He then reports, in response to complaints that he was preaching a "plurality of Gods," that he has been preaching that doctrine since the beginning of his career. With a wink and a nudge, he indicates that his belief in God the Father, Jesus, and the Holy Ghost as distinct "personages" means that he has always been preaching divine plurality. He then re-engages Revelation 1:6 as if it refers both to God the Father *and* the father of God the Father. He then makes his way through a litany of proof texts, including Paul's statement that "there be gods many, and lords many" (1 Corinthians 8:4–6).

Smith then returns to his famously conciliar reading of the first sentence of the Bible, emphasizing that "beginning" (*bereshit*) refers to the "head" of the plural god *Elohim*. He then, in a subtle but still reasonably clear interpretation, suggests that Jesus prays that his followers will be made one with him, an exegesis of John 17:9–11. If they will be made one with Christ on the Trinitarian model, Smith suggests, "it wo[ul]d. make the biggest God in all the world—he is a wonderful big God—he would be a Giant." In his brash frontier logic, Smith is arguing that Trinitarianism has to be polytheistic if it is to be biblical.[124] And, he notes with a smirk, he is perfectly happy with polytheism.

However, Smith constrains that plurality by invoking the divine hierarchy revealed in the Book of Abraham. In any comparison, he says, there's always a greater and a lesser (Abraham 3:16–18). This hierarchy is meant to apply genealogically—everyone has a father, including God the Father, and his father (Jesus's grandfather by this logic), and so on. Smith employs the principle of correspondence from Paul's writings (e.g., 1 Corinthians 15:46–48) again to argue that if Jesus is God and Jesus both has a father and is the perfect son of the Father, then God the Father must also have a father. Otherwise Jesus would not be the perfect son of the father. If Elohim had no father, then Elohim and Jesus would differ in a fundamental way, and Jesus would thus imperfectly follow the Father.

In the King Follett Discourse and the Sermon in the Grove, Smith runs through a laundry list of suggestive proof texts that throw out fascinating hints into the possibility that humans could be considered gods and that God stood

---

[124] He may also have been rejecting Swedenborg's *Maximus Homo*, although that is much less certain.

among an assembly in the creation of the world. In those fateful sermons, Smith ties up the loose ends of his prior, relatively discreet preaching on the plurality of Gods.[125] He uses the language and rituals of the temple to make his point.[126] Divine plurality is the necessary endpoint for the translation of human beings within the temple.

The correspondent logic of plurality also provided another line of evidence for divine embodiment. If Christ is a God made flesh, and he did everything his father did, then God the Father must also have been flesh. In other words, the Incarnation is not unique to Christ. It includes Christ's Father, and those who came before. Implicitly in that sermon and explicitly in the temple rituals, human beings themselves participate in divine enfleshment. This is the divine plurality of Smith's Chain of Belonging.

Smith believed that his temple priesthood was the mechanism by which humans and gods could share their identity. True enough, they were all born into the species *Ahman*, but the developmental stages were radically different. Smith didn't believe that he and his followers had the same power, wisdom, and purity as God. That discrepancy was obvious. But over the long arc of eternity, Smith did expect that through temple priesthood all would partake of the eternal identity of the gods. While he made these pronouncements in many sermons, the interaction with Mary Fielding in Kirtland in 1837 (discussed in chapter 3) is illuminating. In her dream, the "Priesthood of the Son of God" united Smith with Christ. The intense identity with Christ was mediated by priesthood.

The relevant antecedents shouldn't be overlooked. Smith belonged among other visionaries and rebels of the period, including some unexpected bedfellows who also believed in divine plurality. The learned Presbyterian, Horace Bushnell, believed in a Trinity with angels that spanned the gap between them, what some call "a type of polytheism," like an infinite Brahmin as the background for a variety of gods.[127] Swedenborg taught that "The angels, taken together, are called heaven, because they constitute it."[128] The popular Scottish theologian Thomas Dick wasn't quite as radical, although he was also open to a universe full of angelic, suprahuman beings.[129] According to an excerpt from Dick published in the Latter-day Saint newspaper, there existed "a class of intelligences endowed with physical energies, powers of rapid motion, and a grasp of intellect, incomparably superior to those which are possessed by any of the beings which belong to our sublunary system."[130] When these disparate thinkers discussed angelic

---

[125] Thus, e.g., Smith's January 1842 preaching on God the Father as paradigmatic redeemer: Woodruff, "Revelations," 4–5.
[126] *WJS*, 340–62, 378–83.
[127] Conkin, *Uneasy Center*, 243.
[128] Swedenborg, *Heaven and Hell*, 11.
[129] On Dick, see Park, "Thomas Dick."
[130] *M&A* 3:5 (February 1837): 461, and *M&A* 3:3 (December 1836): 423–25.

beings, they were sticking close to the standard Chain of Being, which always placed angels above humans and closer to heaven. They were not suggesting that angels were identical with gods, even if they hinted vaguely at polytheism.[131] Because the temple was the ritual venue in which the final acts of transformation occurred, it was a factory for the generation of divine beings.

Smith pushed out onto the extreme edges, apparently happy with disturbing the balance between gods and humans. He promulgated an ontology that united heaven and earth in order to support a plurality of actual divine beings. His was a metaphysically charged ontology that radically transformed the *e pluribus unum* of the new nation's official seal (out of many, one). Instead, Smith was proposing *ex uno plures* (out of one, many)—opening the world to a robust divine plurality.

Conclusion

In the temple liturgy he completed in Nauvoo, Smith brought to an idiosyncratic fruition his twin projects of metaphysical translation: the transformation of texts and humans. His followers worshiped according to a script that deposited them directly into the scriptural scenes that Smith had been targumizing his entire career. They found themselves bodily within the Garden of Eden, witnesses to the creation of heaven, earth, and humanity. As they became direct participants in cosmic history, welding their own links to their ancestors the same way scripture did, they were themselves transformed. They became queens and priestesses, kings and priests, and in that royal priesthood they witnessed the full flowering of their genetically divine nature. These Latter-day Saint worshipers simulated Elijah's and Enoch's translation into the presence of God, newly able to bear the divine glory.

Smith was murdered by a vigilante mob before the physical structure of the Nauvoo temple could be completed, and he never reduced the liturgy to written form. Completing the temple and its endowment was a project for his successors. But he'd still managed to find a way to embody the theologies he had been pondering, testing, and fine-tuning for most of his adult life. It is fitting that his grand project for rereading the Bible would find its way finally into a community in a sacred location on earth that proved to its participants to be a portal into heaven. This was the apogee of scripture and the fruition of a religious career.

---

[131] Marshall and Walsham, *Angels*.

Epilogue

I began *Joseph Smith's Translation* with the image of the nervously and delightfully strange coelacanths discovered off the coast of South Africa in 1938. The analogy to Smith's Latter-day Restoration feels apt as a mark and reminder of the many distances between his worlds and ours. Smith cultivated, I think intentionally, a life that didn't fit well in antebellum America. He especially defied many aspects of nineteenth-century culture that are most congruent with our modern world. He was working to free himself and his followers from the prisons of human language, secular time, and modern individualism. He believed that the path to such liberation would be effected not by entire escape, as the Gnostics would have it, but by the dynamic merger of complementary realms. The path of this liberation circled back through the primordium, even as that beginning had been transformed by the integration of human history into a kind of eternal present. That eternal present came vividly to life in Smith's translations, targums of the Hebrew Bible's primeval history that pulsed with metaphysical power.

Smith's process of targumizing the Bible—generating revelatory oral transformations of the written text—fused ancient and modern, physics and metaphysics, texts and humans. It created an array of scriptural texts intended to push past the Protestant Bible into the primordial truths behind it. This process of reaching through scripture to realities beyond it was fundamentally concerned with kindling and maintaining relationships with the dead that could in turn transform the living.

Smith did his religious work in both texts and sociocultural acts, categories that overlapped substantially in his hands as he built sacred settlements and temple liturgies directly from his scripture. He was audacious enough to generate novel scriptures and establish local "theodemocracies" in the simultaneous throes of the revivals called the Second Great Awakening and the promotion of Scottish Enlightenment principles in the United States.

Whatever we may think of Smith's Bible targums, of the Church he founded, and of its current heirs, his translation projects are fascinating. This autodidact intellectual and mystical prophet from western New York shouldered his way into old and new conversations from the margins, unencumbered by the weight of Protestant tradition. He was eclectic and esoteric but also practical and commonsensical. In the phrase of a disciple who had taught him in Kirtland, he was "the calf that sucked three cows," an avid and almost indiscriminate learner driven constantly to discover but not constrained by the polite expectations of the modern age.[1]

While the early Saints were people of their age, they aggressively failed to fit in. The world looked very different to the Latter-day Saints than it did to most of their neighbors—Protestant, Catholic, freethought skeptic, or otherwise. Smith had a knack for employing modern tools, techniques, and images for deeply antique ends. His indifference to the conceptual partitions that should have prevented such improvisation is part of what makes the concept of a living fossil relevant to understanding Smith. He highlighted and consummated the secular with his theologies of body and heaven, and he refused to allow the secular to function without its sacred complement in the realm of gods and angels. The early Latter-day Saints show us what it looks like to resist—in full enjoyment of modernity—the modernist demand that the world be firmly split in two.

In my view, understanding the early Latter-day Saint traditions requires being willing to follow them outside simplistic historical or conceptual categories. Even as Smith and his disciples enjoyed many aspects of modern culture, they were unwilling to be locked in the "iron cage" of exclusively immanent frames of reference.[2] In other words, they would not agree to be merely this-worldly. They demanded the freedom to engage the divine realm without thereby capitulating to some strict division between immanent and transcendent. Without allowing that freedom to inhabit both realms—if only as a sympathetic thought experiment—it's unlikely we will understand the early Latter-day Saints. Without that freedom, there's a decent chance we won't understand ourselves either.

Above all, Smith and his disciples point out the contingency and artificiality of the culture we now associate with Western secular modernity. The world we inhabit was not inevitable, and the world the early Saints disclose is a suggestion of alternative paths that could have been taken. The usual trade-offs required by dominant cultural assumptions in the modern West are not, in fact, necessary. Admitting language's imprecision does not mandate rejection of the possibility of metaphysical power in special forms of language. Stepping away from liturgical calendars need not restrict time to flat linear sequence. Embracing human potential and moral agency need not buffer people against the claims of community, whether earthly or heavenly. Recognizing that Charles Taylor's philosophical treatment of "secularity" forces a fundamental reconfiguration of the secular and its contexts, the Latter-day Saints' failure to fit into modern dichotomies highlights the relevance of Taylor's treatment. We cannot rest confident in the nature of modern secularity.

---

[1] Wyl, *Mormon Portraits*, 25.
[2] The term "iron cage" has been appropriated from Weber, *Protestant Ethic*, 123, with discussion in Smith, *Secular Discourse*, esp. 23, 25, 61.

Few other Americans of the era dissolved so entirely into the metaphysical plasma of word and being as Smith and his followers did. The ancient principle of correspondence told them that objects and essences could be interconnected in deep and nonphysical ways. The Saints' commitment to correspondence provided an infrastructure for that merger of worlds and is a necessary context for understanding Smith's thought. Through his conception of translation as the transformation of human beings, Smith presented what critics would see as a deeply distorted revision of the secular modern worldview. His was a wholly enchanted world that incorporated an anthropomorphic God. He sanctified the everyday, turning marriage and family life into blueprints for heaven—reaching even to God, who was it turns out, married—but he did so because humans were themselves divine beings. He militated as strongly for individual power as many of his peers and predecessors did, but he did so because humans were gods in embryo, not because hierarchy was intrinsically corrupt. Human selves were only fully real in community. Everyone in Smith's Chain of Belonging was a child and a parent, in eternal relation. Everyone had a priesthood to bear.

Smith's radical rereading of the Bible and his theology of texts and humans, of words and worlds, culminated in the Nauvoo temple liturgies. Those rituals became the time and place where worshipers entered eternally durable relation as they themselves became scriptural. At long last, as early Latter-day Saints were wont to say, believers and the world were "one eternal round."

Bibliography

Works Cited

Sydney Ahlstrom, "The Scottish Philosophy and American Theology," *Church History* 24:3 (September 1955), 257–72.

Catherine Albanese, *A Republic of Mind and Spirit: A Cultural History of American Metaphysical Religion* (New Haven, CT: Yale University Press, 2007).

Thomas Alexander, "The Reconstruction of Mormon Doctrine: From Joseph Smith to Progressive Theology," *Sunstone* 10:5 (May 1985): 8–19.

John Allen, *A Spiritual Exposition of the Old Testament, or, The Christian's Gospel Treasure* (London: L. I. Higham, 1816).

Devery Anderson and Gary Bergera, eds., *Joseph Smith's Quorum of the Anointed 1842-1845: A Documentary History* (Salt Lake City: Signature Books, 2005).

Richard L. Anderson, "Joseph Smith's New York Reputation Reappraised," *BYU Studies* 10:3 (Spring 1970) : 283–314.

William Andrews, *Sisters of the Spirit: Three Black Women's Autobiographies of the Nineteenth Century* (Bloomington: Indiana University Press, 1986).

Leonard Arrington, ed., "Oliver Cowdery's Kirtland, Ohio, 'Sketchbook,'" *BYU Studies* 12:4 (Summer 1972): 410–26.

Leonard Arrington, Feramorz Fox, and Dean May. *Building the City of God: Community and Cooperation among the Mormons* (Champaign: University of Illinois Press, 1992).

Mark Ashurst-McGee, "A Pathway to Prophethood: Joseph Smith Junior as Rodsman, Village Seer, and Judeo-Christian Prophet." MA thesis, Utah State University, 2000.

Jan Assmann, *Moses the Egyptian: The Memory of Egypt in Western Monotheism* (Cambridge, MA: Harvard University Press, 1997).

Augustine, *Confessions*, trans. F. J. Sheed, 2nd ed. (Indianapolis: Hackett, 2006).

Michael Austin, "How the Book of Mormon Reads the Bible: A Theory of Types," *Journal of Book of Mormon Studies* 26 (2017): 48–81.

Origen Bacheler, *Mormonism Exposed, Internally and Externally* (New York: n.p.,1838).

Klaus Baer, "The Breathing Permit of Hor: A Translation of the Apparent Source of the Book of Abraham," *Dialogue* 33 (Autumn 1968): 109–34.

Bernard Bailyn, *The Ideological Origins of the American Revolution* (Cambridge, MA: Harvard University Press, 1967).

Philip Barlow, "Toward a Mormon Sense of Time," *Journal of Mormon History* 33:1 (Spring 2007): 1–37.

Philip Barlow, "To Mend a Fractured Reality: Joseph Smith's Project," *Journal of Mormon History* 38:3 (Summer 2012): 28–50.

Philip Barlow, *Mormons and the Bible: The Place of the Latter-day Saints in American Religion*, 2nd ed. (New York: Oxford University Press, 2013).

Kevin Barney, "The Joseph Smith Translation and Ancient Texts of the Bible," *Dialogue* 19:3 (Fall 1986): 85–102.
Kevin Barney, "Joseph Smith's Emendation of Genesis 1:1," *Dialogue* 30:4 (Winter 1997): 103–35.Michael Barton, *Something New* (Boston: [the author], 1833).
Irene Bates and E. Gary Smith, *Lost Legacy: the Mormon Office of Presiding Patriarch* (Champaign: University of Illinois Press, 1996).
Alexander Baugh, *A Call to Arms: The 1838 Mormon Defense of Northern Missouri* (Provo, UT: Brigham Young University Press, 2000).
Richard Bauman, *Let Your Words Be Few: Symbolism of Speaking and Silence among Seventeenth-Century Quakers* (Tucson: Wheatmark, 2009).
Francis Beckwith and Stephen Parrish, *The Mormon Concept of God: A Philosophical Analysis* (Lewiston, NY: Edwin Mellen, 1991).
Maureen Ursenbach Beecher, "The Eliza Enigma," *Dialogue* 11:1 (Spring 1978): 31–43.
Maureen Ursenbach Beecher, ed., "'All Things Move in Order in the City': The Nauvoo Diary of Zina Diantha Huntington Jacobs," *BYU Studies* 19:3 (Spring 1979): 285–320.Robert Bellah et al., *Habits of the Heart: Individualism and Commitment in American Life, with a New Preface* (Berkeley: University of California Press, 2007).
John Bellamy, *The History of All Religions* (Boston: Charles Ewer, 1820).
James Beniger, *The Control Revolution: Technological and Economic Origins of the Information Society* (Cambridge, MA: Harvard University Press, 1989).
John C. Bennett, *The History of the Saints; or, An Expose of Joe Smith and Mormonism* (Boston: Leland and Whiting, 1842).
RoseAnn Benson, *Alexander Campbell and Joseph Smith: Nineteenth-Century Restorationists* (Provo: BYU Studies Press, 2017).
David Bernard, *Light on Masonry* (Utica: William Williams, 1829).
Hans Dieter Betz, ed., *The Greek Magical Papyri in Translation, Including the Demotic Spells*, Vol. 1, 2nd ed. (Chicago: University of Chicago Press, 1992).
Joseph Blenkinsopp, *Opening the Sealed Book* (Grand Rapids, MI: Eerdmans, 2006).
Joseph Blenkinsopp, *Creation Un-Creation Re-Creation: A Discursive Commentary on Genesis 1–11* (London: T&T Clark, 2011).
Harold Bloom, *The American Religion* (New York: Simon & Schuster, 2006).
John Bossy, *Christianity in the West, 1400–1700* (New York: Oxford University Press, 1987).
Gregory Bowen, "Sounding Sacred: The Adoption of Biblical Archaisms in the Book of Mormon and Other 19th Century Texts" (2016). Open Access Dissertations. 945. http://docs.lib.purdue.edu/open_access_dissertations/945.
Matthew Bowman, "Eternal Progression: Mormonism and American Progressivism," in Jana Riess and Randall Balmer, eds., *Mormonism and American Politics* (New York: Columbia University Press, 2015), 53–70.
Matthew Bowman and Samuel Brown, "The Reverend Buck's *Theological Dictionary* and the Struggle to Define American Evangelicalism, 1802–1851," *Journal of the Early Republic* 29:3 (Fall 2009): 441–73.
George Box, *An Accidental Statistician: The Life and Memories of George E. P. Box* (Hoboken, NJ: Wiley, 2013).
Theodore Bozeman, *To Live Ancient Lives: The Primitivist Dimension in Puritanism* (Chapel Hill: University of North Carolina Press, 1988).
Remi Brague, *The Wisdom of the World: The Human Experience of the Universe in Western Thought*, trans. Teresa Fagan (Chicago: University of Chicago Press, 2003).

Catherine Brekus, *Strangers and Pilgrims: Female Preaching in America, 1740–1845* (Chapel Hill: University of North Carolina Press, 1998).

Catherine Brekus, *Sarah Osborn's World: The Rise of Evangelical Christianity in Early America* (New Haven, CT: Yale University Press, 2013).

Hugh Brogan, *Alexis de Tocqueville: A Life* (New Haven, CT: Yale University Press, 2007).

John Brooke, *The Refiner's Fire: The Making of Mormon Cosmology, 1644–1844* (New York: Cambridge University Press, 1994).

Richard Brothers, *A Revealed Knowledge of the Prophecies and Times* (Albany, NY: Webster, 1796).

Candy Gunther Brown, *The Word in the World: Evangelical Writing, Publishing, and Reading in America, 1789–1880* (Chapel Hill: University of North Carolina Press, 2004).

Peter Brown, *The Body and Society: Men, Women, and Sexual Renunciation in Early Christianity* (New York: Columbia University Press, 2008).

Samuel M. Brown, "The Translator and the Ghostwriter: Joseph Smith and William Phelps," *Journal of Mormon History* 33:4 (Winter 2007): 26–62.

Samuel M. Brown, "Escaping the Destroying Angel: Immortality and the Word of Wisdom in Early Mormonism" (paper presented at the Mormon History Association, Springfield, IL, May 22, 2009).

Samuel M. Brown, "Joseph (Smith) in Egypt: Babel, Hieroglyphs, and the Pure Language of Eden," *Church History* 78:1 (March 2009): 26–65.

Samuel M. Brown, "William Phelps's 'Paracletes': An Early Witness to Joseph Smith's Divine Anthropology," *International Journal of Mormon Studies* 2:1 (Spring 2009): 62–81.

Samuel M. Brown, "Early Mormon Adoption Theology and the Mechanics of Salvation," *Journal of Mormon History* 37:3 (Summer 2011): 3–52.

Samuel M. Brown, "The Early Mormon Chain of Belonging," *Dialogue* 44:1 (Spring 2011): 1–52.

Samuel M. Brown, *In Heaven as It Is on Earth: Joseph Smith and the Early Mormon Conquest of Death* (New York: Oxford University Press, 2012).

Samuel M. Brown, "The Language of Heaven: Prolegomenon to the Study of Smithian Translation," *Journal of Mormon History* 38:1 (Summer 2012): 51–71.

Samuel M. Brown, "The Olive Leaf and the Family of Heaven," in Scott Esplin, Richard Cowan, and Rachel Cope, eds., *You Shall Have My Word: Exploring the Text of the Doctrine and Covenants* (Provo, UT: BYU Religious Studies Center, 2012), 182–91.

Samuel M. Brown, "Joseph Smith, Polygamy, and the Levirate Widow," *Dialogue* 49:3 (Fall 2016): 41–60.

Samuel M. Brown, "Mormons Probably Aren't Materialists," *Dialogue* 50:3 (Fall 2017): 39–72.

Samuel M. Brown, "'To Read the Round of Eternity': Speech, Text, and Scripture in The Book of Mormon," in Fenton and Hickman, eds., *Americanist Approaches*, (New York: Oxford University Press, 2019), 159–83.

Samuel M. Brown, "Seeing the Voice of God: The Book of Mormon on Its Own Translation," in MacKay et al., *Producing Ancient Scripture*, (Salt Lake City: University of Utah Press, 2020), 137–68.

Charles Buck, *A Theological Dictionary* (Philadelphia: Edwin T. Scott, 1823).

David Buerger, *The Mysteries of Godliness: A History of Mormon Temple Worship* (San Francisco: Smith Research Associates, 1994).

Steven Bullock, *Revolutionary Brotherhood: Freemasonry and the Transformation of the American Social Order, 1730–1840* (Chapel Hill: University of North Carolina Press, 1996).

Walter Burkert, *Ancient Mystery Cults* (Cambridge, MA: Harvard University Press, 1987).
James Burnett, *Antient Metaphysics: or, The Science of Universals* (Edinburgh: J. Balfour, 1779-1799).
James Burnett, *Of the Origin and Progress of Language* (London: T. Cadell, 1773-1792).
Richard Bushman, *Joseph Smith: Rough Stone Rolling* (New York: Knopf, 2005).
Horace Bushnell, *God in Christ: Three Discourses Delivered* (Hartford: Brown and Parsons, 1849).
Diana Butler, *Standing against the Whirlwind: Evangelical Episcopalians in Nineteenth-Century America* (New York: Oxford University Press, 1995).
Jon Butler, *Awash in a Sea of Faith: Christianizing the American People* (Cambridge, MA: Harvard University Press, 1990).
Jon Butler, "Disquieting History in *A Secular Age*," in Warner et al., eds., *Varieties of Secularism in a Secular Age* (Cambridge, MA: Harvard University Press, 2010), 193-216.
Alexander Campbell, *Sacred Writings of the Apostles and Evangelists of Jesus Christ*, 4th ed. (Bethany, VA: McVay and Ewing, 1835).
James Carey, *Communication as Culture: Essays on Media and Society* (New York: Routledge, 1989).
Henry Caswall, *The Prophet of the Nineteenth Century* (London: Rivington, 1843).
Salvatore Cirillo, "Joseph Smith, Mormonism and Enochic Tradition," Durham theses, Durham University, 2010. http://etheses.dur.ac.uk/236/.
Adam Clarke, *The Holy Bible, Containing the Old and New Testaments* (New York: T. Mason and G. Lane, 1837), 6 vols.
Adam Clarke, *The New Testament of Our Lord and Saviour Jesus Christ* (Philadelphia: Thomas, Cowperthwait, and Co., 1838).
Kenneth Cmiel, *Democratic Eloquence: The Fight for Public Speech in Nineteenth-Century America* (New York: William Morrow, 1990).
Marc Coenen, "An Introduction to the Document of Breathing Made By Isis," *Revue D'egyptologie* 49 (1998): 37-45.
Charles Cohen, "Religion, Print Culture, and the Bible before 1876," in *Religion and the Culture of Print in Modern America*, ed. Charles L. Cohen and Paul S. Boyer (University of Wisconsin Press, 2008), 3-13.
Thomas Coke, *A Commentary on the Holy Bible* (London: G. Whitfield, 1802).
Samuel Cole, *The Freemasons' Library and Ahiman Rezon* (Baltimore: Benjamin Edes, 1817).
Charly Coleman, "Resacralizing the World: The Fate of Secularization in Enlightenment Historiography," *Journal of Modern History* 82 (June 2010): 368-95.
Paul Conkin, *The Uneasy Center: Reformed Christianity in Antebellum America* (Chapel Hill: University of North Carolina Press, 1995).
John Cooper and D. S. Hutchinson, eds., *Plato: Complete Works* (Cambridge: Hackett, 1997).
Rex Cooper, *Promises Made to the Fathers: Mormon Covenant Organization* (Salt Lake City: University of Utah Press, 1990).
Lee Copeland, "Speaking in Tongues in the Restoration Churches," *Dialogue* 24:1 (Spring 1991): 13-32.
Paul Cornelius, *Languages in Seventeenth and Early Eighteenth-Century Imaginary Voyages* (Geneva: Droz, 1965).

John Corrill, *A Brief History of the Church of Christ of Latter Day Saints* (St. Louis: for the Author, 1839).
Alexander Cory, *The Hieroglyphics of Horapollo Nilous* (London: William Pickering, 1840).
James Creighton, ed., *The Sacred and Profane History of the World*, 4 vols. (Philadelphia: Woodward, 1824).
Richard Cummings, "Quintessential Mormonism: Literal-Mindedness as a Way of Life," *Dialogue* 15:4 (Winter 1982): 92–102.
David Daniell, *The Bible in English: Its History and Influence* (New Haven, CT: Yale University Press, 2003).
Douglas Davies, *The Mormon Culture of Salvation* (Aldershot, UK: Ashgate, 2000).
Owen Davies, *Popular Magic: Cunning-folk in English History* (London: Continuum, 2003).
Owen Davies, *Grimoires: A History of Magic Books* (New York: Oxford University Press, 2009).
Andrew Jackson Davis, *The Philosophy of Spiritual Intercourse; Being an Explanation of Modern Mysteries* (New York: Fowler and Wells, 1851).
Andrew Jackson Davis, *The Great Harmonia concerning the Seven Mental States* (Boston: Benjamin Mussey, 1853).
David Brion Davis, "The New England Origins of Mormonism," *New England Quarterly* 26:2 (June 1953): 147–68.
Jasmine Day, *The Mummy's Curse: Mummymania in the English-Speaking World* (London: Routledge, 2006).
John Day, *Yahweh and the Gods and Goddesses of Canaan* (London: Sheffield Academic, 2002).
Kathryn Daynes, *More Wives Than One: Transformation of the Mormon Marriage System, 1840–1910* (Champaign: University of Illinois Press, 2001).
Ronald Delph, "From Venetian Visitor to Curial Humanist: The Development of Agostino Steuco's 'Counter'-Reformation Thought," *Renaissance Quarterly* 47:1 (Spring 1994): 102–39.
Mario DePillis, "The Development of Mormon Communitarianism, 1826–1846," PhD dissertation, Yale University, 1960.
Jill Mulvay Derr and Karen Lynn Davidson, eds., *Eliza R. Snow: The Complete Poetry*. (Provo: Brigham Young University Press, 2009).
Jill Mulvay Derr, Carol Cornwall Madsen, Kate Holbrook, and Matt Grow, eds., *The First Fifty Years of Relief Society: Key Documents in Latter-day Saint Women's History* (Salt Lake City: Church Historian's Press, 2016).
William Dever, *Did God Have a Wife? Archaeology and Folk Religion in Ancient Israel* (Grand Rapids: Eerdmans, 2008).
Johannes Dillinger, *Magical Treasure Hunting in Europe and North America: A History* (Basingstoke: Palgrave Macmillan, 2012).
Robert Divett, "His Chastening Rod: Cholera Epidemics and the Mormons," *Dialogue* 12 (Fall 1979) 3:6–15.
Eamon Duffy, *The Stripping of the Altars: Traditional Religion in England, 1400–1580* (New Haven, CT: Yale University Press, 1992).
Harold Durfee, "Language and Religion: Horace Bushnell and Rowland G. Hazard," *American Quarterly* 5:1 (Spring 1953): 57–70.
Florian Ebeling, *The Secret History of Hermes Trismegistus: Hermeticism from Ancient to Modern Times*, trans. David Lorton (Ithaca: Cornell University Press, 2007).

James Egan, "A Flood of Light and An Abyss of Darkness: Mormons, Heathens, and Bringing Truth Home to Zion," Maxwell Institute Summer Seminar paper, 2013, copy in author's possession.

Andrew Ehat, "They Might Have Known That He Was Not a Fallen Prophet—The Nauvoo Journal of Joseph Fielding," *BYU Studies* 19:2 (Winter 1979): 133–66.

Andrew Ehat, "Joseph Smith's Introduction of Temple Ordinances and the 1844 Mormon Succession Question." MA Thesis, BYU, 1982.

Mircea Eliade, "Paradise and Utopia: Mythical Geography and Eschatology," in Frank Manuel, ed., *Utopia and Utopian Thought* (New York: Houghton Mifflin, 1966), 261–69.

Janet Ellingson, "Becoming a People: The Beliefs and Practices of the Early Mormons, 1830–1845," PhD dissertation, University of Utah, 1997.

Ralph Waldo Emerson, *Nature. Addresses, and Lectures* (Boston: James Munroe, 1836).

Ralph Waldo Emerson, *Essays* (Boston: James Munroe, 1850).

Eugene England, ed., "George Laub's Nauvoo Journal," *BYU Studies* 18:2 (Winter 1978): 151–78.

John Ernest, "The Governing Spirit: African American Writers in the Antebellum City on a Hill," in Susan Juster and Lisa MacFarlane, eds., *A Mighty Baptism: Race, Gender, and the Creation of American Protestantism* (Ithaca: Cornell University Press, 1996), 259–79.

Jared Farmer, *On Zion's Mount: Mormons, Indians, and the American Landscape* (Cambridge, MA: Harvard University Press, 2008).

James Farrell, *Inventing the American Way of Death, 1830–1920* (Philadelphia: Temple University Press, 1980).

Denis Feeney, *Caesar's Calendar: Ancient Times and the Beginnings of History* (Berkeley: University of California Press, 2007).

John Fellows, *An Exposition of the Mysteries* (New York: for the author, 1835).

Elizabeth Fenton, "Open Canons: Sacred History and American History in *The Book of Mormon*," *J19* 1:2 (Fall 2013): 339–61.

Elizabeth Fenton and Jared Hickman, eds., *Americanist Approaches to the Book of Mormon* (New York: Oxford University Press, 2019).

Elizabeth Fenton and Jared Hickman, "Learning to Read with *The Book of Mormon*," in Fenton and Hickman, eds., *Americanist Approaches*, (New York: Oxford University Press, 2019), 1–20.

Kathleen Flake, "'Not to be Riten': The Mormon Temple Rite as Oral Canon," *Journal of Ritual Studies* 9:2 (1995): 1–21.

Kathleen Flake, "Translating Time: The Nature and Function of Joseph Smith's Narrative Canon," *Journal of Religion* 87 (October 2007): 497–527.

Kathleen Flake, Utah State University Press, "The Emotional and Priestly Logic of Plural Marriage" (2009). Arrington Annual Lecture. Paper 15. https://digitalcommons.usu.edu/arrington_lecture/15.

Robert Flanders, "To *Transform History*: Early Mormon Culture and the Concept of Time and Space," *Church History* 40 (March 1971): 108–17.

William Fleming, *The Scripture Gazetteer*, 2 vols. (Edinburgh: The Edinburgh Printing and Publishing Company, 1837).

Spencer Fluhman, *"A Peculiar People": Anti-Mormonism and the Making of Religion in Nineteenth-Century America* (Chapel Hill: University of North Carolina Press, 2012).

Jarl Fossum, *The Name of God and the Angel of the Lord: Samaritan and Jewish Concepts of Intermediation and the Origin of Gnosticism* (Waco: Baylor University Press, 2017).

Nicholas Frederick, *The Bible, Mormon Scripture, and the Rhetoric of Allusivity* (Madison, NJ: Fairleigh Dickinson University Press, 2016).

Nicholas Frederick, "The Book of Mormon and Its Redaction of the King James New Testament," *Journal of Book of Mormon Studies* 27 (2018): 44–87.

Clarke Garrett, *Spirit Possession and Popular Religion: From the Camisards to the Shakers* (Baltimore: Johns Hopkins University Press, 1987).

John Gee, "A Tragedy of Errors," *FARMS Review of Books* 4:1 (1992): 93–119.

John Gee, "Some Puzzles from the Joseph Smith Papyri," *FARMS Review* 20:1 (2008): 113–37.

John Gee, *An Introduction to the Book of Abraham* (Provo: Religious Studies Center and Deseret Book, 2017).

John Gee, William Hamblin, and Daniel Peterson, "'And I Saw the Stars': The Book of Abraham and Geocentric Astonomy," in John Gee and Brian Hauglid, eds., *Astronomy, Papyrus and Covenant* (Provo: FARMS, 2005), 1–16.

Michael Gillespie, *The Theological Origins of Modernity* (Chicago: University of Chicago Press Press, 2008).

Terryl Givens, *By the Hand of Mormon: the American Scripture That Launched a New World Religion* (New York: Oxford University Press, 2002).

Terryl Givens, *When Souls Had Wings: Pre-Mortal Existence in Western Thought* (New York: Oxford University Press, 2009).

Terryl Givens, *Wrestling the Angel: The Foundations of Mormon Thought: Cosmos, God, Humanity* (New York: Oxford University Press, 2014).

Terryl Givens, *Feeding the Flock: The Foundations of Mormon Thought: Church and Praxis* (New York: Oxford University Press, 2017).

Terryl Givens, *The Pearl of Greatest Price: Mormonism's Most Controversial Scripture* (New York: Oxford University Press, 2020).

Shalom Goldman, *God's Sacred Tongue: Hebrew and the American Imagination* (Chapel Hill: University of North Carolina Press, 2004).

Shalom Goldman, "Joshua/James Seixas (1802–1874): Jewish Apostasy and Christian Hebraism in Early Nineteenth-Century America," *Jewish History* 7:1 (March 1993): 65–88.

Nicholas Goodrick-Clarke, *The Western Esoteric Traditions: A Historical Introduction* (New York: Oxford University Press, 2008).

Brett Grainger, *Church in the Wild: Evangelicals in Antebellum America* (Cambridge, MA: Harvard University Press, 2019).

Christopher Grasso, "The Religious and the Secular in the Early American Republic," *Journal of the Early Republic* 36 (Summer 2016): 359–88.

Christopher Grasso, *Skepticism and American Faith: from the Revolution to the Civil War* (New York: Oxford University Press, 2018).

Edward Gray, *New World Babel: Languages and Nations in Early America* (Princeton, NJ: Princeton University Press, 1999).

Thomas Gray, *The Confessions of Nat Turner* (Baltimore: Thomas R. Gray, 1831).

Steven Green, *The Second Disestablishment: Church and State in Nineteenth-Century America* (New York: Oxford University Press, 2010).

Brad Gregory, *The Unintended Reformation: How a Religious Revolution Secularized Society* (Cambridge, MA: Harvard University Press, 2012).

Matthew Grey, "'The Word of the Lord in the Original': Joseph Smith's Study of Hebrew in Kirtland," in *Approaching Antiquity: Joseph Smith and the Ancient World*, edited by

Lincoln H. Blumell, Matthew J. Grey, and Andrew H. Hedges (Provo, UT: Religious Studies Center; Salt Lake City: Deseret Book, 2015), 249–302.

Matthew Grey, "Approaching Egyptian Papyri through Biblical Language: Joseph Smith's Use of Hebrew in His Translation of the Book of Abraham," in MacKay et al., *Producing Ancient Scripture*, (Salt Lake City: University of Utah Press, 2020), chapter 16.

Philip Gura, *American Transcendentalism: A History* (New York: Hill & Wang, 2007).

Paul Gutjahr, "The Golden Bible in the Bible's Golden Age: The Book of Mormon and Antebellum Print Culture," *American Transcendental Quarterly* 12:4 (December 1998): 275–93.

Paul Gutjahr, *An American Bible: A History of the Good Book in the United States, 1777–1880*. (Stanford, CA: Stanford University Press, 1999).

David Hackett, *That Religion in Which All Men Agree: Freemasonry in American Culture* (Berkeley: University of California Press: 2014).

David Hall, *Worlds of Wonder, Days of Judgment* (New York: Knopf, 1989).

Wouter Hanegraaff, *Esotericism and the Academy: Rejected Knowledge in Western Culture* (Cambridge: Cambridge University Press, 2012).

Carmon Hardy, *Solemn Covenant: The Mormon Polygamous Passage* (Champaign: University of Illinois Press, 1992).

Grant Hardy, *Understanding the Book of Mormon: A Reader's Guide* (New York: Oxford University Press, 2010).

Grant Hardy, "The Book of Mormon and the Bible," in Fenton and Hickman, eds., *Americanist Approaches*, (New York: Oxford University Press, 2019), 107–35.

Heather Hardy and Grant Hardy, "How Nephi Shapes His Readers' Perceptions of Isaiah," in Joseph Spencer and Jenny Webb, eds., *Reading Nephi Reading Isaiah: Reading 2 Nephi 26–27* (Salem: Salt Press, 2011).

D. E. Harkness, *John Dee's Conversations with Angels: Cabala, Alchemy, and the End of Nature* (New York: Cambridge University Press, 1999).

Craig Harline, *Sunday: A History of the First Day from Babylonia to the Super Bowl*, (New Haven, CT: Yale University Press, 2011).

Steven C. Harper, "Infallible Proofs, Both Human and Divine: The Persuasiveness of Mormonism for Early Converts. *Religion and American Culture* 10:1 (Winter 2000): 99–118.

Steven C. Harper, "Pentecost Continued: A Contemporaneous Account of the Kirtland Temple Dedication," *BYU Studies* 42:2 (2003): 5–22.

William Harris, *Mormonism Portrayed* (Warsaw, IL: Sharp & Gamble, 1841).

William Hartley, *Stand by My Servant Joseph: The Story of the Joseph Knight Family and the Restoration* (Salt Lake City: Deseret Book, 2003).

Nathan Hatch, *The Democratization of American Christianity*, (New Haven, CT: Yale University Press, 1989).

Brian Hauglid, *A Textual History of the Book of Abraham: Manuscripts and Editions* (Provo, UT: Maxwell Institute, 2010).

Brian Hauglid, "Book of Abraham and Egyptian Project," in *Approaching Antiquity: Joseph Smith and the Ancient World*, edited by Lincoln H. Blumell, Matthew J. Grey, and Andrew H. Hedges (Provo, UT: Religious Studies Center; Salt Lake City: Deseret Book, 2015), 474–511.

Charlotte Haven, "A Girl's Letters from Nauvoo," *Overland Monthly* 16 (December 1890): 616–38.

Craig Hazen, *The Village Enlightenment in America: Popular Religion and Science in the Nineteenth Century* (Champaign: University of Illinois Press, 2000).

R. A. Heavlin, *The Mysteries of Isis: or, The Science of Mythematics* (New York: John F. Trow, 1858).
Jared Hickman, "Amerindian Apocalypse," *American Literature* 86:3 (2014): 429–61.
Jared Hickman, "'Bringing Forth' the Book of Mormon: Translation as the Reconfiguration of Bodies in Space-Time," in MacKay et al., *Producing Ancient Scripture*, chapter 3.
Bruce Hindmarsh, *The Spirit of Early Evangelicalism: True Religion in a Modern World* (New York: Oxford University Press, 2018).
Marvin Hill, *Quest for Refuge: The Mormon Flight from American Pluralism* (Salt Lake City: Signature Books, 1989).
Marvin Hill, et al., "The Kirtland Economy Revisited: A Market Critique of Sectarian Economics," *BYU Studies* 17:4 (Summer 1977): 391–475.
E. Brooks Holifield, *Theology in America: Christian Thought from the Age of the Puritans to the Civil War*, (New Haven, CT: Yale University Press, 2003).
David Holland, *Sacred Borders: Continuing Revelation and Canonical Restraint in Early America* (New York: Oxford University Press, 2010).
Michael Homer, "'Similarity of Priesthood in Masonry': The Relationship Between Freemasonry and Mormonism," *Dialogue* 27 (Fall 1994) 3:1–113.
Daniel Walker Howe, *What Hath God Wrought: The Transformation of America, 1815–1848* (New York: Oxford University Press, 2007).
E. D. Howe, *Mormonism Unvailed*, (Painesville: for the author, 1834).
David Howlett, *The Kirtland Temple* (Champaign: University of Illinois Press, 2016).
Ronald Huggins, "Joseph Smith's 'Inspired Translation' of Romans 7," *Dialogue* 26:4 (Winter 1993): 159–82.
Ronald Huggins, "'Without a Cause' and 'Ships of Tarshish': A Possible Contemporary Source for Two Unexplained Readings from Joseph Smith," *Dialogue* 36:1 (Spring 2003): 157–79.
Richard Hughes, ed., *The American Quest for the Primitive Church* (Champaign: University of Illinois Press, 1988).
Richard Hughes, "Soaring with the Gods: Early Mormons and the Eclipse of Religious Pluralism," in Eric Eliason, ed., *Mormons and Mormonism: An Introduction to an American World Religion* (Champaign: University of Illinois Press, 2001).
Richard Hughes and Leonard Allen, *Illusions of Innocence: Protestant Primitivism, 1630–1875* (Chicago: University of Chicago Press Press, 1988).
Arnold Huijgen, "Divine Accommodation in Calvin: Myth and Reality," in Peter Opitz, ed., *The Myth of the Reformation* (Gottingen: Vandenhoeck & Ruprecht, 2013), 248–59.
James Hunt, *Mormonism: Embracing the Origin, Rise and Progress of the Sect, With an Examination of the Book of Mormon* (St. Louis, MO: Ustick and Davies, 1844).
William Hunter, *Edward Hunter: Faithful Steward* (Salt Lake City: Hunter, 1970).
William Hutchinson, *The Spirit of Masonry* (Carlisle: F. Jollie, 1796), 2nd ed.
John Irwin, *American Hieroglyphics: The Symbol of the Egyptian Hieroglyphics in the American Renaissance* (New Haven, CT: Yale University Press, 1980).
Erik Iversen, *The Myth of Egypt and its Hieroglyphs in European Tradition*, 2nd ed. (Princeton, NJ: Princeton University Press, 1993).
Kent Jackson, *The Book of Moses and the Joseph Smith Translation Manuscripts* (Provo: BYU Religious Studies Center, 2005).
Kent Jackson, "Joseph Smith Translating Genesis," *BYU Studies* 56:4 (Winter 2017): 7–28.
Margaret Jacob, *The Radical Enlightenment: Pantheists, Freemasons and Republicans* (London: George Allen and Unwin, 1981).

Soame Jenyns, *A View of the Internal Evidence of the Christian Religion*, 3d edition (London: J. Dodsley, 1776).
Hollis Johnson, "One Day to a Cubit," *Interpreter* 3 (2013): 223–30.
Paul Johnson, *A Shopkeeper's Millennium: Society and Revivals in Rochester, New York, 1815-1837*, rev. ed. (New York: Hill and Wang, 2004).
Janiece Johnson, *"Give It All Up and Follow Your Lord": Mormon Female Religiosity, 1831-1843* (Provo: BYU Studies, 2008).
Janiece Johnson, "Becoming a People of the Books: Toward an Understanding of Early Mormon Converts and the New Word of the Lord," *Journal of Book of Mormon Studies* 27 (2018): 1–43.
Timothy Johnson, *Religious Experience in Earliest Christianity: a Missing Dimension in New Testament Studies* (Minneapolis: Fortress, 1998).
Christopher C. Jones, "The Complete Record of the Nauvoo Library and Literary Institute," *Mormon Historical Studies* 10:1 (Spring 2009): 153–76.
Flavius Josephus, *Antiquities of the Jews*, Vol. 1, trans. William Whiston (New York: Evert Duyckinck, John Tiebout, and M. & W. Ward, 1810).
Flavius Josephus, *The Works of Flavius Josephus*, trans. William Whiston (Baltimore: Armstrong & Berry, 1839).
Susan Juster, *Doomsayers: Anglo-American Prophecy in the Age of Revolution*. (Philadelphia: University of Pennsylvania Press, 2003).
Daniel Kidder, *Mormonism and the Mormons* (New York Lane & Sandford for the Methodist Episcopal Church, 1842).
Stanley Kimball, "The Anthon Transcript," *BYU Studies* 10:3 (Spring 1970): 325–352.
James Knowlson, *Universal Language Schemes in England and France 1600-1800*. (University of Toronto Press, 1975).
Erazim Kohák, *The Embers and the Stars: A Philosophical Inquiry into the Moral Sense of Nature* (Chicago: University of Chicago Press Press, 1987).
Paul Kosmin, *Time and its Adversaries in the Seleucid Empire* (Cambridge, MA: Harvard University Press, 2018).
Bradley Kramer, "Keeping the Sacred: Structured Silence in the Enactment of Priesthood Authority, Gendered Worship, and Sacramental Kinship in Mormonism," PhD Dissertation, University of Michigan, 2014.
James Kugel, *The God of Old: Inside the Lost World of the Bible* (New York: Free Press, 2003).
James Kugel, *How to Read the Bible: A Guide to Scripture, Then and Now* (New York: Free Press, 2007).
Manuel Lacunza and Edward Irving, *The Coming of Messiah in Glory and Majesty*, Volume 2 (London: L.B. Seely and Son, 1827).
David Rich Lamson, *Two Years' Experience among the Shakers* (West Boylston: for the author, 1848).
Charles Larson, *By His Own Hand upon Papyrus: A New Look at the Joseph Smith Papyri* (Grand Rapids, MI: Institute for Religious Research, 1992).
Stanley Larson, "A Study of Some Textual Variations in the Book of Mormon Comparing the Original and the Printer's Manuscripts and the 1830, the 1837, and the 1840 Editions," MA thesis, Brigham Young University, 1974.
Richard Laurence, *The Book of Enoch the Prophet* (New York: Oxford University Press, 1821).
E. G. Lee, *The Mormons, or, Knavery Exposed* (Philadelphia: George Webber and William Fenimore, 1841).

Michael Lee, *The Erosion of Biblical Certainty: Battles over Authority and Interpretation in America* (New York: Palgrave Macmillian, 2013).
Chris Lehmann, *The Money Cult: Capitalism, Chrsitianity, and the Unmaking of the American Dream* (New York: Melville House, 2016).
Stephen LeSueur, *The 1838 Mormon War in Missouri* (University of Missouri Press, 1990).
Herbert Leventhal, *In the Shadow of the Enlightenment: Occultism and Renaissance Science in Eighteenth-century America* (New York: New York University Press, 1976).
Catherine Lewis, *Narrative of Some of the Proceedings of the Mormons* (Lynn, MA: for the author, 1848).
Rhodri Lewis, *Language, Mind and Nature: Artificial Languages in England from Bacon to Locke* (New York: Cambridge University Press, 2007).
Arthur Lovejoy, *The Great Chain of Being: A Study of the History of an Idea* (Cambridge, MA: Harvard University Press, 1948).
Sally MacDonald and Michael Rice, eds., *Consuming Ancient Egypt* (Walnut Creek: Left Coast Press, 2003).
Michael MacKay, "'Git them Translated': Translating the Characters on the Gold Plates," in Lincoln Blumell et al., eds., *Approaching Antiquity: Joseph Smith and the Ancient World,* (Salt Lake City: Deseret Book, 2015), 83–116.
Michael MacKay, et al., "The 'Caractors' Document: New Light on an Early Transcription of the Book of Mormon Characters," *Mormon Historical Studies* 14:1 (Spring 2013): 131–52.
Michael MacKay, et al., eds., *Producing Ancient Scripture: Joseph Smith's Translation Projects and the Making of Mormonism* (Salt Lake City: University of Utah Press, 2020).
Carol Cornwall Madsen, *Journey to Zion: Voices from the Mormon Trail* (Salt Lake City: Deseret Book, 1997).
George M. Marsden, "Everyone One's Own Interpreter? The Bible, Science, and Authority in Mid-Nineteenth-Century America," in Mark Noll and Nathan Hatch, ed., *The Bible in America: Essays in Cultural History* (New York: Oxford University Press, 1982).
George M. Marsden, *Jonathan Edwards: A Life* (New Haven, CT: Yale University Press, 2004).
Peter Marshall and Alexandra Walsham, eds., *Angels in the Early Modern World* (New York: Cambridge University Press, 2006).
Martin Marty, "Living with Establishment and Disestablishment in Nineteenth-century Anglo-America," *Journal of Church and State* 18:1 (Winter 1976): 61–77.
Patrick Mason, "God and the People: Theodemocracy in Nineteenth-Century Mormonism," *Journal of Church and State* 53:3 (September 2011): 349–75.
Armand L. Mauss, *All Abraham's Children: Changing Mormon Conceptions of Race and Lineage* (Champaign: University of Illinois Press, 2003).
Matthew McBride, *A House for the Most High: The Story of the Original Nauvoo Temple* (Salt Lake City: Kofford Books, 2007).
Eugene McCarraher, "God and Mammon, Incorporated," *Raritan* 37:1 (Summer 2017): 101–17.
Eugene McCarraher, *The Enchantments of Mammon: Capitalism as the Religion of Modernity* (Cambridge, MA: Harvard University Press, 2019).
D.P. McCarthy, "The Biblical Chronology of James Ussher," *Irish Astronomical Journal* 24:1 (1997): 73–82.
Daniel McLellan, "Cognitive Perspectives on Early Christology," *Biblical Interpretation* 25 (2017): 647–62.

Daniel McLellan, "Abraham 1:1–3 and the Prophet Joseph Smith as Translator," Church History Translation Symposium, Salt Lake City, 2018, electronic copy in my possession.

Kirstie McClure, *Judging Rights: Lockean Politics and the Limits of Consent* (Ithaca, NY: Cornell University Press, 1996).

Colleen McDannell and Bernhard Lang. *Heaven: A History*, 2nd ed. (New Haven, CT: Yale University Press, 2001).

Gerald McDermott, *Jonathan Edwards Confronts the Gods: Christian Theology, Enlightenment Religion, and Non-Christian Faiths* (New York: Oxford University Press, 2000).

Ben McGuire, "Nephi and Goliath: A Case Study of Literary Allusion in the Book of Mormon," *Journal of the Book of Mormon and Other Restoration Scripture* 18:1 (2009): 16–31.

Sidney Mead, *The Lively Experiment: The Shaping of Christianity in America* (New York: Harper and Row, 1963).

Alton Merrill and Amos Merrill, "Changing Thought on the Book of Mormon," *Improvement Era* 45 (September 1942): 568.

Brent Metcalfe, "The Curious Textual History of '*Egyptus*' the Wife of Ham," *The John Whitmer Historical Association Journal* 34:2 (2014): 1–11.

Brent Metcalfe, "Newly Discovered Copies of JS's Adamic Q&A," *Mormon Studies Podcast*, December 19, 2015, http://www.mormonstudiespodcast.org/newly-discovered-copies-of-jss-adamic-qa/#hn8.

Marvin Meyer, ed., *The Ancient Mysteries: A Sourcebook of Sacred Texts* (Philadelphia: University of Pennsylvania Press, 1999 [1987]).

Marvin Meyer, et al., *Ancient Christian Magic: Coptic Texts of Ritual Power* (New York: HarperCollins, 1994).

Mary Ann Meyers, *A New World Jerusalem: The Swedenborgian Experience in Community Construction* (Westport, CT: Greenwood, 1983).

Samuel Miller, *A Brief Retrospect of the Eighteenth Century*, 2 vols. (New York: T. and J. Swords, 1803).

Watson Mills, ed., *Speaking in Tongues: A Guide to Research on Glossolalia* (Grand Rapids, Michigan: Eerdmans, 1986).

John Lardas Modern, *Secularism in Antebellum America* (Chicago: University of Chicago Press Press, 2011).

R. Laurence Moore, "Religion, Secularization, and the Shaping of the Culture Industry in Antebellum America," *American Quarterly* 41 (June 1989): 216–42.

Kerry Muhlestein and Megan Hansen, "'The Work of Translating': The Book of Abraham's Translation Chronology," in *Let Us Reason Together: Essays in Honor of the Life's Work of Robert L. Millet*, ed. J. Spencer Fluhman and Brent L. Top (Provo, UT: Religious Studies Center; Salt Lake City: 2016), 139–62.

William Mulder and Russell Mortensen, eds., *Among the Mormons: Historic Accounts by Contemporary Observers* (New York: Alfred A. Knopf, 1958).

Lincoln Mullen, *The Chance of Salvation: A History of Conversion in America* (Cambridge, MA: Harvard University Press, 2018).

Robert Mullin, *Miracles and the Modern Religious Imagination* (New Haven, CT: Yale University Press, 1996).

Lewis Mumford, *Technics and Civilization* (New York: Harcourt Brace, & Co., 1934).

Peter Nabokov, *A Forest of Time: American Indian Ways of History* (New York: Cambridge University Press, 2002).

John Narrien, *An Historical Account of the Origin and Progress of Astronomy* (London: Baldwin and Cradock, 1833).

"The New Translation," *The Christian Baptist*, 7 vols. in 1 (Cincinnati: D.S. Burnett, 1835).
Linda Newell, "Gifts of the Spirit: Women's Share," *Sisters in Spirit: Mormon Women in Historical and Cultural Perspective*, ed. Lavina Fielding Anderson and Maureen Ursenbach Beecher (Champaign: University of Illinois Press, 1987), 111-50.
Hugh Nibley, *Enoch the Prophet* (Salt Lake City: Deseret Book, 1986).
Hugh Nibley, "The Meaning of the Kirtland Egyptian Papers," *BYU Studies* 11 (Summer 1971) 4: 350-99.
Hugh Nibley, *The Message of the Joseph Smith Papyri: an Egyptian Endowment* (Salt Lake City: Deseret Book, 1975).
Max Nolan, "Materialism and the Mormon Faith," *Dialogue* 22:4 (Winter 1989): 62-75.
Mark Noll, "Common Sense Traditions and American Evangelical Thought," *American Quarterly* 37:2 (Summer 1985): 216-38.
Mark Noll, *America's God: From Jonathan Edwards to Abraham Lincoln* (New York: Oxford University Press, 2002).
Mark Noll, *In the Beginning Was the Word: The Bible in American Public Life, 1492-1783* (New York: Oxford University Press, 2015).
Andrews Norton, *A Statement of Reasons for not Believing the Doctrines of Trinitarians* (Cambridge: Brown, Shattuck, and Co., 1833).
Thomas O'Dea, "Mormonism and the American Experience of Time," *Western Humanities Review* 8:3 (Summer 1954): 181-90.
George Oliver, *Antiquities of Free-Masonry* (London: G. and W.B. Whittaker, 1823).
"Origin of Sneezing Customs," *Current Literature: A Magazine of Contemporary Record* 17:6 (June 1895).
Robert Orsi, *Between Heaven and Earth: The Religious Worlds People Make and the Scholars Who Study Them* (Princeton, NJ: Princeton University Press, 2004).
Robert Orsi, *Cambridge Companion to Religious Studies* (New York: Cambridge University Press, 2012).
Robert Orsi, *History and Presence* (Cambridge, MA: Harvard University Press, 2016).
Thomas Paine, *Age of Reason* (London: D.I. Eaton, 1794).
Benjamin Park, "'Reasonings Sufficient': Joseph Smith, Thomas Dick, and the Context(s) of Early Mormonism," *Journal of Mormon History* 38 (Summer 2012): 210-24.
Benjamin Park, "Joseph Smith's Kingdom of God: The Council of Fifty and the Mormon Challenge to American Politics." *Church History* 87:4 (December 2018): 1029-55.
Max Parkin, "Joseph Smith and the United Firm: The Growth and Decline of the Church's First Master Plan of Business and Finance, Ohio and Missouri, 1832-1834," *BYU Studies* 46:3 (2007): 5-66.
William Paul, *English Language Bible Translators* (Jefferson, NC: McFarland, 2009).
John Peck and John Lawton, *An Historical Sketch of The Baptist Missionary Convention of the State of New York* (Utica: Bennett and Bright, 1837).
Seth Perry, "The Many Bibles of Joseph Smith: Textual, Prophetic, and Scholarly Authority in Early-National Bible Culture," *Journal of the American Academy of Religion* 84:3 (September 2016): 750-75.
John Durham Peters, *Speaking into the Air: A History of the Idea of Communication* (Chicago: University of Chicago Press Press, 1999).
John Durham Peters, *The Marvelous Clouds: Toward a Philosophy of Elemental Media* (Chicago: University of Chicago Press Press, 2015).
John Durham Peters, "Recording beyond the Grave: Joseph Smith's Celestial Bookkeeping," *Critical Inquiry* 42:4 (Summer 2016): 842-64.

H. Donl Peterson, *The Story of the Book of Abraham; Mummies, Manuscripts, and Mormonism* (Salt Lake City: Deseret Book Company: 1995).
Geraldine Pinch, *Magic in Ancient Egypt: Revised Edition* (Austin: University of Texas Press, 2010).
William Pitts, *The Gospel Witness* (Catskill, NY: Lewis and Co., 1818).
Amanda Porterfield, *Conceived in Doubt: Religion and Politics in the New American Nation* (Chicago: University of Chicago Press Press, 2012).
Barry Powell, *Writing: Theory and History of the Technology of Civilization* (Malden, MA: Wiley-Blackwell, 2009).
Parley Pratt, *Mormonism Unveiled* (New York City: for the author, 1838).
Parley Pratt, *A Voice of Warning*, 2nd edn., (New York: J.W. Harrison, 1839).
Parley Pratt, *The Millennium, and Other Poems* (New York: W. Molineux, 1840).
Parley Pratt, *Plain Facts* (Manchester: W.R. Thomas, 1840).
Robert Price, "Prophecy and Palimpsest," *Dialogue* 35:3 (Fall 2002): 67–82.
Josiah Priest, *American Antiquities, and Discoveries in the West*, 2nd ed., revised. (Albany, NY: Hoffman and White, 1833).
Joseph Priestley, *An History of the Corruptions of Christianity* (Birmingham: Piercy and Jones, 1782).
Theda Purdue and Michael Green, *The Cherokee Nation and the Trail of Tears* (New York: Penguin, 2008).
D. Michael Quinn, *Early Mormonism and the Magic World View* (Salt Lake City: Signature Books, 1987).
D. Michael Quinn, "Latter-day Saint Prayer Circles," *BYU Studies* 19:1 (1978): 79–105.
Chevalier Ramsay, *The Travels of Cyrus*, 2nd ed. (Albany, NY: Pratt and Doubleday, 1814).
Karl Reinhold, *The Hebrew Mysteries, or the Oldest Religious Freemasonry* (Leipzig, 1788).
Jules Remy and Julius Brenchley, *A Journey to Great-Salt-Lake City* (London: W. Jeffs, 1861).
Noel Reynolds, "The Coming Forth of the Book of Mormon in the Twentieth Century," *Brigham Young University Studies* 38:2 (1999): 6–47.
Michael Rhodes, *The Hor Book of Breathings: A Translation and Commentary* (Provo, UT: FARMS, 2002).
Michael Rhodes, *Books of the Dead Belonging to Tschemmin and Neferirnub: A Translation and Commentary* (Provo, UT: Maxwell Institute, 2010).
Daniel Richter, *Facing East from Indian Country* (Cambridge, MA: Harvard University Press, 2001).
Robert Ritner, "'The Breathing Permit of Hor' Thirty-Four Years Later," *Dialogue* 33:4 (Winter 2000): 91–119.
Robert Ritner, *The Joseph Smith Egyptian Papyri: A Complete Edition* (Salt Lake City: Signature Books, 2013).
Sarah Rivett, *The Science of the Soul in Colonial New England* (Chapel Hill: University of North Carolina Press, 2011).
Charles Rollins, *Ancient History* (New York: Robert Carter, 1844).
Michael Russell, *View of Ancient and Modern Egypt* (Edinburgh: Oliver and Boyd, 1831).
Charles Sanford, *The Quest for Paradise: Europe and the American Moral Imagination* (Champaign: University of Illinois Press, 1961).
Lewis Saum, *The Popular Mood of Pre-Civil War America* (Westport, CT: Greenwood Press, 1980).
John Sawyer, *The Fifth Gospel: Isaiah in the History of Christianity* (New York: Cambridge University Press, 1996).

Jillian Sayre, "Books Buried in the Earth: *The Book of Mormon*, Revelation, and the Humic Foundations of the Nation," in Fenton and Hickman, eds., *Americanist Approaches*, 21–44.

Mark Schantz, "Religious Tracts, Evangelical Reform, and the Market Revolution in Antebellum America," *Journal of the Early Republic* 17:3 (Autumn 1997): 425–66.

Leigh Schmidt, *Consumer Rites: The Buying and Selling of American Holidays*, (Princeton, NJ: Princeton University Press, 1997).

Leigh Schmidt, *Hearing Things: Religion, Illusion, and the American Enlightenment* (Cambridge, MA: Harvard University Press, 2000).

Leigh Schmidt, *Holy Fairs: Scotland and the Making of American Revivalism*, 2nd ed. (Grand Rapids, MI: Eerdmans, 2001).

Leigh Schmidt, *Village Atheists: How America's Unbelievers Made Their Way in a Godly Nation* (Princeton, NJ: Princeton University Press, 2016).

Wilhelm Schmidt-Biggermann, *Philosophia perennis: Historical Outlines of Western Spirituality in Ancient, Medieval, and Early Modern Thought*, (Dordrecht: Springer, 2004).

Charles Schmitt, "Perennial Philosophy: from Agostino Steuco to Leibniz," *Journal of the History of Ideas* 27:4 (Oct–Dec 1966): 505–32.

Jerrold Seigel, *The Idea of the Self: Thought and Experience in Western Europe since the Seventeenth Century* (New York: Cambridge University Press, 2005).

Charles Sellers, *The Market Revolution: Jacksonian America, 1815–1846* (New York: Oxford University Press, 1991).

John Seymer, *The Romance of Ancient Egypt* (London: Whittaker & Co., 1835).

Gregory Shaw, *Theurgy and the Soul: The Neoplatonism of Iamblichus* (University Park: Penn State University Press, 2003).

Jane Shaw, *Miracles in Enlightenment England* (New Haven, CT: Yale University Press, 2006).

Jonathan Sheehan, *The Enlightenment Bible: Translation, Scholarship, Culture* (Princeton, NJ: Princeton University Press, 2005).

Jan Shipps, *Mormonism: The Story of a New Religious Tradition* (Champaign: University of Illinois Press, 1987).

William Simmons, *Spirit of the New England Tribes: Indian History and Folklore, 1620–1984* (Lebanon, NH: University Press of New England, 1986).

Christopher Smith, "The Dependence of Abraham 1:1–3 on the Egyptian Alphabet and Grammar," *John Whitmer Historical Association Journal* 29 (2009): 38–54.

Christopher Smith, "Joseph Smith in Hermeneutical Crisis," *Dialogue* 43:2 (Summer 2010): 86–108.

Emma Smith, *A Collection of Sacred Hymns for the Church of the Latter Day Saints* (Kirtland, OH: F.G. Williams, 1835).

George Smith, ed., *An Intimate Chronicle: The Journals of William Clayton* (Salt Lake City: Signature Books, 1995).

Jonathan Z. Smith, *To Take Place: Toward Theory in Ritual* (Chicago: University of Chicago Press Press, 1987).

Jonathan Z. Smith, *Drudgery Divine: On the Comparison of Early Christianities and the Religions of Late Antiquity* (Chicago: University of Chicago Press Press, 1990).

Jonathan Z. Smith, *Map Is Not Territory: Studies in the History of Religions* (1978; repr., Chicago: University of Chicago Press, 1993).

Jonathan Z. Smith, *Relating Religion: Essays in the Study of Religion* (Chicago: University of Chicago Press Press, 2004).

Mark Smith, *The Origins of Biblical Monotheism: Israel's Polytheistic Background and the Ugaritic Texts* (New York: Oxford University Press, 2001).
Steven Smith, *The Disenchantment of Secular Discourse* (Cambridge, MA: Harvard University press, 2010).
Timothy Smith, "The Book of Mormon in a Biblical Culture," *Journal of Mormon History* 7 (1980): 3–21.
William Smith, "Early Mormon Priesthood Revelations: Text, Impact, and Evolution," *Dialogue* 46.4 (Winter 2013): 1–84.
Charles Piazzi Smyth, *Our Inheritance in the Great Pyramid* (London: A. Strahan, 1864).
F. S. Spalding, *Joseph Smith, Jr., as a Translator* (Salt Lake City: The Arrow Press, 1912).
Joseph Spencer, *The Vision of All: Twenty-five Lectures on Isaiah in Nephi's Record* (Salt Lake City: Greg Kofford Books, 2016).
Sidney Sperry, "Joseph Smith as an Egyptologist," *Deseret News*, April 6, 1935, 1.
Mark Staker, *Hearken O Ye People: The Historical Setting of Joseph Smith's Ohio Revelations* (Salt Lake City: Greg Kofford Books, 2009).
Jonathan Stapley, "Adoptive Sealing Ritual in Mormonism," *Journal of Mormon History* 37:3 (Summer 2011): 53–118.
Jonathan Stapley, *The Power of Godliness: Mormon Liturgy and Cosmology* (New York: Oxford University Press, 2018).
John Stearns, *An Inquiry into the Nature and Tendency of Speculative Freemasonry* (Utica, NY: T.W. Seward, 1869).
Stephen Stein, *The Shaker Experience in America* (New Haven, CT: Yale University Press, 1992).
Stephen Stein, "America's Bibles: Canon, Commentary, and Community," *Church History* 64 (1995): 169–84.
Krister Stendahl, "The Sermon on the Mount and Third Nephi," in *Reflections on Mormonism: Judaeo-Christian Parallels*, ed. Truman G. Madsen (Brigham Young University, 1978), 139–54.
David Stevenson, *The Origins of Freemasonry: Scotland's Century, 1590-1710* (New York: Cambridge University Press, 1988).
Joseph Stuart, "'A More Powerful Effect upon the Body': Early Mormonism's Theory of Racial Redemption and American Religious Theories of Race," *Church History* 87:3 (September 2018): 768–96.
Moses Stuart, *Grammar of the Hebrew Language* (Andover, MA: Flagg and Gould, 1831).
Randall Styers, *Making Magic: Religion, Magic, and Science in the Modern World* (New York: Oxford University Press, 2004).
William Swartzell, *Mormonism Exposed* (Pekin, OH: for the author, 1840).
Emanuel Swedenborg, *Concerning Heaven and Its Wonders, and Concerning Hell* [1758] (Boston: Otis Clapp, 1837).
Ann Taves, *Revelatory Events: Three Case Studies of the Emergence of New Spiritual Paths* (Princeton, NJ: Princeton University Press, 2016).
Alan Taylor, "The Early Republic's Supernatural Economy," *American Quarterly* 38.1 (Spring 1986): 6–34.
Alan Taylor, "Rediscovering the Context of Joseph Smith's Treasure Seeking," *Dialogue* 19.4 (Winter 1986): 18–28.
Charles Taylor, *Sources of the Self: the Making of the Modern Identity* (Cambridge, MA: Harvard University Press, 1989).
Charles Taylor, *A Secular Age* (Cambridge, MA: Harvard University Press, 2007).

Charles Taylor, *The Language Animal: The Full Shape of the Human Linguistic Capacity* (Cambridge, MA: Harvard University Press, 2016).
Lori Taylor, *Telling Stories about Mormons and Indians*, Ph.D. dissertation, State University of New York at Buffalo, 2000.
Stephen Taysom, "Abundant Events or Narrative Abundance: Robert Orsi and the Academic Study of Mormonism," *Dialogue* 45:4 (Winter 2012): 1–26.
Stephen Taysom, "'Satan Mourns Naked Upon the Earth': Locating Mormon Possession and Exorcism Rituals in the American Religious Landscape, 1830–1977," *Religion and American Culture* 27:1 (Winter 2017): 57–94.
Cecil Thomas, *Alexander Campbell and his New Version* (St. Louis, MO: Bethany Press, 1958).
E. P. Thompson, "Time, Work-Discipline, and Industrial Capitalism," *Past and Present* 38 (December 1967): 56–97.
Jason Thompson, *Wonderful Things: A History of Egyptology*, 3 vols (Cairo: American University of Cairo, 2015–2016).
Keith Thomson, *Living Fossil: The Story of the Coelacanth* (New York: Norton, 1991).
Stephen Thompson, "Egyptology and the Book of Abraham," *Dialogue* 28:1 (Spring 1995): 143–60.
Ryan Tobler, "'Saviors on Mount Zion': Mormon Sacramentalism, Mortality, and the Baptism for the Dead," *Journal of Mormon History* 39:4 (Fall 2013): 182–238.
Alexis de Tocqueville, *Democracy in America*, trans. Philips Bradley (New York: Knopf, 1994).
Jay Todd, *The Saga of the Book of Abraham* (Salt Lake City: Deseret Book, 1969).
Salem Town, *System of Speculative Masonry* (New York: H. Dodd and Co, 1822).
Scott Trafton, *Egypt Land: Race and Nineteenth-Century American Egyptomania* (Durham, NC: Duke University Press, 2004).
Frances Trollope, *Domestic Manners of the Americans* (New York reprint, fourth edition: Reprinted for the booksellers, 1832).
John G. Turner, *The Mormon Jesus: A Biography* (Cambridge, MA: Harvard University Press, 2016).
John Tvedtnes, "The Critics of the Book of Abraham," in *Book of Abraham Symposium* (Salt Lake City: Salt Lake Institute of Religion, 1971), 70–76.
Laurel Thatcher Ulrich, *A House Full of Females: Plural Marriage and Women's Rights in Early Mormonism, 1835–1870* (New York: Knopf, 2017).
Laurel Thatcher Ulrich, "Early Diaries of Wilford Woodruff," in Mark Ashurst-McGee, et al., eds., *Foundational Texts of Mormonism* (New York: Oxford University Press, 2018), chapter 10.
Grant Underwood, "Book of Mormon Usage in Early LDS Theology," *Dialogue* 17:3 (Autumn 1984): 35–74.
Grant Underwood, "Relishing the Revisions: The Doctrine and Covenants and the Revelatory Process," in Blair Van Dyke, Brian Birch, and Boyd Petersen, eds., *The Expanded Canon: Perspectives on Mormonism and Sacred Texts* (Salt Lake City: Kofford, 2018), 171–83.
Yulia Ustinova, "To Live in Joy and Die with Hope: Experiential Aspects of Ancient Greek Mystery Rites," *Bulletin of the Institute of Classical Studies*, 56:2 (December 2013): 105–23.
Robbert Van Den Berg, "'Becoming Like God' According to Proclus' Interpretations of the *Timaeus*, the Eleusinian Mysteries, and the *Chaldean Oracles*," *Bulletin of the Institute of Classical Studies*, 46:S78 (January 2003): 189–202.

Increase McGee Van Dusen and Maria Van Dusen, *Positively True* (Albany: C. Killmer, 1847).

Bruce Van Orden, ed., "Writing to Zion: the William W. Phelps Kirtland Letters (1835–1836)," *BYU Studies* 33:3 (1993): 542–93.

Michael Van Wagenen, "Singular Phenomena: The Evolving Mormon Interpretation of Unidentified Flying Objects," in Michael Van Wagenen and Paul Reeve, eds., *Between Pulpit and Pew: The Supernatural World in Mormon Folklore* (Logan: Utah State University, 2011), 97–124.

Richard Van Wagoner, *Sidney Rigdon: A Portrait of Religious Excess* (Salt Lake City: Signature Books, 1994).

Richard Van Wagoner, Steven C. Walker, and Allen D. Roberts, "The 'Lectures on Faith': A Case Study in Decanonization," *Dialogue* 20:3 (Fall 1987): 71–77.

Dan Vogel, "Mormonism's Anti-Masonick Bible," *John Whitmer Historical Association Journal* 9 (1989): 17–29.

Dan Vogel and Brent Metcalfe, "Joseph Smith's Scriptural Cosmology," in Vogel, ed., *The Word of God: Essays on Mormon Scripture* (Salt Lake City: Signature, 1990), 187–220.

Jeremy Waldron, *One Another's Equals: the Basis of Human Equality* (Cambridge, MA: Harvard University Press, 2017).

Jeffrey Walker, "The Kirtland Safety Society and the Fraud of Grandison Newell: A Legal Examination," *BYU Studies* 54:3 (2015): 32–148.

James Walsh, "Holy Time and Sacred Space in Puritan New England," *American Quarterly* 32:1 (Spring 1980): 79–95.

Michael Walton, "Professor Seixas, the Hebrew Bible, and the Book of Abraham," *Sunstone* 6 (March-April 1981): 41–43.

William Warburton, *The Divine Legation of Moses Demonstrated in Nine Books*, 4th edn. (London: Millar and Tonson, 1765).

Ronald G. Watt, *The Mormon Passage of George D. Watt: First British Convert, Scribe for Zion* (Logan: Utah State University Press, 2009).

Robert Wauchope, *Lost Tribes and Sunken Continents: Myth and Method in the Study of American Indians* (Chicago: University of Chicago Press Press, 1962).

Thomas Wayment and Haley Lemmon, "A Recently Recovered Source: The Use of Adam Clarke's Bible Commentary in Joseph Smith's Bible Translation," in MacKay et al., *Producing Ancient Scripture*, chapter 11.

Thomas Wayment and Tyson Yost, "The Joseph Smith Translation and Italicized Words in the King James Version," *Religious Educator* 6:1 (2005): 51–64.

Max Weber, *The Protestant Ethic and the Spirit of Capitalism*, trans. Talcott Parsons (New York: Routledge Classics, 2005).

Noah Webster, *An American Dictionary of the English Language* (New York: S. Converse, 1828).

John Welch, "The Miraculous Translation of the Book of Mormon," ed., *Opening the Heavens: Accounts of Divine Manifestations, 1820–1844* (Provo, UT: BYU Press, 2005), 76–213.

Anita Wells, "Bare Record: The Nephite Archivist, the Record of Records, and the Book of Mormon Provenance," *Interpreter* 24 (2017): 99–122.

John Wesley, *Explanatory Notes Upon the Old Testament* (Bristol: Printed by William Pine, 1765).

Ellen White, *Yahweh's Council: Its Structure and Membership* (Philadelphia: Coronet Books, 2014).

Nathan Whiting, *The Good News of Our Lord Jesus, the Anointed* (Boston: Joshua V. Himes, 1849).

Robert Wilken, *Liberty in the Things of God: the Christian Origins of Religious Freedom* (New Haven, CT: Yale University Press, 2019).

Lynn Wilkinson, *The Dream of an Absolute Language: Emanuel Swedenborg and French Literary Culture* (Albany: SUNY Press, 1996).

Cyril Williams, *Tongues of the Spirit: a Study of Pentecostal Glossolalia and Related Phenomena* (Cardiff: University of Wales Press, 1981).

Catherine Wilson, *Epicureanism at the Origins of Modernity* (New York: Oxford University Press, 2008).

John Wilson, "The Joseph Smith Egyptian Papyri: Translations and Interpretations: A Summary Report," *Dialogue* 3:2 (Summer 1968): 67-85.

Kenneth Winn, *Exiles in a Land of Liberty: Mormons in America, 1830-1846* (Chapel Hill: University of North Carolina Press, 1989).

Wilford Woodruff, "Book of Revelations" [manuscript, ca. 23 December 1837-1860], CHL.

Fred Woods, "'A Mormon and Still a Jew': The Life of Alexander Neibaur," *Mormon Historical Studies* 7:1-2 (Spring-Fall 2006): 22-34.

David Wright, "'In Plain Terms That We May Understand': Joseph Smith's Transformation of Hebrews in Alma 12-13," in Brent Metcalfe, ed., *New Approaches to the Book of Mormon* (Salt Lake City: Signature Books, 1993), 165-229.

Wilhelm Wyl, *Mormon Portraits, or the Truth about Mormon Leaders from 1830 to 1886* (Salt Lake City: Tribune, 1886).

Thomas Young, "Egypt," in *Supplement to the Fourth, Fifth, and Sixth Editions of the Encyclopaedia Britannica*, vol. 4 (Edinburgh: Archibald Constable and Company, 1824), 38-73.

Louis Zucker, "Joseph Smith as a Student of Hebrew," *Dialogue* 3 (Summer 1968) 2: 41-55.

Index

Figures are indicated by *f* following the page number
For the benefit of digital users, indexed terms that span two pages (e.g., 52–53) may, on occasion, appear on only one of those pages.

Abiff, Hiram, 78, 255
Abinadi, 148
Abraham, 105–8, 187, 212, 223–24
Adam, 22–23, 40, 41, 64, 67, 93–94, 104–5, 244–45, 247–49, 252–53
Adam-ondi-Ahman, 45, 246, 247
agency, 85–86, 93–95, 181–82
Ahman, 107, 252–53, 266, 268. *See also* God: names of; Jesus Christ: names of
alienation. *See* separation
American Bible Society, 132
American Indians:
    Book of Mormon and, 133
    negation of history, 61
    Timpanogos Nuche band, 19
angels, 244–45, 249–50, 268–69
    Book of Mormon and, 139
    Michael, 110, 247, 266
    ministering, 103
animal sacrifice, 71–74
anointing, 238, 252, 260. *See also* Kirtland temple *and* Nauvoo temple
Arminianism, 85–86
Articles and Covenants, 133–34, 160, 174
astronomy, 225–29, 248–49
Atiya, Aziz, 193

Babel:
    American religious pluralism, 35–36
    Book of Mormon and, 33–34
    curse of, 7, 23, 32–33, 48–49
    Joseph Smith Translation (Bible), 34
Bacheler, Origen, 166
Baptism, 172
    for the dead, 66, 189, 241–42, 250–51
Baptists, 6, 85
Beecher, Lyman, 150
Belsham, Thomas, 171–72
Bible, 130–32, *See also* New Translation (Bible)
    criticism of, 130–32

Doctrine and Covenants and, 173–78
    errancy of translation, 137–40
    King James Version, 22, 49, 123–25, 129, 136, 145, 149, 163, 171, 186, 190–91
    nineteenth-century translations of, 136–72
    translation of, 144–45
Biblical exegesis, 42, 52–53, 77, 94, 101, 103, 142, 184–90
Bloom, Harold, 120, 129–30
Book of Abraham, 193–95, 204–9. *See also* Egyptian Bible
    Bible, relation to, 205–9
    creation, 206–8
    facsimiles, 209–11
    Hebrew language and, 212–15
    human agency, 94, 206
    plurality of gods, 267
    premortal life, 206
    Urim and Thummin and, 101–2, 206
Book of Breathings, 210
Book of Commandments. *See* Doctrine and Covenants
Book of Mormon, 3–4, 76, 127, 160–61
    Bible, relationship to, 129–30, 132–35, 138–41, 147–49, 153–54, 163–64
    canonization, 141
    cessationism, 65–66, 157
    Christocentrism, 153
    communitarianism, 112–13
    critics of, 129
    ecclesiology, 158–60
    editions of, 140–41
    Fall of Adam and Eve, 179
    gold plates, 3, 29–30, 132–35, 151, 175, 179
    human agency, 93
    human depravity, 90
    human potential, 90
    Isaiah, 148
    language and, 38, 135–37
    location, 134–35

Book of Mormon (*cont.*)
  lost books, 143, 149
  miracles, 155–57
  priesthood and, 73
  quotation of Bible, 129, 134, 148, 154
  Reformed Egyptian and, 31, 198, 200–1
  secrecy, 258
  stick of Joseph, 186–87
  temples, 235–36
  temporality, 68–69
  title page, 128*f*
  transforming power, 154–55
  translation, 101
  witnesses, 151
Book of Remembrance, 40–41, 113, 167
Brague, Remi, 246
Brothers, Richard, 172
Brown, John, 146–47
Brownson, Orestes, 86
Buck, Charles, 73, 74–75, 138
Buckminster, Joseph, 130–31, 144
Bushnell, Horace, 30–31, 135, 268–69

calendar, 56, 57
Calvinism, 23–24, 81, 85–86, 96, 108–9, 135, 263–64
Camp of Israel, 109–10
Campbell, Alexander, 134–35, 136, 140–75
  bible translation, 171
canonization, 141–43
Catholicism, 15–16, 57, 60–61, 131–32, 146–47, 250
celestial marriage, 106, 260
cessationism, 5, 63, 145, 155
Chain of Belonging, 173, 189–90, 206, 210–11, 231–32, 247, 250–51, 261–62, 266, 273.
  See also Egyptian Bible
Champollion, Jean-François, 229–30
Chandler, Michael, 193, 196
Chicago, fire of, 193
cholera, 109–10
The Church of Jesus Christ of Latter-day Saints, 2
  name of, 2n.2, 159
city of righteousness. *See* Enoch: city of Zion
Clark, Gen. John, 118
Clarke, Adam, 171–72, 183–84, 253–54
  Egyptian hieroglyphics, 29
Cleveland, Sarah, 47–48
coelacanth, 1, 271
Coltrin, Zebedee, 98
Combs, Abel, 193
communal salvation, 106, 112

communitarianism, 114–16
cosmic order, 246
Council of Fifty, 119
covenants, 174
Covey, Almira Mack Scobey, 85–86
Cowdery, Oliver, 116–17, 160, 168, 176–77, 197–98, 200–1, 212–13
creation, 22, 67–68, 91–92, 93–94, 167, 180–81, 182, 185, 206–8
Cutlerite sect, 259

Davis, Andrew Jackson, 30, 99–100
Deism, 144
Deseret Alphabet, 47
Dick, Thomas, 268–69
discernment. *See* spiritual gifts
dispensation, 62–64, 181
divine anthropology, 10, 89–93, 185, 236–37, 248–52, 255–56
Doctrine and Covenants, 173–78
  Book of Commandments, 173
  New Translation of Bible and (*see* New Translation [Bible])
  time and, 66

Edenic language. *See* Pure language
Edwards, Jonathan, 94, 152
Egypt, 195–96, 213
  cultural persistence, 195–96, 227–28, 229–30
  discovery of, 216–18
Egyptian Bible, 199, 211–29, 230–32
  Chain of Belonging and, 223–29
  female power and, 215–23
  Katumin, 219–21
  light and, 227
  pictography, 211–15
Egyptian language, 229–31
Eichhorn, Johann, 144
Elaw, Zilpha, 24
election, 95, 108–9
Eliade, Mircea, 55
Elias, 223–24
Elijah, 98–99, 175, 264
Elohim. *See* God *and* plurality of gods
Emerson, Ralph Waldo, 30–31, 36–37, 59–60, 88–89
endowment. *See* Nauvoo Temple
Enoch, 18, 39, 99, 112–14, 181–83, 247–48
  city of Zion, 18, 42–43, 112–13, 264
  prophecy of, 44, 90–91, 94, 113–14, 167 (*see also* New Translation [Bible])
  Song of Zion, 182–83

Erasmus, 137–38
Eve, 41, 71–72, 94, 100, 178, 180, 208, 215, 221, 233–34, 244–45
evidential Christianity, 150–58
exaltation. *See* divine anthropology
exodus to the West, 260–62

Fall of Adam and Eve, 71–72, 98, 113, 178–81
Far West, Missouri, 116
Female Relief Society, 107–8, 240, 242–44, 257
Fenn, Lucius, 133
Fielding, Joseph, 262
Fielding, Mary, 107, 239–40, 256, 268–69
Flake, Kathleen, 74, 259
Frederick, Nicholas, 186
Freemasonry, 233, 242–44, 257
    in antebellum America, 26–27
    friendship and, 97
    handshake and, 110, 255
    language and, 27–28
    name of God in, 27, 252–53, 255
    names and, 255
    Prisca theologia and, 75

Garden of Eden, 244–45, 246, 269
Gazelem, 145
Gilbert, Eli, 134
Givens, Terryl, 151
glossolalia, 47–48, 182–83, 202–3, 239–40
Gnosticism, 98
God, 263–69
    body of, 82, 92
    justice of, 180
    names of, 42–46, 252–53, 254
    nature of, 66
    presence of, 100–1, 249, 250–51, 259–60
    time and, 54–55, 65–69
gold plates. *See* Book of Mormon
Grammar and Alphabet of the Egyptian Language (GAEL), 200–4, 228–29
    image, 201*f*
Grandin printing press, 132
Griesbach, Jakob, 137–38
Grotius, Hugo, 85

handshake, 110–11
Hatch, Nathan, 60, 95
Heavenly Mother, 89–90
Helaman, 153
Hickman, Jared, 140–41
hieroglyphs, 29–31
"historylessness," 60
Holy Ghost, 169, 187

human potential. *See* divine anthropology
human saviors, 107–9, 251
human will. *See* agency
Hunt, William, 188–89
Huntington, Zina Diantha, 98–99, 157–58
Hyde, Orson, 252
hymns, 66, 251–52

illud tempus. *See* yon time
individualism, 83–89, 96–97

Jackson County, Missouri, 114, 236
Jaredite narrative, 38–39, 81–82, 136, 145
    Moriancumer in, 100, 182
Jesus Christ, 248–49, 268
    Book of Mormon, 140–41, 143
    names of, 42, 43–44, 254
    Second Coming of, 99, 119, 235–36
    visions of, 239
John, Gospel of, 43, 175–76, 267
Joseph of Egypt, 198, 227

Kabbalah, 184–85
Katumin. *See* Egyptian Bible
Kayser, Johann, 148–49
Kimball, Heber C., 96–97, 262
Kimball, Presendia Huntington, 99
Kimball, Rebecca Swain Williams, 114–15
Kimball, Vilate, 241
King Benjamin, 93
King Follett Discourse, 255–56, 267–68
King James Bible. *See* Bible
Kirtland Hebrew School, 266
Kirtland, Ohio, 114, 193, 197, 200, 239, 256
Kirtland temple, 236–40, 248–49
    dedication, 238
    image, 237*f*
    Pentecostal season, 238–39
    rites, 197, 236, 239–40
Kolob, 67, 98–99, 101–2, 194–229
Kramer, Brad, 259

Laban, 127
Lacour, Pierre, 212–13
language:
    corrupted, 34, 186
    problem of, 135–37
Laub, George, 249–50
Laws of the Church, 160, 176–77, 235–36, 256
Lebolo, Antonio, 193
Lectures on Faith, 75, 107–8, 174
Lee, Ann, 99–100, 172
Lee, E.G., 134

Lee, Jarena, 24, 37
Lehi, 90, 127, 179
Lehman, Chris, 119
Liberty, Missouri, 118
Locke, John, 85, 117, 144, 231–32
Luther, Martin, 136–37, 145, 146–47

marriage, 188, 224–25
marvelous literalism, 185–90
metaphysical correspondence, 8, 97, 184, 214–15, 241–42, 246–47, 273
Methodism, 6, 85–86, 92–93, 95, 176–77
Michaelis, Johannes, 146–47
Missouri-Mormon War, 1838, 117–18, 239
modernity, 4, 12–13, 185, 272
    time and, 54
Moriancumer. *See* Jaredite narrative
Mormon (Book of Mormon prophet), 133, 139, 141–42
Moroni, 38, 65–66, 76, 81, 82, 136–37, 156, 159, 163–64, 175
Moses, 179, 247–48, 254
    transfiguration, 100
    Visions of, 44, 71–73, 90–91, 93–94, 167 (*see also* New Translation [Bible])
Mount Shelem. *See* Jaredite narrative

names, 252–56
Napoleon, 195–96
Nauvoo, Illinois, 52, 114
Nauvoo temple, 73, 125, 241–44, 264
    endowment, 233–34, 242, 244–52
    image, 243*f*
    liturgy, 187, 194, 229, 241–44, 250–52, 260–63, 269
    rumors, 233
Neibaur, Alexander, 165
Nelson, Russell M., 2n.2
Nephi, 127, 136–37, 153–54, 157
    the Bible and, 142–43
    vision of, 139–40
New Jerusalem, 52, 76–77, 236. *See also* Jackson County, Missouri
New Translation (Bible), 163
    completion of, 170
    esoteric approach to, 165–66
    Genesis, 178–81
    lost books and, 167
    Prophecy of Enoch, 167, 181–83
    Sidney Rigdon and, 168–70
    Visions of Moses, 167
New York Metropolitan Museum of Art, 193
Nibley, Hugh, 194
Norton, Andrews, 130–31, 135–36

Olive Leaf Revelation (D&C 88), 66, 90–91, 100, 107–8, 175–76, 223–24, 227, 236–37
Orsi, Robert, 250
Owen, Robert, 263–64

Paine, Thomas, 87, 138
Palmyra, New York, 132
papyri, 193–95, 199
Parrish, Warren, 197–98
patriarchal blessings, 98–99, 106, 238, 241
Peck, Phebe Crosby, 114–15
pedilavium, 238. *See also* Kirtland Temple
Pelagianism, 85–86
Pentecost. *See* Kirtland Temple
Perry, Seth, 129–30
Peters, John Durham, 142, 184–85
Phelps, William Wines, 197–98, 262
    Bible and, 163–64
    Book of Mormon and, 133–34, 151–0
    Egyptian Project and, 31, 200–1, 214
    Enoch's people and, 101
    pure language and, 46, 211
    time and, 67
Philo of Alexandria, 144–45
pictogram. *See* hieroglyphs
Plan of Salvation, 95
pluralism, 146–47
plurality of gods, 265–69
polygamy, 69–71, 249–50, 260, 261–62. *See also* celestial marriage
Pratt, Parley P., 157
    "One Hundred Years Hence. 1945," 51–53, 62–63, 76–77
pre-earth life, 91–92, 111, 205–6, 224
priest, 73
priestcraft, 160
priestess. *See* priesthood: female power
priesthood, 3–4, 40–41, 64, 73, 76, 100–1, 104–9, 189, 221–23, 225–26, 242, 246–48
    Abraham and, 105–8, 221–22
    cosmic, 104, 209
    female power, 215–23, 240, 262–63
    genealogy, 105–6, 114, 223, 246–48 (*see also* sacerdotal genealogy)
    hierarchy, 187, 222, 228–29
    human connection and, 104, 231, 241, 251, 261–62, 268
    revelation on, 183
    translation and, 103–4
primordial language. *See* Pure language
prisca theologia, 74–76
pseudepigrapha, 10
Public Universal Friend. *See* Jemima Wilkinson

Pure language, 20–21, 253–54, 259–60
  Adam and, 22–23
  gift of tongues and (*see* glossolalia)
  loss of (*see* Babel)
  names of God (*see* God: names of)
  primordial, 21, 203–4
  sample of, 42–48, 46*f*, 211
  Second Coming of Christ and, 47
  Zephaniah and, 23–25

Quakers, 257–58

Religious Right, 2–3
Restorationist movements, 158
resurrection, 102–3, 177–78
Revelation, Book of, 166–67, 188, 253–54, 267
  books (life, judgement etc.), 188, 189
Rich, Sarah Dearmon Pea, 261
Richards, Willard, 204
Rigdon, Sidney, 42, 168–69, 258
  Bible translation, 163, 168–70

sacerdotal genealogy, 104, 108–9, 210, 219, 224–23, 238
Samuel the Lamanite, 93
Satan, 179
School of the Prophets, 236
sealing, 246–47
Second Anointing, 260
Second Great Awakening, 85
secrecy, 256–60
secularization, 15–17, 272
seer, 145
seer stone, 52–53
Seixas, Joshua, 37, 200
separation, 7, 32–33, 68–69, 96
  from God, 98–71
sexuality, 187–88
Shakers, 172
Sharp, Thomas, 233
Sheehan, Jonathan, 130–31
Smith, Emma Hale, 193, 240
  relationship with Joseph Smith, Jr., 96
Smith, Hyrum, 239–40
Smith, Joseph, Jr., 3, 271–73
  astronomy, 77
  Bible, view of, 130, 131–32
  Bible translation, 3–4, 123, 124–25, 169, 183–85, 190–91, 255–56 (*see also* New Translation [Bible])
  Book of Abraham and, 3–4, 123, 125, 193 (*see also* Book of Abraham)
  Book of Mormon and, 3–4, 123–25, 145–46, 160–61 (*see also* Book of Mormon)
  curse of Babel and (*see* Babel)
  death of, 133–34, 161, 233, 256, 258, 269
  dispensationalism, 181
  Doctrine and Covenants and, 3–4
  dualism and, 263–65
  Egypt and, 196, 231–32
  endowment on, 245
  escaping individualism and, 97
  Freemasonry and (*see* Freemasonry)
  human agency and, 89, 95
  human potential, 89–93
  human spirit, 91–92
  names and, 252–56
  "Observation of the Sectarian God," 91–92
  plural marriage and, 69–70
  problems with language, 32–33, 255–56
  Pure Language and, 20–21, 42–48
  Relief Society and, 240
  resurrection and, 103
  secrecy and, 257 (*see also* secrecy)
  study of Biblical languages, 36–37, 212–15
  theodemocracy and, 118–19, 271
  time and, 53–54, 62–65
  translator, 123–25, 140–41, 145–46, 170, 173, 177–78, 182–83
  treasure seeking and, 26
  U.S. presidential campaign, 119
Smith, Joseph, Sr., 105
Smith, Lucy Mack, 142, 193, 198
Snow, Eliza R., 19–20, 67–68, 235–36
  image, 20*f*
sola scriptura, 131–32
soul. *See* spirit
spirit, 91, 225–26, 253
spiritual gifts, 157–58, 176
  discernment, 110–11
  tongues (*see* glossolalia)
  translation, 146
Stapley, Jonathan, 104
stars, 227–29. *See also* astronomy *and* Kolob
Stein, Stephen, 153
Stuart, Joseph, 104
Stuart, Moses, 130–31
succession crisis, 258
supernatural forces, 109–11
Swedenborg, Emmanuel, 28, 268–69

targum, 10, 106, 123–25, 148–49, 164–65, 175–76, 197, 205–9, 218, 227, 229, 234, 241, 269, 271
Taylor, Charles, 16–17, 55–56, 83–84, 272
temple. *See also* Kirtland Temple *and* Nauvoo temple
  history of, 235–46
  liturgy of, 46–47, 77–78, 125, 194, 210, 256

temple (*cont.*)
　metaphysical correspondence, 234–35
　secrecy, 256, 257, 259–60
tetragrammaton, 254. *See also* God: names of
theogony. *See* divine anthropology
Thompson, Mercy Fielding, 262
time, 225–27, 231, 234–35
　dispensationalism and (*see* dispensations)
　nineteenth century views and, 58–59
　primordialism and, 59–61
　secular, 55–56
Tocqueville, Alexis de, 4–6, 34, 60, 86–89
translation, 7, 123–25, 245–46
　bodily, 98–104, 249
　definition of, 9
　human essence and, 8–9, 82
travel, 98–104
Trinitarianism, 44–45, 92–93
True Light Revelation (D&C 93), 175–76, 227
Turner, John, 133–34
Turner, Jonathan B., 150
Turner, Nat, 29–30

Unitarianism, 44–45, 144, 263–64
United Firm, 114
Urim and Thummin, 101–2, 252–54
Utah, 260

"The Vision" (D&C 76), 42–43, 100–1, 113–14, 175–76, 223–25, 251–52

Waldron, Jeremy, 264–65
War in Heaven. *See* pre-earth life
Washington, D.C., 131–32
Wayment, Thomas, 183–84
Weber, Max, 96
Webster, Noah, 171–72
Wesley, John, 171
Western Esotericism, 25–29, 242–44
　language and, 25, 28–29
Whiting, Nathan, 136–37, 172
Whitmer, John, 167
Wilkinson, Jemima, 99–100
Williams, Frederick G., 169–70, 197–98, 200–1
Wilson, Lovina Fairchild, 47–48
Winchester, Benjamin, 98–99
women, 262–63
　divinity of, 215–23
　Egyptian project (*see* Egyptian Bible)
　exclusion from Kirtland temple, 239–40
Woodruff, Phebe, 241
Woodruff, Wilford, 98
Word of Wisdom, 109–10

yon time, 55, 56, 61–62, 69–74
Young, Brigham, 119, 230–31, 244–45, 252, 260

Zephaniah. *See* Pure Language
Zion, 114

 www.ingramcontent.com/pod-product-compliance
Ingram Content Group UK Ltd.
Pitfield, Milton Keynes, MK11 3LW, UK
UKHW022155230426
12049UKWH00004BA/111